W9-CEV-514

VERMONT   COLLEGE
MONTPELIER, VT.

WITHDRAWN

WITHDRAWN

THE KREMLIN

VERMONT COLLEGE MONTPELIER
GARY
MEMORIAL
LIBRARY
IVA B. FIFIELD

1   St Basil's and the Red Square from the Kremlin Walls   [photo: S.C.R.]

THE KREMLIN

Nerve-Centre of Russian History

BY

VICTOR ALEXANDROV

TRANSLATED BY

ROY MONKCOM

ST MARTIN'S PRESS

NEW YORK

FIRST PUBLISHED IN USA 1963

This book is copyright under the Berne
Convention. Apart from any fair dealing
for the purpose of private study, research,
criticism or review, as permitted under
the Copyright Act, 1956, no portion may
be reproduced by any process without
written permission. Enquiry should be
made to the publisher.

This translation
© George Allen & Unwin Ltd., London, 1963

Translated from
Les Mystères du Kremlin
© Librairie Arthème Fayard
Paris 1960

Library of Congress Catalog Card No. 63-7280
All Rights Reserved

PRINTED IN GREAT BRITAIN
in 11 on 12 point Juliana type
BY THE BLACKFRIARS PRESS LTD
LEICESTER

947
Al383 k

Strange and unusual is the history of the Russian people, of the Russian nation. Immense and vague ideas make their way through the centuries—ideas of world domination, of life according to a divine 'truth'. Insolent designs of grandeur, unknown up to this time, emerge which confuse the western world. And it is with terror and indignation that the Occident scrutinizes this Oriental monster, weak and powerful at the same time, miserably and infinitely rich, whose fertile womb is giving birth to tomorrow's colossal ideas.

ALEXIS TOLSTOY
1941

18561

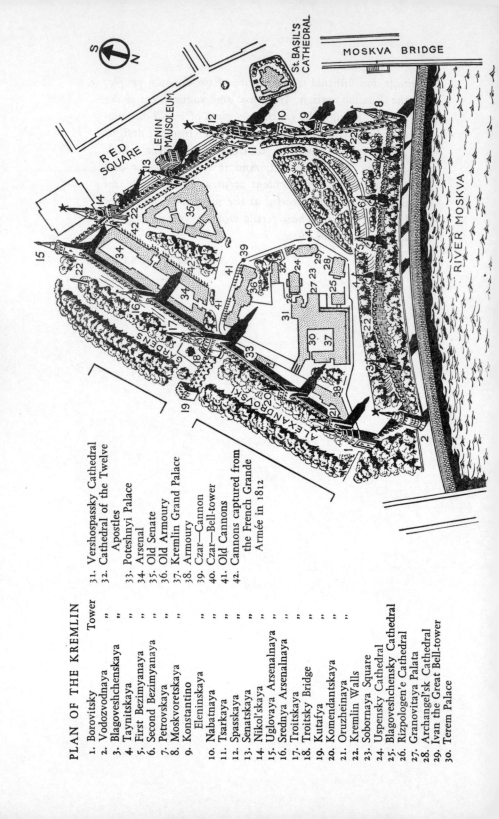

PLAN OF THE KREMLIN

1. Borovitsky   Tower
2. Vodozvodnaya   "
3. Blagoveshchenskaya   "
4. Taynitskaya   "
5. First Bezimyanaya   "
6. Second Bezimyanaya   "
7. Petrovskaya   "
8. Moskvoretskaya   "
9. Konstantino
    Eleninskaya   "
10. Nabatnaya   "
11. Tsarkaya   "
12. Spasskaya   "
13. Senatskaya   "
14. Nikol'skaya   "
15. Uglovaya Arsenalnaya   "
16. Srednya Arsenalnaya   "
17. Troitskaya   "
18. Troitsky Bridge   "
19. Kutafya   "
20. Komendantskaya   "
21. Oruzheinaya   "
22. Kremlin Walls
23. Sobornaya Square
24. Uspensky Cathedral
25. Blagoveshchensky Cathedral
26. Rizpologen'e Cathedral
27. Granovitaya Palata
28. Archangel'sk Cathedral
29. Ivan the Great Bell-tower
30. Terem Palace
31. Vershospassky Cathedral
32. Cathedral of the Twelve
    Apostles
33. Poteshnyi Palace
34. Arsenal
35. Old Senate
36. Old Armoury
37. Kremlin Grand Palace
38. Armoury
39. Czar—Cannon
40. Czar—Bell-tower
41. Old Cannons
42. Cannons captured from
    the French Grande
    Armée in 1812

INTRODUCTION

The Kremlin, once a hunting venue like Versailles, has for centuries been the nerve-centre of Russian history. Everything has had its origin in its precincts; autocracy, religious faith and cruel repression. The history of Russia from the twelfth century, with a brief interval during which power was transferred to Petrograd, is inextricably bound up with its development. It was there that the czars were crowned and buried; it was on many occasions the scene of their assassination. Everything was nurtured there: religion, dreams of power, absolutism, favouritism, felony and sheer insanity, and plans for the future. Through triumphs, setbacks, and tragic periods of chaos, the rulers, whatever their names, pursued the same policy. Their victories, the lessons drawn from their defeats, everything reverted to the Kremlin, where cathedrals stood as monuments of devotion or expiation and where *prikazes* and ministries became manifold. It was the symbol both of increasing schism and of encroaching bureaucracy. Its record abounds in orgies, murders, impulsive renunciation and harsh rectification. Behind its battlements Slavonic society in its most crushing form has given free rein to the best and the worst in its genius. Year after year, throughout the centuries, blood has bonded its stones and stained its ikons.

The Red Square—the time-honoured name has nothing to do with the Revolution—is rightly so called. The doves of today have taken the place of the crows and birds of prey which came to tear at the hanging bodies that dangled there from the twelfth to the seventeenth century. But there came a time after Peter the Great when the Kremlin, with its legal conspiracies, appeared to the czars as something just as unsafe as was the Louvre to the French monarchy. Another Versailles came into being hundreds of miles away; that was St Petersburg.

Henceforth, the Kremlin became nothing but a castle given over to other purposes, a silent and colourful witness of the events of history. Everything that happened took place far away and its mysteries no longer excited public interest. No

9

more was it involved in Russian history. Once the stronghold
of faith, it was now merely a storage-house for political
records. For 177 years, until Lenin returned to it in March
1918, it had no part to play. In the chancelleries of the world
only St Petersburg had any significance, a town owing its
origin to the whim of a prince. In the following pages, therefore, in so far as power has been identified with the Kremlin,
the objective has been to trace as faithfully as possible, with
the help of anecdotes and documentary evidence, the history
of the czars. For the period 1741 to March 1918, when the
Kremlin had little importance save as a sacred monument, the
attempt has been made to summarize with all possible brevity
the story of the Russian people and nation. There is no point
in trying on every page to ring the bells which were silent
for nearly two centuries. Today the Kremlin has regained all
its importance.

CONTENTS

ILLUSTRATIONS

PART I

FROM ITS FOUNDATION TO THE ACCESSION OF ELIZABETH

(1100 to 1741)

CHAPTER 1

THE LEGEND

The story of the Kremlin begins with this legend from an ancient Russian anthology:

'It was a dark, stormy night when the boyar Stephen, son of Ivan Kuchka, came upon a thicket near the River Yauza, a tributary of the Moskva. The boyar and his followers spent the night in a hunting-lodge. The following morning, when the sun was beginning to gild the tops of the birches and the fir-trees, Kuchka had his horns sound the boar-hunt. The huge, savage boar suddenly appeared. The hunters were about to flee, when they saw a bird come out of the sky and swoop down upon the beast. It was a bird of prey of strange shape, having apparently two heads. Its claws and its two beaks reminded one of a fork. The boyar and his men became more afraid of this monster than of the boar. They immediately called off the hunt. The bird pounced upon the boar, seized it in its powerful claws and set it down on the hill which overlooks the Moskva and its tributary the Neglinnaya. Followed by his men, Stephen Kuchka went up to the top of the hill and there found the mangled remains of the boar.

'Very much impressed by this occurrence, the boyar decided to build a hunting-village on this hill and call it Kuchkovo.'

It was this village of Kuchkovo or Kutzkovo that was to become the town of Moscow. On top of the hill where the two-headed bird, the ancestor of the Russo-Byzantine double eagle,[1] had left the mangled boar, the Kremlin[2] was later erected.

Whether eagle, falcon or hawk, the bird of the legend had chosen a good spot to appear. Indeed, the place where the boyar Kuchka saw it for the first time is almost in the exact

[1] Two Soviet scholars, V. A. Alexandrov and A. A. Zimin, have collected this legend. In their view, it is steeped in Byzantinism, in that Byzantinism of the time of Ivan III, the Muscovite Grand Duke who married Sophia Zoë Paleolog and adopted as his coat of arms the double-headed eagle of the Emperor of Byzantium. Alexandrov and Zimin have unearthed another, very similar, text of still earlier date, which also treats of this bird of prey with the huge head and strange shape.

[2] *Kreml*, in Russian, means 'fortress' generally. Every fortified Russian town had its Kremlin.

17

geographical centre of European Russia. It was surrounded on all sides by forests and peat-bogs, being thus provided with effective protection against enemies from outside. The Moskva, which wound its way through the settlement, could be used from the beginning of the first 'Muscovite era' as a link between the Volga and the Oka, both these great rivers rising near it.

The boyar Kuchka had no idea of the consequences of his historical action when he went after the boar and the double-headed bird.

The legend continues:

'When evening came, the bag was so impressive that his servants found it very difficult to set out the slaughtered animals. The forest teemed with nocturnal birds and rats with handsome reddish fur, now extinct. There were also at that time foxes in great number, more plentiful than dogs (if an old twelfth-century Russian manuscript can be believed) and bears, wolves, lynxes, civet-cats, all lying in wait for their prey.

'Stephen Kuchka gave orders for a sort of trench to be dug quite close to the Neglinnaya and disguised with leafy branches and tree-trunks. The trench was dug and trees were cut down. In the middle of a patch of grass[1] a temporary wooden hut was built.

*　　　*　　　*　　　*

'So, Stephen Kuchka, happy at having laid the foundations of the future Kuchkovo, went to sleep on the hill, after drinking many glasses of braga[2] with his friends.

'A strong wind was blowing over the hill that night. The smell of the dismembered boar mingled with the scent of the berries and the fir-trees. Kuchka's sleep was disturbed by a troublesome nightmare, in which he saw a huge town built on the site of the settlement; a magnificent fortress with white battlements stretched away as far as the Neglinnaya. This fortress had a strange appearance; its roofs resembled those to be seen in the lands of the Bassurmans.[3]

'Many tents and wonderful gold-domed churches stretched down to the Moskva. Thousands of human creatures were being brought in chains to the white walls and while the church bells were sounding the tocsin their decapitated bodies were flung

---

[1] This grass-plot was given the name of Kuchkovo Field in the fifteenth century and retained it until the nineteenth century.

[2] A Russian drink resembling beer.

[3] In old Russian the word Bassurman means 'Infidel', i.e. 'Moslem'.

into the pits. Men, bound hand and foot, crawling along on their knees and wailing in front of a huge gallows, were begging mercy of a tall, gaunt skeleton of a man. The sun was already well up when the boyar awoke. He summoned his friends and servants to him and urged them to continue with the hunting, which he desired to be a joyful occasion. But he could not manage to regain his customary calm; there was sadness in his heart.'

In a few years the small settlement of Kuchkovo became a flourishing village. Craft, coming from the Volga and making their way towards the Oka, were moored by a jetty of pine-trunks. A little church called 'Paraskeva' raised its steeple on the very spot where the two-headed eagle had set down its prey. The boyar had merely to count the moneys coming to him from the toll-dues levied upon the boatmen. But the income from these dues had aroused the jealousy of Yuri, Prince of Suzdal. This Prince of Suzdal coveted Stephen Kuchka's village. Its position on the highroad joining the cities of Rostov and Vladimir was excellent. Yuri had an ally in the person of Svyatoslav-Olgovich, Prince of Novgorod Seversk, whom he had easily convinced of the importance of having a fortified township half-way between the two cities. This prince had himself built a 'small Kremlin' in the village of Lopasnaya, some forty-five miles south of Kuch-kovo, but this village standing on marshy ground had little to commend it. Prince Yuri Dolgoruki therefore determined to take Kuchkovo by force. He one day informed the boyar Stephen of his intended visit: he wished to hunt wild animals in the great forest. The sokol'nichiy, the head fowler, followed Prince Yuri with seventy-five falcons trained for hunting. It was the boyar Stephen's responsibility to provide all that was needed by the sokol'nichiy and his assistants.

Stephen Kuchka did his best to entertain his guests in a suit-able manner. The braga flowed copiously while Yuri's coming was awaited. Casks of the best Greek wine had been brought from Kiev for him. It was not until a very late hour that the boyar and his guests lay down to sleep on the Kremlin hill, in a newly-built hut of tree-trunks, with mica windows from the Kama. Tired from his copious drinking, the boyar fell into a deep sleep. He was rudely awakened in the middle of the night. The moon was hidden by small thickets on the Sparrow Hills. The stars were twinkling in the silvery northern sky. Suddenly the boyar Stephen became aware of the *sokol'nichiy's* face quite close to his own. 'Wake up!' the fowler was calling. 'Can't you hear that wailing cry?' It was the brown bear of the virgin Russian forest pouring out its lamentations in the night.

'Come, boyar! Take your *rogatina*![1] We are going to make Prince Yuri a handsome present!'

Stephen Kuchka got up, dressed hurriedly and set out. He did not realize that several of the *sokol'nichiy's* assistants were following him. He was completely unaware that the *smerde*[2] Stiopka, Prince Yuri's general serving-man, had a wonderfully trained bear which began howling whenever its master gave it the word of command. The following morning, on the greensward, was found the boyar's body, stabbed through and through and strangled. The ill-fated Stephen Kuchka was the first of the Kremlin's victims.

[1] A kind of three-pronged spear used in bear hunting.
[2] Peasant servant.

CHAPTER 2

THE FOUNDATION OF MOSCOW

By 1147 Kuchkovo was in the possession of Prince Yuri Dolgoruki.[1] It was in the same year that the Prince of Suzdal invited
his friend and ally, the Prince of Novgorod-Seversk, to visit him.

'I need to see you urgently, brother; other princes are casting
greedy eyes upon Russian lands. We must discuss the dangers
which beset us both. I will await your arrival at the fortress on
the common frontier of our two domains, the town of Moscow.'

The name Moscow is here mentioned for the first time. The
year 1147 may therefore be regarded as that of the foundation
of the capital of Russia.

It is quite understandable that Prince Yuri, after disposing of
the lord of Kuchkovo in so unchivalrous a manner, was not keen
to perpetuate his victim's name. He simply adopted the name of
the river, the Moskva, which flowed through the town. The
name 'Moskva' was already more than a thousand years old at
that date. It was first used by Finnish tribes who had settled in
the region between Lakes Ladoga and Seliger on the one side and
the River Oka on the other.

Like all Russian nobles of the age, Prince Yuri had at his court
a *kudesnik*, or soothsayer. At the time of meeting his friend
Svyatoslav Olgovich, Prince Yuri took his *kudesnik* with him.
It was his wish that the soothsayer should there and then foretell
the outcome of his alliance with the Prince of Novgorod-Seversk.
When he arrived at the river bank, the *kudesnik* took a piece of
glass obtained from 'beyond the River Ural', the purpose of
which was to conjure up in the water strange shapes in which
he could read the future.

That day, the water of the Moskva was more than usually
turbid. Nothing appeared in the piece of glass and the soothsayer had nothing to tell. Angrily, Yuri flung the glass into the
stream with the words, 'May this river be known for all time as
turbid water!' The small frontier town was of little importance
at that time and the prince could not have imagined that the

---

[1] *Dolgoruki* in Russian means 'long-armed', a nickname given him in view
of his intentions to appropriate cities as far distant as Kiev and Novgorod.

strange name would later be borne by one of the greatest capital cities in the world.

Svyatoslav Olgovich was escorted by four hundred soldiers of his *druzhina* (a detachment of guards). These men were themselves accompanied by young women. Unlike the Teutonic soldiery, the Russian fighting-men did not wait for death before visiting Valhalla and enjoying the company of the Valkyries; they preferred the companionship of the fair sex in their own lifetime.

An imposing banquet was held, the first in Moscow.[1] But let us hear the words of the ambassador-extraordinary of the caliph of Baghdad who was at that time passing through the principalities of Novgorod-Seversk and Suzdal to pay a visit to the Bulgarian King beyond the Volga.

'I, Ahmad ibn Fudlan ibn 'Abbas, desirous that the truth concerning these mysterious peoples should be known, declare that the Prince of the Novgorod-Seversk Russians has among his subjects four hundred of the bravest and most dependable men-at-arms to be met with. They form part of his retinue and accompany him in his travels. These men are prepared to give their lives for their prince or to die with him. Each of them has a girl to wait upon him, to wash his hair, pour his drink and share his bed. These girls sit at floor level, at the foot of the great, high princely dais, which is studded with precious stones brought from beyond the Ityl, from the River Ural, where emeralds, turquoises, rubies, amethysts and sapphires are found. Forty young women, intended to grace the prince's bed, are privileged to sit near him in this exalted place, where he occasionally disports himself with one or another of them before the eyes of his guards and attendants. The prince rarely comes down from the dais, except to obey a call of nature.'

His Excellency Ahmad ibn Fudlan ibn 'Abbas, ambassador-extraordinary of the caliph of Baghdad, had slightly misrepresented the facts concerning the 'mysterious peoples' he had seen. His oriental imagination is the reason. After Vladimir's baptism, the Russian princes had abolished polygamy and avoided appearing in public surrounded by a harem. The princes were content with the occasional discreet choice of a few of their *druzhinniki* girls for their amusement. The first Moscow banquet, held in 1147, was a sumptuous affair. Heaped at the foot of the Kremlin

---

[1] According to ancient records, this first Kremlin banquet was given in honour of the Prince of Chernigov.

was a huge quantity of slaughtered cattle, game, bear hams and casks of *braga* and mead. The negotiations between the two princes were preceded by a drinking bout which lasted at least three days and nights.

'When Russian princes begin diplomatic negotiations,' continues Ahmad ibn Fudlan ibn 'Abbas, 'they first have a drinking party in the presence of their *druzhina*. They take to the wine in a reckless manner, drinking day and night. It is not uncommon for one of the guests to die of indigestion or apoplexy, goblet in hand. And yet I noticed that the Russian princes sometimes made a pretence of drinking or drank just water, while plying their guests with large quantities of mead. No doubt they hoped in that way to dull the wits of those with whom they were dealing. I have witnessed the conclusion of an agreement between two Russian princes, one of whom signed a document without in the least being able to understand what he was doing. Moreover, when he was sober again he was anxious to refute the signature. Likewise I have noticed that the girls who are present at these orgies come to their master's assistance by practising their wiles upon those on the other side of the negotiations. This is done in a place specially fitted out for the purpose, a wooden chalet of rough external appearance but of sumptuous refinement within. There the girls get busy administering cold water to sober the men down and offer themselves with the purpose of detaining the guests.'

Once again, the caliph's ambassador had allowed himself to be carried away by his oriental imagination.

However that may be, the Yuri-Svyatoslav banquet was completely successful. The two princes and their *druzhini* had indulged in wine, women and song before proceeding to conclude an agreement which was to strengthen the union of the principalities (*udels*) of Suzdal-Rostov and Novgorod-Seversk. But a certain distrust prevailed. The Prince of Suzdal's *lazutchiki* ('spies', in old Russian) brought him disquieting news: large-scale fortifications were being put in hand in the village of Lobassnaya in the Principality of Novgorod-Seversk. What was the purpose in erecting these fortifications? Did not the Prince of Novgorod-Seversk intend one day to penetrate as far as Moscow, not as an ally but as a foe? Prince Yuri's spies gathered irrefutable proofs of Svyatoslav's double-dealing.

The conference of the two so-called allies at an end, Prince Yuri ordered the building of a fortress, a Kremlin, on the hill near the mouth of the River Neglinnaya.

The year 1156 is the date given in Russian history as that of the completion of the 'little Kremlin', on boyar Stephen Kuchka's hill.

CHAPTER 3

THE MONGOL VICTORY

The Kremlin was born. Moscow was certainly not yet the 'white stone capital' as it was later to be called, nor yet the holy city of the Russians which centuries of time were to make it. The wooden Kremlin was not the imposing building it became under the early czars.

The sole historical source of that age mentions 'a town downstream from the confluence of the Neglinnaya and the Moskva'. Prince Yuri's court was protected by a wooden fence, furnished with posts and strengthened with a few towers, also of wood. On the hill an enclosure had been contrived, surrounded by walls made of stones or badly-kilned bricks. This fortified enclosure was the 'little Kremlin', later on to become great.

The 'little Kremlin' occupied only the western slope of the hill which ran steeply down towards the confluence of the Neglinnaya near the present 'Borovitsky' gate. The name of this gate, which contains the word 'bor', shows that a forest of pines or firs must have existed there. The site which Prince Yuri had surrounded with wooden walls was triangular in shape. Its area was barely a third of that of the present-day Kremlin.

The Moscow of those times was neither a capital nor even a real town. At the very most it was a frontier fortress, a place on the route from north to south and a junction for river traffic.

The Moskva was an important highway. The Kremlin, built almost upon its banks, was primarily a stronghold for the purpose of protecting that highway, a kind of Russian freshwater Gibraltar.

Yuri Dolgoruki was not to enjoy his ill-gotten gains for very long; fate decreed that he should not see the development and improvement of the future capital of Russia. In 1157, one year after the building of the 'little Kremlin', Prince Yuri died. His son, Andrey Bogolyubsky, succeeded him as ruler of Suzdal Rostov-Vladimir.

Although the Kremlin in Moscow had so far played no important part in this period of Russian history, Andrey had nevertheless made occasional use of his father's freshwater

Gibraltar to settle the fate of certain of his enemies. The latter used the Kremlin to hatch a large-scale plot, the outcome of which was the death of Bogolyubsky.

Andrey's death had brought about civil war. His brothers Mikhail and Vsevolod arrived at Vladimir, where they were acclaimed Russian Grand Princes by the populace. On the other hand, the towns of Rostov and Suzdal never would acknowledge Andrey's younger brothers. These towns called upon Andrey's nephews, the sons of his deceased brother, as their rulers.

The civil war between the Russian towns degenerated into the war of the 'uncles and nephews', a cruel and bloody conflict. It ended in victory for Vsevolod III, Prince of Vladimir-Suzdal, after which the Kremlin enjoyed a long period of comparative peace.

A Russian chronicle states: '1237 was a fateful year in the history of the town of Moscow and its Kremlin. In the winter of 1237-1238 the hosts of Tartary, under the leadership of Baty Khan, came to Moscow and captured and burned the town, destroying the Kremlin. But in the spring of 1237 another event had taken place: many of the boyars in the service of the Grand Prince Yuri Vsevolodovich of Vladimir, who governed Moscow and had chosen the Kremlin as his palace, proved false to the Christian faith. This perfidy was the reason for the curse which descended upon the town and its Kremlin.

In the spring of 1237, a small craft sailed down the Moskva and moored by the wooden bridge opposite the Kremlin gate. It carried a cargo of precious fabrics, velvets and woven silks. The boyars' wives and the Grand Prince of Vladimir invited the owner of the vessel to dine with them. He was a certain Isaac, also known as Rabbi Yehuda, who hailed from Egypt and was a pupil and disciple of the late Moshe ben Maymun, Jewish physician and rabbi who lived and died in that land. Rabbi Yehuda was undoubtedly a sorcerer, for he brought with him the book of zelie (drugs) and claimed as its author Moshe ben Maymun himself. With the help of this book he began to treat the Grand Prince of Vladimir and his wife, as well as the boyars and their wives. He asserted that he knew the secret of youth, which he proposed to apply in treating Prince Yuri's wife; but she refused the treatment on account of the indecency of Isaac's methods. Rabbi Yehuda stayed in Moscow for a year, living in the Kremlin.'

The chronicle later continues: 'We must confess to our disgrace! Many of the Prince of Vladimir's retainers, his boyars and their wives, tempted by the "Evil One", allowed themselves to be imposed upon by Rabbi Yehuda. They renounced our holy faith, our orthodox beliefs, and embraced the foreign religion of the ungodly, the Jews and Moslems and Moorish Arabs from Spain and the Caliphate. They thought that by so doing they would be members of *a chosen race, believers blessed of God, who would once again send the Messiah into this world,* although our Lord Jesus Christ, crucified under Pontius Pilate and raised from the dead, remains the only Messiah recognized by the whole of Christendom.'

It has been thought worth while to disclose this little-known episode in the history of Russia and the Kremlin. Russian historians often refer to the 'sect of Judaists' in their country, in Kiev and Novgorod, and to the success which the sect achieved with the Russian aristocracy of those days. But one is never told that Judaism nearly possessed Muscovite Russia at the dawn of the Kremlin's existence, although the chronicle from which the details are taken had been known in Russia and read and re-read by Czar Alexander I in person during his spells of 'pantheistic mysticism'.

As it chanced, Rabbi Yehuda arrived at the Kremlin on the eve of the terrible catastrophe which occurred in the winter of 1237-8. The hordes of Gengis Khan, under the leadership of his nephew Baty Khan, swept over the Russian plain, burning towns and villages, looting, raping, butchering. As he made his way north-westward, where he hoped to reach Novgorod, that town 'overflowing with riches', of which his spies had informed him, he had drawn near to Moscow. From the heights of the Sparrow Hills, at the very spot where, in 1812, Napoleon cherished the dream of receiving the boyars bearing the keys of the Kremlin as a token of the city's surrender, the Mongol had beheld the Kremlin; it was made only of wood and did not yet possess its 'forty times forty' churches. Gengis Khan's nephew had no hopes of finding rich booty in Moscow, but as an experienced tactician he realized the strategical importance of the town as a cover for his left flank in the invasion of the 'soil of Novgorod', which abounded in wealth. He quickly made up his mind. With a motion of his gloved hand he signed to Barsadal, in charge of his cavalry. To the accompaniment of flutes made of reeds from the River Amur Darya, the 'cavalry-marshal' launched the attack upon the little fortress. One hundred and twenty thousand

Tartars flung their weight against the three thousand defenders of the Kremlin.

In the course of the evening, the town and the Kremlin fell to Baty Khan. Sitting in the hall of the Kremlin before setting fire to it, he and his officers celebrated the victory with heavy drinking. Gengis Khan's nephew drank from a vessel fashioned from the skull of the Grand Duke Yuri II of Vladimir, who had been killed by the Mongolian cavalry in the battle of Siti. All the prisoners of importance were laid out underneath planks, and the Tartars, in accordance with time-honoured custom, went on with their carousel, leaping and dancing on top of the planks so as to crush their prisoners; they smothered them, listened to their cries and the final rattle in their throats; and all the while they drank to Baty Khan, who was preparing to march upon Novgorod and Kiev, in the direction of western Europe. The boyars' wives, ravished by the Tartars, subsequently fell into the hands of the slave-traders who followed in the wake of the invaders.

The feasting at an end, Baty Khan went out and ordered all the prisoners who had not been smothered beneath the planks to be piled up in a heap in the Kremlin courtyard and burnt, together with the town, until all were dead beneath the smoking ruins. Rabbi Yehuda perished in the flames with his books by Ben Maymun and the Jewish religious scrolls.

So ended the attempt at messianic conversion, but it had left deep and permanent scars on the mentality of the Russian nation.

CHAPTER 4

THE REBUILDING OF MOSCOW

For Russia, with Moscow devastated and its Kremlin destroyed, the Tartar era had begun, with all its cruel savagery. Baty Khan's hordes, together with their cavalry which was bogged in the northern marshlands, had turned back without reaching Novgorod and marched on Kiev, which they captured and pillaged in 1240, before continuing westwards to carry death and destruction into Moravia, Croatia and Dalmatia. Prince Yaroslav, the brother of Yuri II who had been killed at the battle of Siti, entreated the Great Khan, Ugedey, third son of Gengis Khan, the paramount chief of all the hordes, to invest him with the title of 'Grand Prince' of Suzdal-Vladimir.

The Great Khan, who was busy attending to matters of war, was in no hurry to grant this favour. In the meantime, Yaroslav set about the work of rebuilding Moscow and the Kremlin; he clung to this town as if he already foresaw its great importance.

The Great Khan ordered the Prince of Vladimir-Suzdal to come in person to his chief city, the headquarters of the Golden Horde. Although a sick man, Yaroslav was compelled to undertake the long and difficult journey. On his arrival at the Golden Horde he did not find the Khan. The Russian prince was instructed to go further on, to Karakum in eastern Mongolia, to render homage to the paramount chief. Yaroslav resumed his exhausting journey across the Karakum desert, and died of the plague on the way.

While he was breathing his last in a wretched Mongolian village, his younger son, Mikhail 'Khorobrit',[1] the brawler, had come to Moscow to supervise the reconstruction of the town. The 'Khorobrit' was a reckless young prince, nearly always at loggerheads with other Russian princes, despite the Tartar yoke and the Mongolian threat hanging over Russia. And yet he remained faithful to the task entrusted to him by his father; the rebuilding of Moscow and the Kremlin, the improvement of the one and the fortification of the other. The Tartar yoke, cruel and

[1] Not to be confused with Evpati Kolvrit (Khrabri), the legendary Russian hero of the Tartar war (Klyuchevsky).

29

barbarous though it was, had almost no effect upon the administration of the conquered country, nor yet upon its established
customs or its religion. The nomadic barbarians of Mongolia,
crude and uncouth, were little concerned to know who the
prince of that country and the metropolitan were to be. Pagan,
ignorant, superstitious, they had only one interest: tribute-
money. Whoever organised the payment of tribute to their
greatest advantage was held in high favour with the Golden
Horde. In a Russian chronicle, these Mongols are described as
'armed monkeys with cavalry to serve them'. They remained so
until they were converted to the faith of Islam and were baptized
into the great Arabic civilization which had an invigorating
and beneficial influence on the west at the time of the crusades.

The 'Khorobrit' was not master of the Kremlin for long.
Wounded in one of his many skirmishes, he died as a result of
his wound in 1248, ten years after the burning of Moscow. In
1250 appeared the following description of the 'Khorobrit's'
rebuilding of the Kremlin:

'The prince (Mikhail, the 'Khorobrit') was energetic and
courageous in his work of reconstruction,' writes the abbot of
the monastery at Kolomna Wood. 'He worked with all his might
to rebuild his beloved Kremlin. It was from there that he often
used to watch the Moskva winding away into the distance and
the Neglinnaya joining its waters with it. He supervised the
work of reconstruction in person, occasionally taking pick or axe
and working alongside the labourers or helping the carpenters
and joiners. To those who did good work the prince would distribute bonuses from his own pocket. Careless workers were
punished; they were denied Mass and did not receive the bene-
diction from the coadjutor (Vikariy) on Sundays or feast-days.'

The prince made a success of his undertaking. The common
people were genuinely grieved when he died and the coadjutor
delivered a funeral oration, comparing him with the builders of
the Temple of Jerusalem.

'The prince has left us a restored and enlarged Kremlin, with
six gates in the place of four, five churches instead of two, a new
palace with many-coloured mica windows and buildings for the
druzhina and the boyars.' 'Moscow and the Kremlin have a most
peculiar quality,' said Count Rostopshin, the general who
ordered the burning of Moscow six centuries later, in 1812.
'They rise again from their ashes like a phoenix! And what is
more, they are more beautiful when they do so!'

Perhaps Count Rostopshin spoke in that way in the hope that his responsibility for burning the capital would be forgotten. But the story of the Kremlin which was rebuilt between 1238 and 1248 could have testified in favour of the Rostopshin theory. The Kremlin, restored and beautified by the 'Khorobrit', was used meanwhile by the Khan's tax-gatherers, his *baskaks*, who compelled the Russians to live in poverty and rags in order to pay the poll-tax. This tax was very heavy. The *baskaks* arrived with a detachment of cavalry intended for dragooning recalcitrant villages. The *baskaks* had the power of life and death over the prince's officials whose business it was to aid the Khan's tax-collectors. Wherever these officials did not 'furnish aid and assistance', as directed by the Grand Treasurer of the Golden Horde, the *baskak* had an executioner's block brought to the spot and cut off the head of the official who had shown such reluctance. But the Great Khan had also given orders that there should be no meddling in the affairs of the Church. His assistants were exempted from all taxes and levies, even from the 'chimney tax',[1] which was so ruthlessly applied by the Golden Horde during the Russian fratricidal wars. This particular tax fell most heavily upon the boyars and the wealthy inhabitants, since the poor people's *izbas*[2] of those times had neither chimneys nor even windows; the smoke came out through holes in the roof and walls.

The privileges enjoyed by the Russian Church were in no sense due to tolerance on the part of the Tartars or to political flexibility. As far as the Khan was concerned, the Russian metropolitan was nothing but the 'master magician', a spell-binder with the power of inflicting curses, and it was as well to have him on one's side. The Russian clergy often took advantage of these Tartar superstitions. The case is known of one coadjutor of the Kremlin who managed to compel a *baskak* to make a valuable donation to the building of a large Kremlin church by promising him that on his return to the Golden Horde his wife would give birth to a son, an event that had long been awaited in vain. As the *baskaks* were frequently changed by the Khan, so that they should not, as a result of greed and bribery, act in league with the Russians, the bishop ran no risk of seeing the same *baskak* return deluded and bent on vengeance.

The continued presence of the Tartar *baskaks* in the Kremlin

---

[1] *Dimnaya poda*: smoke tax.
[2] Peasants' cottages.

brought about increasingly marked disruption in the Russian way of life. The Russian princess, who enjoyed great freedom before the Tartar yoke was felt, had become a sort of prisoner in a place apart known as the *Terem*. There she lived, without the right to go out unaccompanied. Gradually, further restrictions to her freedom had been imposed. She was compelled to wear the veil, as is customary in Asia, to hide her face from men other than her husband and never more to take part in any gathering of men. To married women were attached female attendants who kept a close watch on their mistresses. The next stage to the *Terem* attendants' practice of passing information was denouncement from the prince's palace itself. This unhealthy atmosphere, originating in the Kremlin under the influence of the *baskaks*, was spreading through the land. The mental habit of the whole nation was beginning to change because of the moral deterioration of the princes who, in adapting their lives to the Tartar occupation, had recourse to deception and increasingly widespread hypocrisy, in politics to begin with and eventually extending to the cultural, moral and religious aspects of life. The springs of spiritual life, so plentiful before the Tartar control of Russia, were drying up from year to year. The Monasteries were mostly concerned with material things, becoming landowners on a large scale, exempt from taxation but harshly exploiting the peasantry. The dire poverty of the communities in the Moscow area created a system of credit buying, on the security of one's personal freedom. A peasant who did not manage to pay his debts became a *Kabalnyi*, the mere chattel of his creditor. This system had spread to the town, where free craftsmen gave up their positions to the men belonging to a prince's court, or in the service of a boyar or a free attendant to the prince, such as his hunt-master, his falconer, his armiger or his accredited usurer.

This moral corruption was already noticeable in the second half of the thirteenth century, at the time of the death of Yaroslav, Prince of Vladimir-Suzdal.

Vassili, Prince of Moscow, in his work of improving the Kremlin had built the first *Great Terem* for the women. To a foreign visitor he gave the explanation that it had been necessary to do so in order to keep the Russian women out of sight of the 'lustful invader'.

Ivan III, the Great; 1440-1505
[*photo: Radio Times*]

Ivan the Terrible, after the painting
by Vasnetsov   [*photo: Radio Times*]

Ivan IV, the Terrible; an early print; 1530-84
[*photo: Radio Times*]

Theodore III 1661-82 [photo: *Radio Times*]

III

Alexei Mihailovich 1629-76 [photo: *Radio Times*]

CHAPTER 5

ALEXANDER NEVSKY AND
YURI DANILOVICH

It is beyond doubt that the character and mental attitude of the Russian noblewoman, sometimes seemingly full of mystery to the western observer, felt the effects of the bondage of the *Terem*, with its system of continual observation and denouncement, the superiority of a husband strict and often cruel and the 'spiritual evasions' sought in prayer, meditation and long winter evenings given up to dreams begotten of unrelieved repression. But it is worthy of note that Alexander of Novgorod, known as Nevsky (second son of Yaroslav II), the great hero of thirteenth century Russian history, when visiting Moscow in the year of his accession as Grand Prince, refused to go to the *Terem* with the Prince of Moscow to see his wife. Nevsky declared that he would like to see the princess by her husband's side at the banqueting-table, as befitted a Russian woman.

Alexander Nevsky's visit to Moscow and the Kremlin was very significant. Appointed Grand Prince on the death of Yaroslav II, he was about to leave for the Golden Horde, in the flush of his victories over the Swedes and the Teutonic Knights, won when he was only as yet a prince with limited rights. When the Tartar invasion broke upon Russia in 1240 and brought about the destruction of Kiev, the 'mother of Russian cities', the Pope requested Alexander Nevsky to submit his lands to the authority of the Vatican, but Nevsky refused. To punish him for this refusal the Pope urged a crusade against the 'schismatics', instructing the Swedes to attack and destroy the town of Novgorod. Nevsky turned to the neighbouring principalities and with their support beat the Swedes on the banks of the Neva (whence the name Nevsky). Two years later he routed the Teutonic Knights at Lake Peypus, so saving Novgorod from the second wave of the papal 'Crusade'.

Now, in these two battles of enduring fame, the detachment from the Principality of Moscow had played a great part. This

B   33

otryad[1] had fought with outstanding bravery and had returned to the Kremlin with rich booty, enemy flags and a number of important prisoners.

Upon his arrival in Moscow, Nevsky celebrated his victories in the new Paraskeva Church which replaced the one destroyed by fire in 1238.

He told his son Daniel: 'Look upon this Kremlin, my son! When I die, you will have to come here and take control of the Moscow dependency. I believe it is here that the revival of our Russian land and the greatness of our country will have their beginning.'[2]

In 1263, on the death of Alexander Nevsky at St Fedor Monastery on the Volga, Daniel succeeded to the Kremlin and became the appanaged Prince of Moscow. Daniel made great efforts to improve the Kremlin and make it a seat worthy of such a prince. He had new churches and small palaces built and enlarged the Terem.

Daniel's son, Yuri Danilovich, continued his father's work of building and inherited the rôle of dangerous neighbour. Adopting his father's technique (when dealing with the Prince of Ryazan), Yuri attacked the Prince of Mozhaysk without warning, killed him and relieved him of his udel near the source of the Moskva.

Prince Yuri's insufferable nature had brought him to grips with the appanaged Prince of Tver, his neighbour and most dangerous rival, Prince Mikhail. Mikhail was a reticent but courageous man, and above all an experienced soldier with a sound knowledge of the military science of his day. There could be no question of Yuri's defeating Mikhail in open combat.

Yuri had chosen another means, which was to make Moscow a great principality and the Kremlin the sacred place of Russia after his death. Giving up all idea, therefore, of an open struggle with Mikhail, Yuri undertook a pilgrimage to the Golden Horde with the intention of accusing him (once again) of conspiracy against the Tartars and so discrediting him in the eyes of the Great Khan. This was not difficult to achieve, for at about the same time the people of Tver, the Tverichi, had butchered the

---

[1] From the thirteenth to the fifteenth century this name was often applied to a special reserve force (zasada) which played an outstanding part in battles like those of the Neva, Lake Peypus and Kulikovo, in which the zasada of the Voevoda Bobrok had given victory to the Russians.

[2] 'Russkaya Starina'.

members of a mission which the Mongolian despot was sending
to Louis XI of France in return for a visit paid to 'Great Tartary'
by an unofficial plenipotentiary, Guillaume de Rubriquis, a
Franciscan friar. The *baskaks*, the bodyguard, the great
ambassador himself—all lost their lives. The *Tverichi* had not
forgotten their treatment at the hands of a *baskak* who, in a
temperature of minus forty degrees, had stripped them naked in
the open in order to persuade them to pay tribute-money.

Yuri was received with honour at the Golden Horde, where
he arrived bringing wagons weighed down with sumptuous
gifts. After passing beneath the 'arch of obedience', the Tartar
equivalent of the Roman 'yoke', he was ostentatiously welcomed
to the great Khan's tent. The Prince of Tver, after his denunciation by Yuri, had fallen into the hands of a Tartar detachment,
urgently dispatched, and had been brought in chains to the
Golden Horde. He attempted to escape and was shut up in a
bear cage, just as Cardinal La Ballu was caged at about the same
time. But just then the Mongol ruler was concerned with other
troubles. An expedition to China claimed his attention. He
abandoned his guest and left his prisoner to be dealt with by a
Regency Council, which included the *khansha* who had the
reputation for winning everybody's heart. Yuri, who, according
to the 'Russkaya Starina', was a man 'as handsome as Czar
David' (*sic*), did not remain indifferent to her charms, just as
she could hardly resist his. Meanwhile, the Prince of Tver was
sentenced to death by the Regency Council, decapitated and
impaled.

Yuri received his investiture as Prince of Tver but the
irresistible *khansha* detained him for many months, both in her
bed and on her council, on the plea of 'important business dealings with her vassal'. The Prince of Moscow had appointed
boyars to govern Tver on his behalf and the people were showing
resentment against them. Mikhail's sons, who had fled, lodged
an unsuccessful complaint with the Metropolitan of Kiev against
the 'base and treacherous servant of the Tartars'. The Church
remained unresponsive: it paid no tax. Nobody dared to engage
in open conflict with the complacent and ageing Great Khan or
with Yuri, who so adequately filled the *khansha's* desires. The
aged Mongolian despot was prepared to sign the *yarlyk* granting
Yuri's investiture as a Russian Grand Prince, sealed with the
'great Mongolian Dragon'. But his wife was watching events.
She, too, was getting old—she was over thirty—and was fading,

as an Oriental woman does. On the occasion of Yuri's second journey she had the impression that her 'David' was wearying of her endearments. She permitted him a certain degree of freedom with the Khan's harem, among those 'beauties for a night', whose indulgence was not without danger. And there ends, or almost ends, this eastern tale, in which a favourite and an empire were at stake. Legend has it that she knew her charming Muscovite prince would be unfaithful no more. When he left, he was suffering from a sickness, the symptoms of which had become apparent at a banquet given by his 'old' mistress, when he had drunk 'the drink of the isles'. On the way back he spat blood and from day to day his strength deserted him. When he returned to Moscow, he was in such a state of ill-health that the Kremlin 'healer' forbade him to leave his bed. But Yuri, although suspecting that the 'drink of the isles' held some slow-acting but effective poison, wished to obtain the promised *yarlyk* before he died. Ill and in pain, he set out a third time for the Golden Horde, but Prince Mikhail's sons had decided to avenge their father. They got together a *druzhina*, and when he was fording the River Kolocha a rain of arrows descended upon the dying Yuri and he collapsed upon his white charger.

So died the traitor, too well loved and not a little hated, without receiving the investiture of Grand Prince. But his stay as the guest of the Golden Horde had opened the way to his brother Ivan, who, on becoming the first Muscovite Grand Prince, set about gathering together the Russian estates around the Kremlin.

CHAPTER 6

IVAN I KALITA

The early days of the reign of Ivan Danilovich, the grandson of Alexander Nevsky and the future Ivan I Kalita, were stormy times of bloodshed. After their assassination of Yuri, the sons of Mikhail of Tver sought refuge in Novgorod, the free Republic saved by Alexander Nevsky from the Swedes and the Teutonic Knights. But not long afterwards the body of one of Mikhail's sons was taken from the River Volkhov. This drowning coincided strangely with the arrival in Novgorod of a boyar from the Moscow Kremlin, Kvashnin, Prince Ivan's confidential agent.

The dead man's brother, Alexander, sent a violently-worded letter to Ivan accusing him of his brother's death and promising that he 'would meet him at the Last Judgment, unless he killed him first like a dog, as he had killed his brother Yuri, the lackey of a *bassurman* Khan'.

This same Alexander addressed another letter to several Russian princes:

'Are we Russians or, like Ivan of Moscow, have we become the servants of the Tartar infidels?' he wrote. 'Are we prepared to help one another, to die for one another, to show mutual friendship and brotherliness by uniting our efforts to fight the Tartars, or are we going to betray our brethren to the *bassurmans*, as did the ungodly prince who now rules in the Moscow Kremlin? For my part, I shall fight to the death and resist the Tartars and their lackey! I am ready to defend Russian soil and Christendom!'

These inflammatory words from Alexander caused a new revolt in Tver. For the second time the *Tverichi* massacred the *baskaks* and their Tartar bodyguard. When he heard of the massacre Prince Ivan Danilovich left with all haste for the Golden Horde, bearing precious gifts, just as his brother Yuri had done before him. He found the Great Khan Uzbek, who was ageing noticeably, and the *Khansha*, fat and bloated, looking for a new fair-haired lover.

The Khan was furious with the town of Tver and proposed
sending against the Russians a large expeditionary force under
the command of his best cavalry marshal, Eldegaz, the descendant of a line of Gengis Khan's marshals.

A great danger hung over Moscow and the Kremlin, greater
perhaps than that of the ill-fated winter of 1238.

Prince Ivan fell on his knees before the Khan, begging him to
show magnanimity. That same day the Prince of Moscow had
distributed many gifts to the *murza*. He had also been received
in audience with the *khansha* and had presented her with a gold
bracelet of Swedish workmanship, studded with diamonds and
sapphires. Some historical sources claim that Ivan Danilovich,
who bore a close resemblance to his brother Yuri, so impressed
the *khansha* that she resumed with him the relationship she had
had with the brother whom she had poisoned. The outcome of
Ivan's visit to the Golden Horde was that the Great Khan
decided to put the Prince of Moscow in charge of the Tartar
forces sent to punish the Russians for the death of the *baskaks*.

The master of the Kremlin had achieved a diplomatic coup,
but at a heavy price: a Russian prince in command of infidel
armies which were about to massacre, pillage and burn Russian
principalities on their way. The cavalry-marshal Eldegaz was
the subordinate of Ivan but it was he who was in fact in command. This expedition proved even more bloody than Baty
Khan's invasion, but if Ivan had not been in command of the
Tartar forces Russia would have become one vast graveyard.
Nothing would have been left of the towns and villages.

Ivan restrained Eldegaz to the best of his ability without
utterly compromising his position with the Golden Horde. The
only respect in which he was completely successful was in
sparing the Principality of Moscow and its Kremlin. The people
of the other principalities learnt their lesson: they transferred
themselves bodily to the district which came under Ivan's control. Immigrants, with their families and households, came
pouring into Moscow from all directions.

Having carried out his task of repression, Ivan left again for
the Golden Horde to bow the knee and pay tribute to the Khan.
At last, in 1328, Uzbek Khan's *yarlyk* was issued in his favour
and he became Grand Prince of Vladimir. So Moscow was made
the capital and its Kremlin became the 'heart of Russia', ninety
years after the town was captured and destroyed by Baty Khan!
It was almost a miracle. A small township, lost among the

forests and marshes, governed by a prince of little importance, had risen rapidly to the dignity of a capital city, comparable with glorious old towns like Kiev, wealthy commercial towns like Novgorod or religious centres such as Vladimir.

A new era was beginning, although not without its obstacles. The new Prince, thrifty by nature, shrewd and niggardly in his dealing, used to walk about wearing a sable-lined coat, frayed at the collar and cuffs, with a huge money-bag attached to his belt, making loans at high interest rates to tradesmen and artisans, encouraging them to construct new buildings for the Kremlin, to improve the appearance of his capital and make it attractive to the traders and boyars of other principalities.

But, while Moscow was growing, a permanent danger hung over the town and the whole of Russia: if another revolt should break out somewhere and a massacre of *baskaks* should result, the old Khan might put into execution his terrible threat 'to transform the land of Russia into hard mud!' His cavalry-marshal, Eldegaz, did not conceal from Ivan that he had already received instructions for meeting such a contingency.

Therefore, scenting the danger to Russia, Ivan spent most of his time at the Golden Horde and continued his relationship with the *khansha*, to whom the Khan, old and ailing, relinquished his authority as a ruler. Eldegaz, wholly devoted to her sovereignty, was waiting only for the death of Uzbek Khan in order to become Great Khan himself by a *coup d'état* and marry Uzbek's widow.

Ivan Kalita's[1] frequent visits to the Tartar capital brought him diplomatic success.

Uzbek Khan, urged on by the *khansha*, had consented to Ivan's replacing the *baskaks* for the collection of the Khan's tax. Ivan guaranteed him a certain minimum sum and was to share with him anything above this minimum. In this way the Khan would no longer be obliged to send punitive expeditions against rebels who were also taxpayers and customers and whose death stopped the flow of wealth into the coffers of the Golden Horde.

Ivan Kalita had thus become the Tartars' tax-gatherer. He used a large part of the share of the money for improving Moscow and obviously did his utmost to tax most heavily those principalities which were his political or commercial rivals.

A Russian *letopis'* records that at this time an Italian architect

[1] 'Kalita' means 'money-bag' in old Russian.

called Solario arrived in Moscow from 'the land of the Poles'. This architect[1] constructed several buildings of brick and stone, two of them being churches, and they all disappeared during the Kremlin fire in the first half of the fourteenth century.

Ivan went on with his work of unification. He took over his neighbours' estates, by virtue of the Khan's *yarlyk* and the first *ukases*. The Russian *yarlyks* were countersigned by the Khan, his treasurer, his Regency Council or his cavalry-marshal, who had been promoted to the position of Marshal of the Court. Ivan bought back from the Tartars Russian, Bulgarian and Finnish prisoners, to whom he distributed territories. By offering subsidies he attracted settlers to his lands. The forests and marshes of the Moscow region were becoming more populous than the old districts of the country which were well known for the fertility of their soil.

But the speed of Kalita's undertaking was not matched by an improvement in the way of life. The beautiful Russian tongue, with its melodic inflexions, was being spoilt by Tartar neologisms and crude, guttural words from the uncultured conquerors. The coarsest oriental abuses invaded the language. The boyars quickly assimilated such oaths and their council meetings often ended with floods of abusive terms worse than those to be heard at the meetings of the Golden Horde.

Since police and legal authority were practically non-existent in those days, the Kremlin chronicle of the times has little information to provide. There are just a few items dealing with poisoning 'affairs' through the *zelie*, murders committed during hunting expeditions and some cases of severely punished 'witchcraft', such as evil incantations pronounced over models of intended victims.

[1] Not to be confused with Pietro Antonio Solario who, together with Marco Ruffo, built the famous 'Palace of Facets' or 'Granovitaya Palata' of the Kremlin in the fifteenth century, during the reign of Ivan III.

CHAPTER 7

SIMEON THE PROUD AND IVAN II

Before he died, Ivan Kalita summoned the Metropolitan Theognost to the Kremlin in order to make his 'private' and his 'political' wills. Ivan Kalita was, in fact, responsible for instituting the custom of making two. While the crowd was praying in the Kremlin courtyard for the health of the Prince, he revised the text of a will he had made in 1327, before his last journey to the Golden Horde at Saraï:

'In the name of the Father, the Son and the Holy Ghost, I, Ivan, a sinner and the humble servant of God, make this will and testament without compulsion of any kind and being sound of mind and body. When it shall please God to call me I bequeathe my possessions to my sons and to my beloved Princess. To all my sons I leave my appanage of Moscow, with the exception of the Kremlin, which will go to my eldest son Simeon, the Grand Prince of Moscow.'

This will, witnessed by the boyars of the court and the Metropolitan, made the Kremlin the private property of the Grand Prince who succeeded his father.

In referring to Ivan Kalita's will, the historian Klyuchevsky somewhat ironically notes the following extract from the document:

'As for my two fur-lined coats, slightly moth-eaten, which are in the small clothes cupboard in the basement of the *Terem* in the Kremlin, I make a gift of these to my wife, that she may offer them to her most zealous and devoted attendants.'

So it was (says Klyuchevsky) that Ivan Kalita, the 'unifier of Russian estates', at the hour of his death did not forget the two moth-eaten coats, while mentioning in his will most important affairs of state. Kalita's successors also were later to reveal in their wills the same parsimony.

Every age has its heroes who are in keeping with that age. The thirteenth and fourteenth centuries were a period of widespread corruption due to the Tartar influence upon Russia. It

was a period of self-seeking narrow-mindedness. Almost all the
princes of the 'Kremlin period' possessed this historic characteristic. They succeeded in making Russia out of the Principality
of Moscow, but their achievement was not due to their personal
qualities. They were merely the tools of Russian history, which
developed of its own accord along the lines of its own laws and
the character of the Russian nation.

Simeon I, Ivan's successor, wished to achieve greater power
and glory than his father's. His personal castle, the Kremlin,
became the scene of continuous and merciless conflict during the
thirteen years of his reign. Before everything else Simeon desired
to be acknowledged by the Metropolitan Theognost as a prince
'in a class apart'; he gave instructions for an Easter sermon in
which the Metropolitan was to sing the praises of Ivan's successor. The crafty Theognost, while seeming to obey, made a
point of referring in his sermon to the debasement of morals and
the poisonings which still continued to corrupt the Kremlin :

'Give thanks to God, you men of the Holy Church, and
glorify our Grand Prince Simeon Ivanovich, while yet confessing
the terrible sins which are rife in Moscow and the Kremlin ! For
women are no longer protected from the evil spirit of their husbands and husbands must stand in awe of their wives' wicked-
ness, for both husbands and wives have become the servants of
the Evil One, as did Adam and Eve in the Garden at the coming
of original sin. My brothers and sisters, Satan stalks the Kremlin ! He wields his fork to drive into Hell the Christians of our
Church. Do penance ! Cast aside the lust which lurks in the
Terems.'

This sermon recalls another, by Father Johan of Kronstadt,
the miracle-worker and 'saint' acknowledged and revered by the
last Czar Nicholas II and his wife Alexandra Feodorovna.

But Simeon the Proud was cast in a very different mould from
the ill-fated Nicholas II. He did not forget the sermon in which
he detected a personal reference, since he himself was very much
inclined to the sin of lechery : his wives very conveniently died
every time he wished to find another mate among the boyars'
daughters gathered at the Kremlin for the smotriny, the bridal-
fair. The troublesome Metropolitan himself died soon after the
sacring.

The smotriny had become an indispensable custom in the
Kremlin. The candidates offering themselves in marriage were

brought from every corner of the land, being chosen from among the boyars' daughters. The *Terem* was enlarged by the addition of a new room, the 'brides' hall', and a building apart, the 'brides' hostel', which also had its baths and a *gornitza*[1] in which the candidates prepared for the *smotriny*. It was the duty of a specially-appointed woman official to supervise the Kremlin's *devichnik*.[2] She was supported in her task by a dozen assistants who helped the 'brides' to 'beautify themselves', to bathe and to beguile their time without having to leave the *Terem*. This official guardian had also to make a 'detailed inventory' of all the candidates. This inventory was in each case presented to the intended husband before the final display of the 'brides'. It gave a general idea of the candidate, her moral and intellectual qualities (literate or illiterate, religious or not, ability to play musical instruments, disposition, etc.). It also gave detailed 'anatomical' characteristics, including 'freckles or warts', if such markings were of strange, suspicious-looking shape, so that a witch should not become a Princess of Moscow. Obviously, the protection of the brides' virginity was very strict. The rivalry between the noble families presenting candidates was so keen, such effective means were employed (and these included bribes) to inflict upon the Prince the daughter of some particular rich or noble boyar, that it was too much for him and he was obliged to appoint the Metropolitan as 'inspector-extraordinary'. The aged head of the Church begged to be excused from this duty, offering a preposterous explanation of his request:

'I am no St Anthony,' he rapped out, when he was commissioned to witness the verification of the brides' virginity. As the Grand Prince insisted, the prelate, who was something of a wit, said, 'Do not think, Prince, that I am like the "companion", either!'[3]

Having failed in his attempt to make the Metropolitan his 'inspector-extraordinary' of the brides' virginity, the Prince entrusted this task to a special boyar, chosen, in the words of the *letopis'*, 'from among those whose hair was whitened by age and who were known for their monastic deportment'. Despite this 'guarantee of moral behaviour', the notorious Kremlin

[1] Young women's recreation-room.
[2] The *Terem* living-quarters for the unmarried daughters or female staff of a boyar or the Grand Prince.
[3] According to legend, St Anthony had as his companion a pig.

chronicle recorded several instances in which the candidate-brides brought their charms to bear in order to win over the boyar acting as 'inspector-extraordinary'.

From motives of decency the Grand Prince refrained from attending the inspection of the brides, but he reserved for himself certain means of keeping watch on his 'inspector'. A small opening was contrived in the wall of the corridor through which the brides were taken, so that the Prince might observe them in their ordinary clothes, without make-up or *rumyana*.[1] A little later this 'princely privilege' was extended to include the *Terem* baths. Several small openings had been arranged there for the benefit of the 'intended', who could by that means see the candidates completely naked.

To return to Simeon, he died in 1353 and his widow, who was still young, proved not to be inconsolable.

Along with this 'sidelight' on the Kremlin the greater history of the Grand Duchy of Moscow developed. Although they were recognized as 'Grand Dukes' by the Khans, the Princes of Moscow and the Kremlin found themselves on many occasions in conflict with the other princes. They were obliged to make countless journeys to Saraï, the new capital of the Golden Horde, with presents for the Khan, his first wife and the many *murzas* of Saraï. The road from the Kremlin to the great tent of the Khan in Saraï became the 'pupils' path' for each new Prince. Along this same road, from Saraï to Moscow, travelled the Tartar *murzas*, the treasurer-auditors, the Khan's ambassadors-extraordinary, the officers in charge of the 'security guards' who stayed a long time in Russian principalities that were not completely 'pacified'. As the Grand Prince of Moscow had become the tax-gatherer, it was possible for him to distribute gifts in plenty, but it was often difficult for him to prevent the Khan's suppression of the regions in revolt. These revolts were provoked by the population census undertaken on the average once every twelve years to verify the total of the tribute-money. The treasurer-auditors,[2] with the help of a whole army of officials, counted the Russians as sheep are counted in the fields of Mongolia: the people were collected together, men, women and

[1] Red colouring for the lips and cheeks. Russian women have always been very skilled in make-up. The habit was adopted even by the women of the common people, who made excessive use of *belila*, a whitish substance making the face appear very pale.

[2] *Chislenikki*, in Russian.

children, in separate pens similar to those used for sheep. The Russian tallymen helped the Tartars so as to prevent the latter from cheating the Grand Duke by submitting a fanciful total, a number in excess of the real one. A special building in the Kremlin contained the 'counting-house',[1] where the Tartars learned to reckon. Being very primitive, they used pebbles[2] for the purpose. The pebbles were brought to the Kremlin after the census and their number compared with the result reached by the Russian tallymen. But the matter did not end there; the Mongols, who could not write, were not able at once to record the result of the count and the Moscow Prince's officials took advantage of the fact to make away with some of the Tartars' bags of pebbles and so reduce the total figure. A free fight developed in the Kremlin in 1353, when Ivan II, the Debonair, succeeded Simeon the Proud. The Tartars who had come to count the population had an argument with the Russian officials and came to blows with them beneath the windows of the *Terem*. The Metropolitan came out of his Cathedral with the intention of calming down the disputants, but when he was attacked by the Tartars he was compelled to seek refuge behind the altar.

It may be affirmed from the study of Russian historical sources that it was the Russians who intended to trick the Tartars in the Kremlin in 1353, and not the reverse. Suspecting that the Russians had cheated them in previous censuses, the Tartars brought with them a Chinese expert who made a written record of the aggregate. So it was established that some of the pebbles in the Tartars' bags, carried to the Kremlin in huge wains, had been removed by the Russian officials, unaware that thanks to the 'learned Chinese' the result of the census was already recorded.

Ivan II, the Debonair, left with the Tartar treasures for Saraï with tribute-money for the Great Khan. On the way the caravan made frequent halts at inns, called *bardaks*,[3] where the female staff were very forthcoming. The Prince paid the treasurers'

[1] *Chislennaya Palata.*

[2] This system was already known to antiquity; the numbers were represented by means of small pebbles, *calculi* in Latin, whence the word 'calculate'.

[3] In those times, hostelries used as their inn-sign a 'pitcher' (*kuvshin* in Russian) set up on a post in front of the inn. In the Tartar tongue, the word for 'pitcher' is *bardak*. As the female staff of the inns was very accessible to visitors, the Russians became accustomed to using the term *bardak* as the equivalent of 'brothel'.

expenses in full so as to keep on the right side of them, thus avoiding having to pay forfeit to the Grand Treasurer or being deprived of his right as tax-gatherer.

Ivan II's journey to Saraï was therefore highly successful, thanks to the hospitable *bardaks* on the way. When he had received the *yarlyk*, Ivan requested the Khan to mete out punishment to several of the Russian princes who had taken it into their heads to oppose him. The Khan dispatched his 'grand *murza*' to bring these princes to Saraï, where they were ruthlessly put to death. Their stripped and mangled corpses lay in the dust near the Khan's tent for more than a week. Ivan II, coming to make his bow before the Mongol, had to walk on the bodies of the princes murdered by his orders.

On his return to Moscow Ivan II built a 'church of thanksgiving' in the Kremlin as an acknowledgement to the Holy Trinity of the success of his mission. He then summoned to the Kremlin some of the younger sons of the princes murdered in Saraï and had them shut up in a prison by the east wall. Several of these embarrassing prisoners died there.

Having first overthrown the Prince of Bryansk, Ivan II then took up arms against the Princes of Obolensk and Novossilsk. The latter readily submitted, from fear of the Prince of Tver, the chief enemy of the Kremlin. This prince had, with Tartar support, occasionally sought the help of the Grand Duke of Lithuania, who regularly invaded Russian territories. The Great Khan approved so highly of Ivan's policy that a '*murza* of the court and seal' came to the Kremlin to confer upon him the order of the 'grand *yarlyk*', which gave him the right to try all Russian princes and act as judge in their political and personal differences. A kind of Court of Appeal was set up in the Kremlin and the Russian princes were henceforth to attend there instead of going to Saraï.

The Kremlin was increasingly becoming a second Saraï, the centre of political power of the whole of Russia. Ivan II turned the situation to good account by compelling the princes to establish a sort of 'Russian joint financial society', which was both economic and monetary in purpose. The coinage of Russia as a whole was now beginning to be struck in the Mint at the Kremlin. So it was that the Grand Princes of Moscow suddenly found themselves in possession of a powerful means of binding the princes to them. For his part, the Metropolitan required of them blind obedience to Ivan II, 'not merely from fear but more especially in good Christian faith'.[1]

The second part of Ivan's reign contrasted strangely with its early years. When he had made peace with his enemies, the Princes of Tver and the 'Svyatoslavich of Chernigov' line,[2] Ivan changed his attitude towards them, as if he wished to blot out the story of his tragic rise to power in Saraï. Apparently, he was highly successful in this, for he went down in Russian history as 'the Debonair'; which fact has its amusing side.

As he became increasingly rich and powerful, 'the Debonair' Prince began to plot against the Great Khan, trading on the state of affairs at Saraï, where several bodies were vying with each other for power. The *murzas* broke away from the Khan's authority and, since they were accustomed to being paid at the Kremlin, they came to the ruler of Moscow in increasingly large numbers, peddling secret information concerning Saraï and offering him their services.

In 1359, the year in which Ivan II died, the Grand Treasurer himself came to the Kremlin with a tempting proposal: the Council of *murzas*, whose chief concern of the moment was the raising of an army to invade China, asked the Prince of Moscow for a loan from the Mongol tribute-moneys and for this loan offered security—yesterday's conqueror now begging at the gate of the Kremlin.

Ivan II gave his consent but was stricken down with an intestinal disorder and died at Saraï a few weeks later, in 1359. Only four years after his death, his son Dmitri was crowned Grand Prince of Moscow in the Kremlin. He determined to make the most of the weakness revealed in Saraï; but, instead of 'striking through gold', which was his father's intention, he flung out a challenge to the Great Khan. For the first time in history the Kremlin was becoming aware of its military strength.

[1] This formula persisted even to the end of the Romanov dynasty. Even as late as 1916, the soldiers of the Russian army repeated after their *pope*: 'The Czar of Russia is an absolute czar: God himself had ordained that he shall be obeyed, not merely from fear but more especially in good Christian faith'.

[2] This 'line' consisted of the Principalities of Obolensk, Bryansk and Novossilsk; whence the names of the Princes: Obolensky, Bryansky, Novossilsky.

CHAPTER 8

DMITRI DONSKOY AND THE DEFEAT OF THE TARTARS

The 'lesser coronation' of Prince Dmitri Ivanovich, son of Ivan II and grandson of Ivan Kalita, was celebrated in 1363. All Russian historians hold that Dmitri Ivanovich, who mounted the Kremlin throne at eleven years of age and was to remain there until 1389, possessed remarkable qualities: he was handsome, tall, slight, courageous, clever, devout, very polite and shy.[1]

He began his reign by making a few raids upon his neighbours' territory and occupying the towns of Starodub-on-Klyazma,[2] Dmitrov and Galich. The reigning princes of these *udels* were driven out and *voevodas* were appointed as Dmitri Ivanovich's first governors.

But, as a 'very polite' person, the young Prince decided to pay a 'retirement pension' to the evicted princes and instituted a special 'pensioners' fund'. From that day onwards, the Grand Prince could not possibly drive the princes from their towns and dispossess them of their goods without paying compensation! The political problem of the struggle against feudalism in Russia was thus greatly simplified and many of these princes came and settled with their *dvor* in Moscow, living like lords upon their incomes.

Dmitri Ivanovich also engaged in much diplomatic activity with those who were unwilling to give up their *udels* in order to come and live at the Kremlin. It was his intention to enlarge the 'joint financial society' established by his father. His method was to send *gontzi*[3] to the four corners of Russia to offer loans to princes. If the loans were not repaid by the agreed date, the Grand Prince would request a 'parcel of land' in payment. A large building was erected in the Kremlin (later burned down in the days of Ivan the Terrible), a kind of hostelry for the purpose of lodging the appanaged princes who came to Moscow to ask

[1] According to Klyuchevsky.

[2] Not to be confused with the southern town of Starodub in the Principality of Chernigov. Starodub-on-Klyazma was founded by settlers from South Russia.

[3] Couriers.

for money. To the Moscow *Terem* was added a south wing for housing the wives and daughters of their attendants. The princes were in the habit of taking their daughters with them, for it was easier for them to make a 'good match' in Moscow than in the country. To the bachelor Dmitri Ivanovich the boyars brought candidates from all corners of Russia in anticipation of bringing off a marriage with the Grand Prince. But the 'very polite' young man was also 'very celibate' and avoided female society. The Metropolitan himself felt constrained to step in and persuade Dmitri of the necessity of getting married, in the interests of politics at least.

The Princes of Tver, recovering from defeat and the catastrophes they had suffered at the hands of Moscow and Saraï, resumed the struggle. Michael of Tver, who was energetic and intelligent, and cultured for those days (unlike Dmitri, who could neither read nor write at the time of his accession[1]), had determined to avenge his principality's misfortunes and to make an attack upon Moscow. Michael sought by all means in his power to obtain some backing at Saraï, but he had not at his disposal, as his adversary had, the money necessary to pay the *murzas* and the *khatun*.[2] In the end, having had no success with Saraï, Michael turned to his neighbour Olgerd, Grand Duke of Lithuania. In response to this move, Dmitri called to a great conference in the Kremlin nineteen Russian princes[3] in order to form a 'holy alliance' against Tver.

After signing the Holy Alliance and sworn on the Metropolitan's cross to remain faithful to their oath, the princes decided upon the day for the expedition against Tver. Nineteen detachments from the surrounding principalities joined the Grand Prince's army for the attack. Michael dispatched his ambassador to Vilno, the capital of Lithuania, begging his ally's help. At the same time, an envoy from Dmitri left the Kremlin for Vilno, with costly gifts for the Grand Duke Olgerd and the proposal of a permanent alliance between Moscow and Vilno to replace the armistice arranged with Dmitri's uncle, Simeon the Proud, at the conclusion of the Russo-Lithuanian war which was settled by Olgerd's annexation of Kiev, Chernigov, Severia and Podolia.

[1] He later learned to read and write.
[2] The Great Khan's principal wife.
[3] The Princes of Rostov, Beloozero, Starodub, Bryansk, Smolensk, Novossilsk, Ryazan, Mozhaysk, Kolomna, Serpukhov, Kaluga, Meshchera, Galich and others.

Dmitri had chosen a good moment for suggesting an alliance. Lithuania had been continually at war with the Teutonic Knights since 1340, when the Grand Duke Gediminas had been killed in combat against these knights. Olgerd, who had come to the throne in 1345 and had attacked Moscow on three occasions, had been converted to the Orthodox Church, while still remaining the grim enemy of Russia. But the Order of Teutonic Knights was growing in size and strength and the Lithuanians, faced by this threat, disregarded their old enmity and Olgerd chose the Russian alliance. So the situation was saved for Dmitri Ivanovich.

The new Great Khan of Saraï, Mamay, disturbed at the intelligence brought to him by his *murza* Kalchok, who claimed that Dmitri was plotting against him, decided to agree to Michael of Tver's proposal to displace Dmitri, summon him to Saraï and put him to death before his tent, as required by established tradition. For his part, Dmitri, after signing an armistice with Olgerd, who was covering the north-west flank of Moscow, began to make preparations for open conflict with the Great Khan by refusing to go to Saraï and by having his ambassadors murdered.

But Dmitri, inexperienced in the art of war,[1] realized very clearly that to fight the Tartars he needed a great *voevoda* to lead his armies. For this purpose he considered his first cousin Vladimir Andreyevich, Prince of Serpukhov, 'a man of indomitable courage'. But courage was not enough. He needed to find a leader of wide experience and skill.

At the time of the Tartar oppression, the Russian princes fought among themselves but there was little of the real art of warfare in these conflicts.

Dmitri finally settled upon his *voevoda*: old Bobrok, who had gained his experience in Lithuania against the Teutonic Knights as the commanding officer of an auxiliary Muscovite detachment sent to Vilno after Olgerd's conversion. Dmitri left for Serpukhov to see his cousin Vladimir Andreyevich and prepare his plan of campaign, taking the *voevoda* Bobrok with him. A rare occurrence, indeed, in the annals of Moscow for a Grand Duke to call upon his vassal in the 'little Kremlin' of Serpukhov!

One can see the town of Serpukhov from the top of a hill, after crossing the bridge over the Oka. It lies along a spur of land at a turn in the river. A huge panorama unfolds to the visitor's

[1] *The Grand Duchy of Moscow in the 14th century*, by Soloviev.

gaze: the Oka, green fields, the valley and, in the distance, a forest still untouched in those times. The town of Serpukhov, with its Kremlin and its monastery, stretches as far as the eye can see.

Dmitri and Bobrok were received with honour by the appanaged prince attended by his boyars and the clergy. On a hot day at the end of August 1380, there began a council of war to decide upon the plan of campaign against the powerful Mamay and his Golden Horde.

It is curious that this meeting has passed almost unnoticed by historians, who refer to many less important subjects, such as the case of the two monks Peresvete and Oslyabya, who were sent to the aid of Dmitri by the Holy See itself, or the story of the Princes of Kozel'sk and Mozhaysk, who were blessed by the holy ikons from a *skite*[1] in the Mozhaysk forest.

The battle between the Russians and the Tartars which took place on September 8, 1380, on the Kulikovo Field, was decisive, thanks to the plans worked out at Serpukhov and the appointment of Bobrok to the command of the reserve army, *zasadnaya rat'*. Kulikovo Pole! The 'Field of Stilts'! In the eyes of Russian historians this day is comparable with the great occasions, like the battle of Poitiers, that have decided the fate of nations.

The Great Khan Mamay and Kochuk, his marshal, flung against the Russians their fearless, untiring horsemen on their small Mongolian mounts. The Russian infantry, feebly supported by a badly-trained cavalry and consisting of *zemsky sbrod*—rabble from the villages—could not withstand the latest Tartar onslaught and fell back a few *versts*.[2] The Grand Duke and his cousin, standing on the hill with the Kremlin flag and, behind them, the standards of Dmitri's twenty-two princely allies, believed that the battle was already lost. Dmitri ordered Bobrok's reserves to throw themselves without delay into the thick of the fight to ease the pressure on his army. But the Prince of Serpukhov strongly interposed. 'No, Dmitri Ivanovich,' he cried. 'Wait a little, until the sun is shining straight in the Tartars' eyes! Then, let Bobrok loose on them!'

As soon as the sun began to come down near the line of the forests in which Bobrok was waiting with his reserves, his men attacked the blinded Tartars. The Russians, with terrible oaths streaming from their lips, hacked their way through the panic-

[1] A small monastery hidden in the woods.

[2] A *verst* is approximately two-thirds of a mile.

stricken Tartar cavalry, killing, and finishing off those already wounded. The Great Khan, wounded by the Prince of Kozel'sk himself, succeeded in making his escape, but left on the field of Kulikovo the flower of a hitherto invincible army.

Dmitri, henceforth known as Dmitri Donskoy, gave orders for 'the colours to be flown over the blood and bones and the bugles to sound the victory call'. On his return to Moscow he made the monasteries a grant from his personal treasure-house and did likewise to the Metropolitan for his Cathedral.[1]

[1] It is interesting that the van of the Tartar army in the Battle of Kulikovo Pole was composed largely of Genoese; an important detachment from this Italian republic had been sent to the Crimea and from there passed on to the Golden Horde. One may wonder why Italians fought on the side of the Tartars. Sufficient reason is given by the fact that Mamay Khan had proposed to the Genoese a military alliance against the Russians. In exchange, the Republic of Genoa had agreed to surrender the town of Sudak on the Black Sea. The animosity felt by the Russians against Roman Catholicism dates from this alliance.

The importance of the Russian victory was more far-reaching than may be imagined, for Mamay Khan had ensured the help of Sweden and the Finnish tribes of the Baltic coast. It was therefore a great combination of forces which marched against Russia to break up the young Grand Duchy of Moscow. If Dmitri Donskoy had failed at Kulikovo-Pole, the Genoese would have established themselves permanently on the Black Sea coast, the Swedes on the Baltic and the Lithuanians on the Dnepr. Dmitri Donskoy's victory was for Russia a turning-point in history as important as Stalingrad.

CHAPTER 9

VASSILI I

Following on the Russian victory at Kulikovo Field a conflict broke out at the Golden Horde, in which the *murzas* surrounded Mamay's green tent and slew him. An emissary was sent to the Kremlin by the 'Council of *murzas*' to inform Dmitri that the Golden Horde would not harbour resentment against him and would forget the bloodshed if he formally acknowledged the sovereignty of Saraï. With one consent the Kremlin boyars decided to cut off the messenger's head and send it back to Saraï. But the Metropolitan intervened, recommending restraint: when all was said and done, the Tartars were asking for no more than symbolical obedience and modest payment, while guaranteeing the Moscow Prince, in exchange, a lasting peace on his eastern frontier. The Metropolitan had valid reasons for urging moderation: a new enemy threatened Moscow on the western side. This was the Grand Duke Yagellon, the Lithuanian who meant to gain control over the plain between the Dvina and the Oka.

The Lithuanian race, one of the oldest branches of the Indo-European families, had settled, before the time of the Slavs, in the swampy, boggy region which stretches from East Prussia to Lake Peypus. Of the other two representatives of this ethnological family, one, the Borussian group (of the Koenigsberg-Krelevec region) has disappeared; the other, consisting of the Letts (in Kurland and Livonia), has persisted to the present day. The rather obscure history of the combined Lithuanian, Latvian and Borussian races was cleared up to some extent by German writers after the crusades carried out by the Sword-bearer Knights on the banks of the Dvina. When, at Yalta, Stalin requested the annexation of East Prussia by the USSR as far as the 'Koenigsberg Line', Roosevelt raised the question of the USSR's historic rights to this region. Molotov answered, 'The Slavs have always inhabited that region; the Prussians are only Germanized Slavs'.

'When,' asked Roosevelt, 'do you consider the Prussian Slavs to have settled there?'

'I cannot remember exactly,' said Molotov. 'It happened some seven hundred years ago.'

Roosevelt observed with some amusement, 'That kind of reason for annexing territories alarms me, for in that case Churchill might have claimed the annexation of the United States, since the British were still there in the seventeenth century—much later than your Prussian Slavs were in Koenigsberg!'

Molotov was adapting history to his advantage.

Until the death of Olgerd, Moscow and Vilno had worked out a policy of 'armed neutrality'. Yagellon, who had just been converted to the Orthodox Church, had rejected Mamay Khan's proposal that he should give up to him part of the Grand Duchy of Moscow as a token of their alliance. Advised of the Khan's intrigues by Yagellon's nephew, Dmitri offered him a magnificent present: the ikon of the Blessed Virgin of Mozhaysk, studded with diamonds and precious stones. But, not long after the burning of Moscow and the massacring of its inhabitants by the new Great Khan, Toshtamysh, in 1382, Yagellon resumed his father's policy.

Russo-Lithuanian relations were upset by a woman, the Franco-Polono-Hungarian Princess Yadwiga. It is said that she was a woman of remarkable beauty, who captivated the heart of the Grand Duke of Vilno with no trouble at all. This princess, who was Queen of Poland, had for a very long time the power to beguile all men. She was the daughter of Louis the Great of Hungary, of the House of Anjou. She combined the charm of her French ancestry with the heady beauty of a Hungarian and the seductive quality of a Polish woman. When the Polish emissaries came to Vilno bearing the young woman's portrait and showed it to Yagellon, he set out with galloping horse and heart for Warsaw.

Dmitri Ivanovich, Grand Duke of Moscow, tried his best to prevent their marriage and made Yagellon a tardy offer of the hand of one of his sisters, Praskovya, pointing out to him all the possible advantages of a union between Russia and Lithuania.

The first respect in which the Queen of Poland, Grand Duchess of Lithuania, had her own way was to persuade her husband to renounce the Orthodox Church in favour of Roman Catholicism. Having accepted the Polish throne under the name of Vladislas, and urged on by his wife, he indulged in an 'antiorthodox campaign on Polish and Lithuanian territories. This marked the beginning of ill-feeling between Russia and Poland which has lasted ever since.

The Holy See of Rome considered it opportune to send to the Kremlin a papal representative who suggested that Dmitri Donskoy should become a Catholic, so repeating the proposal made to Alexander Nevsky in 1240. The Grand Duke refused the offer and had all the trouble in the world to ensure the safety of the pontifical representative, for several boyars were determined to prove by direct strong-arm action that the Orthodox religion was superior to Catholicism. Lodged at the Kremlin, alongside the 'visitors' little palace', the Roman nuncio was obliged to take refuge in Dmitri Donskoy's private apartments. It was Dmitri's son, Vassili Dmitrievich, the future Vassili I, who accompanied the unsuccessful emissary with an armed escort.

Despite the striking victory of Kulikovo Field, the change in the political situation and the tension which prevailed over the whole of the western frontier compelled the Kremlin once again to submit to the 'symbolical yoke' of Saraï and resume payment of tribute-money to the Great Khan.

Dmitri's son, Vassili I, acceded to the throne in 1389. He continued his father's policy of armed neutrality in respect of Vilno and Saraï. But an ever-widening rift was developing between Russia on the one hand and Lithuania and Poland on the other, because of the policy adopted by the beautiful Yadwiga.

In 1958, Khrushchev, speaking to Gomulka and the Polish delegation which had come to the USSR, said, 'We Russians and Poles must one day settle our differences! Let us establish once and for all that you are no more responsible for your Queen Yadwiga than we are for our Czarina Catherine II.'

The Russian princes soon became aware of Moscow's difficult position and took advantage of it. Intrigue increased at the Kremlin. Emissaries from Warsaw boasted to the boyars and the Russian princes of the importance of the power of the Polish nobility over the king. The Warsaw aristocracy attracted the nobility which was beginning to take shape in the Kremlin. Of course, this nobility was as yet in statu nascendi, and so Vassili was able more easily to contend with the intrigues. But the appanaged princes thought of their privileges as private to their families. The boyars who were given lands by the Moscow Prince in return for their services desired above all to be the

ruling class. It was their wish to base their power on the new
legal code which had long been promised by Moscow and always
postponed.

Two sorts of landed property were recognized under Vassili I:
(1) inherited estates—*votchina*; (2) life estates—*pomestie*, which
the Sovereign had the right to pass on or not, as he wished, to
the son of the holder—*pomeshchik*, who was under obligation
to meet the demands of military requisitioning.

As for the common people, they no longer held electoral meetings, either in the towns or in the country districts! From being
subjects, they were becoming 'objects', without being able to
understand why their legal position was deteriorating. But, a
feeling, vague as yet, was beginning to penetrate the mind of
the public, exploited by the *pomeshchiki* — the boyars continually in conflict with the Grand Duke:

'The Grand Duke and we have enemies in common. Therefore
we have common interests! Long live the Grand Duke who
opposes the princes and who is our protecting father —
batyushka. The Kremlin is the *Chertog* (Palace), the seat of
justice! It will be the source of our deliverance!'

It was, then, the masters of the grand-ducal Kremlin who
originated that ideology, at first vague and mystical, which was
later to enable the czars to make their power felt in Russia.
'Justice for the people' is the concern of the Kremlin! It is only
in recent times that that justice ought, in the opinion of the
inhabitants of the USSR, to be also 'justice by the people'.

In 1408, Vassili I had once again to stand up to the Golden
Horde. A new Grand Khan, Edighaï, a Turk by origin, now
reigned in Saraï, after eliminating all rivals. This erstwhile
marshal of Mongol cavalry got together a horde and, having
arrived at the approaches to Moscow, pitched his tents on the
Sparrow Hills. Then, by way of a 'solemn *yarlyk*' to Vassili, he
requested payment of a huge tribute in pieces of silver within
one week. Refusal would mean the total destruction of Moscow
and the Kremlin. 'I will have your homes destroyed and your
women raped,' wrote Edighaï. 'I will turn your churches and
cathedrals into stables and spread dung in the holy places of
your land. My riders will kill the whole of the male population
of Moscow and fling the bodies into the cesspools.'

Faced with such an attractive prospect, Vassili I gave the
alarm and ordered defence measures to be taken. It was an almost
hopeless position. Against 85,000 Tartar horsemen Vassili I

could raise only some 50,000 defenders of his capital, and half of them were men unusued to handling weapons.

The Moscow boyars decided upon a stratagem. The Mint was given the order to strike coins consisting half of silver and half of white alloy. A few hours before the time-limit expired the tribute-money was paid, and Edighaï set off again for Saraï. Immediately the Tartars had left, Vassili ordered the Kremlin defences to be strengthened and brought into Moscow a great garrison of troops amounting to an army of horsemen. Vassili I thought that the Tartars would renew their invasion as soon as the false money had been detected by experts at the court of Saraï. How great was his astonishment to receive from the Treasurer-General of the Golden Horde notification that the amount of money was correct and in accordance with the 'Great Khan's requirements'!

Vassili I died in 1425, while his son Vassili II was just a child. The princes and boyars used the occasion to stir up trouble, the 'Minor Disturbances' which heralded the 'Major Disturbances' of the sixteenth and seventeenth centuries.

CHAPTER 10

VASSILI THE BLIND

The period of 'Minor Disturbances' began with a fight which took place on the occasion of the Grand Duke Vassili's funeral in the Cathedral of the Assumption. Vassili I's brother Yuri, Prince of Galich, who had come to the funeral with his sons Vassili the One-Eyed and Dmitri Chemyaka, caught the ten-year-old Prince Vassili by the ears with the intention of throwing him over the high wall of the Kremlin. Yuri would not recognize the right of his nephew Vassili, the son of Vassili I, to the throne and he chose this way to show his displeasure and his strength to the princes and boyars. Owing to the intervention of the Metropolitan, *popes* of the Church and pacificatory deacons created because of the troubles which periodically disturbed the Kremlin, the young prince managed to get away from the hands of his uncle and cousins, after they had heaped abuse upon him and tried to assault him.

The historical records are quite clear about this fight: Prince Yuri's right hand was broken and his teeth knocked out, his son Vassili's eye was put out — which earned him the nickname 'One-Eyed'. Then Prince Yuri's breeches were pulled off and the deacons beat him at some length, beneath the windows of the *Terem*, to the great delight of the inmates. On the day following this memorable occasion, the Metropolitan, with blackened eyes, hastily proceeded to perform the prince's 'lesser sacring'. A Regency Council, presided over by the Metropolitan, was created and Prince Yuri went back to Galich with his sons, declaring that he did not acknowledge the rights claimed by his nephew. The fight provided the Muscovites with the excuse and the opportunity to settle the fate of those people of Galich who were in Moscow; a wholesale drowning was arranged and dozens of Galichans were thrown into the Moskva.

Prince Yuri decided to take his revenge and he invited all the disgruntled princes and boyars to Galich to elect a new ruler in place of the one appointed. The guests were in two minds how to act. Samoylo, a boyar who hailed from the south, began to speak: 'What is the good of making an exchange which might

58

mean our jumping from the frying-pan into the fire? Let us take
advantage of the fact that this prince is young and "settle" him
so that he cannot stand against us.'

It was no sooner said than done! The conspirators went back
to Moscow and succeeded in kidnapping the young Prince. They
took him into the basement of Prince Meshchersky's *Terem* in
Uglich. The little boy, in tears, begged them to let him go,
promising to give up the throne and enter a monastery. But
Prince Meshchersky said 'We must finish it, or the Metropolitan
will send his *popes* and deacons and they will tear our insides
out'.

Just then, Prince Mozhaysky's wife, the child's cousin, suggested that they should spare his life but put out his eyes. A
white-hot bar of iron was brought. Several boyars and princes
held the child and his eyes were burnt out. The unfortunate
Prince was henceforth known as 'Vassili the Blind'. For more
than thirty years, from 1425 to 1462, he was the obedient tool
of the boyars.

On the night of the atrocity a small party of Prince Mozhaysky's *ratniki* entered the Kremlin and took possession of the
Metropolitan's residence. When the blinded Prince was brought
to him he died of heart-failure on the spot.

So began the reign of Vassili II. Prince Yuri of Galich, who
was not content with the 'compromise', began what amounted
to civil war by setting fire to the houses belonging to the princes
and boyars who would not acknowledge him as master of the
Kremlin. Before he died (of indigestion), Yuri set up his son
Chemyaka as claimant to the throne of the great Principality of
Moscow. Followed by his detachments of troops, Chemyaka
spread the civil war over the whole extent of Russia. He dis-
pensed prompt justice by having all his adversaries hanged. Once
again Moscow was torn by bloody strife. The historian
Klyuchevsky states that between 1245 and 1445 the Principality
of Moscow suffered ninety-eight internal rebellions and sixty-five
military clashes among the princes or between the princes and
the Grand Prince.

The new Metropolitan determined to put an end to this state
of affairs and suggested that he should mediate between Chemyaka and Vassili the Blind. Chemyaka rejected this proposal in
an insulting letter, in which he called the Metropolitan 'a lewd
old goat', 'an arrant liar', 'a glutton who eats meat on Good
Friday' and 'a dirty, foul-arsed pig', etc. The Princes Tarusky and

Muromsky, whose appanages had been taken from them by
Vassili I, broke down the Metropolitan's door and flogged him.
Their parting words to him were, 'You should be pleased, you
dirty, foul-arsed pig, that we should deal with you as Jesus
Christ was treated under Pontius Pilate!'

The other princes, fearing that the brutal Chemyaka[1] might
become their sovereign, moved up their troops to Moscow,
where the soldiers from Galich were stationed. There was fighting every day, and the Kremlin became a *vertep*, a den of
thieves, as one boyar complains in his memoirs:

'People have become robbers. Nobody can be trusted. The
archpriest of the Troitsko-Sergeyevsky monastery robbed his own
deacon and the latter set about him with a strap, during Mass.
The archpriest's wife has turned her *Terem* into a disorderly
house visited in the middle of the night by men who pay for
their lustful pleasure. From the fen quarter — *boloto* — the
butchers, armed to the teeth, set out for the country districts,
where they go plundering and killing people; so they get their
cattle for nothing. Many people are said to die after eating
mushrooms from the market at Glokhova. It seems that the
population of that place, so often looted by *ratniki* (Moscow
soldiers), take their revenge by selling poisonous mushrooms. In
the Kuchkovo-Pole district, on the road to Tula, a leaflet was
found advising people not to go out on Palm Sunday, as some of
Prince Tarusky's *ratniki* were expected then, and it was his
intention, so they said, to kill anybody found in the streets.

On the Moskva-Neglinnaya bridge there was a brawl among
the inhabitants of that neighbourhood; they fought for the
pleasure and amusement of it and many were killed with
hatchets or thrown into the water.'

Seeing no end to the civil war which threatened to destroy
the principality, Vassili the Blind made up his mind to appeal to
the Great Khan of Saraï, to judge whether the right to the
princedom was his or Chemyaka's. So it was that in 1431, fifty-
one years after the victory of Kulikovo Field, a ruler of Moscow,
brought to bay by civil war, acknowledged anew the Great Khan
as overlord of Russia. A diplomatic mission, with the Metropolitan's blessing, left for Saraï with costly presents for the Khan
and his *Khatun*. A boyar Vsevolozhsky, a great scholar and

---

[1] The Russian word is connected with the verb 'to lynch'. *Chemyakin Sud*
means 'The justice of Chemyaka', i.e. 'lynch law'.

noted expert in jurisprudence, led the mission. For his part, Chemyaka sent his boyar Kachinsky, a former *chislennik* who spoke the infidels'[1] language well.

The Great Khan received the two boyars in his tent. Kachinsky had brought with him a copy of Dmitri Donskoy's will in which the Grand Duke referred to Yuri as the heir presumptive in the event of Vassili I's death: 'If it be the will of God that our beloved son and heir, Vassili Dmitrievich, should be called by Him, we, Dmitri Ivanovich, Grand Duke of Moscow, bequeath to our son Yuri our *votchina*[2] and *pozhitki*'.[3]

The boyar Vsevolozhsky also took from his pocket a copy of Dmitri Donskoy's will and began to read from it: 'If Vassili Dmitrievich were called to God with no issue to receive his inheritance . . .'

At that moment Kachinsky interrupted him. The two boyars had a very heated argument, full of insults. The Great Khan, a Tartar from Astrakhan, steeped in Persian culture, was both intelligent and shrewd. He asked to see the two wills. There could be no doubt of it: Dmitri Donskoy's will was a forgery! This was the first instance of a false will in Russian history, and there are ten such forgeries on record, the most recent being Stalin's. Rejecting the evidence, the boyar Kachinsky obstinately maintained that he had in his possession the original of Dmitri Donskoy's will. The Great Khan showed some hesitancy in pronouncing judgement and the boyar Vsevolozhsky began to plead his case:[4]

'Thou, O Khan, art powerful and mighty. Thou art the Great Khan and as our sovereign Lord thou dost give judgment of our disputes, being the fount of wisdom and justice. The writings of the old *letopistzi* and the letters which the dead have left behind are unavailing before the Great Khan's justice. Vouchsafe a word of wisdom and we shall bow to thy will.'

The amusing thing in this situation was that the Great Khan should be invited by a boyar to disregard the will of Dmitri, the victor of Kulikovo Field. A decision was given in favour of Vassili the Blind, but Chemyaka refused to accept the verdict which, in his view, concerned only Prince Yuri. He went on

[1] The language of the Tartars.
[2] Permanent inheritance.
[3] Life income from estates.
[4] According to Klyuchevsky.

with the civil war. Vassili the Blind then consulted the Metropolitan, who set up a court consisting of five bishops and three archimandrites to judge the Vassili-Chemyaka case. After much deliberation the tribunal decided to dispossess Chemyaka of the Principality of Galich if he continued the civil war. As for Vassili, his claims were fully recognized. The records of the tribunal state:

'He (Prince Yuri) wished to possess the Principality of Moscow and the Kremlin, without the least right to do so, in which respect he appeared like his ancestor Adam, who meant to become the equal of God, having been prompted by Satan to this terrible and inexpiable sin.'[2]

The Metropolitan confirmed the judgement of his bishops and archimandrites in a circular letter to the princes, forbidding them to support Chemyaka and requesting them to 'restore peace to the land of the Russians'. Thus an honorable solution was found and the war ended.

Vassili II was succeeded by his son, Ivan III, who in 1453 became the first Prince of Moscow to assume the title of Grand Duke of Russia and incorporated the emblem of the double-headed eagle in the coat of arms of the Grand Duchy of Moscow.

[1] In the reasons adduced the bishops and archimandrites emphasized that Yuri had committed many wanton sins. (This was not a reference to the torturing of Vassili II.)

CHAPTER 11

IVAN III

On the day of Vassili the Blind's funeral, his son Ivan Vassile-vich went to the Metropolitan's residence for the reading of his father's will. The document was brief. In his lifetime, Vassili had appointed his son as regent and so conferred his authority upon him. The ceremony of proclaiming the regent had been followed by the reading of the deed which defined Ivan's rights in Vassili's lifetime and subsequent to his death. The will was therefore merely a straightforward confirmation of the deed. The blind Grand Duke, who had suffered so much after his father's death, thereby spared his son the difficulties of succession to the grand-ducal throne.

The Metropolitan, so devoted to Vassili, hated Ivan III and took him to task for his pride and his insubordination to the Church; and he did not forget that Ivan had ruined the citizens of Novgorod by demanding from the Russian republic payment of tribute-money three times as great as that required by the Khan: 'You are worse than the Tartars! Fear God, for he will not spare you on the Judgment Day.'

Ivan III did not allow himself to be influenced by the Metropolitan's execrations but continued his systematic exploitation of Novgorod. He set about the German traders who held their market near the German church of St. Peter.[1] Ivan informed the church members that the celebration of the Mass was a concession which had to be paid for; when the Germans refused to pay the extra tax, he instructed the *posadnik*—the president of the Novgorod Republic—to seize all objects of value in the basilica. The Orthodox Metropolitan of the Kremlin protested vigorously against Ivan's *ukase*; objects of Catholic worship could not be seized and sold like ordinary goods.

In view of the presidential election, Ivan now showed a close interest in the two contending sides in Novgorod. The presidency

[1] When the dispute broke out between Ivan and the German traders, German commerce in Novgorod was administered by the town of Lübeck, which directed the Hanseatic union. Lübeck had completely ousted the Scandinavian merchants from the Russian towns. These merchants, who also worked in Novgorod, built the Church of St Olaf there.

63

was hotly contested by the *Mikhalchichi* and the *Nezdinichi*, so called because of the names of their leaders, two boyars of the town, Mikhail Stepanich Michalchich and Miroshka Nezdinich. Ivan, who had received a large sum of money from a *Mikhalchich*, invited the leader of the *Nezdinichi* to the Kremlin and had him thrown into the *yama* — 'the hole' — dug on the very spot where Stephen Kutchka was buried.

Not long afterwards, there came to the Kremlin a beautiful German girl from Lübeck who had been converted to the Orthodox Church; she was betrothed to the leader of the *Nezdinichi*. This girl made a deep impression on Ivan; he set free the leader of the *Nezdinichi*, who was immediately appointed president instead of the *Mikhalchich*. But when the new *posadnik's* betrothed would have gone with him to Novgorod, Ivan kept her in the *Terem*, where he installed some magnificent *pokoy* for her, despite protestations from clergy and boyars. Only the intended husband maintained a discreet silence.

The Grand Duke meant to exercise his 'sovereign rights' in the pursuit of ignoble ends. Once again, the Metropolitan intervened and took Ivan to task for his conduct. In the presence of the archpriest of the Cathedral of the Assumption and a group of boyars, Ivan hurled abuse at the leader of the Church. But the Metropolitan stood firm and, taking advantage of the scandalous situation caused by Ivan's making the betrothed girl his mistress, he demanded that Ivan 'should enter upon no undertaking without first consulting him'—as Vassili the Blind had done—and that he 'should bind himself to refrain from spilling the blood of members of the faith'. Ivan III was compelled to sign a *gramota*, which was lodged in the Cathedral.

One month later, in 1462, Ivan had to face a riot which broke out in Novgorod.[1] He gave orders for a general recruitment for the purpose of restoring peace. But the Metropolitan, in his sermons, protested so violently against the recruitment that only five hundred *ratniki* answered Ivan's appeal. It was close to the town of Russa[2] that Ivan III's *polk* came to grips with the *rat* from Novgorod. In spite of their numerical superiority, the

---

[1] This riot was an extension of the revolt of 1456, when two hundred Muscovite *ratniki* wiped out the five-thousand-strong Novgorod *rat'* (of traders who, it must be admitted, fought reluctantly).

[2] It was near Russa also that the Muscovites defeated the Novgorodians in 1456.

IV   Arabesque arch in the Terem Palace, founded by Ivan the Great

[photo: Educational and TV Films]

v   Ancient Throne Room in the Palace of Facets

[photo: Educational and TV Films]

Novgorodians, under bad leadership, were beaten. Betraying his *gramota*, Ivan III ordered the decapitation of a goodly number of prisoners, among them many boyars.

As soon as the Grand Duke returned to the Kremlin, the Metropolitan invited him to give an explanation for having broken his oath. Before the boyars of his *Duma* and the arch-priest of the cathedral Ivan III solemnly averred that he had never signed the document of which the prelate spoke. So shame-less a falsehood filled the archpriest with such indignation that he sent immediately for the document. But it had vanished. According to the Ryazan letopis', the document was removed, on Ivan's orders, by Prince Kozlovsky, the vice-president of the 'Council of Boyars'.[1] The infuriated Metropolitan threatened to anathematize Ivan III, but a few days later he died suddenly, after eating mushroom soup, the usual fare of the clergy who were under vow not to eat meat. His sudden death almost resulted in a veritable revolution among the black clergy[2] of the Kremlin.

The Archbishop of Ryazan made a speech in honour of the departed Metropolitan, comparing him with the 'martyrs of Tiberius'. The Metropolitan's housekeeper, Nastya, the daughter of a boyar of Murom, was accused of having put poisonous mushrooms in his soup; the coadjutor of the Kremlin asked for an emergency meeting of a Church tribunal to be convened in order to make an inquiry into the death. But Ivan III forestalled the clergy; the housekeeper was brought before the Kremlin tribunal, composed of five boyars and presided over by the same Kozlovsky who was responsible for the disappearance of the *gramota*. Nastya collapsed during the trial. There then took place a great meeting of the black clergy, in the *pokoy* of the archbishop acting temporarily in place of the deceased Metro-politan. An account of this meeting may be found in the Ryazan

[1] The Grand Duke's Council of Boyars.

[2] The Russian clergy consist of 'white clergy' and 'black clergy'. The white clergy include the *popes*, who have the right to marry, but only once; as widowers they may not marry a second time, which gives rise to the proverb: 'There is only one unrepeatable thing—a *pope's* wife'. The black, or monastic, clergy are made up of those who take vows of celibacy, purity, moderation in eating, etc. (The drinking of vodka is not forbidden.) The leaders of the Orthodox Church are recruited from the black clergy. The highest grade attainable by a *pope* of the white clergy is that of archpriest. The bishops, archbishops and metropolitans are recruited from the black clergy exclusively. A *pope*, having become a widower, may join the black clergy if he wishes to extend his ecclesiastical career.

C

letopis': 'Bratya',[1] cried the assembly in unison, mourning the dead man. 'What are we to do now if scoundrels put mushrooms in our soup? Are we to be obliged to eat no more mushrooms, the food-allowance of all consecrated men in the land of Russia? The meanest peasant of the land may eat them but the black clergy would be denied that right! How may one eat fish in Holy Week without mushrooms?'

In his turn the archimandrite of the monastery of Kolomna, who was at the meeting, declared: 'Mushrooms are the food and the medicine of the Russians. Our monastery has cured hundreds of wounded and sick people with our *nastoyka* (infusion) of mushrooms and *kvass*.'[2]

The early days of the reign were disturbed by the scandals of the Kremlin and vicissitudes of foreign policy. The struggle with Novgorod was worsening. Ivan III was contemplating the complete discarding of the Tartar yoke; the great Golden Horde, which had been non-existent for some time, had broken down into the Khanates of Kazan, Astrakhan and Crimea. Ivan III decided to conclude an alliance with the Khan of Crimea so as to be rid of the Tartars from the Volga. The Girey dynasty had settled at Bakhchisaray, the khanate's summer capital. Bakhchisaray, the 'town of gardens', was in competition with Kazan and Astrakhan. Ivan planned to show open defiance to the Khan of Kazan, the most despotic of the three Khans; but before getting involved in a war against him he had first to reach a definite settlement of the Novgorod question.

In February of 1471, Ivan III convened a meeting of his *Duma* and the princes of the *udels* and asked them: 'How can we put an end to the arrogance of Norgorod, whose alliance with Lithuania constitutes a betrayal in the eyes of Russia?' He was forgetting that he had concluded an alliance with the Khan of Crimea and that he had sent a Russian army to destroy his

[1] *Bratya*, literally translated, means 'the brotherhood'. Ecclesiastics always uttered this word on the occasions of their oecumenical councils or meetings. It denotes the 'corporate body' and in the present connection stands for the 'ecclesiastical body of the black clergy'.

[2] A Russian drink noted for hundreds of years. It is prepared by steeping pieces of dried rye-bread in the infusion and allowing them to develop a mould. The unfermented liquid of *kvass* was used in Russia in the middle ages for treating wounds and intestinal ailments. This mushroom mould is the *penicillum glaucum* used in France in the making of Roquefort cheese. Russian monasteries had thaumaturgists who treated patients with an infusion of the same species of mushroom as that used today in the preparation of penicillin.

enemies, the Volga Tartars. So it happened that when he protested against the *posadnik*, the free city and the Council of
Elders[1] of Novgorod, this Council passed a resolution to the
effect that 'the Grand Duke of Moscow must be regarded as a
traitor to the Christian faith, for he has bound himself to the
infidel Khan Girey who pillages and burns the lands and
churches of Russia'.

In a letter to the Metropolitan, the Archbishop of Novgorod
suggested the excommunication of the 'scoundrel of the
Kremlin'. But the new Metropolitan had not forgotten the fate
of his predecessor and he replied to the Archbishop reminding
him of the scriptural decree: 'Render unto Caesar the things
which are Caesar's.' However, he added that, like his predecessor,
he would exhort the Grand Duke not to spill 'Orthodox
Christian blood'.

A solemn procession, headed by the Metropolitan, left the
cathedral and made its way to the palace. The clergy made a
most vigorous request of the Grand Duke that he should settle
his differences with Novgorod and come to an amicable arrange-
ment: 'Thou, who are our Prince and master, the Grand Duke
of Russia, show thy Christian clemency.' That was the first time
in Russian history that the title of the Grand Duke of Russia
was used in the Kremlin.

The day following the demonstration by the clergy Ivan III
summoned his private Council, a newly inaugurated institution,
and announced: 'We shall force the Novgorod *kramolnik*[2] to
their knees, as God brought down the Egyptians in the time of
Moses! Novgorod is a town that has betrayed the Russian cause.
We shall bring famine upon that town. Henceforth, no *telega*[3]
of wheat will be able to get into Novgorod. Let them repent or
let them perish like the heathen Egyptians who would have held
Moses and his people in Egypt.'

The blockade of Novgorod had begun. Barricades were set up
at all the approaches to the town and cavalry detachments put
in control of them. Not a grain of wheat entered the Republic.
This was the beginning of a terrible famine. The poor were the
first to revolt in Novgorod; they raided the German *dvor*, the

---

[1] The Council was made up of some fifty or sixty members, called boyars.
It was presided over by the Archbishop of Novgorod and it met in his private
pokoy (residence).

[2] Traitors, rioters, rebels.

[3] Wagon.

boyars' establishments and the archbishop's *pokoy*. They threw wealthy traders and *gosti*[1] into the River Volkhov, forced their way into the 'Herrenrath' chancellery and carried off the seal of the Republic.

The *posadnik* and his Council determined to break the blockade. Some fifteen thousand Novgordians were recruited and handsomely paid to go and fight the Muscovites. The artisans and tradesmen were for the most part badly led and quite inexperienced in the art of warfare, and in view of this the *posadnik* asked the King of Poland and Lithuania to send horsemen and seasoned soldiers. As soon as the Novgorod *opolchenie*, under 'catholic' command, left to face the Muscovites, a huge crowd rushed into Prussia Street,[2] looting the boyars' homes and killing those who had remained in Novgorod. The Viceroy of Lithuania, who was there at the time, had to make his escape by night disguised as an itinerant merchant. The crowd roared, 'To the gallows with the catholics!'

The *posadnik* heard of the 'pogrom', which had resulted in about three thousand deaths, just as his army was awaiting the arrival of a strong Muscovite force of 5,000 *ratniki*. He determined to take immediate steps to put down this revolt, which was the work of Ivan III's agents, and sent back part of his troops towards Novgorod. It was his undoing; the Muscovites immediately took advantage of the situation, encircled the Novgorod army and took 10,000 prisoners.

The boyars of Novgorod were taken to the Red Square and executed, and their headless bodies were thrown into the many ponds around Moscow. Many officers, soldiers and 'catholic leaders' were beaten like cattle and fed to the crayfish. The way was now open and the Muscovite armies thrust into the province of Novgorod, taking thousands of prisoners among the civilian population. The women-folk were sent to the Tartar harems in Crimea and the men drowned in the Volkhov, the lakes of the region, the Yauza, the Oka, the Volga, the Moskva.

A pond in the neighbourhood of the Kremlin became notorious; for two years it was 'fed' with the prisoners! As in the days of the Roman emperors and the Borgias, the Grand Duke had the Kremlin supplied with fish fed on the bodies of traitors. The expression 'to feed the *kramolniki* to the fishes'

[1] Foreigners, merchants or visitors.

[2] The residential quarter of the well-to-do Novgorodians.

became legendary. It was employed in Russian folklore until the nineteenth century.

Ivan III crushed the rebellious town a second time in 1478 with a cruelty and savagery worthy of the Tartars. The example of Gengis Khan and his successors, who piled up pyramids of human heads in the squares of the conquered capitals, provided the model for the behaviour of Ivan III, his son Vassili and his grandson Ivan the Terrible. But Ivan III could be an able politician as well; he employed guile and secrecy to maintain his authority.

It has been seen how the Novgorod riots eased the way to conquest of the great northern Republic. Ivan III applied his policy of 'corruption from within' to Tver also, to Ryazan and to the other principalities lying to the north, south and east of Moscow. At Ryazan, Ivan III had an ally in the person of the boyar Korobin. When he came to Moscow, the Grand Duke entertained him for more than a year and married him to one of his god-daughters. On his return to Ryazan, Korobin became Ivan's faithful agent. Thanks to such methods Ivan III succeeded in annexing the Principalities of Rostov, Yaroslavl, Vyatka, Perm and Chernigov.

Nevertheless, what was most noteworthy in his reign was neither the annexations achieved through diplomacy or espionage nor the terrible massacres of the *kramolniki*.

In the year 1470 a strange character, ostensibly from Rome, appeared on the scene. He appeared to be a senior church official and at the same time an adventurer. He was tall and slim, an expert swordsman, remarkably conversant with eastern and western history and fluent in Latin and Greek. He arrived at the Grand Duke's chancellery and introduced himself as Anthony Paleolog, second cousin of Thomas Paleolog, who was the brother of the last Emperor of Byzantium, Basileus Constantine, killed at the taking of Constantinople by the Turks in 1453.

Anthony Paleolog had a mission to fulfill. Thomas Paleolog's daughter, Princess Sophia, was of marriageable age and her father was offering her in marriage to the Grand Duke of Russia.

It was known in Rome that Ivan III had lost his first wife, Maria Borisovna, Princess of Tver, in 1467, and that he was seeking a princess of the highest standing to succeed her. The Pope considered that by this marriage he might reconcile the Orthodox Church and Roman Catholicism. The Pope's scheme found favour with Ivan III. Would it not provide an opportunity for him, who was still subject to the Khan's authority, to become the successor of the Byzantine emperors?

Sophia Paleolog arrived in Moscow in 1472 with a large body of retainers. She was a woman who weighed about twenty-five stone. According to the *letopis'*, she was 'very ugly, intelligent and scheming'. On the night of her arrival in Moscow the magnificent bed of the grand duchesses of Moscow broke down under her weight. During an intimate talk with Prince Odoevsky, Ivan III expressed doubts of his ability to father a child of the huge Byzantine princess, but as he already had several children by his first wife the problem was of secondary importance. The marriage was solemnized without delay.

The new Grand Duchess had brought with her from Rome some architects: Fioravanti, Aleviso, Giuliani and Masconi. It was they who built in the Kremlin the Grand Duke's new palace of brick and stone instead of the usual wooden palace. They also constructed the new cathedrals of Blagoveschensky, Uspensky, Arkhangelsk, and the Palace of Facets, the place where foreign ambassadors were received.

After his marriage to Sophia, Ivan III devised a new coat of arms, with the Byzantine double-headed eagle and the addition of the figure of St. George slaying the dragon.

The new Grand Duchess asked Ivan III to be rid of the Volga khan with all speed. Ivan, supported by Menghli-Girey, the Crimea khan, declared war on Akhmet Khan, nicknamed *Trusishka* ('the timid one'). The latter and his army were camped for more than a month by the Ugra, a tributary of the Oka, waiting for the attack to come from the Russian force on the opposite bank. Neither side was eager to open the fighting. One morning, at dawn, a host of birds came screaming out of the dense fog. Each of the two armies imagined that the other was launching an attack and took to flight, the Tartars making for the Volga and the Russians for the Moskva. So, in the most incredible fashion, was lifted the Tartar yoke that had bound Russia for more than 200 years.

Ivan III was becoming increasingly aware of his power. In 1486, a German Knight named Poppel, an untiring traveller, arrived in Moscow and was very well received there. When he returned home, the richer by a magnificent fur-lined coat, the gift of Ivan, he told the Emperor Frederick III about his visit. Poppel returned to the Kremlin as an ambassador with the mission of asking Ivan III for the hand of one of his daughters on behalf of his master's nephew. In return, the German monarch undertook to concede to Ivan the title of 'King of Russia'. The Grand Duke, while thanking the Emperor for his 'kindness' and declining the offer, replied that he held his rights from God himself. When he took his leave, the German ambassador— the first ambassador of a foreign power to come to the Kremlin —was the bearer of a letter to the Emperor. In this letter, Ivan III referred to himself as 'Supreme Ruler of all the Russias' and 'Byzantine Emperor'. But, believing that no absolute monarch could be called 'Ivan', the Grand Duke, assumed the title of 'Johann, by the Grace of God, Absolute Ruler of all the Russias'.

This ambition of limitless personal power led Ivan III to make serious blunders. On the example of his father, he appointed his eldest son, the child of his first marriage to Princess Maria Borissovna of Tver, to be his heir and co-regent. When Ivan the Young died in 1490 Sophia Paleolog asked that her son Vassili should be the sole heir, but Ivan III, after much hesitation, followed the Russian law, by which the succession fell to the son of Ivan the Young, his grandson Dmitri. Dmitri was anointed co-Grand Duke in the Cathedral of Uspenie in 1498. His grandfather placed the crown and the hat upon his head and around his shoulders the ermine collar, all insignia of his power.

Sophia Paleolog, in spite of her weight, was an extremely enterprising woman. She contrived to be rid of Dmitri, whom she accused of trying to spy upon her while she was taking a bath. Ivan III, in his annoyance, had the youth shut up in the Kremlin *yama* and appointed his son, Vassili, co-Grand Duke.[1]

By this thoughtless act, the first Grand Duke of Russia showed that he was a law unto himself. An heir to the throne, anointed in the Cathedral of Uspenie, was thrown into the terrible, stinking *yama* of the Kremlin, without trial and without the power to defend himself before a Council of boyars or make an appeal to the Metropolitan.

It was at this time that there first appeared in the Russian language the new word *samodur*,[2] related to the word

---

[1] The boyars, who hated Sophia, claimed that Vassili was not the son of Ivan III but of his steward, an Italian whom Sophia had brought with her from Rome and kept for ten years. His name was Borgia. If he was related to the Borgias and to Pope Alexander VI, certain characteristics of Ivan the Terrible, Sophia's grandson, become comprehensible.

[2] *Samodur* is derived from two words: *sam* ('alone') and *dur*, from the verb *durit*, that is 'to act in a foolish, irresponsible manner'. *Samoderzhetz* comes from two words: *sam* and *derzhat*. *Derzhat* means 'to hold'.

samoderzhetz (autocrat), which played an important part in
Russian history.

Even those Czars like Ivan the Terrible and Peter the Great,
who brought far-reaching reforms to their country, behaved like
people for whom no human or divine law had any validity.

Ivan III died in 1505. The Kremlin personnel witnessed the
sacring of Vassili III, son of Sophia Paleolog and 'possibly' of the
Grand Duke, 'by the Grace of God, Absolute Ruler of all the
Russias'.

CHAPTER 12

VASSILI III

Old habits die hard. The death of Ivan III almost resulted in yet another outbreak of civil war in the Grand Duchy of Moscow.

The Grand Duke had given up his soul to God, the passing-bell tolled from the Cathedral and the boyars arrived from all directions. They walked in close ranks, in accordance with the strictest hierarchy and etiquette.[1] The most powerful headed the procession, followed by those who were less endowed; the bearing of each rank was in accordance with its degree of nobility; the order of precedence was matched by graded differences of gait in the cortège, so that, whereas the leaders of the procession strode forward majestically, those bringing up the rear adopted a shambling jog-trot. The order of the boyars procession was settled by the senior boyar, Prince Penkov of Yaroslavl. The Princes Shuysky of Suzdal, the Princes Rostovsky, the Lithuanian princes who had sought refuge in Moscow, Belsky, Mstislavsky and Patrikeyev, with their descendants Golitzin and Kurakin, followed after Penkov and preceded Zakharin and other powerful boyars descended from the Koshkin-Yurev-Romanov[2] family, which, although it had no noble title, was reckoned among the most eminent families of the Grand Duchy.

The Kremlin boyars, Saburov, Valyaminov, Davydov, Buturlin, Golovin, Chelyadrin and Beklemishev headed the second column of titled nobility and untitled boyars.

When the procession came level with the rostrum from which the Metropolitan was to deliver his funeral speech, a scream

---

[1] This etiquette, which was very complicated, established the precise degree of the boyars' seniority by making comparisons of the official positions held by each boyar's ancestors. A ministry, specially created for the purpose of such verification, gave close attention to this etiquette and was regarded as one of the most important ministries in the Kremlin. The tradition has been maintained until the present day. In Stalin's time a fixed order of precedence was laid down and it is still in force.

[2] This family was founded by Theodore The Cat, whose descendants served the Princes of Moscow and the Kremlin. The excessively long name of Koshkin-Zakharin-Yurev-Romanov was shortened to Romanov. When Anastasya, the daughter of Nikita Romanov, became the wife of Ivan the Terrible, the Romanovs became known throughout Russia.

73

rent the air and was followed by other cries: 'Prince Ryapolov-sky-Starodubsky! Prince Simeon Ryapolovsky-Starodubsky! Prince Simeon!'

The Metropolitan came down from his rostrum and took refuge in the cathedral.

The shouts redoubled in intensity: 'Prince Simeon! Where is our prince? Hey there, you Greek whore! Sophia, you whore, answer! Into the Moskva with her, the whore!'

The Kremlin *voevoda*[1] ordered the *ratniki* to form up in front of the palace to prevent the nobility from ill-treating or slaughtering the Grand Duchess. At that very moment the Metropolitan reappeared, brandishing the sacrosanct cross of the Orthodox Church. 'Bow before the Holy Cross, you pack of *Bassurmans*!'[2] he yelled.

The nobles fell to their knees in the muddy, rain-sodden earth. Old Prince Penkov was the first to kneel, in the middle of a puddle of water. The massacre had been avoided just in time.

The enquiry conducted by the young Grand Duke, Vassili III, established the fact of a real conspiracy which had as its objectives the burning of the palace and the murder of the Grand Duchess Sophia. The instigator of the revolt was the son of Prince Ryapolovsky-Starodubsky. The father had been arrested, tortured and beheaded in 1500 on Ivan III's orders. He could not endure the 'Greek' and did not scruple to call the Grand Duchess 'Graeco-Ferrarese[3] dung' and 'Roman whore' and to apply to her even more offensive terms. The list is to be found in the archives of the Kremlin.

Following upon Prince Simeon Ryapolovsky-Starodubsky's punishment his friends were brought to trial. They were sentenced to deportation or to oblivion in a monastery. Among them was one Ivan, a prince of the Patrikeyev line, and his son Vassili who, under the name Vassian Kosoy, became the leader of a strange religious sect related to the 'iconoclasts'.

Right at the beginning of his reign, Vassili III had to hand over to the executioner another character who reviled his mother even more coarsely and systematically than old Prince Ryapolovsky-Starodubsky, the Kremlin boyar, Ivan Nikitich Bersen Beklemeshev. This able, quarrelsome man was a member

[1] The chief officer of the palace guard, the Kremlin commandant.

[2] Infidels.

[3] Sophia Paleolog was the daughter of Thomas Paleolog and his wife, the Grand Duchess of Ferrara by birth.

of the Council of Kremlin Boyars until the day when Vassili
turned him out of the assembled *Duma*. With an oath, Vassili
cried, 'You *smerde*,[1] I don't need you here at the Kremlin!'

The *smerde*, driven from the Kremlin, sought refuge in the
monastery of Semenov, near Moscow. In this monastery lived a
Greek monk named Maxim, who had come to Moscow at the
invitation of the Grand Duke and the Metropolitan to translate
into Russian the holy books of the Greek Orthodox Church.
Maxim and Bersen struck up a friendship. When Bersen was
arrested, after his denunciation by his former assistant Saburov
(who replaced him in the *prikaz*[2]), 'Maxim the Greek' had to
testify and repeat the conversations he had had with Bersen. The
latter had said, 'Our Grand Dukes are worse than the Turkish
sultans who rule the land of Greece today. In your homeland,
justice is harsh, but it is justice of a sort, whereas here in Russia
there is greater cruelty and there is no justice. The power of the
Grand Duke is boundless; even if the Grand Duke is a madman
or a complete idiot, one has to submit to his will! Ours will
always be an unhappy land, for the princes will always be the
masters and the people will always be the martyrs.' 'And what
of the Metropolitan?' asked the Greek monk, 'Can he not curtail
this power?' 'No', answered Bersen. 'Most often the Metropolitan is lined up with the stronger side. One crow does not
peck out the eyes of another. There is nothing to hope for from
him.' 'And the Grand Duke's mother?' asked the Greek monk.
This question startled Bersen, who turned pale with anger. Livid
with rage he poured forth a stream of the greatest insults. 'It is
because of Sophia', he said, 'that Russia will soon perish, overwhelmed by the mendacity and the infamy of her reigning
princes'. Mendacity and infamy, in the words of a monk of those
times, constitute the cesspool of all crimes.

The trial of the Bersen affair by the 'secret *prikaz*' ended in
the execution of the culprit in the Red Square.

The Kremlin was becoming a 'vast flea-market in which the
boyars reviled one another and abused the Grand Duke like
fishwives'. Most ingenuously, Vassili III called together the
Grand Council and put before it the following questions: (1)
how to put an end to the boyars' everlasting quarrels and their
plotting against the throne. (2) how to save the army from the
consequences of those quarrels.

[1] Low-grade peasant.
[2] The ministry.

The Grand Council, inevitably, reached no firm decision, for the greater part of it consisted of the very boyars and princes who were conspiring against the throne; the clergy were weak; the merchants formed but an ineffectual minority. The Grand Council did succeed, however, in restoring order to the military heirarchy; it decided that the Grand Duke's army should consist of five 'polk' army units, in the terminology of the day. (Nowadays the 'polk' indicates a regiment). These five units were to be, in order of seniority:

I. the Grand Polk (the centre or nucleus of the army), the *bolshoy polk*.

II. the Right Hand (the right wing of the army), the *pravaya ruka*.

III. the Advance Guard, the *peredovoy polk*.

IV. the Rear Guard, the *storozhevoy polk*.

V. the Left Hand (the left wing of the army), the *levaya ruka*.

The *polk* army unit was divided into 'centuries' (*sotnya*), but the number of soldiers in each often exceeded a hundred and sometimes varied between 300 and 500. Each *polk* had several *voevodas* (generals): 1st *voevoda*, 2nd *voevoda*, 3rd *voevoda*, the number depending on the number of 'centuries' in the unit. The title *voevoda* of the army', standing for the commander-in-chief, was abolished. This position was henceforth to be occupied by the 1st *voevoda* of the Grand Polk. In the event of his death, the 1st *voevoda* of the Right Hand became commander-in-chief. If he, in turn, died, lots were to be drawn on the field of battle to determine which of the generals of the Advance Guard and the Rear Guard should be appointed. It was agreed that they were equal in seniority. The strange decision concerning the seniority of the various army units of the Grand Duke's *rat'* is explained by the disposition of battle-troops as adopted by the Russians in imitation of the Tartars. The Advance Guard, Grand Polk and Rear Guard were drawn up on a straight line at right angles to the supposed front and distant five to seven versts from one to the next. The Right Hand was placed on a line parallel to the Grand Polk and some four versts from it. The position of the Left Hand was equidistant from the Grand Polk and the Rear Guard on a perpendicular parallel to the 'base-line'¹ and eight or nine versts from it. Thus, the Left Hand filled the rôle of a reserve force with a well-defined function. The first *voevoda* of

---

¹ This base-line, or base-perpendicular, is that on which the centre, the advance-guard and the rear-guard of the army was disposed.

this reserve force was chosen from among elderly men, known for their coolness and steadiness of nerve. Such a man was the *voevoda* Bobrok at the Battle of Kulikovo Field.

Having settled the military question at the meeting of the Grand Council, Vassili III turned his attention to putting an end to the boyars' disputes. In May of 1521, there was published a *ukase* (edict) from the Grand Duke, forbidding them to make unaided attempts to administer the departments and ministries of the Grand Duchy. They were now to have with them clerics, Called *Dyaks*,[2] as expert advisers. The *dyaks* were to be chosen on the grounds of 'outstanding ability', without regard to their social position.

Immediately the system of dyaks was instituted, Vassili III ceased consulting his boyars. A merciless purge of the Grand Duke's establishment removed the *kramolniki* (traitors). There were still some of them there. The Grand Duke's orders could not be questioned, on penalty of banishment, oblivion or death. The first Kremlin purge had been carried out.

Baron Sigismund von Herberstein, the Emperor Maximilian's representative to the court of Vassili III, has left this interesting testimony:

'It was not possible to have private conversation with the Grand Duke's boyars on subjects that were within their province; there were always two or three *dyaks* present, who listened closely to all that was said and whispered to the boyars the answers they should give me. The *dyaks* did not scruple to quarrel with a boyar, their hierarchical superior, about what reply he should make. In the great Palace of Facets,[2] I once saw the *dyaks* surround the chief of the *prikaz*, who would not give way to them, and drag him off by force to the Grand Duke.

'On another occasion, when I was crossing the small courtyard of the Kremlin, I saw several boyars flogging a refractory *dyak* who would not sign a contract agreed upon the previous day. The *dyak* was struggling and threatening that he would complain to the Grand Duke. Those cursed *dyaks* made it impossible to negotiate, for they continually went back on what they had agreed to the day before and were for ever making new demands, always in the name of Vassili III.

[1] Not to be confused with *Dyakon*, meaning 'deacon'.

[2] Foreign ambassadors were received and negotiations undertaken in a special office reserved for informal business discussions. This office consisted of six rooms separated by small compartments for private consultations.

'Arrogant and uncompromising, the *dyaks* always required bribes and signed no agreements until they had received them. During a conversation I had with the boyar Tuchkov, he referred to the *dyaks* as *Krapivnoe Semiy*.[1] The *dyaks* were ever fighting the boyars, who could not escape their vigilance, as they were usually more intelligent than their superiors, having been chosen by Vassili III. Without exaggeration, it may be said that fifty per cent of the people to be met with inside the Kremlin were *dyaks*.'

So was born Russian bureaucracy. These new officials' fidelity to the Grand Duke enabled them to reach the highest stages in the administration; gradually they became the real masters of the administrative machinery. Often their advice was sound. It was on their advice that Vassili III decided to do away with the franchises of the Republic of Pskov, by finally settling the fate of the North Russians, who were preventing the extension of the Grand Duchy's possessions in the north-west and the north-east. Thus there were joined to the Grand Duchy the extremely rich lands of the northern Urals, which abounded in iron, coal, copper, precious stones, asbestos, mica, platinum, silver and lead. The epic of Peter the Great would not have been possible without this annexation by the Kremlin, and the annexation was made possible only by the new caste of officials who replaced the ministeries of the Grand Duke and each of whom replied to Baron von Herberstein's tactless questions, 'I know nothing of it, Highness. Only God and our Great Sovereign know!'

Vassili III, however, did not listen to good advice only; the *dyaks* urged him to repudiate his wife, Salomonya, and marry Princess Helen Glinsky, niece of Michael Glinsky, the former comrade in arms of the Emperor Maximilian and Albert of Saxe.

Salomonya belonged to a younger branch of a family of Suzdal boyars, the Saburov-Shuyskys. Vassili III was still an adolescent when his mother, Sophia Paleolog, decided to marry him to a princess who was the descendant of one of the oldest families in Russia, a true Ryurikovich. As a youth, Vassili III was self-indulgent and wild, and his mother made up her mind to choose for him a princess of outstanding beauty who could keep him to the Kremlin *Terem*.

The *smotriny* of all girls of the nobility were announced, so that Vassili Ivanovich might select his future wife. More than

[1] Nettle seed.

500 hundred applicants arrived from all parts of the Grand
Duchy. Sophia Paleolog, as a Byzantine, was more knowledge-
able than the Russians of the day, and was anxious to be present
at the inspection of the young women held in the Kremlin
baths.

Sophia chose young Salomonya, the sixteen-year-old princess,
who, according to the records, was bewitching in her beauty. In
addition to the large, green and slightly oblique eyes of the
women of the Oka she had a mat complexion, a perfect oval
of a face and the body of Diana.

Soon after the death of Sophia Paleolog, Salomonya became
the prey to attacks by the boyars, who accused her of not accept-
ing the *Terem* regulations, of indulging in horsemanship and
changing by night into a witch so as to celebrate the black Mass
on the Valday hills. Her morals were suspect. But Salomonya
suffered most from her lack of children, in spite of the love which
Vassili showed her.

The Czar had no heir. Then an unexpected event took place.
The Lithuanian Prince Glinsky, appanaged Prince of Smolensk,
suggested to Vassili III that he would give up that town to him
if he would leave Salomonya and marry Helen Glinsky, his niece.
Vassili III sought the advice of the Metropolitan, who declared
categorically that Vassili must break his marriage with the
Grand Duchess Salomonya, since politics were of greater importance than religion and the well-known sacred bonds of matri-
mony.

According to the historian Kostomarov, a real Shakespearian
drama was enacted in the Kremlin; the break took the form of a
tragedy. The Grand Duchess told her husband that endless misfortunes would come to Russia if he broke the marriage.

Vassili put aside Salomonya and married Helen. The deserted
wife was obliged to enter the convent at Suzdal. Soon, however,
she disappeared. Monks and travellers from the South of Russia
told how they had seen 'the former Grand Duchess begging on
the roads leading to the Don and the Volga'. The monks also
related that she had with her 'a young boy who said he was the
son of Vassili III'.

In 1513, the Russian troops appeared on the Lithuanian border. The Grand Duke's *rat'* broke down the resistance of the
Lithuanians, who did not mean to give up to the Grand Duke
what Prince Glinsky had so readily offered him, and Vassili,
followed by Prince Glinsky, who had been appointed *voevoda* of

the Left Hand, made a triumphal entry into the town of Smolensk and proclaimed himself its sovereign Lord. Intrigues and conspiracies were not mitigated by his return to Moscow. The town of Nizhni-Novgorod rebelled again, but the revolt was quickly put down. In accordance with a *ukase* from Vassili III, 'gibbet rafts' were constructed and on them more than one thousand rebels were hanged. After the hanging, the rafts were turned adrift on the Volga, the corpses intended as a warning.

Suddenly there was a sinister rumour in the Kremlin: a horde of Tartars and Cossacks were descending upon Moscow, under the leadership of a young Cossack named Kudeyar' and the khan Mazgol Tokhtamysh. It was reported that the Tartars and Cossacks were destroying everything in their path. A dozen towns in the Grand Duchy were already sacked and burnt; but the panic reached its height when it was heard that the Cossack Kudeyar' claimed to be the son of Vassili and Salomonya! After killing and looting in the captured towns, he held funeral services to the memory of his mother, who had died of starvation on the highroad between Kaluga and Veronezh. He swore that when he had taken Moscow he would have his father beheaded in the Red Square.

A wind of terror blew through the Kremlin. Vassili III, the Grand Duchess Helen and most of the boyars escaped to the provinces, there to get together an army with all speed to march against Kudeyar' and Mazgol Tokhtamysh. The *voevodas* Prozorovsky, Kholmsky and Obolensky-Repnin were sent to the Suzdal region, Salomonya's homeland, to prevent a possible uprising.

Kudeyar' advanced rapidly and succeeded in breaking through *voevoda* Mikulinsky's army which barred his way at the approach to Moscow and he laid siege to the town and the Kremlin. On the third day of the siege the town's fortifications[1] were stormed and the Cossacks broke into the White City.[2] A furious attack was launched against the walls of Kitay-Gorod.[3] A few Tartar groups who had got in through the Borovitsky Gate set up their ladders against the Kremlin walls and flung

---

[1] These defences were called the *Ziemlyanie Vorota*.

[2] The artisan quarter in the centre of Moscow, comprising twelve wards.

[3] The 'Chinese City', the trading district of the capital, situated beyond the Kremlin and the White City. Because it had a battlemented wall, it was known as the 'Chinese City of the Battlements'.

burning missiles, pieces of wood impregnated with resin, into the enclosure.

At the eleventh hour Vassili sent to the Khan a representative in the person of the turncoat Sayn-Bulat, with a large sum of money, and he promised, moreover, to resume payment of the tribute discontinued in 1480. The Khan ordered his horde to cease hostilities and withdraw towards the Oka and the Tzna, where there was a small Tartar fort at Orlum.[1] Betrayed by the Khan, Kudyar' and his Cossacks were obliged to quit Moscow after setting fire to several hundred buildings. During the withdrawal, Kudeyar', the 'son' of Salomonya, took his life by throwing himself, dead drunk, into the Oka. Behind him the flames still licked at the Borovitsky and Taynitsky gates.

In 1553 Vassili III died, and Helen remained alone with her two children, Ivan, aged three, and Yuri, a year younger.

[1] Orel.

CHAPTER 13

IVAN THE TERRIBLE

Vassili's death gave free rein to the most tragic, wild and fantastic stories. The Princes Glinsky were suspected of having helped fate to take a hand and the widow's attitude gave support to all the gravest accusations. She refused to remain a prisoner of the *Terem* and that fact seemed unpardonable. While they were there, the mother of the Grand Duchess, who had three young male attendants sleeping in her bedroom, was accused of the grossest immorality, not to mention the black Mass, and those who claimed to have seen her by night on her brother's grave in a cemetery, conversing with his ghost in an infidel tongue and making the 'strangest remarks'! She had also been observed among the tombs, tearing out the hearts from the bodies of her enemies so as to steep them and make an ungodly liquid with which she sprinkled the walls of those whose death she desired. And finally, the nurses—the *nyani*—had seen her bathing the four-year-old Ivan IV 'in an indecent manner for an Orthodox Christian princess'.

The young Ivan IV, it was stated, took pleasure at the age of five in ill-treating animals, tearing the wings from flies and setting fire to ants' nests after sprinkling them with 'oil intended for the lamps in front of the ikons'. He used to beat the boyars' children who played with him and on one occasion, coolly, without a sign of compunction, broke the leg of one of them.

Caesar Borgia's young days and those of Ivan IV have some points of similarity. (Sophia Paleolog's relations with Antonio Borgia must not be forgotten!)

Ivan IV's precocious sensuality was the cause of several incidents which took place in the Kremlin, when he was entering upon his twelfth year, and of which the women-servants of the *Terem* were the victims. At that time Princess Helen had already died from poisoning and the Boyars' Regency Council was in control. The chief boyar, Shuysky, received a detailed report on the conduct of the young prince. 'The serving-girl', said the report, 'complains that her clothing was torn (her skirts and the lace of her bust-bodice); one sleeve of her dress is missing and her girdle is of no further use; moreover, her neck, chest, knees and thighs are covered in bruises. She further complains that in her virgin state she was to become the wife of the *sotnik* (captain) Pavlushka Krat and that she now risks staying a spinster and being obliged to enter a convent.'

The chief boyar considered it unnecessary to approach the young Grand Duke for his treatment of the servant but he criticized his general behaviour. In a letter from Ivan IV to Prince Kurbsky is found a passage dealing with this attitude shown towards him when he was young!

'I recall how the boyars, and particularly the chief boyar, behaved towards me and my young brother Yuri; how they kept us in dire poverty and prevented us from eating our fill; how Shuysky compelled me, the Czar, to wear his son's old clothes. One day Shuysky called me in order to remonstrate with me; he was in my father's bedroom and, sitting on the bed with his foot on the pillow, he flouted me and adopted towards me, the Czar and Sovereign, a contemptuous attitude.'[1]

Ivan IV lost no time in taking his revenge upon Shuysky. When he was twelve years old (a year after the ravishment of the *Terem* serving-maid), the young Grand Duke of Russia gave orders for his mentor to be bound and thrown into his kennels. Shuysky was devoured by the pack. (According to the Suzdal *letopis*', this took place in 1543). What was left of the body was flung into the pit, the *yama*, of the prison cemetery in the Kremlin, among the bleached bones of its creator.

'It was from that day,' say the *letopis*' chronicler, 'that became apparent the fear and respect on the part of the boyars towards our Czar and Great Sovereign; Russia suddenly became aware that she had discovered her master'. It was likewise from that day that the Grand Duke began to acquire the habit of riding full gallop through Moscow, trampling people beneath his horse's hooves. There could be no doubt of it: the Kremlin harboured within its crenelated walls a true despot, Ivan IV.

Then, suddenly, this wild, violent youth, underwent a change: he turned to study, meditating upon the Holy Scriptures and reading the works of the Fathers of the Church, Roman history and Russian *letopis*' and chronicles. In 1547, four years after the chief boyar had been thrown to the hounds, Ivan

[1] Quoted by the historian Klyuchcvsky and Karamzin in the *History of the Russian State*.

IV was solemnly crowned and assumed the title of Czar (derived from the Latin 'Caesar'). The youth explained to the dumb-founded boyars that by so doing he wished to draw attention to the beginning of a new era of absolute power in Russia, one which would take no further account of the titles and privileges then in force.

To the Patriarch of Constantinople Ivan sent a letter in which he canvassed support for his investiture as Czar. This support—handsomely paid for—was not forthcoming until 1561, when the Greek Patriarch of Constantinople had received three times the sum agreed upon; but he did not do things by halves: 'I certify that by this investiture the power of the Czar implies sovereignty by divine right, which is answerable neither to the people nor to the monastic orders. This sovereignty proceeds from the sixth law of Justinian.'

Once he had become Czar, Ivan IV expressed his intention of marrying. The Czar's grandmother, Anna Glinska organized the *smotriny*. Never had such numbers of applicants been seen coming to the Kremlin. Since the *Terem* could not accommodate them all, it was enlarged. The baths also were enlarged and wide windows of Venetian glass were fitted to the dividing walls. A new church was erected. Ivan IV's choice fell upon a beautiful and intelligent girl, Anastasya Romanova Zakharina-Yureva-Koshkina, and the marriage was celebrated with great ceremony.

Later in the same year fire destroyed three-quarters of the capital and part of the Kremlin, causing the death of some thousands of people. There was nothing new in this; a foreign visitor declared that in the sixteenth century the town of Moscow was completely burnt every twenty years. But on this occasion the story that the fire was the work of the Glinskys was spread about by the parents of the boyar Shuysky, who wanted to avenge the terrible death of their son. And the old Princess Anna did not escape calumny.

In front of the Kremlin several thousand people demanded that the Princess Anna should be publicly castigated.

The Czar sent his *voevodas* to request the crowd to withdraw but the shouts were redoubled and he gave the order to charge the rioters. The massacre was horrible, resulting in more deaths than were caused by the fire. Those responsible for the riot were hanged in the Red Square, where a huge gallows had been erec-ted. Ivan IV came out of the palace with his boyars and *dyaks* and for more than an hour viewed the swaying bodies. Then, to

Philip, the Metropolitan, he gave his purse containing a large sum of money and asked that every year, at the anniversary of the execution, he should pray for the souls of the dead men. The public, gathered in the Red Square and surrounded by the Czar's *ratniki*, began to applaud his action in honouring those who had died in the 'Anna riot'.

When he returned to the palace, the Czar was confronted by a strange character who requested an audience. He was a certain Ivan Peresvetov, a Lithuanian deserter, who had come to Moscow in 1537 to offer his services as an army officer.[1] A former Polono-Lithuanian *condottiere*, who had served three kings, Hungarian, Polish and Czech, this Ivan Peresvetov, having been expelled as a result of looting in Silesia, came to Moscow and claimed to be the descendant of the famous monk Peresvet, the hero of Kulikovo-Pole, and a 'prostitute of the battle-field', Nastya Semenova.[2]

'What do you require of me?' asked Ivan IV of the *condottiere*. For reply, the latter handed him a long letter: 'You are the greatest Monarch that Russia has known, but in order that you may fulfil the will of God, who has chosen you as His divine instrument, you must once for all exterminate the foul vermin of boyars, who do nothing but conspire against you and the country. The only people who might be faithful to you are those of modest station, who have succeeded by virtue of their excellent qualities rather than of their birth. The nobles, who are nothing but . . . (here follow some indecent expressions), are all traitors and scoundrels. Remember the Czar Mehmet-Saltan,[3] who had all his *murzas* thrown into the Volga.'

Ivan IV, standing by a casement window, his tall fur cap touching the vault of the ceiling, read and reread the letter carefully, thanked the *condottiere*, handed him a sable collar 'from his shoulder'[4] and said, 'Thank you, my good fellow. Go and rest in your *sobyaka*.[5] Sooner or later I will call you.'

[1] So states Klyuchevsky.

[2] Solovyev states that, according to Russian custom, a soldier could spend the night before the battle with a woman, often a common prostitute. The monk Peresvet, absolved by his abbot, the holy Serge Radonezhsky, from his vow of celibacy before he left for battle, took advantage of the custom and his absolution.

[3] A Khan of the Tartar Kingdom of Astrakhan, who was responsible for the intermittent bloodthirsty purges of his dignitaries.

[4] It was a Muscovite custom for the Czar to show his benevolence to the one he wished to reward, by handing him a 'sable collar from the shoulders of the Czar'.

[5] The property awarded by the Czar for services rendered.

Peresvetov made his departure with a remark which was intended for the Czar's ministers and which Ivan IV never forgot, 'Remember, O Czar: those who attain high positions by virtue of their noble birth and not through police or military services rendered to their Great Sovereign are nothing but sorcerers and, as such, should be burnt'.

At the time of the 'Anna Riot', Ivan IV had not yet become known as Ivan the Terrible. At his side was the gentle, beautiful, virtuous Anastasya Romanova, who had the gift of making him more human and more understanding. At Anastasya's residence Ivan often saw Father Sylvester, the *pope* of the Kremlin cathedral, who would often read and narrate the Gospel to the Czarina. Ivan IV attached the *pope* to himself and made him his personal adviser. He also made a friend of one of the lesser nobles of the Kremlin, a *stolnik*[1] called Adashev. The two advisers often held council with the young ruler and prompted him to take measures either to show clemency or to effect far-reaching reforms.

So, in 1550, there was created within the confines of the Kremlin, the *Sobor*.[2] The *Sobor* adopted the draft of a new compendium of laws, the *Sudebnik of Ivan IV*. The *Sudebnik* laws, copied from Tartar legislation, were terribly harsh, and some of the cruellest, most inhuman punishments became part of Russian legal practice. The most dreadful torture was quite customary during criminal investigation. But, on the other hand, the magistrates, elected by the people of the towns and villages, were appointed to supervise legal procedure, which was henceforth separate from administrative action. The magistrates were to meet at the Kremlin every ten years to make known to the Czar the most interesting 'acts of justice'.

The *Sobor* also decided to replace the governor (*voevoda*) of certain localities by an official elected by the populace, provided the inhabitants were prepared to guarantee full payment of tax without the central authority being obliged to intervene.

The years 1550 and 1551 were dominated by intense activity on the part of the Czar and his advisers. The midnight oil burnt long in the palace. In the ministries, no work was done in the

[1] The administrative grade equivalent to that of a departmental chief in a ministry and of rather modest standing at court.

[2] *Sobor*, in Russian, means 'cathedral'. The same word also stands for an oecumenical council. Ivan IV adopted the term to indicate the States-General (or Diet) which he convened in 1550.

afternoon. The working hours in the Kremlin were: in summer, from half an hour after sunrise; in winter, from one hour after sunrise. Foreigners who came to Moscow were amazed at this habit which the officials had of working at dawn. Captain Margeret, the French military adviser to the Kremlin, has given a picturesque description of these ministries which 'begin their work, as our peasants do, with the first cock-crow'.

When it had dealt with questions of State reform, Ivan ordered the *Sobor* to turn its attention to ecclesiastical reforms. A list of religious regulations was solemnly read in the Uspenie Cathedral of the Kremlin. They were known as the *Hundred Chapters* and contained what was, for the age, a very democratic law: each group of a hundred priests was to elect an 'elder'[1] whose duty it was to call his group periodically to a meeting in the Kremlin in order to settle administrative questions.

Concerning the 'establishment of elders' Ivan IV delivered an important speech before the States General: 'From now on it will be the custom of our country and a tradition for our children to consult the 'elders'[2] every time events make it necessary to do so. I swear by the Holy Cross that I will strictly respect this custom and not allow it to decline.'[3]

The *Sobor* would not dissolve before it had required the Great Sovereign to 'set free from Tartar bondage the thousands of our Russian brothers, sold to Kazan in the service of the infidels'.

After much deliberation and many solemn masses, Ivan IV set out with his army in the direction of the Volga to take possession of Kazan. The Czar was accompanied by foreign military advisers and specialists in artillery and in 'underground knowledge'.[4] The Russian artillery and the explosions from a dozen barrels of gunpowder beneath the walls of Kazan brought about the fall of the town on October 2, 1552, after a six weeks' siege. Some time later, in 1556, the Russian army captured the Tartar

[1] 'Elder', in Russian, is *starshina*. The *starshiny* establishment was maintained in Russia during the three centuries of the Romanov dynasty. All corporations had their *starshiny*; the merchants, town burgesses, peasantry and also the nobility under the direction of their 'marshal' (*predvoditel dvoryanstva*).

[2] Even today in the USSR the 'Council of Elders' appears every time the Congress of Soviets, or the Party Congress, is convened for the elections of the Supreme Soviet or the Central Committee of the Party.

[3] Ivan the Terrible broke his oath when he created his political police.

[4] That is, of underground explosions which undermined the foundations of the fortress.

fortress of Astrakhan at the mouth of the Volga. The Ityl, the sacred river of the Tartars, became the Mother Volga or Volga Matushka, the sacred river of the Russians.

After the conquest of Kazan and Astrakhan and the changing of the Volga into a 'respectable Russian river', an imposing mass was said in the Kremlin. The Czar and Philip, the Metropolitan, made fiery speeches to the populace. Three new towers were built in acknowledgement of the victory and Ivan IV decided to erect the cathedral which would surpass any that existed within the walls. Several achitects were summoned from Italy. The names of only three of them appear in the Russian archives: Julian Aristo, Philip Manzio and Marcellini. The name of the chief architect who produced a masterpiece in the building of St. Basil Cathedral was never known. One thing about him is known: Ivan the Terrible had his eyes gouged out so that he might never build elsewhere another cathedral like it.

The taking of Kazan and Astrakhan had brought the Tartar invasions to an end; the regions of eastern Russia could now enjoy reasonable security. But there still existed, in the south of the Crimean Peninsula, a Tartar khanate which continued its murderous and devastating raids. This khanate had fallen under the power of the Turkish Sultan of Constantinople in 1475, when the Genoese Republic lost its colonies in Crimea, Kaffa (now called Theodosia) and Sudak. Having become the Sultan's vassal, the Crimean khan resumed his invasions of Russian territory with increased intensity; thirty per cent of the slave-prisoners taken in Russia by the Tartars were given up to the Sultan as the khan's *ulus* (tribute payment). After two hundred years of war with Russia, the Tartars had found ways of penetrating deep into Russia, burning towns and villages, carrying off men and women and of effecting a very rapid withdrawal.

A Kremlin historian, the abbot Kassyan, gives precise details of these invasions in the *letopis*': the Tartars herded together the boys and girls whose parents they had killed and carried them away in nets tied to their saddles. A Lithuanian, who was travelling from Kiev to the Crimea, witnessed this awful spectacle in the Crimean Isthmus, which links the Crimea to the mainland. In order to isolate themselves, the Tartars had dug a very wide moat nearly four miles long. 'Returning from an expedition to Russia, the Tartar band were bringing back thousands of children of both sexes, in nets tied to their saddles. The children were weeping and wailing. Their hands and feet

were bound with leather thongs. Just before they came to Perekope, the Tartar commander gave a sign, at which the horsemen
stopped and killed all those children who were sick. They threw
the children's bodies into the cess-pit, mutilated and sometimes
defiled before their slaughter.'

Prince Kurbsky, Ivan IV's *voevoda* and hero of the capture of
Kazan and Astrakhan, decided to make a surprise attack on the
Crimea, in spite of the opinion of the Czar, who feared that his
army might suffer from the heat and lack of water if it marched
through the Ukrainian steppes. Kurbsky intercepted a Tartar
army unit returning from an expedition to Russia. The Tartars
were decimated and the prisoners were freed from their nets.
There seem to have been about 25,000 prisoners, of whom 15,000
were children.

Kurbsky opened the bombardment of the Perekope Isthmus
with his artillery and his famous 'Rhinoceros'.' The Tartars gave
ground and the Russians forced their way into the Crimea to a
depth of more than sixty versts. The Sultan, alarmed, ordered
his fleet to set course for the Crimea and to land troops at
Ochakov. Afraid of being cut off from the mainland, Kurbsky
halted the invasion and contented himself with setting fire to
the Khan's capital and his splendid summer palace at Bakhchis-
saray with its wonderful fountains. Kurbsky took back a magnificent present for the Czar, a block of pink Carrara marble,
which was used to make one of the columns of the Grand Palace.
So may the stones of the Kremlin stand as witnesses of each
reign.

The Crimean Khan made a pilgrimage to the tomb of
Mahomet, where he vowed vengeance. Twelve years after the
Russian expedition of 1559, the Khan, taking advantage of the
absence of the Czar's armies, which were fighting a war in
Livonia, laid waste to Russia. The Tartar forces, supported by the
Sultan's artillery, entered Moscow in 1571. The looting lasted
for two days. The Russian armies returned from Livonia with all
haste, but not before more than 50,000 Muscovites had been
butchered. The Tartars took 100,000 prisoners.

Some time after the conquest of Astrakhan, an important
mission arrived at the Kremlin with a present from the Shah to
Ivan IV; it was a huge elephant. The elephant was led by its
mahout, who claimed to have trained the creature and taught
it how to bow before the Great Sovereign of Russia. Public

---

¹ This gun is now to be seen in the Kremlin Museum.

merry-making was organized in the Red Square and people came from all parts to admire the animal, the like of which had never been seen. Towards the end of the festivities the Czar made a state appearance followed by his boyars and streltzi.[1] He waited, seated upon a huge throne in the middle of the Square, until the elephant should pay its respects by bowing before him. But that day the elephant behaved like a veritable kramolnik and obstinately refused to bow the knee before the Czar of all the Russias. 'Cut it to pieces!' ordered Ivan IV, livid with rage. And the Shah's present crumpled beneath the axes and lances of the streltzi.

The situation in the Kremlin was deteriorating. Anastasya Zakharina Romanova, the beloved wife of the Czar, fell ill. Ivan's personal advisers, Adashev and Sylvester, had quarrelled violently with the Czarina's parents, the Zakharins, who endeavoured to obtain important posts outside their scope. During a dispute with Adashev, the Czarina was overcome with an apoplectic seizure and was immediately taken to her pokoy, where she died. Her death (1560) caused the Czar great distress. He burned hundreds of candles to her memory and for days together, prostrated, he bewailed her loss. When Adashev came to see him, Ivan IV shouted at him, 'May all the fiends possess you! I want no more of you, you murderer!'

The pope Sylvester had a similar reception, and the boyars were no longer allowed inside the Sovereign's pokoy. What his intentions were in encircling the Kremlin with his streltzi gave cause for speculation.

As soon as the Czarina was in her grave, Ivan IV showed a complete change of front; he began to offer violent insults to the boyars, threatening to tumble their heads about the Red Square. He had not forgotten, he said, that the boyars had, on the occasion of his illness, refused to take the oath of allegiance to his son Ivan, when he had requested them to do so.

Then, one day, the people of Moscow saw a great number of carts enter the courtyard of the Kremlin; the Czar was leaving the following night, with his family and attendants, for an unknown destination. The Muscovites were dumbfounded. The shops closed, bakers sold no bread and panic spread through the capital. Three days after the Czar's departure, a courier arrived

[1] Ivan IV had formed a new unit which was stationed in the Kremlin. These soldiers were called streltzi, the equivalent of 'musketeers'. They were made up of a 'select body' of twenty-three regiments.

with a message from the Czar informing the Metropolitan and the boyars that he proposed to spend some time in the township of Alexandrovskaya Sloboda, near Moscow. A strange procession made its way there, a procession consisting of thousands of Muscovites headed by the Metropolitan and all floundering in the snow. The monks and clergy carried lighted candles. The Metropolitan found the Czar at prayer in a wretched hut filled with holy ikons and he begged him to return to the Kremlin. 'I will give my answer in a few days' time,' said Ivan IV. And in fact a few days later a reply did arrive in Moscow: the Czar requested the Metropolitan, the boyars and nobles, to sign a solemn deed giving the Czar full powers to deal with questions of treason.

Ivan IV returned to the Kremlin with his waggons, assuming full autocratic powers. The court ministry had already presented to the Muscovites a note 'for reimbursing the Czar and Great Sovereign for the expenses he had incurred because of his subjects who, unworthy of so devoted a ruler, had made it necessary for him to leave the Kremlin and go roving like a beggar'.[1] He even requested compensation in respect of three horses which had died on the journey.[2]

Full payment was made immediately, but it was not enough to calm the anger which the Sovereign felt for his people.

The British ambassador, Fletcher,[3] gives further disturbing details of Ivan the Terrible's regime:

'The only method of investigation employed is torture, for here one feels obliged to compel the alleged offender to confess his guilt. Without such confession a conviction is impossible. The culprit is whipped with ox nerves or leather lashes as thick as one's finger, which bite into the flesh; or else he is tied to a spit and roasted. Alternatively, he may have a rib broken and twisted with red-hot tongs or the flesh beneath his nails may be cut away.

'The results of the investigation are handed to the prefect of the chetverte (district), who places them upon the council table, after which they are read by a tribunal of justices who neither see nor hear the accused.

---

[1] Klyuchevsky.

[2] The Kremlin archives.

[3] The ambassadors of Her Britannic Majesty in the time of Ivan IV were in turn, Richard Chancellor, Thomas Randolph, Jenkinson, Robert Best.

'Capital punishment takes the following forms: hanging, decapitation, bludgeoning, impalement, drowning, freezing under the ice, burning, etc. Often, those who are sentenced in summer are kept in custody until the winter so that they may be frozen to death.'

Such was justice under Ivan the Terrible. However, he did not consider it sufficiently expeditious or terrifying for the *kramolniki*. He gave considerations to a new project, a political secret police force, the *Oprichnina*, in imitation of the Spanish Inquisition.

In his correspondence with Prince Kurbsky, the Czar's *voevoda* (who later fled to the court of the Grand Duke of Lithuania), Ivan IV gives a clear account of his project, together with his reasons for wishing to organize the *Oprichnina*: he can no longer trust anybody, associates, boyars, dyaks or *okolnichi*; that is why he must create a special force, a State within the State, one over which he will hold supreme authority by the mortal terror which he inspires in his enemies. In his writing, Ivan IV gives the name of Ivan Peresvetov as the originator of the *Oprichnina*.

What is quite surprising is that the Czar should continue his correspondence with his best friend and *voevoda*, Prince Kurbsky, even after he had heaped the latter with insults and called him a 'turncoat *kramolnik*'. This correspondence was made possible thanks to one of Kurbsky's servants, Vasska Shiganov, who was provided with a pass. He was able to enter the Kremlin at any hour of the day or night. Ivan IV who, at that time, was having thousands of people investigated on the slightest suspicion of *kramola*, allowed the right of entry to the personal servant of the greatest *kramolnik* in his realm, Prince Kurbsky ! One of Ivan IV's most pleasurable occupations was to drive his terrible staff into Shiganov's foot and watch the expression of anguish on the face of his enemy's faithful servant, while reading the letter from Kurbsky who took no pains to disguise home-truths from him.

The Kremlin chronicles of the age leave no room for doubt concerning the sadism of Ivan IV. He was attacked by persecution mania in its most terrible form; nightmares and hallucinations invaded him from all sides and allowed him no respite.

The *Oprichnina* was created, and Ivan IV recruited some 10,000 people, former bandits, felons and itinerent monks known as *yuradivye* (feeble-minded). Ivan left the Kremlin to go and live among his 'supporters' in a district of Moscow where the streets called Preshistenskaya, Sivtzeva and Nikitskaya meet those surrounding the monastery of Novo-Devichi. Ivan and Feodor, the Czar's sons, lived there with their father. As for the police force and its leaders, the Princes Vyazemsky, Basmanov and Plescheyev, they lived in the Sloboda Alexandrovsk, a kind of 'monastery', in which a sucession of the wildest orgies took place. The Czar's police wore black from head to foot, including the cowl. Their horses' harness, too, was black. A broom and a dog's head were embroidered on a pennon fixed to the saddle. These were the insignia of the order; like dogs, the police were to nose out the *kramola* and sweep it away with their brooms!

This strange force behaved in Moscow and the Kremlin with exceptional cruelty; they practised torture and rape, looted tradesmen's stores and set fire to the shops of those who would not pay tribute-money levied by the *oprichniki*.

Ivan was becoming increasingly unbalanced. In his monastery he preached the need for fasting to the *oprichniki*, who were always carousing. He preached abstinence from carnal indulgence at a time of mass raping of boyars' daughters who had been captured in searches and arrests. The Czar was losing his reason, such as was left to him; he contracted marriages, to be followed by divorce, either in the presence of the Metropolitan or in his monastery before his chief of police, Malyuta Shuratov, who acted as priest and gave his blessing to the marriages![1]

All his life Ivan IV held the religious view of 'prayer for the victims of assassination', said at his request by the Metropolitan, whom he supplied with a full list of his victims.[2] However, when Philip the Metropolitan decided he should intervene on behalf of certain prisoners, Ivan IV became enraged and ordered Skuratov to arrest him and have him tried as a *kramolnik*. He was brought by Alexandrovskaya Sloboda and barbarously tortured by Vyazemsky, Basmanov and Skuratov, after which he was hanged on a hook in the cellar of the *Oprichnina* monastery.

The death of the Metropolitan, who was well liked by the Muscovites, made a deep impression on Ivan IV. In a fit of anger he ordered the execution of Prince Vyazemsky and Basmanov. Skuratov, who was an extremely cunning individual, managed to escape the fate of his associates. A terrible 'purge'

---

[1] Ivan IV had five legal wives, whose marriages were solemnized by the Metropolitan, and two others blessed by Skuratov or Vyazemsky.

[2] The number of Ivan IV's victims is estimated at 5,000.

decimated the *Oprichnina*; all the police agents against whom the population offered testimony were as savagely attacked as their victims had been at their hands. But others filled their places and the terror went on.

During the ominous period of the *Oprichnina* there was enacted a drama, the details of which historians have not yet elucidated. The Czar, insane and completely unrestrained, murdered Ivan, his son and heir, in 1582. This murder, a terrible deed even for Ivan IV, who dearly loved his son and was preparing him for his eventual assumption of supreme power, took place at the Kremlin, in the *Terem* of the Czarevich's wife.

It seems that, one feast-day, Ivan IV appeared unexpectedly in the *Terem*, to see whether the Czarevna was ready to leave for the cathedral. He found his daughter-in-law, who was pregnant at that time, not made up or properly dressed, but still wearing her wrap. Ivan IV, wild with rage, kicked her repeatedly in the stomach. Hearing his wife's cries, the Czarevich ran up and attempted to defend her. Ivan IV, who was furious at finding his son standing up to him, struck him on the temple with his staff. The Czarevich died in his wife's *Terem*.

This death very nearly resulted in Ivan IV's suicide. That same night he went up to the bell-tower of St. Basil Cathedral with his younger son Feodor and tolled the passing-bell. Howling with distress, he attempted to fling himself into the void but fell unconscious. He fully realized the political importance to Russia of the death of his elder son. In bringing his dynasty to an end, the Czar exposed Russia to the dangers of anarchy, that 'Great Anarchy' of Russian history, which began early in the seventeenth century, for his younger son Feodor was half-witted and incurable, incapable of continuing the line of descent.

Having lost all hope of founding the 'mare and cat'[1] dynasty, Ivan IV's mind became so unhinged that he even considered leaving the country and finding asylum in England, with Elizabeth I.[2] In a letter, the Czar suggested to the Queen that he should marry her! In a courteous reply Elizabeth declined the offer. The daughter of Henry VIII and Anne Boleyn, whom her

---

[1] By adding to the early Romanovs a certain Andrey Kobyla (kobyla means 'mare') as well as Fedor Koshka (koshka means 'cat') Ivan IV had wished to create a new dynasty; whence his marriage to Anastasya-Zakharina-Yureva-Koshkina-Romanova, which his son's murder made useless.

[2] According to Klyuchevsky.

husband in his jealousy had had beheaded, had no desire to marry a man whose exploits had gone far beyond those of her father. Nevertheless, Ivan continued his correspondence with Elizabeth, always with the view of securing a haven in England, to which country he meant to escape from his enemies. The suggestions put forward by Elizabeth on May 18, 1570, did not meet with his approval, and Ivan's reply, made in October of that year, was cutting and offensive:

'Your mouzhiks do as they like with you. I spit on you and your Palace.'

One could hardly be more gallant!

The defeats sustained by the Czar in Livonia drove him to resume communication with Elizabeth. In 1580 he instructed Jerome Holsey to find him a wife among the close relatives of Her Brittannic Majesty. Elizabeth recommended her grand-niece Mary Hastings.

The marriage did not take place, however. After this matrimonial and political failure, Ivan IV thought to find comfort in military success. The war which had long been raging in Livonia flared up with renewed intensity. The Czar's troops were beaten by the army of Poland's King Batory, in 1579, near Polotsk. Nevertheless, Pskov, under siege, held out. By the truce of 1582, Russia lost all her towns near the Baltic, all the Russian part of Livonia as well as the towns of Polotsk and Smolensk, which had come to Vassili III by his marriage.

At home there were rumblings of rebellion; Ivan IV's informers told him that the towns of Novgorod and Pskov wished to secede from Muscovy. Having been defeated on his north-west frontier and hearing that the Sultan was equipping a new fleet at Constantinople, Ivan IV reacted violently; he sent armies to Novgorod and Pskov with orders to show merciless repression. For the fifth time in Russian history these 'martyr towns' were burnt, the glory of Russian architecture was destroyed, thousands perished by the sword or in the flames.

The persecution mania from which Ivan IV suffered reached such a pitch that the Czar shunned his boyars and avoided speaking to them or listening to their advice. He was afraid, afraid of everything. The great courtyard of the Kremlin, the huge cathedrals, the cellars and the long empty corridors of his palaces—all held terrors for him. In his will he states:

'I am physically and mentally sick. The hurt in my soul and

my bodily ills increase day by day; and there is no physician who can cure me! In vain have I waited for someone with whom I might share my troubles, but nobody has come. Nobody. No comforter. All have repaid with evil the good that I have shown them. All. There is no justice in this world. Even Czars cannot find it in their subjects and servants.

'My subjects cannot understand me. Ignorant as they are, they are incapable of understanding that there is no power but that which comes from God and that it is given only where God wills. And I, what should I have done, confronted by these barbarians who cannot rise to the conception of eternal life? What ought I to have done, faced with those greedy, thieving boyars, the men who pillage the property of the Realm, the men who are beyond the reach of God's word? I smote them, as God smote the Ammonites and the Moabites; and then they called me fierce and cruel, me, the instrument of divine justice. There is no more rest for me on this earth; my eyes, which soon will no longer behold the light of earthly day, seek in vain the light of the celestial City. All seems lost to me. My very heart has turned to stone. May God forgive me, for it is He who sent me, the Czar, as the bearer of His message to my people.'

After writing this pathetic introduction, Ivan sets out in his letter instructions for the allocation of his possessions. He forgets nothing, not even a pair of shoes, the gift of Queen Elizabeth, which he bequeaths to his equerry.

Of Ivan IV's will the historian Klyuchevsky wrote in 1907 : 'When these dramatic words were read, one cannot help being moved by the poor martyr of the Kremlin, this martyr who wore a crown !' Yet this 'martyr' had just destroyed, on mere suspicion and stupid, slanderous denunciation, an old Russian town. In the best Tartar tradition he had brutally wiped out tens of thousands of citizens of Novgorod and demolished the historical monuments of Russian culture. Ivan IV was but a comedian—a tragic comedian, who could shed crocodile tears over the mutilated bodies of his victims. A comedian, and a consummate hypocrite.

VI Peter III, 1728-62, from a painting by G.C. Groth
[photo: Radio Times]

Peter I, the Great, 1672-1725, after a painting by Kneller
[photo: Radio Times]

Catherine II, 1729-96, drawn and engraved

Elizabeth I, 1709-62, engraved by Stenglin [photo: Radio Times]

CHAPTER 14

BORIS GODUNOV

On the day of Ivan the Terrible's death, his successor Feodor Ivanovich (or Fedor), who was regarded as half-witted, was not at his father's deathbed. He was sought high and low to be told that he was proclaimed Czar Feodor I. After searching in every corner of the Kremlin, the boyars were unable to find their new Czar. Then it occurred to one of them to send the *streltzi* up to the bell-tower of the Uspenie Cathedral; the new sovereign was snoring peacefully there near the great bell. When he was awakened, he said he would not appear before the boyars and high dignitaries until he had personally rung the bell for evening Mass!

The people dubbed Feodor the 'Bell-ringer'. He was a gentle, humble person, who had lived remote from his father's crimes, going off alone to the bell-towers and chattering away to the pigeons and storks. When he became Czar of all the Russias, he avoided taking any part in the government of his country. A grand Regency Council was formed to direct affairs of state. The chief boyar of this Council (Duma) was Boris Godunov, who became the real sovereign of Russia. A special residence was built for him and his family in the Kremlin, where he received ambassadors from abroad, acted for the Czar and signed all documents relating to home and foreign policies.

Boris Godunov was a strange character. Although blessed with remarkable intelligence, he had not thought it necessary to learn to read or write! When he signed documents, he did so by scribbling something which looked like a tiny field-bird (*godun*, in Tartar, means 'lark'). Of Tartar origin, he married the daughter of Malyuta Skuratov, the chief of Ivan IV's terrible secret police, in order to follow a political career. In that way he managed, with the consummate skill of an eastern statesman, to insinuate himself during the *Oprichnina* terror and yet run no risk.

To strengthen his position with the Czar, Boris Godunov decided to bring about a marriage between Feodor and his sister. He made arrangements for the *smotriny*, but poor Feodor, who was shy and afraid of women, would not attend. Godunov, in conjunction with his friend, the Metropolitan Job, calmly announced on behalf of Feodor that the Czar had chosen to marry his sister. The marriage was celebrated in the Kremlin cathedral with unparalleled ostentation.

His 'idiocy' notwithstanding, Feodor succeeded, with Godunov's aid, in getting back from the Swedes the Russian Baltic towns of Yam, Ivangorod and Kapore which had been lost by his father. He also succeeded, again thanks to Godunov, in obtaining 'promotion' for the Metropolitan Job; he officially invited the Patriarch of Constantinople to the Kremlin and obtained from him the solemn consecration of Job as Patriarch of Russia, for which he was handsomely paid.

The only arbitrary act of which Feodor might be accused was his confirmation of the decision made by his father to burn to death Gavrila, the Pskov blacksmith, the bird-man, the first Russian flying-man. In 1584, the year of Ivan IV's death, Gavrila had invented a kind of glider with which he launched himself from the Pskov bell-tower and glided for a few hundred yards. The *voevoda* of Pskov reported the event to the Czar, who gave orders for the blacksmith to be burnt. At the instigation of Godunov, Feodor confirmed the order. But did he know what he was ordering?

Feodor I died in 1598, leaving no heir. Godunov, as chief boyar, convened the *Sobor* to elect a new Czar. The Patriarch Job nominated Godunov. After taking part in an impressive Mass in the Kremlin cathedral, the crowd, under the direction of the Patriarch, set off for the convent of Novo-Devichi, to which the Czarina, Godunov's sister, had retired. Police armed with cudgels, says Klyuchevsky, marched at the back of the crowd. The pilgrims had been ordered to fall to their knees as soon as they arrived at the convent gates and to make lamentation, by weeping and wailing, to prove to the Czarina the depth of their affection. Those who were slow to call out lamentations were beaten with the cudgels until they decided to weep. The Patriarch made his entry with all solemnity and, pointing to the crowd, said to the Czarina. 'Behold your people! They are imploring you to speak to the *Sobor* and request that the Czar to be elected shall be your brother—Boris'. After this scene, which would not have disgraced the *commedia dell'arte*, the Czarina addressed the *Sobor* and Boris Godunov was elected Czar of all the Russias, 1598.

The coronation ceremony, which took place in the Uspenie Cathedral, was an even more solemn occasion than the coronation of Ivan the Terrible. But it was hardly concluded when the boyars and high-ranking nobles were already scheming and working up a whole series of plots. The conspirators reproached the new Czar with his Tartar birth and also alleged that he had had a hand in the murder of Ivan's young son, the Czarevich Dmitri, whose mother, Maria Nagaya, the fifth legal wife of Ivan the Terrible, was living in exile in the little town of Uglich.

The Shuyskys and the Romanovs were foremost in accusing this 'erstwhile slave, this Tartar, this hangman's son-in-law, himself a hangman in his soul',[1] of having seized the throne as the result of an assassination. They recalled that Dmitri, Ivan's young son, was the sole legal claimant to the throne of Russia and that Boris Godunov had played a part in the murder of Dmitri at Uglich in 1591.

The air in the Kremlin became unbreathable. Boris Godunov, that 'elder' of the *Oprichnina*, organized his secret police, which was not so fierce as Ivan IV's, but more efficient. A network of delation spread through the whole Empire. Serfs had the right to inform against their masters. They were rewarded with large sums of money and their emancipation. From this time date the confiscation of the boyars' goods, the exile of offenders and the deportation to Siberia, which had become a Russian province during the reign of Godunov's formidable predecessor, thanks to the Cossack Yermak. It soon became a mass of prisons, whose inmates worked the iron and coal mines.

Boris Godunov's police faithfully reported to him the rumours accusing him of the death of the Czarevich and the growing disaffection of the boyars and the nobility. He decided to act. In 1602, he called to the Kremlin the Patriarch, a few carefully selected representatives of the nobility, some merchants and delegates of the 'black hundreds'.[2] The Czar took the important decision to exile the opposition leaders, the Shuyskys and the Romanovs. After giving the reasons why he had been obliged to act against the *kramola* instigators, Boris Godunov stated that he had no other objective but to rule for the 'good of the nation'. As famine was raging in Moscow, he had free food distributed

---

[1] According to Pushkin.

[2] The name given to the free artisans, small traders and well-to-do free peasants, etc. In 1905, during the first Russian revolution, it was applied to ultra-nationalistic and anti-Semitic associations.

and, at the State's expense, he rebuilt all the houses which had just been burnt down in a fire. In the years 1602 and 1603, this illiterate Czar created 'work-shops' in Moscow, 250 years before the establishment of the Parisian work-shops in 1848!

Boris Godunov announced to his subjects his intention of marrying his daughter to Waldemar, the heir to the Danish throne. This Prince let it be understood that Russia and Denmark might combine to go to war against Sweden and so enable Russia to 'set up her standards on the shores of the Baltic'.

The untutored Boris Godunov decided to send nineteen Russians abroad, all chosen from the highest nobility in the land, to study science, western techniques, navigation, management, military science, etc.

A weary man, this Czar, so full of good intentions, was dogged by ill luck which became proverbial. The Danish Prince died in the Kremlin of a malignant fever; a new fire destroyed the town's food depots; the nineteen Russians, sent abroad, preferred to stay there.

The Czar's stubbornness was as well known as his bad luck and it is likely that Boris Godunov would have risen above these tricks of fate if terrible news had not arrived in Moscow in 1604: Polish, Ukrainian and Cossack detachments had just crossed the Dnepr. They were led by a man who claimed to be the Czar Dmitri and who said he had escaped the clutches of the soldiers sent by Boris Godunov to Uglich to assassinate him! This 'Dmitri' was determined to dethrone Godunov and replace him as 'rightful Czar of all the Russias'.

This was the beginning of the Kremlin's greatest adventure.

CHAPTER 15

THE FALSE DMITRI

It was after the first military successes by the false Dmitri that the extent of Boris Godunov's unpopularity was realized. The Czar's regiments surrendered to the false Dmitri, on the pretext that they were unwilling to fight against the 'Czarevich'. Confronted with this state of affairs, the Patriarch gave instructions to the *popes* to read in the churches a manifesto signed by all the dignitaries of the Greek Orthodox Church and proclaiming that the sham Dmitri was the 'Antichrist' and 'servant of the Devil'. But this manifesto had no effect upon the public who, instead of listening to the *popes*, flogged them and called them 'enemies of the Russian Czarevich'.

In 1605, the news according to which Basmanov, one of the best of the Czar's *voevoda*, had gone over bag and baggage to the side of the 'impostor' broke suddenly upon Moscow. The bells of the Kremlin and the cathedrals of the town sounded the tocsin summoning the Muscovites to form a troop in defence of the capital.

Boris Godunov, accompanied by the Patriarch, went to the Red Square[1] and began to make a speech. He was interrupted by the booing of the crowd and was suddenly taken ill and fainted. He was carried to his *pokoy*. The same night he passed away, after horrible suffering. Pushkin believed that it was a natural death following a heart attack, but today the more probable version is that it was a case of poisoning.

Another mystery which historians have never succeeded in clearing up is that of Dmitri's identity. The Patriarch's manifesto stated that the impostor was a lesser noble from Galich, Yuri Otrepev, who had become a monk and had taken the name of 'Grigori', better known in its diminutive form of 'Grishka'. This so-called 'Grishka Otrepev' was employed as an attendant by the Romanovs. It therefore appears that it was the Romanovs

---

[1] It was not until about the second half of the sixteenth century that the Red Square was so called. Before that time it was called *Pozhar* (conflagration), by reason of the innumerable fires which drove the Muscovites from their burning homes to camp in the great square.

who had staged the 'fake Dmitri' affair in order to be rid of Boris Godunov! This false Czar was apparently just an invention of the Romanov family who coveted the Russian throne. It is evident, moreover, from the archives of Boris Godunov's secret police that a certain 'Grishka' had made his escape from Moscow, soon after the police had arrested the Romanovs, and had taken refuge in Lithuania and Poland. It was in fact while he was with the wealthy Polish grandees that Grishka Otrepev decided to proclaim himself Czar and march on Moscow, after he had asked Prince Mniszek, the Polish governor of Sandomerz, for the hand of his daughter, Marina, in marriage.

In his *Boris Godunov*, Pushkin shows Dmitri speaking to Marina in Prince Mniszek's garden, when Dmitri confesses to his betrothed that he is not the Czarevich but has represented himself as such to the Prince so as to be in a position to ask for his daughter's hand.

Here are the words of the historian Klyuchevsky concerning Dmitri, who entered Moscow and ascended the throne in June, 1605.

'The false Czar always behaved like a true, legal Czar, with confidence in his birth and his right to the throne; never—as all who had dealings with him agree—did Dmitri for a moment doubt the authenticity of his ancestry. So firm was his belief that when the Princes Shuysky, who wished to succeed Boris Godunov, began to spread stories of the 'impostor', stories invented by Godunov's police, the assumed Dmitri convened the *Sobor* (the Russian States-General), the most democratic *Sobor* ever known in Russia and consisting of merchants, artisans and even peasants, in order to place before it the dispute between him and the Shuyskys. The *Sobor* condemned the Shuyskys' behaviour and sentenced them to be quartered, but the false Dmitri reprieved them and sent them into temporary exile. Then he brought them back to Moscow and restored to them their estates and titles. How could an impostor knowingly have acted in that way? How and why it was possible for this bogus Czar to imagine that he was the true Czar is one of the greatest enigmas in Russian history, an enigma which is as psychological as it is historical!'

He was a young man (Klyuchevsky continues) a little below average height, rather ugly, with red hair and a shy, sad expression. His outward appearance gave no hint of his nature or of his intelligence. Unlike Boris Godunov, he was literate. A gifted, shrewd, individual, he was able to solve the most complex problems in the boyars' *duma*. He was of a lively disposition and quick-tempered; he was courageous when danger threatened; he liked healthy amusements. He was skilled in making speeches in a happy vein; he had a thorough knowledge of Russia and her history. The 'false' Czar was unpretentious and available to the least of his subjects, and so totally changed the medieval nature of the relationship between the lords of the Kremlin and those who served them. He also brought about a radical transformation in the way of life of the Russian monarchs and in their habits; he did not sleep after meals, he often went to the baths— and not only on feast days. He was a generous man. He liked to be abreast of all that was happening in the chancelleries and would make unexpected appearances at administrative assemblies and in the *prikazes*, where he would glance through the files. Every day he came to the *duma* to take personal charge of affairs of state. And finally, he was keen to direct military exercises himself; he was a great leader of men, a learned and capable military chief.

Occasionally Dmitri would criticize his advisers and the boyars of the *duma* for their ignorance of foreign lands and would ask them, very politely, if it would not be useful for them to travel a little so as to improve their knowledge. He did not command; he advised.

It will be seen that Dmitri was far superior to all the authentic Czars of Muscovy; he had none of the frightful and barbarous cruelty of Ivan the Terrible, he outshone even Peter the Great, 'whose bold reforms and thin layer of western culture were overlaid with the most genuine barbarism'.

Every man has his Achilles heel. Unfortunately for him, Dmitri felt a strange and deep sympathy for the Vatican and catholics, the pet aversion of the Russians. He appointed a new Metropolitan, Philaret Romanov, a former boyar exiled by Boris Godunov. After this appointment, Dmitri called a solemn session of the *duma* in the Palace of Facets and made a pathetic speech: 'It is *necessary*', he said, 'to *combine all Christian churches* to fight the Turks and Islam'. In his speech he criticized the dogmatic formalism of the Russian churches, the lack of depth in their religious thought and their fondness for the most absurd superstitions.

This unusual harangue caused a stir. The Metropolitan spoke in his turn and expressed the idea that 'if union with the catholics were achieved and the Moslems overthrown, it would be possible to reconsider the question of the churches and restore the universal church'. The boyars heaped abuse upon him. In plain, unvarnished terms Dmitri accused them of 'unchristian' cruelty, and reminded them how, immediately after Boris Godunov had fainted, they had burst into the Czar's palace, strangled his son and thrown the body in the *Yama*. 'If all Christians were like you,' concluded Dmitri in a voice shaking with anger, 'the Moslem religion would long since have wiped out our holy faith'.

The boyars greeted this speech with such howls that the Czar had to suspend the assembly. After the session, the Metropolitan said to Dmitri, 'Arrest and impale all that howling scum and the others will be as gentle as lambs'. 'For shame, Metropolitan, you are the servant of God and you speak like a hangman!' answered Dmitri.

The false Czar was also accused of adopting a distant attitude towards the boyars and of discouraging familiarity on their part. What is more, he was clean-shaven and refused to drink the brandy and mead—the only alcoholic drink of those times. He rarely went to church and refused to observe the lengthy fasts; he crossed himself, as all Russians do,[1] but not without vague movements of the hand showing that he was accustomed to doing so in another manner. Nations like great men in their own image!

All this gave an opportunity to the boyars, led by those same Shuyskys Dmitri had just reprieved, to accuse him secretly of being 'a servant of the ungodly catholic religion'. The Poles who had come to Moscow with him had settled in the Kremlin and were in occupation of half the palaces. They continually molested the women of the *Terem*. They and the Cossack detachment constituted a veritable plague.

Dmitri had been obliged, when recruiting his troops in Lithuania and Poland, to apply to adventurers and mercenaries; the Polish grandees, like Wiczniewiecki, who were financing Dmitri, had 'lent' him as a *voevoda* a certain Rozinsky. This Rozinsky, a mixture of adventurer and felon, was appointed *hetman*; but, as neither the Poles nor the Cossacks obeyed him,

---

[1] At that time the Russians used two fingers in crossing themselves; today they use three fingers in doing so.

Moscow was becoming the scene of brawls and scuffles. The Russians often attacked the Poles in the middle of the night when the latter, hopelessly drunk, were on their way back to the Kremlin after spending a few hours in bawdy-houses. The girls in these establishments sometimes poisoned their customers by putting a few *zelie* in their drinks. As for the Cossacks, they plundered the Russians as much as they did the Poles and stole precious objects from the cathedrals, while still remaining 'orthodox Christians and defenders of the faith'. Anarchy was beginning to take root in the Kremlin; the Poles, under orders from their *hetman*, shut themselves up in their barracks and posted guards at the Kremlin gates with instructions to kill any-one who tried to get in without a pass from *hetman* Rozinsky. For their part, the Cossacks occupied the *Kitay-Gorod*, situated between the Kremlin and the Centre, barricaded themselves in and killed off the Poles who passed through to *Kitay-Gorod* by night.

This anarchy allowed the boyars to organize their conspiracy against Dmitri. Their plan was simple: to force their way into the Kremlin with the Cossacks on the pretext of defending Dmitri, whom the Poles were threatening to kill.

At dawn on May 17, 1606, the 150 churches in Moscow[1] sounded the tocsin. 'The Poles are attacking the Czar's residence and mean to kill him,' shouted the sacristans. Faithful to Shuysky, the *streltzi*, together with some fifty conspirators from among the boyars and Cossacks under the command of Prince Trubetzkoy, invaded the inner courtyard of the Kremlin. Making an onslaught upon the Czar's residence the boyars forced their way into the spurious Dmitri's sleeping-quarters. Dmitri leaped out of bed, in his night attire, and with his curved Cossack sword in hand, managed to get free of his assailants. But the latter were too many for him; he had to jump out of the window, and he broke a leg as he fell. He tried to drag himself to the barracks of the Polish regiment, but he was too late; the pack had caught up with him. He was kicked and bludgeoned to death like a mad dog, and his attackers screamed, 'The Poles are murdering our Czar!' The frightfully mutilated body of Dmitri was flung upon a brazier. His ashes were handed over to the *streltzi*, who were ordered to 'fire a shot from the Kremlin'.

[1] In 1606 there were 150 churches in Moscow. By 1812, when the capital was occupied by the *Grande Armée*, the number was three times as great. Moscow became the town of the 'forty times forty' churches (*soroke sorokov*).

The cannon-ball, containing the ashes of the false Czar, was fired in the direction of Warsaw, whence the 'impostor' had come.

So ended the epic reign of the false Dmitri, who might have proved one of the best Czars.

CHAPTER 16

THE POLISH EPOCH

The murder of the spurious Dmitri, the revolt of the Muscovite populace and Shuysky's accession to power on May 19, 1606, marked the beginning of the Kremlin's saddest epoch, the 'Polish epoch'. The Russian sanctuary was for several years occupied by the Polish armies, who plundered the historical treasures, murdered the citizens of Moscow, destroyed the houses, threw the ikons into the gutters, insulted the boyars and outraged the women.

This epoch left gloomy memories in the public mind. The great poet Pushkin reminded the Poles, with regard to the Polish insurrection of 1831 which was severely put down by Nicholas I, that they had been guilty of misdeeds at the Kremlin. 'These crimes', he said, 'will be paid for one day; the burning of the Warsaw suburb of Praga by Suvarov in the reign of Catherine II was merely the answer to the insult suffered by Russia from the defilement of the Kremlin sanctuary by the Polish occupation'.

The boyar, Prince Vassili Shuysky, who led the conspiracy against the false Dmitri, was borne to power by the band of intriguers who had murdered the Czar. The nation had no illusions about the usurper.

Klyuchevsky describes this character in the following terms:

'After the death of the assumed Dmitri, the throne of the Kremlin was occupied by Shuysky the conspiratorial Czar. This queer Shuysky was a boyar, small of stature, about fifty years old and almost blind. He was a crafty man, a liar and a professional schemer, who had many ups and downs but more downs than ups. He would have been beheaded but for the clemency of Dmitri, whom he had sworn on the cross never to oppose.'

The schemer created in the Kremlin a secret chancellery concerned exclusively with denunciations.

The quaintest characteristic of this 'Czar' was his great superstition: he was afraid of witches and black cats! That is the reason why Czar Shuysky suddenly interrupted a session of the boyars' *duma* when a huge black cat got into the hall of the Palace of Facets and mewed distractedly before the Czar and boyars. The Czar hurriedly left his throne and rushed for the door, crossing himself and reciting the prayer to Nicholas the Miracle-worker.

'Shuysky began his reign', continues Klyuchevsky, 'by appending his signature to a series of manifestos, which were displayed on all the walls of the Kremlin. Each of these manifestos contained at least one flagrant falsehood!

Soon after the murder of Dmitri, Shuysky published the testimony of a Polish officer, handsomely paid for the evidence, according to which Dmitri had signed a secret agreement with the Poles: all Russians were to have their beards shaven and be converted to the Catholic or Lutheran religion, either willingly or by compulsion. Shuysky did not hesitate to make use of the most stupid untruths to inflame the ignorant Moscow crowd; did he not inform the public that Dmitri wished to compel the Russians to attend the baths every day and that Dmitri himself bathed twice a day like an ungodly Catholic? Did he not go so far as to claim that Dmitri had decided to have all women shaved in intimate parts of their persons in accordance with the practice of Tartar women?'

Such, then, was the man who sat upon the throne; a Czar who paid the leaders of the Polish troops in the Kremlin to ensure his protection, a Czar who, unlike the courageous soldier Dmitri, feared the sound of cannon and the smell of gunpowder.

The people despised him to such an extent that in 1607, when an habitual criminal who had recently escaped from prison proclaimed himself 'Dmitri, miraculously saved from the murderers sent by Shuysky', a good many Russians applauded this second bogus Dmitri. The new false Czar set up his headquarters in the village of Tushino, not far from the gates of Moscow. The Patriarch himself paid a visit to the 'horse thief of Tushino' to confer his blessing upon him.

The widow of the *real* Dmitri went to Tushino and solemnly identified the 'horse thief' as her husband! This event had the blessing of the Patriarch and the black clergy. The last remaining doubts were dispelled by the intervention of the high clergy and the whole nation decided to place its faith in this new miracle: 'God had saved the false Dmitri from Shuysky's clutches!'

Meanwhile, the war with Poland was resumed. In the autumn of 1609, Sigismund III laid siege to Smolensk, while a revolt caused by famine broke out in Moscow.

Shuysky doubled the pay of his Polish mercenaries, responsible for defending him from the populace, but the Poles had their own plan, namely to place Prince Ladislas, the son of King Sigismund of Poland, on the Russian throne. Instead of defending Shuysky, they joined forces with the boyar 'collaborators' and threatened to send Shuysky to the 'horse thief' if he refused to sign his abdication in favour of the Pole Ladislas. Shuysky, who always turned green with fear at the mere mention of the 'thief', hastened to sign all that was asked of him and set out for Poland and exile, accompanied by a considerable escort. He was soon dead, of a 'sudden indigestion', probably poisoned by the Poles, who were determined to be rid of a witness so damaging to Ladislas.

Under the command of *hetman* Jolkiewski, the Polish detachment from the Kremlin occupied all bridges and strategical points in Moscow and proclaimed the new Polish Czar.

The Muscovites' resistance, passive at first, now became active. Philaret Romanov, the Metropolitan of Moscow and future co-Czar with his son Michael, fled to Tushino, to the 'thief' whom he proclaimed Czar of all the Russias. For his part, the new 'thief Czar' appointed Philaret Patriarch of all the Russias.

The situation became increasingly involved. While the Poles, who had so far supported the 'thief', suddenly declared him to be a 'usurper' and brought his past to light, the Russians defended the 'thief' as if he were their true 'Russian Czar'.

To punish Philaret Romanov for his support of the 'thief', the Poles exiled him to Poland. Prince Rozinsky, in command of a gang of Polish adventurers in Tushino, received orders from Warsaw to entice the 'thief' to the Kremlin and there murder him. But the sham Dmitri II had wind of the plot and escaped to Kaluga, a town he knew well from having been in prison there! Unfortunately for him, Rozinsky followed him there and had him killed. His body was thrown into the pond of the Archbishopric.

A great celebration was put in hand by *hetman* Jolkiewski to announce to the Muscovites the death of the 'usurper' and the arrival of Prince Ladislas in Moscow as the new Russian Czar. A delegation of boyars, carefully chosen by the Poles and headed by Prince Saltykov, was sent to the neighbourhood of beleaguered Smolensk, where King Sigismund was, to request him to set up his son as Czar of Russia. But, hardly had the delegation left for Smolensk, when a terrible riot broke out in Moscow, a riot called the *babyibunt*,[1] the women's revolt.

The female population of Moscow, joining hands with those shut up for years in their *terems*, took advantage of the anarchy created by the false Dmitri, and took part in the Moscow riots. A traveller had come back from Kaluga with the news that the Poles had assassinated the 'Tushino Czar', and the women met together in front of the Kremlin and attacked the Polish detachment which was coming in to reinforce Jolkiewski's troops. Armed with axes and cudgels, the Russian women succeeded in overthrowing the Poles and killed 100 of them.

The riot of March 1611 played an important part in the fostering of 'Russian anarchy'. The people of Moscow followed the women; the invaders could not get out; pickets with axes surrounded the Kremlin and the *Kitay Gorod*: the beleaguered troops could not get further supplies.

The Polish garrison, which was destined to remain at the Kremlin until October 1612, was faced with starvation. Their small-calibre guns bombarded Moscow, they threw incendiary grenades and the capital was aflame day and night. Inside the Kremlin the Polish soldiers sacked the churches, threw down the ikons, destroyed the Palace of Facets, the Uspenie Cathedral and one wing of St. Basil's Church. The Polish priest Kossinsky made a *kostiol*[2] of one of the churches in order to celebrate his masses, which provoked a new Kremlin assault by the *babas* and Cossacks, who had sworn to 'deliver the sacred ikons from impious humiliation'. The attack was savagely repulsed by the Poles, who violated their women prisoners.

While the battle was raging in the Kremlin, the Muscovites heard from a citizen of Pskov that a man claiming to be the 'Tushino Czar' had managed to avoid the grasp of the Poles! This third false Dmitri was an even more obscure person than the Tushino 'thief'. He was known as 'Sidorka'.[3] The Muscovites sent a delegation to Pskov and invited him to come and occupy

---

[1] *Baba* means 'woman' in popular Russian.

[2] Polish church.

[3] 'Sidorka' is the pejorative diminutive of Isidor. Sidorka was a former nightwatchman of a meat warehouse, from which position he had been dismissed because of illicit dealings. The Russian false Czars were certainly recruited from the lowest classes.

the throne of his father, Ivan the Terrible.[1] The Poles acted with bewildering speed and put Sidorka to death. His body was thrown into the lake at Pskov.

In the meantime, King Sigismund had told Prince Saltykov's delegation that he did not wish to see his son on the Kremlin throne but that he would occupy it himself. Hetman Shodkiewicz[2] was sent to Moscow to free the Polish garrison surrounded in the Kremlin. For that purpose he had at his disposal strong bodies of cavalry, but after a bloody battle at Mozhaysk,[3] Paleolog's Cossacks crushed the hetman's army. The Polish garrison at the Kremlin therefore remained surrounded, without reinforcements or food. The Muscovites and the Cossacks offered to evacuate the Kremlin on condition of a safe-conduct, but the garrison proudly refused and valiantly threw back all Russian assaults.

Now began an ominous period for Jolkiewski and his garrison; they were driven to eating the bodies of their comrades who had fallen in the skirmishes. It is one of the rare instances of cannibalism known in the Kremlin. Historians have had a great deal to say about it and have supplied horrible details.

The Russian 'Great Anarchy' went on. The Cossacks, with the help of women from the common people, engaged in a fresh attack on the Kremlin, but it was in vain. Jolkiewski, in order to establish himself as defender of the Russians against the Cossacks, who were looting the traders in the capital, invited Prince Mstislavsky to form a provisional government, while awaiting the decision of the Sobor. For their part, the Cossacks formed a triumvirate based in the Kitay Gorod, near the Kremlin and sheltered from the Polish artillery. This triumvirate was made up of Prince Trubetskoy, Zarutsky and a noble, Prokop Lyapunov. The trio formed a territorial guard in Moscow and proclaimed the 'People's Council'. A few nobles, like Princes Shakhovskoy and Volkonsky, who had joined the Cossacks, and Russo-Polish nobles, like Kakhevsky, Muraviev, Bestuzhev,

[1] All false Czars of this period of Russian anarchy were, naturally, sons of Ivan the Terrible.

[2] Polish supreme commander. There were two hetmans in Poland; the Koronny hetman and the hetman of the Grand-Duchy of Lithuania.

[3] By a strange coincidence, this battle which saved Moscow from Polish occupation was fought on the Volokolamsk road, at the very spot where Zhukov saved Moscow from occupation by the Wehrmacht in 1941.

Tolshinsky, Sukhomlin and others,[1] became the leaders of the first 'Soviet of Moscow and the Kremlin.'[2]

The Council appointed a delegation on which the *bolotnikovtzi*[3] were represented. The latter were Bolotnikov's supporters, who were asking for the merchants' estates and money to be divided up immediately.

It was the first programme of the 'social revolution', copied in part—and, moreover, by Bolotnikov—from that of the sixteenth century peasant revolt in Germany and the registered grievances of the French peasants of Meaux in the fourteenth century. This programme concluded with the wholesale confiscation of the possessions of the wealthy traders of the towns.

The delegation began negotiations with the Patriarch Philaret Romanov, who agreed to submit their complaints to King Sigismund. The Poles arrested the Patriarch and deported him to Poland. Then a monk, Abraham Palitzin, took upon himself the role of 'defender of the poor' and addressed to all Russian towns a proclamation in which he asked for the recruitment of an 'army of liberation from the Polish yoke'.

The army was raised in the Volga region. Under the command of Prince Pozharsky and the magistrate representing the traders of Nizhni Novgorod, Kuzma Minin, it came to Moscow and laid siege to the Kremlin; but the Cossacks, displeased with Pozharsky and Lyapunov, rose in revolt and requested the

[1] The names of the nobles who decided to profit from the Great Anarchy in order to make Russia a popular and democratic State, like the *Sech* of the Zaporog Cossacks, occur again among those who determined to impose a democratic constitution upon Nicholas I on December 2, 1825. Such are Volkonsky, Trubetskoy, Shakhovskoy, Muraviev, Kakhevsky, Bestuzhev, etc.

[2] Lenin, who knew Russian history as well as he did Karl Marx's *Kapital*, reminded Trotsky of this when the latter thought that the 1905 'Soviet' was the first in Russian history.

[3] Bolotnikov was a picturesque character. A former serf of the Telyatevsky princes, who had escaped and settled in the Cossack Republic of Zaporog, he became the chief of an army unit. Taken in battle by the Tartars, he was sold to a Turkish Pasha in Constantinople and adopted as his son. After learning Turkish in a Constantinople school and at the Moslem University of Skutari, Bolotnikov was sent by the Turks to fight in the Balkans, where he attempted to stir up revolt among the troops. He was arrested and sentenced to death, but was pardoned by the Sultan. He became a galley-slave, but escaped during a Turco-Venetian naval battle and went to live in Poland. At the time of the Great Anarchy he became a boyar at the court of the false Tushino Czar, who sent him to seek Cossack aid against the Poles. The Cossack leader, Prince Shakhovskoy, made him his adjutant, but Bolotnikov, true to his stock, preferred to lead the peasant uprising. This great seventeenth-century adventurer was killed in battle.

immediate convocation of a *Sobor* to elect the new Czar of all the Russias. By threatening the Poles, who were still held within the Kremlin, that all their throats would be cut if they did not accept an honourable capitulation, the Cossacks managed to bring about the evacuation of the Kremlin on October 26, 1612. It must be stated that the Poles had already eaten all their horses and a third of their men !

The Cossack leaders, who represented the dominating force in the army of liberation, put forward Michael Romanov, Philaret's son, as candidate for the Russian throne. When the Poles heard of this proposal they sent a specially picked body of men to the Ipatev monastery,[1] where young Michael Romanov was living. They had very clear instructions to murder him.

The detachment lost its way in the forests of Kostroma, which were famous for their huge brown bears. The Poles captured a peasant hunter, Ivan Susanin, and compelled him to lead them to the Ipatev monastery, but Susanin took them into the depths of forest and swamps, where gangs of armed peasants decimated the Polish horsemen. The Poles killed Susanin, but they themselves perished in the snow-storms.

This event became legendary. The composer Glinka used it as the text of his opera, *A Life for the Czar,* better known today under the title *Ivan Susanin.*

The Muscovites sought out Michael Romanov and took him to Moscow, but he refused to live there and he went instead to live with his mother in a convent not far distant.

Meanwhile, the *Sobor* was debating the question of the appointment of the Czar. The Russian Princes came to the Kremlin with the greatest possible number of their friends in tow and each spent enormous sums of money to influence the *Sobor's* decision in favour of one or another of the candidates. It was Prince Trubetskoy's Cossack army which settled the fate of the election. It was camped at the gates of Moscow and a guard of honour was posted to watch over the voting. The names of several candidates were put up during the meeting of the Council of Elders of the *Sobor*: Michael Romanov and the Princes Golitzin, Mstislavsky, Vorotinsky, Trubetskoy, Dmitri Pozharsky, Dolgoruki and Obolensky-Pepnin. There were foreigners also among the candidates: King Sigismund of

[1] It is a strange fact that the Romanov dynasty began in the Ipatev monastery and came to an end in the Ipatev house at Ekaterinburg where Nicholas II and all his family were massacred.

Poland, his son Ladislas and Prince Gustav of Sweden, who commanded the Swedish garrison of Novgorod.

The cathedral bells of the Kremlin pealed out from morning to evening while the members of the *Sobor* went on with their debating. The discussion was winding up and the Council of Elders was about to vote, when the *Sotnik* Struysky, the leader of the Cossack detachment, suddenly came into the hall of the Kremlin Palace, followed by ten Cossacks armed to the teeth.

'What do you want?' asked Prince Pozharsky.

The *sotnik* read out the motion voted by the Cossacks: 'We desire as our Czar the son of the Tushino sovereign!'

The members of the *Sobor* were obliged to vote on the candidature of the 'thief's' offspring, a child of four.

This outrageous trick played on the *Sobor* was due to Prince Trubetskoy, furious that his candidature had been unsuccessful. It appears that this coarse, undaunted man had said to his friend, the *dyak* Korotkov, 'Those sons of bitches won't have me, a Russian Prince and Cossack *hetman*. I'll slip in their way the son of a thief and a Polish whore. Then let them get out of that mess!'

Prince Pozharsky, who shared the leadership of the Povolge army with the municipal representative Minin, found a way out of the difficulty by proposing that henceforth no foreigner or son of a non-Russian mother should be elected Czar. After a lengthy prayer in the Uspenie Cathedral, the members adopted the motion. King Sigismund, his son Ladislas and the child of the thief and Marina Mniczek were thus excluded once and for all from the list of candidates for the Russian throne. The *Sobor* had hardly resumed work, when a scuffle broke out between the Cossacks posted at the gates of Moscow and the *Sobor* guard inside the Kremlin. The *sotnik* Struysky, supported by Prince Trubetskoy, insisted that the Cossacks should be admitted to the Kremlin. Once inside the enclosure, the Cossacks lost no time; the same night they kidnapped Prince Galitzin, the most eminent of the candidates, and handed him over to the Poles in Smolensk, who took him to Warsaw. There he found Prince Shuysky, also of the Galitzin line, and the Patriarch Philaret. The following night the Cossacks carried off Prince Mstislavsky but, this time, did not hand him over to the Poles, for it was well known that the Prince was *persona grata* at the court of Warsaw. The Cossacks simply made him swear to withdraw his candidature for the throne. The kidnappings continued whenever a prince offered himself as a candidate; the elections were at a standstill.

The Cossacks went to find the Abbot Abraham Palitzin, who had been their friend since the day when, on his advice, they had raised the siege of the Monastery of Triad and Sergius, invested by the Poles.

Abraham Palitzin celebrated a thanksgiving Mass in the Kremlin and appeared before the *Sobor*. 'My brethren', he said, 'you are here to elect a Russian Czar and not to enjoy yourselves. But we cannot accept just anybody for the throne. An elected Czar is not an alderman. A Czar is the father of the nation, and he rules from Moscow. Moscow is the mother of the nation. You can neither select nor elect your father or your mother; they are sent to you by God!'

The *Sobor* responded to this wily speech with thunderous applause: '*Amen*, Abraham! *Amen!* You are right! Tell us now who is he that is sent from God to ascend the throne of Russia's Czar?'

'Who other than Michael Romanov?' exclaimed the cunning Abraham. 'Is he not the nephew of Czar Feodor and the son of Czarina Anastasya? God keep her holy soul in Paradise![1] Is he not the grand-nephew of Czar Ivan Vassilevich who sought the presence of God to ask pardon for his sins? God has sent us none other than Michael Romanov. Let us blot out the stain of your foolhardiness in choosing Boris Godunov and Shuysky. Let us elect young Michael Romanov, let us give him our blessing and long may he reign!'

Abraham had hardly finished speaking, when the provincial delegations came through all the Kremlin gates and into the hall where the *Sobor* was in session; and, keeping to the plan previously arranged by Abraham himself, they put forward motions in favour of Michael Romanov. Armed Cossacks followed the delegations. 'Listen to them, my brethren,' went on Abraham; 'heed them, and cast your votes for Czar Michael Romanov'.

At that exact moment, Prince Trubetskoy, the *hetman*, drew his sabre and, leaping on to the dais where Prince Pozharsky was presiding, he shouted[2]: 'The Cossacks are for Michael

[1] Anastasya Romanov, first wife of Ivan the Terrible, was the mother of Feodor.

[2] As a result of this intervention, Michael Romanov was known as the 'Cossacks' Czar'.

Romanov, but they insist that he swear on the Gospel to convene the *Sobor* and govern with the approval of the Russian nation !'

The bells of the Kremlin cathedrals rang out—they had been ringing for days—and on this Friday in Lent, February 19, 1613, the *Sobor* acclaimed the name of Michael Romanov. Each member had mounted the rostrum to deposit his envelope, (156 members were illiterate and requested Abraham to fill in their voting-papers for them). Michael Romanov was unanimously elected Czar of all the Russias.

The following Sunday, from the platform in the Red Square, Abraham Palitzin read out the *Sobor's* decision to the crowd. There was an outburst of joyful shouts: *'Davay tsarem Mikhayla Romanova!'*[1]

The Czar swore on the Gospel in the Uspenie Cathedral to convene the *Sobor* so as to govern in accordance with the wishes of the Russian nation and to be a *narodni Czar*.[2] At a later date Alexis Romanov, son of Michael, and Feodor, son of Alexis, also gave their promise to convene the *Sobor*, in order to consult the nation about the new laws and on the subject of war and peace. But Peter the Great, who succeeded Alexis, put an abrupt end to this tradition by deciding in favour of the Byzantine system of autocracy, a system which came to grief in the cellar of the Ipatev house.

[1] 'Give us Czar Michael Romanov !'
[2] A Czar for the nation, by the nation.

CHAPTER 17

MICHAEL ROMANOV

On July 11, 1613, a huge crowd collected in the Red Square in front of the *Lobnoe Mesto* platform. The new Czar, Michael Romanov, had just been crowned in the Uspenie Cathedral, and as usual all the bells were in full peal.

Michael Romanov was wearing all the imperial emblems: the crown, the Monomah hat, the sceptre, the collar. This sixteen-year-old Czar had nothing of a 'Cossack Czar' about him; he was short, pale and sickly, and he had a slight twitch in his left eye. Michael Romanov then uttered the few phrases which had been prepared for him by Prince Baryatinsky: 'We, the Czar of all the Russias, undertake to give heed to the grievances of our people, to dispel their worries and to defend them against their enemies at home and abroad.'

At that moment a flock of pigeons flew from St. Basil's Church and over the Czar's head. The crowd fell to their knees and kissed the earth. 'It is the Holy Spirit Himself, bringing blessings upon our Czar,' they were heard to say.

A woman, dressed completely in black, strode firmly on to the platform. It was Marfa, Michael's mother, the nun with whom he had been living in the convent at Ipatev. Marfa went up to the young Czar, who was reeling under the weight of his imperial regalia, and kneeling before him she said, 'My blessing be upon you, my son. Reign like a true Russian Czar'.

Michael Romanov, forgetful of court etiquette, bent down to help his mother to her feet, but could not stand up again, so great was the weight of his accoutrements, and he fell on his knees in front of his mother.

Hastily, the boyars formed a circle around the young Czar. 'Get up! Get up!' whispered Prince Mstislavsky. 'Realize that you are the Czar and that Marfa is merely your slave.'

During this scene the Czar's sceptre rolled on the ground and his hat fell off. There was bustling among the boyars and they hurriedly put the insignia back into his shaking hands. The bystanders' indignant murmurings did not reach the ears of the crowd but these are the words of the historian Klyuchevsky on the subject:

'The few incidents that occurred during the coronation of July 11, 1613, had been sufficient to show the boyars that the Czar would always be under the influence of his mother, who was an overbearing, scheming woman. The situation quickly became clear to them: they addressed themselves in future, not to Michael Romanov, but to his mother.'

The new Czar had little liking for kingship; he used to walk about the Kremlin, crossing himself before the churches and cathedrals, and feeding the pigeons. In a general way, he concerned himself little with affairs of state and left to the *Sobor* the trouble of solving the most serious questions.

A special session of the *Sobor* was held. The problem was how to be rid of the Cossacks, who were now unwilling to return home. The Muscovites complained of seeing their womenfolk 'neglecting their homes and wifely duties'. A deputation of wronged husbands—Muscovite traders—was received by the Czar. The husbands expressed their indignation; their wives would not return to their homes, but spent their time in the Cossack camps!

After protracted negotiations, some of the Cossacks returned to the South and Astrakhan, where their leader, Zarutsky, stirred up a revolt. After marrying Marina, the widow of the two false Dmitris, he proclaimed the son of the 'thief' of Tushino Czar of all the Russias. Prince Pozharsky and his army intervened and the 'thief's' son was hanged. Marina was flung into a dungeon of the prison of Astrakhan, where she died. As for Zarutsky, he was taken to the Red Square in Moscow and impaled.

The *Sobor* was still holding endless meetings. The members decided to declare war on Poland and Sweden in order to regain the regions lost during the 'Great Anarchy'. The Russian army defeated Gustav Adolphus near Pskov but failed to reoccupy the Baltic coast.

English and Dutch emissaries arrived in Moscow, charged with the task of offering mediation by their governments between Russia and Sweden. Thanks to them, Gustav Adolphus, who was already making plans for his glorious German expedition of the Thirty Years' War, agreed to sign the Peace of Stolbovo, in 1617. By this treaty the Swedes restored Novgorod, Staraya Russa, Pskov, Porkhov and Ladoga to the Russians but retained the Baltic coast. As a token of friendship Gustav Adolphus sent the Czar a few clocks. He could not have done better. The 'Cossack Czar' spent all his time looking at these objects, repairing and winding them, and became a horological maniac; more than 200 clocks were imported into the Kremlin to decorate the halls and palaces; a repair-shop was installed. There, Michael Romanov spent whole hours admiring the work of the clock-makers he had brought from Germany, Holland and England. In the receptions he held, he insisted on wearing at least three watches. The boyars imitated the Czar and they also wore several watches at the same time.

Carried away by enthusiasm, the Czar brought specialists from Nuremburg to build on the Kremlin towers huge clocks that played hymn-tunes. When these tunes were first played, the crowd fell to their knees shouting, 'A miracle! The angels have come right to the Kremlin to sing their divine melodies! Glory be to our Kremlin and to Czar Michael!'

Less and less did the Czar appear at official functions; no longer did his limbs support him and a partial paralysis made him impotent. A year after the Peace of Stolbovo, he made another appearance, once again in his Czar's full regalia, to preside over the deliberations of the Sobor, which in 1618 decided to sign a peace with Poland. It was, more precisely, a truce of fourteen and a half years. The Poles retained Smolensk and the Severia region and all Russian prisoners were repatriated.

Among those repatriated was the Patriarch Philaret Romanov, the Czar's father. Returning to Moscow in 1619, this stubborn, domineering old man, supported by his wife, the nun Marfa, bestowed upon himself the same rights as those of Michael Romanov; his ukases had the force of laws. Philaret, the 'co-Czar', went so far as to request his coronation but the pretension was rejected, despite the many entreaties addressed to the Sobor by Michael Romanov. Philaret, although uncrowned, remained Czar No. 2 and Patriarch of all the Russias.

A strange procession was seen, then, to pass through the Red Square early in 1620: Philaret, in his patriarchal robes, headed the procession, holding the imperial sceptre, the Czar Michael, wearing the crown, the Monomakh hat and the collar (the barmy), followed behind his father. Suddenly, a strong gust of wind blew off the Monomakh hat and the barmy. Philaret chased the symbols of supreme power, grasped them eagerly and, holding out the royal hat to his son, decked himself in the barmy, without a care for his priestly habit! Michael said not a word but continued to follow his father, with difficulty because of his unsteady legs, and looking submissive.

His mania for clocks and watches brought Michael Romanov into contact with the large number of foreign mechanics and watch-makers who dealt so skilfully with these precious objects; and, while Philaret was presiding over the meetings of the *Sobor,* which he convened with increasing frequency, Michael was inviting to the Kremlin all foreigners who agreed to go there, traders, diplomats, mechanics, engineers, scientists, military men and others.

So it was that, in 1628, he welcomed to the Kremlin the English engineer Bulmer, who was looking for mines—gold, copper, silver and lead—in Russia. Michael Romanov showed Bulmer his 'clock museum' with childlike pride and asked him to do him a 'great service', 'to repair the clock pendulum' in the Borovitsky Tower of the Kremlin. Bulmer tried to explain that he was a mining engineer and not a clock-maker, but the Czar insisted at great length and finally wept and implored him.

On another occasion Michael Romanov received an English soldier who introduced himself as 'Prince' Aston. This prince,[1] a self-styled 'field-marshal', suggested to the Czar the reorganization of the Muscovite army and the formation of six infantry regiments made up entirely of foreign mercenaries. The Czar offered 'Prince' Aston the title of '*voevoda* in chief of the Grand Polk' at an enormous salary.

'Prince' Aston, the '*voevoda* in chief', brought several of his friends to the Kremlin: Colonel Leslie, Lieutenant Vandam and a Dutch businessman, Coet. The Dutchman succeeded in obtaining from the Czar an important mission: the building of a cannon factory in Moscow. Vandam had to form a 'regiment of 1,760 men', chosen from among the German Landsknechts. As for Leslie, he was entrusted with the recruitment of 5,000 soldiers in Sweden and the purchase of the weapons necessary for arming this small army; moreover, he was to find the engineers and qualified personnel for Coet's future factory. Leslie records that Michael Romanov was intensely curious about what was happening abroad and asked for news of the reigning families of Western Europe, while revealing a certain familiarity with Western countries.

Leslie gives this further detail: 'During the receptions, our

[1] He was, in fact, a baronet.

presence in no way inconvenienced the Czar, who would quite calmly be stuffing his fingers in his nose.'

All these foreigners received wonderful presents: sable cloaks, beaver capes, blue fox furs, etc. In return, the Czar asked them to send him all the clocks and watches they could find.

In 1633, the 'co-Czar', Philaret, died. During the obsequies, Michael Romanov sobbed and wept. As he turned away from the embalmed body of his father in the Arkhangelsk Cathedral, he cried, 'Woe is me, defenceless orphan that I am! Let us ask God to call me to Him as soon as possible.'

What was the state of Moscow when Philaret Romanov died? To answer this question it is fitting to refer to the description given by Adam Œlschlager, a German diplomat, who arrived at the Kremlin on the day following the funeral of the Czar No. 2:

'It is a strange town; there was little left of Moscow after the fire started by the Poles during the 'Great Anarchy', and especially after that of 1611. Only the Kremlin remained! And yet, today, there are more than 40,000 houses, and it is certain that Moscow is now one of the largest towns in Europe.

'The Muscovites' negligence and untidiness inside the house is the main reason why not a month passes without fire spreading. It must be stated that the material is so inflammable that with the slightest wind only a few minutes are needed for the fire to reduce several houses, if not whole streets, to ashes. The Muscovites recover with amazing rapidity from the loss of their houses and easily find accommodation in completely finished new houses in the Market, outside the white wall. There, a house can be purchased for next to nothing; it is dismantled, moved and set up again in a very short time on the site of the burned-out house.[1]

'The town citadel known as the Kremlin—is more extensive than some of our towns and is protected by three thick walls, with a very deep moat behind. The Kremlin has a very fine artillery for its defence.

'In front of the citadel is a large square which incorporates the town's chief market and swarms with people, particularly

---

[1] This testimony from a German diplomat confirms the many Russian documents of the day, according to which there appear to have been prefabricated houses in Russia as early as the sixteenth century.

idlers, beggars and ragged monks. What is curious is that each street is occupied by people of the same occupation, so that the silk traders do not mix with the linen or cloth merchants, or the goldsmiths with the saddlers, the bootmakers with the tailors or the furriers with other artisans. Every trade has its own street; there is one street where nothing but pictures of the saints is sold.

'The *stolnik* Alexander Slashkov, who lives in the Kremlin, at the Ministry of Finance, of which he is the director-general, once invited me to dinner. After the meal he took me into a room so as to introduce to me his wife from the *Terem*, and thereby in his view proving his liking, esteem and respect for me and my lord, His Highness, the Duke of Holstein. So his wife appeared, richly apparelled in her wedding garments, followed by a young woman carrying a huge bottle of brandy and a silver goblet. The lady had a full cup poured out, tasted it and obliged me to drink it up. It went down my throat like fire; and I had to repeat the performance three times in succession. After this, my host begged me to kiss his wife, and he was so politely insistent that I should kiss her on the mouth that I had perforce to comply. The countess clasped me to her in such a tight embrace that my bones crunched. My host laughingly said that on one occasion his wife had sprained his arm in bed.'

It should be explained that Œlschlager (Olearius) had come to Russia about the middle of Michael Romanov's reign, at a time when Russian noblewomen had already begun to struggle for their emancipation. In order to get away from the *Terem*, they made frequent attempts to marry foreigners who came to Moscow, especially the Lutherans who admitted that their women-folk were faithful to the Orthodox Church.

The faith of Russian women of orthodox religion did not prevent their attendance, with their husbands, at the Lutheran *kirkha* (from the German *Kirche*). They went there with all the greater pleasure for being tricked out on such occasions in costly materials and displaying the most extraordinary luxury of dress, which continually caused indignation and noisy exhibitions of jealousy on the threshold of the *kirkha*. It happened that one day the new Patriarch, Joseph, had to intervene and settle the ladies' differences in the open street.

Philaret was buried in the Kremlin with all the honours due to a Czar. Immediately after the funeral Michael Romanov convened the *Sobor*, for talk had reached his ears that certain boyars had made the most of their claims to the co-Regency. The *Sobor* sat in the Palace of Facets. All estates of the realm in Muscovy were represented; even peasant bondsmen were seen there! It was 'unique and incomparable', it was said, but it decreed: 'The Czar must govern alone, for if, through inexperience, youth or filial duty, he felt obliged to share his authority, the diarchy would mean the loss of Russia.'

The boyar Hvorostinin made use of this session to put forward his programme in a 'note to the Czar'. 'We Russians', he wrote, 'are perfectly stupid. In Russia, people sow rye and live on falsehoods.' The remainder of this 'note' was drafted in similar terms. The indignant members of the assembly flung themselves upon the boyar, intending to thrash him, but Michael Romanov intervened, saying, 'Whoever brings disgrace upon the *Sobor* by brawling, disgraces his Czar'. Hvorostinin was simply deprived of his electoral mandate. He refused to fast during Holy Week and appeared in the Kremlin cathedral, dead drunk and carrying in his right arm a bottle of brandy which he displayed as 'the blood of Jesus Christ'. He insulted the new Patriarch Joseph, declaring that 'he was not worth the little finger of the Pope in Rome'. That was too much! He was sentenced to exile in a monastery for a period of ten years. The lightness of the sentence—in England, France or Spain, at the beginning of the seventeenth century, Hvorostinin would have been put to death—indicates that Michael Romanov's regime was the most liberal in Europe at that time. The boyar was even pardoned before the expiry of his sentence and he returned to Moscow, where he hanged himself after an attack of delirium tremens. On the body of this first anarchist noble was found a notebook full of poems by François Villon, which he had translated into Russian.

When the incident caused by this aristocratic intellectual of an anarchist was once cleared up, the *Sobor* turned its attention to a more pressing problem. The truce with Poland was nearing its end. What was to be done? Was it to be war or an extension of the treaty? It was war. At the order of the *voevoda* Shein, the Russians invaded the region of Smolensk and Severia. The regiments of mercenaries, the *reitary*[1] and the *draguns*[2] launched several attacks against the Polish army but the siege of Smolensk dragged on. King Ladislas IV's army, which had come to the aid

[1] Cavalry.

[2] Horse-drawn infantry.

of the fortress garrison, inflicted a heavy defeat upon the Russians.[1]

Ladislas could not profit from his victory in order to occupy the Kremlin again, for the international situation was not favourable. England supported the Czar against the Poles. James I had made a loan to Moscow, the first English loan to Russia.

Louis XIII's ambassador, Dehayes de Courmenin, had likewise promised a loan, but on condition that the Czar should allow French merchants to set up a 'company' in Moscow for the purpose of conducting purchases and sales with Persia and Tartary. The Czar politely declined: 'If the subjects of our beloved brother the King of France wish to buy goods from Persia and Tartary, they have only to apply to the subjects of the Czar of Russia, who will sell them what they require, and more cheaply than elsewhere.'

It was rumoured that Turkey was preparing to attack Poland. Ladislas, who was seriously perturbed by these items of news from abroad, proposed a cessation of hostilities and the conclusion of a peace with the Czar. The Peace of Vyazma was signed in 1634, by which Ladislas gave up his attempts on the throne of Russia but retained Smolensk. Not long afterwards, ambassadors from the Cossacks of the Don and those of Zaporog came to advise the Czar that they were going to war with the Sultan of Turkey; 'the armies of Christ, the free Cossacks of the Don and Zaporog', were declaring war on Turkey, the most powerful military power in Europe! They sent a 'letter' to the Sultan to acquaint him of their intention. This historic letter, preserved in the Kremlin archives, is a unique document in diplomatic correspondence. Here are some excerpts, which lent some inspiration to Guillaume Apollinaire in his Chanson du mal-aimé: 'We write to you, Sultan, servant of Beelzebub and Lucifer's lackey, to invite you to begin with to kiss our backsides.' There follow some insults such as 'pig-face' and others. The declaration of war, which concludes the 'letter', is couched in these terms: 'Seeing that you, Sultan, and your allies, the Crimean Tartars, traffic in Christian souls in the slave-markets, we have decided to declare war on you and to go and storm your fortress of Azov. And then we undertake to call upon you at home in Constantinople, to impale you by the shores of the Bosphorus and—all the whores in your harem!'

Needless to say, the Sobor welcomed the Cossack ambassadors

[1] Shein was beheaded as a 'traitor' on his return to the Kremlin.

with enthusiasm. The fortress of Azov was reputed impregnable, but two months after the beginning of the siege the Cossacks took it by storm, attacking by sea and by land, after destroying the Turkish fleet.[1]

The *Sobor* asked the Czar to support the Cossacks and send an army against Azov, but Michael Romanov, who had become very cautious after the defeat of his *voevoda* Shein near Smolensk, was reluctant to embark upon an adventure which might become very dangerous; a Turkish army 150,000 strong and supported by 200,000 Tartars, was marching towards Azov, where the Cossacks had carried out horrible slaughter by killing the whole Moslem population. The Czar wrote to the Sultan, undertaking to get the Cossacks to evacuate Azov. In fact, the 50,000 Cossacks did retire further inland to the frontier regions of the Muscovite empire in 1642.[2]

Michael Romanov's reign was approaching its end; the Czar did not appear except in his wheel-chair, in the courtyards of the Kremlin and surrounded by a crowd of beggars and half-wits, the 'Czar's madmen'. He absolutely refused to deal with affairs of state. His two eldest sons had just died suddenly, poisoned—so it was said again—by mushrooms. On the eve of their death, had not a witch from the Kulikovo-Pole been seen with the two princes? It was suggested that the Czar should appoint a commission to enquire into their death, but he refused. 'The life and death of all people', he said, 'lie in the hand of God'.

Michael Romanov's third son, Alexis, was brought up in the care of Morozov, a boyar and eminent statesman, but a schemer and unscrupulous. Morozov had a friend, Miloslavsky, and he urged Alexis to marry Miloslavsky's daughter. She was tall, healthy and robust, and Morozov maintained that the marriage would 'improve the Romanov stock'.

At one time, consideration was given to the possibility of the Czar's daughter Irina's marriage to the heir to the Danish throne, but the question of religion spoiled the romance.

On his forty-ninth birthday, Michael Romanov went to his clock repair-shop to observe the German Marcelius at work. The latter was repairing the famous singing clock of the Iversky Gate. It was here that the Czar received the Danish ambassador, who

---

[1] The Cossacks employed small rowing-boats, called *chayka*, in which they could come close up to the Turkish ships and set fire to them.

[2] The Cossacks founded many villages in the Ukraine. One of these villages is Kalinovka, the birthplace of Nikita Sergeyevich Khrushchev.

handed him a personal letter from King Christian of Denmark, who politely but firmly declined to marry his son to Irina. Michael Romanov glanced at the letter and thanked the ambassador. Hardly had the Dane left, when Irina came in and read the bad news in the expression on her father's face. 'I shall take the veil this very day', she told him. With tears in his eyes, Michael Romanov looked at his daughter, gave her his blessing, and his head fell back against his chair. He was dead. So ended both a reign and a romance.

CHAPTER 18

ALEXIS MIKHAYLOVICH

The Czarevna Irina was not present at her father's funeral. She criticized his weakness towards the *Sobor* and the Patriarch, who had prevented her marriage, and retired to the village of Semenovskoe to pray, 'alone and remote from the world'. Perhaps she had hoped for an elopement, but her Prince, who had come to Moscow with the ambassador, had been politely escorted back to the frontier.

The new Czar, Alexis Mikhaylovich (1645-1676), aged fifteen years and some months, began his reign with the inevitable convocation of the *Sobor*. His guardian and teacher, the boyar Morozov, with the support of a few courtiers, claimed the appointment of reigning co-Czar in the style of the Patriarch Philaret. The *Sobor* debated the question at length and one cannot say what conclusion would have been reached, if a delegation of Cossacks from Zaporog had not asked for an immediate hearing by the *Sobor*. The Cossacks came in noisily and read out to the assembly, 'We, the Cossacks of Zaporog,[1] make this proclamation: let him who would suffer impalement, the wheel or quartering, for the sake of the Christian faith, or undergo torture, unafraid to die, come to us and fight the ungodly Tartars and Poles'.

The delegation, (the *sidnie* or *gniezdyuki*[2]), was asking the *Sobor* for the Czar's authorization to attack Poland. The *Sobor*, afraid of war with Poland, replied in mild terms. The Cossack delegation was about to leave the hall, when the *sidnie* Hrytzko Shmarkaty decided to put his grievances before the assembly. This Cossack, of disreputable name,[3] complained of the unmarried Cossacks who, on each of his hunting expeditions, took advantage of his absence to visit his *hata*.[4] 'That is why,' he

---

[1] The Cossack capital of Zaporog was situated on an island in the Dnepr, called Khortitza.

[2] The word *sidnie* comes from the verb *sidet*: to be seated; that is, not to go roving with the Cossack looters.

[3] *Shmarkaty*, in Ukrainian means 'snotty'.

[4] *Hata* means 'cottage'. The Russian peasant's cottage is the *izba*.

said, 'not one of my ten children looks like me!' He could not continue with his complaints, for the Cossack delegation, furious that one of their own people should, in public and before strangers, indulge in criticism of their private lives, rushed forward and beat him before the tear-filled eyes of the assembled *Sobor*. The boyar Likachev interrupted this unequal fight, saying, 'When your Cossacks were stationed among us, here at the Kremlin, we could not prevent our wives from showing preference for them. Those devils are kept long in abstinence and know how to make up for lost time when they are with women.'

This Courteline-style scene made the *Sobor* forget that it had been discussing the co-regency of Alexis. Having nothing further on the agenda, the *Sobor* adjourned, with thanks to the Cossacks for the interlude.

It was some years before the Cossacks were heard of again, and then the occasion concerned the most important event in Russian history, the annexation of the Ukraine to Russia.

Apart from the Zaporog Cossacks, who lived in their democratic Republic, the *Sech*, and recognized no foreign power, the Ukraine—which, at that time, belonged to Poland—had at its disposal six regiments of 'registered' Cossacks, who lived in the county[1] towns and fought under the orders of their leaders, the 'colonels'. In 1625, Koniecpolski, the '*hetman* to the Polish Crown', concluded an agreement with these 'colonels', who became the Polish government's representatives. In case of war, the Polish govenment could recruit tens of thousands of Cossacks in the Ukraine; once the war was over, the unregistered Cossacks had to return to their village and their *pan*, the ground landlord, who treated them like human cattle. But the proud, fearless warriors often refused to become slaves again, tortured and exploited by the *pans*, who had absolute authority over their lives. The terrible *gaydamak*[2] insurrections were always fiercely put down; the Ukrainian peasants lacked a leader. One year after the coronation of Alexis, such a leader appeared: the Cossack

[1] The Ukrainian 'county' was called the *polk* (regiment). The colonels were *polkovniki*.

[2] *Gaydamak* is a word of Tartar and Turkish origin, but a Ukrainian historian, Grushevsky, claims that it is derived from the Ukrainian *gayda*, meaning 'go on', and *mak*, meaning 'poppy' (the flower worn by peasants in revolt for the purpose of recognition).

Early nineteenth-century view of Moscow from the Kremlin, after a drawing by A. G. Vickers

[*photo: Radio Times*]

VIII

The Holy Gate of the Kremlin, after a drawing by A. G. Vickers

[*photo: Radio Times*]

Early nineteenth-century view of the Kremlin from the Quay, after a drawing by A. G. Vickers

[*photo: Radio Times*]

IX

The Ivan Velekoi Kloster, after a drawing by A. G. Vickers

[*photo: Radio Times*]

Captain Bogdan Hmelnitsky, who was in command of one of the Polish Count Potocki's[1] regiments.

Hmelnitsky was an outstanding soldier; his only failing was the same as Potocki's: both used to get horribly drunk. So it happened that Potocki, when thoroughly intoxicated, quarrelled with his regimental captain about some trifling matter and beat him black and blue in a *shinok*.[2] Hmelnitsky had to leave for Chighurin, on the Dnepr, but the sub-prefect of this town, the *starost*, kidnapped his young wife and beat his son to death for having resisted him in this act. In revenge, Bogdan Hmelnitsky stirred up the whole country and organized a general uprising of the Ukrainians against the Poles.

The year 1652 saw the arrival of a delegation at the Kremlin, sent by Bogdan Hmelnitsky, the victorious captain who had defeated the Polish troops commanded by his former chief, Count Potocki, and had just proclaimed himself 'grand *hetman* of the Ukraine'. The Czar Alexis received them very pleasantly and gave them many costly presents, but he was not prepared to make any decision until he had consulted the *Sobor*. At that time, everything concerning the Cossacks was considered as dangerous as a powder-magazine. The Cossacks left the Kremlin 'in a very bad mood and sullen'. It was not until 1654 that the *Sobor* declared its readiness to include the Ukraine in the Russian Empire and to open immediate hostilities against Poland. But in 1648 the *Sobor* had other fish to fry. A Cossack delegation had hardly left the Kremlin, when a terrible riot broke out in the capital. At the very moment when the riot, directed against new taxation, was at its peak, both in Moscow and in the neighbouring country districts, the merchants, boyars, wealthy artisans and clergy, in their turn, broke out in revolt, not against the salt tax—which did not inconvenience them—but against the intrigues of the boyar Morozov, the Czar's former tutor and favourite. Thus the fury of the 'common people' was deflected from its objective and they protested *with* the boyars against the 'infringement of Russian customs and traditions'.

About the end of June in the year 1648, more than a hundred thousand people invaded the Kremlin demanding the death of Morozov and his friends. Alexis, who feared for his brother-in-law, summoned the *streltzi*, but the latter refused to butcher the

---

[1] Potocki, who became '*hetman* to the Polish Crown', was beaten by Hmelnitsky at 'Yellow Waters' and Korsun in 1648.

[2] A Ukrainian tavern.

E

people. The panic-stricken Czar decided to grant the people their wish and hand over to them the 'enemies of the people',[1] who were immediately lynched before his eyes. Morozov made his escape by way of a secret underground passage in the Kremlin.[2]

With tears in his eyes, Alexis addressed the crowd: 'My dynasty reigns because it is elected by the nation. I give you my solemn word, for myself and on behalf of my descendants, that the Kremlin is and always will be the place to drive out the "enemies of the people".'

The sight of this Czar, barely nineteen years old and looking so unhappy, moved the demonstrators. The crowd roared, 'Long live our beloved Czar!' Some drunkards who continued to make threats were immediately bound and handed over to the police by the people themselves.

So ended the revolt of June 1648. This revolt made an impression on the whole of Muscovy. Many provincial towns requested the proclamation of new laws and demanded that the scoundrelly boyars should be punished. In Novgorod, the traditionally free town, the revolt had greater consequences than elsewhere; the mob seized the governor and hanged him before the door of St Sophia's Cathedral.

The rioters, consisting for the most part of cobblers, saddlers and butchers, removed the archbishop's breeches when he attempted to interfere and left him inside the Cathedral by the 'Czar's Door',[3] but his intervention saved many foreign traders who lived in Novgorod but whose establishments were nevertheless pillaged and burnt.

In spite of his youth, Alexis attempted to institute reforms. Morozov, his brother-in-law, once he had come out of hiding, hastened to call together in the Kremlin the representatives of the Muscovite artisan corporations and the common people, and plied them with copious draughts of brandy. The streltzi

[1] The expression 'enemies of the people' was first heard by the crowd of June 1648. In beseeching the mob to spare Morozov, Alexis promised to punish the 'enemies of the people' severely.

[2] This passage runs underneath the Taynitsky Gate and was often made use of by those threatened by the anger of the crowd. The false Dmitri meant to reach it in order to avoid his pursuers, but his broken leg prevented his doing so.

In 1812, Napoleon and his marshals used the passage to get away from the Kremlin, which was cut off by the fire which ravaged Moscow.

[3] That consecrated part of the Russian church which contains the altar.

received the Czar's *charka*;[1] Morozov thought thereby to ensure their fidelity.

Several hundreds of these representatives were gathered around long tables at a banquet and, in the middle of the meal, the Czar addressed these words to his brother-in-law: 'Boyar Morozov, my beloved brother-in-law, who have just escaped the wrath of the nation and who are drinking here, safe and sound, in the company of my loyal subjects, your Czar asks you in future to follow a new path in the affairs of the State. Stop this zigzag course of yours and try to walk straight!' Morozov made a deep bow and answered, 'My Czar, Alexis Mikhaylovich, you accuse me of taking a zigzag course and a roundabout way, but you must know that the crow which flies in a straight line never reaches its goal.'[2]

With a laugh, the Czar took his brother-in-law by the arm and led him to a table where the traders of the Gostini Dvor raised their glasses to the young Czar and the boyar Morozov, who was one of the biggest shop owners in the Moscow square.

On July 16, 1648, Alexis presided over an extraordinary Council. This Council decided to convene the 'Grand Sobor' on September 1 for the purpose of formulating a new penal code against the 'enemies of the Czar and the people'. The incredible speed with which Alexis and his Government decided to act after the riot of June 1648 has been pointed out many times by Russian historians. Kotoshkin, a Russian *dyak* of the Ministry of Foreign Affairs, who was obliged to flee to Stockholm after making off with the Ministry funds,[3] has told how Morozov and the Czarina implored the Czar to act at once to calm the people. 'Your Majesty's throne is threatened,' said Morozov in his Russo-Byzantine style. 'I beg you to make concessions *from above*, so that the public will not take *from below*.'

---

[1] The *charka* is the goblet in which brandy or other strong drink is served. Whenever the Czar invited his people to drink, it was referred to as the Czar's *charka*.

[2] The boyar's reply has become proverbial. Khrushchev, when questioned by a journalist about his Berlin policy which was continually changing course, gave the same answer.

[3] Kotoshkin left some very interesting *Memoirs*. This 'scholar', whose advisory services were highly appreciated by the Stockholm chancellery, came to a bad end, being discovered in the act of adultery and then ripping open the deceived husband's stomach with a kitchen knife. He was hanged in Stockholm.

It will be observed that Alexander II's advisers spoke in similar terms at the time of the liberation of the serfs in 1861.

The penal reform measures of 1648-9, the Code known as the *Ulozhenie*, took no account of the needs of the serfs. The Code defended the interests of traders, artisans and 'freemen servants' only. The situation of the peasant-serfs deteriorated. Before the new Code was proclaimed, the bondman peasant who managed to escape and remain undiscovered for ten years became free; the Code annulled the *davnost*—the application of the time-limit.

The Russian 'parliamentary' system which was beginning to develop under Czar Alexis was later on harshly repressed by Peter the Great, who substituted voracious bureaucratic control by officials, strictly graded in fourteen orders of seniority from the 'local government secretary' to the imperial chancellor. What would have happened if the development of a constitutional monarchy had not been prevented by the surgical operation performed by Peter the Great on his country, no-one can say.

In 1652, there appeared at the Kremlin an embassy from Bogdan Hmelnitsky, who had defeated the Poles and established Ukrainian independence. Betrayed by his ally, the Crimean Khan,[1] Hmelnitsky once again suggested to the Czar that there should be union between Russia and the Ukraine. The Czar convened the *Sobor* in the autumn of 1653 to determine whether this proposal was acceptable. The *Sobor* was still undecided and the boyars and *dyaks* paced the Kremlin corridors, praying before casting their votes. Alexis himself hesitated, because war with Poland would not be long delayed if Russia accepted the Ukraine as part of her Empire. There was an all-night session of the *Sobor*. A delegation consisting of the Patriarch Nikon, the boyars Morozov, Matveyev and Prosorovsky, and the *dyaks* Likhachev and Stakov, made its way to the Czar's residence. Alexis was perturbed, because he was no lover of war and hated bloodshed. The boyars and *dyaks* also sought to avoid conflict, but the Patriarch Nikon declared, 'Your duty, Czar Alexis, is to liberate your brethren of the Orthodox Church in Poland. As long as a single member of the Church endures Polish persecution, the Russian Czar will be unable to sleep in peace. Take the Ukraine under your august protection, muster your armies and go to war.'

[1] This Khan, to whom Hmelnitsky was obliged to hand over Count Potocki, the *hetman* to the Polish Crown, set him free in exchange for a large ransom.

The Czar acted on this advice; he accepted the decision of the Ukrainian *Rada* of Pereyaslavl (January 8, 1654) to link the Ukraine with Russia and invited all the orthodox Christians in Poland to rise in revolt, promising them liberation. He left the Patriarch Nikon in Moscow after appointing him *Velikyi gosudar'*—'lord', a title borne by Philaret.

When Alexis had joined his army, a messenger left for the Kremlin to celebrate a Mass, that God might grant victory to the Russians. Once again, all the cathedrals and churches rang out the 'victory Mass'. The Patriarch addressed the crowd: 'I, Nikon, the Patriarch and "great *gosudar'* " of Russia, promise you that my troops will be victorious and crush the ungodly Catholics.' There was muttering from the crowd. Nikon spoke of 'his troops' but it was surely the Czar who, far from Moscow, was leading the armies.

The couriers brought news: the Russian troops were continually winning victories over John Casimir's army; the Czar, supported by the peasants from White Russia who had decided to join forces with him, took possession of Smolensk, Vilno, Kovno and Grodno. At the same time, Bogdan Hmelnitsky invaded Podolia and Volynia and entered Lublin. A temporary peace left the conquered territory in Russian hands. More than a hundred years before the reign of Catherine II and the Russian occupation of Polish territories, a quiet, placid Czar, who did not like war, led his armies to win this striking victory; the Russian troops proved their outstanding merit; the factories in Moscow and Tula made guns and cannon of excellent quality. The Russia of Alexis was on the threshold of becoming a great power.

On his return to Moscow, the Czar asked the boyar Matveyev, his Minister for Foreign Affairs, to send an embassy to Kurland. 'For what purpose, Your Majesty?' asked the boyar. The Czar replied, 'We have no ports on the Baltic Sea, but Kurland has several. Ask if we may rent one for fifty years!'

The peaceable Czar was therefore the first Russian statesman to have the idea of hiring a naval base. But the Duke of Kurland refused to let the port of Riga.

In the margin of history a strange story is told. The Czar shut himself up with greater frequency in his chapel. There he prayed for his family and for himself. His health rapidly declined. The Czarina, too, was ill. His elder son, the Czarevich Feodor, wandered about the Kremlin courtyard and argued with his friends the roof-cats. His second son, Ivan, was simple-minded; sunk for hours in his armchair, he would occasionally make quick snatches as if he were catching flies. Insects were his chief interest. As for the Czar's daughter, Sophia, she was healthy, robust and ugly; but that in no way prevented her from consorting with the *streltzi* officers. The Czar's family lived an unreal life in the Kremlin, out of touch with the nation and its problems.

Frequently, the Patriarch Nikon discussed with the Monarch questions which he considered to be of the greatest importance: the revision of the liturgical books. The Russian scribes who, before the invention of printing, copied the holy Greek scriptures, had made changes in the sacred texts: the name 'Jesus' was written *Iseus*, instead of *Jisus* as in the Greek text. A scribe of the twelfth century, probably after copious potations, had written that the sign of the cross was to be made with two fingers, not three. Other errors concerned the *Alleluya*: was it to be sung in two parts or in several?[1] These 'very serious errors' which had crept into the holy books robbed the Patriarch of the sleep of the just; in desperation he asked the Czar to summon the *Sobor* so as to correct the liturgical texts. The Czar did not answer immediately, for he was just as much attached to his old liturgical books as were his subjects; was it not with these 'errors' that his children had been baptised and his father and grandparents buried? It was, moreover, by virtue of these 'errors' that the Russian soldiers had fought the Tartars and the Poles. The Czar's hesitancy made the Patriarch impatient and he threatened Alexis with eternal damnation if he 'let his subjects pray with Satan's liturgical books'.

The gentle, reluctant Czar could not resist the impetuosity and authority of Nikon, whose life reminded one of the old medieval Russia. Nikon, the peasant's son, the monk, married *pope* and monk again, had been put in charge of a monastery. Received in audience by the Czar, he had made such a great impression on him that Alexis kept him at the Kremlin. Henceforth, Nikon's career was one of staggering rapidity; in 1652, Alexis made this erstwhile monk Metropolitan of Novgorod and later appointed him Patriarch of all the Russias. In the end, the Czar became merely the shadow of the head of the Church and never did anything without Nikon's approval. When Alexis returned from the Polish campaign, he was so convinced that he had won the war because of the Patriarch's prayers that he

[1] *Sugubaya* and *Dvugubaya Alliluya*, in Russian.

could not refuse him anything; after some argument he gave way and authorized Nikon to convene the Synod and correct the 'liturgical errors'. But Nikon, in his concern for orthodoxy, went further than this; he had the ikons removed, as he considered that they brought the churches into discredit, either because the styles of painting were not 'Russian' or because the subjects were indecent.

No doubt, Alexis regretted that he had placed so much power in the hands of his Patriarch, whose religious fervour could only cause trouble in the country, and for days together he would shut himself up in his *pokoy*, spending his time in prayer and consulting the Scriptures.

The business of the correction of the Scriptures was beyond him; he therefore frequently summoned his boyars in order to ask their advice, but they could not come to any understanding or agreement on such a subject.

After long meetings with Miloslavsky, one of his favourite boyars, the Czar decided to create in the Kremlin a new ministry, the *Tayni Prikaz* (a kind of Ministry of Secret State Affairs). The boyars heard of this decision during the dominical mass at the Monastery of Savin-Storozhevsky, of which Alexis was particularly fond. A wind of panic blew through the Kremlin; false news was circulating. All were in the grip of fear. There was again talk of the *Oprichnina*. The days of Ivan the Terrible came to mind. Alexis maintained the deepest silence, but occasionally there was seen on his face a slight enigmatic smile. One day, before a large audience, the Czar cried to his *Okolnichi*[1] Stukov, 'Boyar, you shall head the new *prikaz*'. From that moment, Stukov was surrounded by frantic boyars trying to gain sympathy; even during Mass boyars were observed counting out gold coins and slipping them into Stukov's pockets.

Frenzy still played havoc in the Kremlin. The boyars were running all over the place in search of Miloslavsky, the Czar's father-in-law: could he not tell them what was happening in the new *prikaz*? It was now just a question of future deportations, of proposed executions; excitement ran high. Then the Czar appeared, followed by Stukov, to whom he called out so that all could hear, 'Above all, do not forget to buy the hawks from Vologda. They are the best in the country and the easiest to train'.

The boyars realized that the Czar had been acting a long

[1] A boyar of the second grade.

comedy, a farce for their benefit. The terrible ministry was concerned merely with hunting. Alexis owned thousands of trained birds, three thousand falcons and hawks and more than ten thousand nests of pigeons. So as to increase his 'High Court', the name he gave to his chosen birds, he had created a *prikaz* which he called by a name curiously reminiscent of Ivan the Terrible's secret police. He had provided a dramatic anodyne to the tragi-comedy in *'cent actes divers'* which had held the Kremlin stage for more than a century.

Thank God, the new ministry's first hunt was entirely successful: the falcons and hawks brought back more than 500 animals. In cheerful mood Alexis returned to the Kremlin; but sad news awaited him: the Czarina had just died.

Soon afterwards, the boyars prepared their daughters for their presentation in the *smotriny* and each of them, seeing his daughter as the new Czarina, impatiently waited for the Czar to fix the date; but Alexis was spending many hours in the company of Matveyev, his Minister for Foreign Affairs, whose ward, Nataliya Kirilovna Narychkin, he liked very much. Of humble stock, the daughter of an official of Foreign Affairs and a Russianized Scotswoman, Nataliya Kirilovna could not be considered a beauty, but her lively wit made her a pleasant person; she sang popular Russian and Scottish airs, played the zither and danced remarkably well.

The Czar summoned the Patriarch and informed him of his intention to marry Nataliya. Nikon protested vigorously; a Czar could not marry someone who was half a foreigner. But, for once, Nikon had to give way, although not before he had obtained the Czar's promise that his future wife should prepare for marriage 'in the true faith of the Orthodox Church' and should accept only him, Nikon, the Patriarch of all the Russias, as her 'appointed confessor'. From that day onwards, the Czarina and the Patriarch were frequently seen together, walking through the corridors of the Kremlin.

One of the new Czarina's great gifts was her ability to radiate joy and youth, which did much for Alexis, who was too prone to hypochondria. Nataliya got him accustomed to western forms of entertainment; the first Kremlin theatre was established and dances and concerts enlivened the long winter evenings. Alexis was unwilling to change the strict life of the Kremlin but he prepared to make some reforms; he sent his ambassador Potemkin to study western habits and customs. Potemkin reported that

French morals were unsuited to Christians, and it was likewise he who, having lived at the court of Spain, declared that the Spaniards were 'gipsies in disguise'. The study of western life was no easy undertaking.

In that year 1662, fourteen years after the 'salt riot', a yet more bloody revolt (the 'copper riot') broke out in Moscow. The Minister of Finance had fraudulently put into circulation copper coins which were refused by government services when the Muscovites offered them in payment of their taxes. The immediate outcome of this was that the tradesmen in the shopping district would not accept these coins and rose in revolt. The *streltzi* intervened and yet another riot was drowned in a bloodbath.

A few years later there was talk of Stepan (Stenka) Razin, a Cossack from the upper Volga. This man was in charge of a gang of peasant-serfs who, Cossacks like himself, looted the possessions of the big landowners and boyars, freed the serfs and ransacked and set fire to the large estates. Stepan Razin distributed to the villagers and common people of this vast Russian plain the money which he took from the rich. The *streltzi* were sent to capture this Russian 'Robin Hood', but Razin and his peasant followers slaughtered them. The exploits of this character, who rapidly became a legendary figure, reached the ears of the Muscovites. In the gambling-saloons and in the streets of Moscow secret meetings were organized in which people prayed for the success of the 'Cossack liberator'. The Kremlin had to consider sending, not just detachments of militia, but an expeditionary force, a veritable army, to quell the revolt by the 'brigand Razin', a revolt which was gaining ground all the time and assuming huge proportions, since it threatened to spread over the whole of central Russia.

June 6, 1671, has become a memorable date in Russian history. Muscovites stood with drooping heads around the Red Square. The tower clocks wheezed and chimed hoarsely. The populace felt miserable. Preparations were made in the Red Square for the execution of the Cossack Stenka Razin, the leader of the Volga uprising, who had been captured by the Russian army. Stenka Razin was subjected to torture in the underground chambers of the Kremlin before being sentenced to quartering. In spite of that, he bore himself like a true hero before his executioners. At dawn on June 6 a vast crowd collected in the Red Square and yelled, 'Pardon Stenka! Pardon Stenka!' The *streltzi* could no longer hold the incensed crowd. Prince Yuri Dolgoruki, the boyar *voevoda*, who had overthrown Razin at Simbirsk, ordered the *streltzi* to charge the mob 'with axe and pike'. The crowd was dispersed. Then were heard for the first time a few chords of the 'Song of the Volga', telling of Stenka Razin's heroic deeds, a story which is famous today. This song tells of Razin's expedition against Persia. After attacking and capturing the Persian port of Enzeli, Razin fell in love with one of his women prisoners, the Shah's niece, a Persian princess of striking beauty, and decided to marry her. But his companions in arms would not have this marriage; so, in the presence of his Cossacks, *ataman* Stenka Razin, standing in his *tscheln* (small boat), took the princess in his arms, kissed her and threw her into the Volga.

His attention drawn to the noise, Czar Alexis came out on to the steps of his palace and, hearing the tuneful, nostalgic melody, asked what was happening. A boyar replied that he was listening to the song of the brigand Razin who was about to be quartered alive in the Red Square. Alexis gave orders that Razin should be beheaded but not tortured. 'Tell Stepan Razin,' he said, 'that the Czar forgives his crimes and acts of robbery.' 'Tell the Czar,' replied Razin, 'that I forgive the acts of robbery committed by his *voevodas* as well as the wrongs done to the Russian peasants.'

It appears that this reply made a great impression on the Czar. Did he realize that the Cossack whom he had just put to death as a robber was the heart and soul of a popular revolt, without which he could not have won so many victories or captured fortresses like Astrakhan, Czaritzin, Saratov and Samara? It is not known whether the Czar understood this, but it is certain that after Stepan Razin's execution he made an attempt to improve the lot of the peasant-serfs. The attempt failed, once again because of resistance offered by the boyars and the clergy.

The clergy was represented by Nikon, who held fast to his idea of correcting the liturgical books, a matter which he considered to be of supreme importance. The Patriarch was well aware that the voting of the synod had changed nothing. The people refused to use the amended versions and the *popes* preached in opposition to their leader, although he declared that those who resisted his reforms were the servants of the devil. The inevitable happened: the tragedy of *raskol*, of schism.

The monastery of *Solovetsk* rose up against the reform imposed by the Kremlin and defended itself—for eleven years! —against the Czar's *streltzi*. A sect of 'death volunteers' came into being. The members of this sect threw themselves voluntarily into the flames, carrying under their arms their— unamended — liturgical books. After surrounding their faggot heaps with huge palissades, so that nobody could escape, whole families, singing psalms, gave themselves up to burning.

Nikon persisted in his fanatical obstinacy; he was determined to prove himself more stubborn than the *raskolniki*, the schismatics. In the middle of a Mass celebrated in the Kremlin, Nikon tore up an ancient liturgical text and flung it to the ground. The book contained a few errors in translation. Mad with rage, this giant of a man went purple in the face and shouted, 'This book is the work of Satan!'

Czar Alexis and the boyars who were present at this Mass turned pale: the book was the one used by St Sergius of Radonezh during the Battle of Kulikovo! Trembling with anger and hard put to it to control himself, the Patriarch left the cathedral. Calm returned to Nikon only when he was with the young Czarina, who often went to him to engage in endless discussions of various 'religious topics'; these discussions sometimes lasted until daybreak. Alexis was overjoyed at his wife's attempts to save her 'sinful soul' with this 'holy man', but his entourage and Nikon's enemies whispered that the Czarina was not unaware of the Patriarch's reputation, which was that of an insatiable male. In 1667 relations between the Czar and Nikon became extremely strained. In spite of the Czar's request, Nikon refused to delay the introduction of the new liturgical books. The 'peaceable' Czar lost his temper in earnest and sent Streshnev, his *okolnichi*, to forbid Nikon the title of 'Lord and Sovereign of all the Russias'.

The following day, at Mass, the Patriarch announced that he was terminating his office and retiring to a monastery. He was white as a sheet when he made the announcement, and his tall body quivered with rage.

The synod was urgently convened to consider the Patriarch's unforeseen action. In the years that followed, the Czarina on several occasions visited Nikon in his exile at the Terapontov Monastery. In 1672 the Czarina gave birth to a son, Peter, the future Peter the Great, who bore a remarkable resemblance to Nikon and who grew to a height of over six feet six inches.

The continuous quarrelling seriously undermined the already poor health of Alexis. In a state of great weakness he remained inside his palace. He never recovered, and died in 1676.

CHAPTER 19

FEODOR

The stained glass windows of the Uspenie Cathedral were streaming with rain and snow. The hooves of the *streltzi's* horses were squelching in the mud of the Red Square. Ankle-deep in the slush were thousands of monks who had come from all corners of Muscovy to witness the coronation of the young Czar Feodor.

The fourteen-year-old Czar was too weak to bear the weight of the imperial insignia. He was helped by several of the most eminent boyars, the appanaged princes of ancient lineage. Prince Vassily Golitzin held the crown in his hands but, possibly in jest, put it upon his own head while Feodor was adjusting the 'royal collar'. At this, an imposing figure, Prince Hovansky, stepped forward. 'Vassili Vassilevich,' he whispered, 'do you know that you might pay with your life for the pleasure of wearing the crown for even a single minute? Are you not aware, Prince, that it is high treason?'

There was no answer. Golitzin had been watching the Czarevna Sophia, Feodor's elder sister, a stout girl dressed in gold brocade whose face was pitted with smallpox. The Czarevna smiled and adjusted her high pearl headdress. Those who had noticed the byplay also smiled; they knew that Prince Golitzin went every night to Sophia's *Terem* and did not leave until cock-crow.

The coronation ceremony was hardly concluded, when the *Duma* debated the question of a marriage. It was, indeed, no easy matter to marry so young a Czar. The *smotriny* were arranged. The young Czar—he too was rather backward for his age—was obliged to go to the Kremlin baths to choose his bride. Even more shy and modest than his father, Feodor began to weep and would have made off. Perspiration was streaming down his face. Muttering a prayer, he feverishly crossed himself. The boyars had the girls paraded and urged Feodor to make his choice. Sick at heart and without raising his eyes, Feodor gave a sign. In that way he 'chose' the daughter of a second-grade boyar.

The new Czarina was six years older than Feodor and was possessed of a character as independent as it was overbearing; which did not suit Sophia, who wanted to retain the Regency until Feodor had reached his majority. A few months later, she drew attention to the Czarina's barrenness and requested her repudiation. This was agreed to by the Patriarch Joseph, and once again there was the question of finding a new Czarina. Sophia put forward as her candidate the daughter of a lordling of Ryazan.

In accordance with custom, the Czar was shown this young woman made-up and dressed in her wedding garments. Feodor accepted her with complete indifference. No son came of this union. One daughter died a few days after birth and another was a sickly child who became a lifelong invalid. The Czarina died suddenly, from overeating, a victim of her peculiar vice: gluttony.

After the death of the Czarina, Sophia decided to stake everything: in the greatest secrecy she addressed to the Patriarch a request for the 'dispensation of incest'[1] so as to marry her brother Feodor. But a leakage occurred from the Patriarch's office. Before the whole town could talk of it, Sophia abandoned the project.

Quite determined to take up the matter of the Regency, Sophia appointed her lover, Prince Vassili Vassilevich Golitzin, chancellor - commander-in-chief - prime minister.

He was a well-educated man with a knowledge of other lands and an understanding of the needs of Russian foreign policy. He removed the boyar Matveyev from the Ministry of Foreign Affairs, which he directed in person. Golitzin was quick to observe the military weakness of the 'nobles' *opolchenie*' and he completely reorganized it. In order to impress foreign diplomats and the nation he held the first military parade in the Red Square. He closely superintended the regiments of *streltzi* and foreign mercenaries, the *reitary*, the infantry and the *draguns*.

---

[1] In 1729, an identical request was addressed to the Holy Synod by the adherents of Elizabeth who were anxious to marry her to her nephew, the young Czar Peter II. The Synod gave its approval.

Sophia's letter to the Patriarch was drafted by the *dyak* Kotov. In it the *dyak* gave frequent quotations from the Bible: Did not the sons of Adam wed their own sisters? Did not Eve love her sons as did Adam his daughters?

The letter disappeared when Peter the Great decided to clean out this 'Augean stable' by doing away with the Patriarchate and substituting the Holy Synod. The archives have been destroyed but thinly veiled references to this project of 'legalized incest' are still to be found.

Then he appealed for Russian volunteers to direct the *streltzi*, who were almost always commanded by foreign officers. Remembering the military qualities of the Ukrainian and Zaporog Cossacks, Golitzin turned nearly the whole region then under the government of Kursk into military districts.

Thanks to the Ukrainian Cossacks, the Russian army in time of peace was raised to 225,000 men, an impressive figure for those days.

By 1682, Sophia and her lover felt strong enough to fly under their own power.

On January 13th of that year Feodor had to confirm the abolition of the 'Precedence List' and read out, in the Palace of Facets, a manifesto drawn up by Golitzin: 'The discontinuance of this accursed list will restore peace to Russian hearts, torn by intrigue, and harmony such as is willed in the commandments of divine law'.

In the spring, Feodor, suffering from violent colic pains, died suddenly, from over-indulgence (it was said) in his favourite dish, mulberry pie.

CHAPTER 20

THE REGENT SOPHIA

The long funeral knell, tolled out by the 'forty times forty' Moscow churches, filled with its solemn notes the cathedral where Mass was being celebrated for the repose of the soul of the young Czar. Then the ominous, dreary sound vanished in the Kremlin sky. In the Red Square, the *kitay-gorod* (Chinese town), the Varvarka and the Nikolskaya, the Muscovites crowded in front of the shops packed with goods of every kind, from Persia, Turkey, Holland and England. The most improbable rumours were running through the capital. Had the Naryshkin put poison in the Czar's mulberry pie? Had not a witch from the *Boloto* predicted that the Czar would be poisoned and for doing so had been beaten to death by the Naryshkin police? Was it not known that, just before his death, Feodor had sent a message to the former Patriarch Nikon in his monastery by the White Sea, asking him to pray for his soul and restoring to him his title of Patriarch? Did he not ask Nikon also to pardon his father, Czar Alexis? And had not Nikon replied to the *gonetz* (messenger), who carried his message to Moscow and returned in a single week by making seven changes of horses, 'I pardon you, Feodor. As for your father, the Last Judgment alone will decide. We shall meet, he and I, in the presence of God, and then we shall see'?

The crowd spread the most absurd tales. If Nikon, having returned to favour, should come back to Moscow, the *staroveri* and the *raskolniki*, those sons of Satan, would have to pay for their sins. 'The Patriarch's vengeance', shouted a *yurodivi*[1] at a street corner, 'will be terrible. Terrible will be his vengeance.' Crossing themselves, the crowd repeated, 'Terrible, indeed'.

The *samosogentzy* (those who sought death by burning) in the north of Russia, who heard of Nikon's return, flung themselves with their families into the blaze to prove their attachment to the old Church, the 'one true' Church. The *protopope* Avvakum set the example by throwing himself on the pile of burning faggots with his wife and children. Thousands of old Believers

[1] Feeble-minded.

followed the *protopope* to their death. The smell of charred flesh reached even to Moscow.

The wave of suicide was halted by the death of Nikon. What sudden malady struck down the Patriarch on his way back to Moscow? It is a question that has never been answered. All that is known is that the Metropolitan refused to go to Nikon's bedside to administer the last sacraments.

For a long time now there had been two rival cliques in the Kremlin: one, the Miloslavsky group, surrounding Feodor; the other, the Naryshkin group, attached to the Czarina Nataliya and Peter. The outcome of the struggle was decided by Feodor's death; indeed, a *dyak* supporter of the Naryshkin party, when making an inventory of Feodor's possessions, discovered numerous objects which seemed to him to be profane: a book entitled *The Science of Alchemy*, a cosmography by Dorn, the ambassador to Moscow in the reign of Alexis, two psalms put into verse form by Feodor, a Polish grammar and some letters in Polish from the Czarevna to her brother Feodor. The Polish language was, in the *dyak's* eyes, that of hereditary enemies, and particularly ungodly. He hastened to report his discovery to the Naryshkins, who meant to exploit it to the full. For them, it was of the greatest importance that Feodor's younger brother Ivan should not be proclaimed Czar, unless the Regency fell into the hands of Sophia, 'the Pole'. The Naryshkins persuaded the Patriarch to ask the boyars to acknowledge Peter, ten years of age, as Czar, and appoint his mother, Nataliya, as Regent. As for the *povrezhdenny*[1] Czarevich Ivan, the easiest thing to do would be to shut him up, so that he could never mount the throne.

But the Naryshkins had not reckoned with the Czarevna Sophia. That energetic, domineering woman had the complete support of the *streltzi*, who hated the Naryshkins and the Czarevich Peter, that 'offspring of the cursed Patriarch Nikon'. The *streltzi* never disguised their sympathy for the *raskolniki*,[2] persecuted by Nikon. (It is known that they refused to quell the rioting.) They readily stood behind Sophia and her lover, the handsome Prince Golitzin, especially as Sophia had promised to pay them the salaries which had been owing to them for some five years.

On May 15, 1682, in a classical setting in the Kremlin, a large crowd gathered in the Red Square. The *streltzi* then

[1] Mentally deranged

[2] The 'schismatics'.

entered the palace, where there were gathered together the Naryshkins, Matveyev, Dolgoruki, Romodanovsky, Cherkassky, Saltykov and a few other supporters of Peter and his mother. 'The Naryshkins have murdered the Czarevich Ivan. Let them be delivered up to the people!' cried a *strelitz*.

The Naryshkins had Ivan brought from his room and they showed him to the crowd from the top of the palace steps. 'Behold the Czarevich Ivan!' The *streltzi* answered, 'It is not Ivan, but the son of the *okolnichi* Rtishchev whom you have disguised as the Czarevich'.

The *sotnik* Ibrahimov, of the Mozhaysk regiment, ran up the steps, flourishing a sheet of paper and crying, 'Here is the list of rabble we have decided to do away with. As for you, Czarina Nataliya, and your son, Peter, we shall do you no hurt, but we must find the traitors to our orthodox Christian faith. Otherwise, not a stone of this palace will be left and you will all be hanged like dogs!'

A squad of *streltzi* lined up in front of the steps. The *sotnik* read out the names of the condemned: the boyar, Matveyev, Afanasy and Ivan Naryshkin, Yury and Mikhail Dolgoruki, the *dyaks* Kurnossov and Anikeyev, Fedor Saltykov and Yazikov; other lesser-known names followed. Twenty-five people were immediately seized. The *streltzi* threw them into the air, caught them on their lances and slashed them to pieces. The Kremlin roadway was bloody with heads, arms and legs. Nataliya and Peter had to look on at this horrible butchery. With his lance, the *sotnik* Ibrahimov speared a head which rolled close to him and, turning to Peter, who was ten years old at the time, said, 'Take a good look at this head. It is your uncle's, that blackguard of a Naryshkin!'

Peter evaded the *sotnik* and ran cowering to his mother's arms, trembling in every limb.[1] The terrified Nataliya lifted him up and covered his eyes with her shawl, so that he should see no more of the horrible spectacle.

The *sotnik* Ptitzin, who commanded a regiment of *streltzi*, announced, 'They are not all here. There are five missing.' Furiously, Ibrahimov cried, 'Bring back that whore of a Czarina and her bastard! She shall show us where they are hidden.'

---

[1] This nervous tremor remained with Peter the Great all his life. Thirty years after the massacre, he would still wake up in the dead of night screaming with fright. He still dreamed of that day, May 15, 1682, and this indomitable Czar could never get rid of the nightmare.

The search lasted for four days, and the *streltzi* slaughtered about fifty more people. They ransacked the Czar's cellar and drank all the wine there as well as that in the Cathedral of Archangel'sk, Greek 'Samos', which was used exclusively for the eucharist of the Czar and certain boyars. 'It is not wine we are drinking,' they cried, 'but the blood of those cursed leeches of boyars! Soon we shall be drinking the blood of the Czar himself, if he does not restore our orthodox faith in a befitting manner.'

Prince Golitzin, Sophia and a few boyars of her suite who had left the Kremlin during those bloody days in May, returned and endeavoured to persuade the *streltzi* to evacuate the abode of the Czars. Their opponents, the Naryshkins, had perished in the massacre or fled to distant provinces. Golitzin and Sophia had nothing more to fear. The Miloslavskys had won.

Old Believers appeared in the streets of Moscow. Men versed in theological writings, unshakable in their beliefs, told the *streltzi* and the Moscow populace: 'The only way to salvation is to rid ourselves of the whole Council of Boyars, who have adopted Niconian satanical practices and foreign ways, and go back to our God-fearing faith and our old way of life'.

The Czarevna's project was realized. Ivan and Peter were both to become Czars. Because of their youth, they accepted the Regency until the time of their majority. The women were having their revenge; For the first time a Czarevna was in supreme power over Moscow. The Regency in the hands of married women, Czar's widows, had been known, but never before had it been in the hands of the Czar's unmarried daughter.

Legal justification of the novelty was undertaken by the Ukrainian scholar, Simeon Polotsky, who was summoned to the Kremlin to 'lecture' on female regency in foreign lands. This theologian and historian addressed a large audience of boyars and *dyaks*. He began his talk by enumerating the various instance of female regency in Byzantium: Pulcheria and Theodore II; Irene (daughter of Leo IV) and Constantine VI; Theodora, wife of Justinian.

Here he was interrupted by a *dyak* who said, 'Listen, khohol.[1] You are forgetting to tell us that Irene had her son Constantine's eyes put out, that Theodora was nothing but a *kurva* (whore) and that Pulcheria used to go to bed with all the tramps in Byzantium!'

---

[1] The nickname given to the Ukrainians by the Russians.

The *streltzi* quickly laid hands on the foolhardy *dyak* who was too well versed in Byzantine history and they threw him out into the courtyard of the Palace of Facets.

When Sophia's reign began—it lasted seven years—Nataliya and her family, her parents-in-law, the Kurakin princes and the Romanovs of the Nikita Ivanovich branch, left Moscow to go and live nearby at Preobrazhenskoye, Semenovskoye, Spasso-Ovrazhsk and other villages.

Sophia, who was anxious not to be reckoned a usurpress and who wished to keep up appearances, held two thrones and two crowns on behalf of Ivan and Peter. The imperial regalia: the Monomah hat, the *barmy*, the sceptre and the Czar's Golden Orb, were borne in turns, as follows: the Monomah hat and the sceptre, by one of the Czars; the *barmy* and the Golden Orb, by the other.

Ivan V and Peter I were introduced to the diplomatic corps. A Polish ambassador describes the ceremony thus:

'Czar Peter, aged ten and very tall for his age, was watching us with sad, curious eyes, and moving his head about nervously. It is said that this twitching goes back to the time of his sister Sophia's *coup d'état*, when the *streltzi* would have murdered him. Czar Peter made as if to touch the decoration of the Lion and Sun which the Emperor of Persia had bestowed on the Kurland minister, but he was roughly prevented from doing so by the sinister *dyak* Shaklovity,[1] who took his arm and no doubt pinched it, for the young Czar flushed with anger and pain.

'As for Ivan, he was a strange Czar, who remained motionless all the time, looking up at the ceiling. He made only one movement, to snatch at a fly and at the same time to steady his crown which nearly fell from his head. It was Peter who leapt from his throne and straightened it for him.'

When this solemn introduction was concluded, Sophia set about governing. Her lover, Prince Golitzin, made a lengthy report to the *Duma* of boyars and *dyaks* concerning the policies at home and abroad which it was necessary to adopt. A copy of this report, which was found in the Kremlin archives, clearly indicates this prince's great culture. He was, beyond all possible doubt, the most cultivated Russian statesman of the seventeenth century. In the report, Vassili Golitzin gives proof of his out-

[1] The chief of Sophia's secret police.

standing erudition. He deals with political economy, military strategy, sea communications and the Koran, which he had read in a Polish translation.

'Muscovite Russia is the only Christian power whose Moslem subjects faithfully fulfil their tasks and duties towards the Czar. Our Tartars do not recognize the Sultan of Constantinople as their Caliph. Why should we not be the leaders of a crusade against Turkey? Why neglect those immensely wealthy regions?'

A polonophile like Sophia, Golitzin particularly desired to bring about a reconciliation between Muscovy and Poland so as to join the Holy Catholic League formed by Poland, Austria, Hungary and Venice, and unite with it in its struggle against the Turks. Golitzin's first care was therefore to discipline and reorganize the *streltzi* regiments. The *streltzi* were still going on with their looting and particularly with their killing of foreign officers, the Russian soldiers' favourite pastime in those days.

The Regent Sophia summoned to her palace Prince Hovansky, who was in command of the *streltzi*, and spoke to him as follows: 'Prince, let your *streltzi* concern themselves with war and not with pillage. It is now two months since they carried out an exercise.' Ostentatiously, Hovansky crossed himself, using two fingers in the style of the Old Believers, and answered, 'We will not fight for *popes* who make the sign of the cross of Antichrist and who gobble their *Alleluia* like drunken swine. What is needed is first to re-discover the religion of our ancestors, for it was they who won wars in the name of *Isus*, and to restore the holy ikons to their proper place, instead of those which that devil's minion, Nikon—may he be damned!—has set up in our churches. We request that the desecrated ikons, buried near the Borovitsky prison, shall be unearthed and restored to our churches.' The frightened Czarevna observed, 'But that is impossible! If those ikons are unearthed, the people will burn the Patriarch's palace, his cathedral and his monasteries! I cannot do that. The synod of 1666 severely condemned the Patriarch Nikon's mistakes but it also decided to ratify his reforms. Let us be reconciled and speak no more of Nikon.'

After much discussion, a compromise was found: a council would be called in the Palace of Facets and the monk Nikita Pustosviat, the representative of the Old Believers, be invited to it.

In July 1682 the Kremlin was invaded by a huge crowd, the *raskolniki* who had come to hear the 'debate on the faith'. The monk Nikita was extremely outspoken and did not scruple to hurl insults at the Patriarch, the Metropolitan and the bishops, often in the most abusive terms. The bishops and the archbishop replied in similar vein. Sophia and Golitzin, who were conducting the proceedings, could not restore order. The discussions became disorderly and extremely stormy. Nikita interrupted with these words: 'Let us have done with it! You who call yourselves Patriarch, Metropolitan, Archbishops, Bishops, and who are merely serving that servant of Satan, Nikon, and the beast spoken of in the *Apocalypse of St John*, read that Apocalypse again! What do you see there? Take Chapter 17, where it is written, "Come hither: I will shew unto thee the judgement of the great whore that sitteth upon many waters; with whom the kings of the earth have committed fornication, and the inhabitants of the earth have been made drunk with the wine of her fornication".' And the monk Nikita, quite calmly pointing his finger at the Czarevna and her lover, Prince Golitzin, went on, 'You followers of Nikon are drinking the wine of her fornication, while claiming that it is the blood of our Lord Jesus Christ. Well, you who do nothing but drink the wine from the Kremlin cellar, I, monk Nikita, tell you that it is not even wine that you drink, but *streltzi* piss, piss poured by those true defenders of the faith into your devil's barrels!' roared Nikita.

Wild applause came from the *streltzi* ranks. The populace joined in. Moscow was in an uproar for three days and three nights. The tocsin was ringing incessantly. Shouts were heard in the streets: 'Kill both Czars; kill Sophia and her lover'. The Kremlin was empty. Czars and the Czarevna had fled together with the boyars. From her headquarters at Kolomenskoye, Sophia sent heralds through the countryside to call up the noble militia. Under the command of Stepan Odoevsky, nearly 200,000 militiamen marched on the outskirts of Moscow, closed in upon Prince Hovansky and the rebellious *streltzi*. The Prince was beheaded, while hundreds of Old Believers and *streltzi* were whipped in the Red Square. Many *streltzi* regiments were dissolved or transferred to provincial towns. Once more a revolt of the Muscovites was broken.[1]

At this time, with a view to preventing an ever-possible new popular uprising, Golitzin had Sophia sign a number of *ukases*

---

[1] Historical episode known to the Russians as 'Hovanschina'.

intended to improve the lot of the serfs. Golitzin even prepared the text of a *ukase* for the general freeing of the serfs, among whom would be divided part of the boyars' lands in return for a long-term repayment, the instalments to be spread over seventy-five years. It is not known why Golitzin gave up this project which was broadly adopted some two hundred years later by the Milyutin Commission set up by Alexander II to work out the details of the law for the liberation of the serfs. The Milyutin Commission even made use of the private talks which had taken place on this subject between Golitzin and Neuville, the Polish ambassador.

Sophia's foreign policy can be summed up in one word: it was that of a polonophile. She did not declare war on the Turks until she had signed a peace with the Polish King John Sobieski and the Catholic League. According to this treaty, Poland definitely ceded Kiev, Smolensk and the left bank of the Dnepr to Russia; in return, Russia undertook to defend Poland in the war against the Turks. Sophia's intention was to extend the Holy Alliance and to this end she sent one of the Dolgoruki princes on an extraordinary mission to Versailles, believing that she could win over Louis XIV to her side. But the King of France had other intentions and was just then negotiating a secret alliance with the Sultan. When Dolgoruki disembarked at Dunkirk in 1687, his mission, a complete failure, was already over. 'France views this war in a different light. We feel as much friendliness towards the Turks as unfriendliness towards Austria.' Such was the reply from France.

Sophia's military expeditions proved unfortunate. Golitzin, in his march against the Turks and Crimea Tartars, was betrayed by the Cossacks, who would have none of this war. The Russian army was compelled to halt: a great fire was raging across the Steppe between the Dnepr and the Perekop Isthmus. Ivan Mazeppa, the 'Ukrainian Scribe-general', accused *hetman* Samoylovich of having started the fire because he would not fight against the Khan and the Sultan. For his part, *hetman* Samoylovich claimed that only the Tartars could have been responsible for the fire.

Whose was the responsibility for this first instance of 'burnt earth'? History does not supply an answer, but the outcome of the fire is known: the Russians had to retreat to escape the burning steppe, leaving behind cannon and horses; the Russians' lack of confidence in *hetman* Samoylovich hastened their flight.

On this occasion Golitzin remembered the treason committed by *hetman* Vygovsky, Hmelnitsky's successor, and the Polish massacre of the best troops of Alexis at Konotop.

The Tartars, who were also impeded by the steppe fire,[1] could not catch up with the Russians, who in their retreat succeeded in crossing the River Samara[2] and followed the course of a stream called the Kolomak, which runs into the Vorskla about six miles from Poltava. Shortly before they arrived at the mouth of the Kolomak, the Cossacks and the Russians set up their bivouacs on a vast stretch of greensward which long afterwards remained a place of pilgrimage for the Ukrainians. From this spot can be observed the wooden towers of the fortress of Poltava, the governor of which, Colonel Nosse, invited Prince Golitzin to a reception given in his honour. Hardly had Golitzin left, when the 'Scribe-general' Mazeppa called together the Cossack grand council. *Hetman* Samoylovich was judged responsible for the steppe fire and immediately arrested. Ivan Mazeppa was elected *hetman* of the Ukraine in 1687, some twenty-two years before the Battle of Poltava, where he repeated 'Yygovsky's move', betraying the Russians to the advantage of the Swedes.

The second Crimean expedition (1689) returned on its tracks without attempting to attack the fortress of Perekop.

The Russians suffered another disaster in the Far East: the Chinese besieged and captured the Russian fort of Albazin, on the Amur. A peace treaty was signed, by which the Russians gave up both banks of the Amur, which the Cossacks were colonizing in their name. The Russian defeats in the Crimean campaigns between 1687 and 1689 severely damaged Sophia's prestige. The number of Peter's supporters was increasing.

There were whispers among the Muscovites and *streltzi* that the military reverses were only atonement for the killing of Hovansky. In this atmosphere so favourable to conspiracy the young Peter was growing up, already surrounded by his own regiments of petty soldiery, the *poteshnyi*. He was preparing to strike back at Sophia. Shaklovity, the new chief of the *streltzi* and Sophia's secret police, had obtained a deposition from a *poteshnyi* accusing the young Czar of fostering a *coup d'état* to take place on his seventeenth birthday. A Scottish officer, Patrick

---

[1] The fire covered rather more than 7,000 square miles, an area a little less than 150 miles long by 55 miles wide.

[2] This has no connection with the town of Samara (Kuybyshev) on the Volga.

Gordon, and a Genevese adventurer, Lefort, together with several friends and advisers, were implicated in the plot. Shaklovity, who had succeeded Golitzin in Sophia's affections, requested that Peter and his friends should be arrested, but had to bow before Golitzin's opposition. The latter realized what arguments the *streltzi* and *raskolniki* might draw from such arrest, and he foresaw a general uprising which could be extremely dangerous to the State of Muscovy. Golitzin's attitude is all the more remarkable because the young Czar had just refused to receive him, on his return from the ineffectual expeditions against the Khan.

Peter occasionally came to Moscow and carried away a few arms. Sophia paid no attention to it, in spite of Shaklovity's advice. It was not until August 1689 that she became aware of the danger, and then it was too late.

In the early summer of 1689, Shaklovity presented Sophia with a new report on the activities of Peter and his 'playmates', the *poteshnyi*. There was now no room for doubt; the young Czar wished to drive Sophia from the Kremlin and force her to take the veil. She gave way before Shaklovity's insistent advice: 'Destroy this accursed Naryshkin stock, or the bastard will cause the death of us all'.

During the night of August 3, 1689, Sophia gave Shaklovity a large sum of money to pay the *streltzi* leaders; the *streltzi* were to surround the village of Preobrazhenskoye and destroy Peter, his family and all his retainers. The assassination was to take place on the night of August 7th.

But the *streltzi* would not follow Shaklovity: 'Go away, you and your damned Sophia!' he was told. 'Give us back Nikita and our Prince Hovansky. It is your turn to lose your head.'

On the night of August 5th, two *streltzi* left with all speed to warn Peter of Shaklovity's plot. Peter was so afraid that he jumped on his horse, while wearing only his nightshirt. He took refuge in the convent of Troytsa. The next day, all his friends, his wife, his mother and his *poteshnyi* joined him. A regiment of *streltzi*, led by Sukharev, left the Kremlin for his protection.

Sophia made a fruitless attempt to harangue the *streltzi*, who would not heed her promises. 'Your hands,' they said, 'are stained with Hovansky's blood. You, also, will pay the price, sooner or later. You shall take the veil.' Sophia promised, 'I will reinstate the holy books. I will have the *raskolniki* monks set

free.' 'Believe me!' she implored them. 'It is too late!' was the
reply. 'We have lost confidence. And besides, it is not you, but
your *muzhik* Shaklovity who is in command,' crudely answered
a non-commissioned officer of the *streltzi*. 'He will make you
change your mind again. He is ungodly; you know his idols, you
have seen them in his palace!'[1]

Sophia realized that she was lost and set out at once for the
convent of Troytsa, but Peter refused to receive her and sent her
a message through his friend, Boris Golitzin,[2] an officer of the
poteshnyi: 'Have Shaklovity's head sent to me and then retire
to the convent at Novodevichi.

Deserted by the *streltzi* who had borne her to the throne, and
panic-stricken, Sophia gave up the struggle and withdrew. The
dramatic finish to her Regency was the execution of her lover
and adviser, Shaklovity, in the Red Square before a huge crowd
of *streltzi*. The *dyak* Samsonov put the still bleeding head of
Shaklovity into a drugget sack and took it to Peter in the Troytsa
convent. 'And what news of our sister?' asked Peter. 'She has
gone to the convent at Novodevichi,' was the reply, 'and asks
that Your Majesty will consent to giving her a nun's name.'

The seventeen-year-old adolescent, clad for the occasion in
Russian dress, looked coldly at the *dyak* with his prominent
brown eyes and dryly answered, 'Tell her to learn to dance and
take the name of Salome. I will let her have Fedka Shaklovity's
head.'

Peter began his rule by giving a sumptuous feast in the Kremlin and inviting the common people to take part in it. The
following day he convened the *Sobor*, which confirmed Sophia's
removal until the Czar's majority. Prince Vassili Golitzin—
'Protector of the Great Seal, Comptroller of all Ambassadorial
relations and Viceroy of Novgorod'—was banished to exile in
the north.

Peter made a triumphal entry into Moscow, where 18,000
streltzi awaited him. The church bells were in full peal. Simple-
minded Ivan, supported by two boyars, came and kissed his
brother.

Otherwise little was changed: simply, that the Naryshkins
instead of the Miloslavskys strode about the Kremlin in sumptuous sables, and slammed doors with authority.

[1] Shaklovity had a collection of Hindu and Persian *objets d'art*, among
which were many statuettes made of jade.

[2] A cousin of Vassili Vassilevich Golitzin.

CHAPTER 21

THE ACCESSION OF PETER

Peter was the much-loved only child of Nataliya Kirilovna Naryshkin, the second wife of Czar Alexis. His mother was a carefree, temperamental and fickle woman. The Czarina's many love affairs have been attributed to lack of virility on the part of Czar Alexis, and it is possible that the Czarina's dissatisfaction was, indeed, the reason for her relations with the Patriarch Nikon, probably Peter's father, with the son of the boyar Chelichev, who was fifteen years her junior, and with many others both known and unknown to the Kremlin historians.

In 1676, when Czar Alexis died, the new Czar Feodor, the son of Alexis's first wife, a Miloslavska, had insisted that Nataliya should provide for Peter an excellent teacher, 'a god-fearing man, well educated and, above all, one who was not a drunkard'. Great difficulty was experienced in finding a man answering such a description and especially one 'who was not a drunkard' —a very rare qualification in those days. The boyars searched through all the *prikazes* and, finally, in the *prikaz* of the 'Grand Revenue' (the Ministry of Indirect Taxation, whose main concern was with the tax on *vodka*) they dislodged a rare bird, the *dyak* Nikita Moiseyevich Zotov, head of the *vodka* department. He was a suitably educated man, for those times, but, as departmental head, he had become an inveterate drunkard. The pupil found his teacher in such a state of intoxication that the latter declared—and held to his statement—that seven times seven were fifty-six. Peter's delight was to get his drunken teacher on all fours, to sit astride his back as if he were riding a horse and, in this fashion, go through the long corridors of the Kremlin. In his rare moments of sobriety the teacher instructed Peter in the Russian alphabet, the Gospel, the Old Testament, the liturgical chants, the rudiments of arithmetic and history. But Zotov taught in so monotonous a manner that his pupil often fell asleep in his lap. One day, Zotov showed Peter some pictures; one of them was of Glasgow in Scotland. Peter would have cut it out and kept it, explaining to Zotov that his maternal grandmother came from that country. The frightened Zotov made him promise never to mention it, for a Russian Czar could not have foreign ancestors. It is noteworthy that this view was shared by the Russian historians, who very rarely mentioned the Scottish origin of the creator of the Russian Empire and represented Peter the Great as the perfect type of Russian.

Zotov continued in the rôle of teacher, even after Czar Feodor's death and the revolt of the *streltzi*. He could never cure Peter's nervous state, or the twitching of his head, or the hard, frightened look that could be detected in the depths of his eyes, or, in fact, those attacks which were so like epileptic fits. This 'nervous predisposition' dated from the day when he had witnessed the murder of his uncles and cousins. Never did Peter lose the fierce, boundless hatred which he felt for the *streltzi*, whom he feared just as much as he hated.

It is recorded that after the proclamation of Sophia as Regent in 1682 Nataliya left the Kremlin to go and live in the 'Summer Palace' of the little village of Preobrazhenskoye, not far from Moscow. Zotov followed Nataliya to this village. Occasionally the boyars came to Preobrazhenskoye for Peter in order to show him to the foreign ambassadors and the people of Moscow, and let them see him on his twin throne, alongside his half-witted brother, Ivan. The demonstrations and killings which he witnessed left permanent traces in him. Peter grew up quickly, too quickly, into a precocious youth.

The dowager Czarina Nataliya had at her disposal only a small number of attendants, for the Kremlin granted her little money, but the few women who served her took a keen interest in the young Czar. At twelve years of age, Peter was a tall, good-looking boy. A very old Russian belief attributed curative qualities to contact with the Czar. Peter took full advantage of this belief and his ability to cure; those innocent games which ended in great bursts of laughter from the thickets on the lawns of the 'Summer Palace' had unfortunate results when Peter entered his thirteenth year. The girls complained. Here is the complaint of one of the servant-girls, a complaint which was found in the Kremlin archives, for Nataliya, who was not wealthy, had to apply to the minister of the court and send him this letter:

'I went to the lawn, dressed in my best clothes, and I came back stark-naked, for the Czar tore off my bodice, my skirt and my ribbons. He broke at least one of my ribs, for I defended myself against his desires and did not want to commit deadly sin . . .'

This naïve complaint was not the only one of its kind. That is why Nataliya decided to find a wife for Peter as quickly as possible.

Peter took full advantage of his last years of single life: he frequented the fairs and in public places of entertainment he made acquaintances unsuited to a Czar; as a matter of fact, he did not go there merely to spend his time with prostitutes, but collected a troop of young men for his bodyguard, in case of a new revolt by the *streltzi*, and formed them into 'play regiments' (*poteshnyi*) as if it were a matter, not of soldiers, but of comrades bent on pleasure. Peter had not much money and could not afford the weapons needed to equip his friends. For a few roubles he bribed watchmen from the Kremlin arsenal. For thirty-two roubles and eighty-five kopecks he purchased the silence of a *dyak* of the Ministry of War and from the great armament store of the Kremlin 'abstracted' a few hundred guns, three cannon and an abundance of sabres and pikes. In undertakings of this sort he needed 'special' assistants and enrolled unscrupulous men from among the adventurers in the capital and, more especially, from among the inhabitants of the German quarter, the *Kukuy*, a place which he described as 'clean and civilized, where people smoke a pipe in the western fashion, know the way to work during the week and enjoy themselves on Sundays, shave every day and have none of those stupid Russian prejudices'. It was there that he made the acquaintance of Captain Franz Yakov-levich Lefort, of Genevese stock and a self-styled 'Doctor of Literature'. Lefort enjoyed life and was a great talker[1]; he had the knack of always being impeccably dressed and was never short of ideas to amuse Peter.

One of Peter's contemporaries, an *okolnichi* called Zhelyabin-sky, wrote about Lefort and his friends as follows: 'Most of these foreigners who came to Russia were, in their own coun-tries, arrant scoundrels. They contrived to mingle with those of our boyars and nobles who possessed the same qualities. The young Czar, completely under their influence, takes part in all the most disgraceful amusements of this devilish gang. Nothing stops these people, who have no religious beliefs and are quite

---

[1] Peter the Great visited Paris in April 1717 for negotiations with the Regent and his foreign minister Dubois. Dubois said, 'When I am speaking in French with the Czar, I wonder who in the world could have taught him our language. He is not fluent in French but he knows some expressions that would bring a blush to the cheek of a dragoon of our regiments. I once heard him swear in Versailles in a way that made the stable-hands gape.'

lawless. Some boyars and *okolnichi* in this gang had been sentenced to flogging, for having sworn and used the *matershina* in the presence of the late Czar and his wife Maria Miloslavska. Among their number was Prince Lobanov-Rostovsky who, in the reign of the Czarevna Sophia, lived by highway robbery; it was he who was given a hundred lashes for having robbed the mail coach on the Troytsa road. He was pardoned by the young Czar and promoted captain of the Preobrazhensky regiment. The gang also included murderers, counterfeiters and coiners. Even the wife of the minister Streshnev was to be seen with them.'

Prince Kurakin has described in his *Memoirs* the feasts and orgies which 'Peter I's gang' indulged in, and which took place in the palace built for Lefort on the River Yauza. These feasts were known as the 'battles with Ivashka Hmelnitsky'[1]; each of these battles ended in the death of several of the participants. An iron constitution was necessary to go through the 'ordeal of the Muscovite Hercules', as Franz Lefort called it, which consisted of opening eighteen bottles of wine and seducing eighteen virgins.

On the occasion of one of his mad escapades in the 'Foreign Quarter', during the week of mid-Lent, Peter, influenced by Lefort, dressed Zotov up as Bacchus and got him to drive a sleigh drawn by four beribboned pigs. Thus Peter made a triumphal entry, observed by the motley crowd of the *Kukuy*. Peter brought back with him from this carnival in the German Quarter two men who later distinguished themselves throughout his reign by their contributions to the expansion of the Russian Empire. They were the future 'Prince of the Land of Izhora', Alexander Danilovich Menshikov, and Baron Pyotr Pavlovich Shafirov. This is how Peter made their acquaintance:

Making his way through the motley, drink-excited crowd, Peter, followed by the inseparable Lefort and by his two friends, the Princes Buturlin and Golitzin, saw in the market-place of *Kukuy* a mob of people in front of a textile merchant's shop and heard screams of 'Stop thief! Stop thief!' Elbowing their way forward, Peter and his attendants reached the shop. A young man, short and fat, was holding a youth by the collar of his coat, shaking him and bawling at him, and yelping that the robber had stolen five roubles' worth of cloth. The little man's 'victim' was a tall fellow, curly-haired and broad-shouldered. He was

[1] A play on words: *Hmel* means alcohol.

struggling and protesting his innocence, declaring that he was an 'honest vendor of *pirozhkis*'. The threatening crowd was already closing in on him when Peter intervened and enquired what was happening. Lefort interceded on behalf of the tall youth, saying, '*Mein Herz*, that is Alexander Menshikov, the son of Daniel, squire to boyar Samsonov, a good fellow whom I know well'. 'Oh, so it is you, Menshikov, who have come to fish in the Yauza,' said Peter with a laugh. 'It is you, the one who frightens away his Czar's fish with his damned accordion.' The two young men began to laugh like old friends.

'Let him go,' Peter told the merchant. 'What is he accused of, and why all this bother on a holiday?'

The little merchant appeared not to be too pleased at the intervention by these high-ranking gentlemen (for such they were, to judge from their style of dress) and he did not let go. 'He has stolen a length of silk worth five roubles,' he said. 'If he does not pay me, I am handing him over to the officers of the *Razboyni.*'

Peter took stock of the merchant and said, 'You are obstinate, merchant. Let the man go and come to see me tomorrow at Preobrazhenskoye. Ask for Czar Peter. I will pay you your five roubles.'

Peter went away with the young man, leaving a puzzled shop-keeper behind him. Turning to the youth, he said, 'And that will be enough of fair-grounds for you. You are coming back with me, Alexander Menshikov, son of Daniel. You will be assigned to the artillery of my personal regiment. From today, you are going to serve your Czar, instead of getting yourself caught by the police. That is understood!'

Next day, the shopkeeper, a small man with bright, smiling eyes that expressed a remarkably quick understanding, came to Preobrazhenskoye, to collect his five roubles.

'Where were you born?' asked Peter.

'In Holland,' replied the young man.

'What is your name?'

'Pinkus Isayevich Shapiro, itinerant merchant.'

'Have you travelled much?'

'Yes, Your Majesty, I know the lands beyond the Vistula, the Prut and the Black Sea.'

'Do you know several languages?'

'Yes, Your Majesty.'

'Are you a Jew?'

'Yes, Your Majesty.'

Peter scratched his head. 'Well, I'm hanged! A Jew, straight out of the blue! But I cannot enlist a Jew in my service. Right! I will have you baptized and I will be your godfather. You see? You will be known as Pyotr Pavlovich Shafirov.'

'Very well, Your Majesty.'

Peter took another look at the fat young merchant, who had a slight limp. 'You'll make a poor soldier.'

'Yes, Your Majesty. But I can speak German, Dutch, Latin, Polish, English—and Yiddish, Your Majesty.'

The young Czar slapped his thigh and gave a loud laugh. 'You are right, Jew. One can find soldiers anywhere, but someone who can manage all those foreign tongues, that is quite another matter. One day, I shall make you Minister of Foreign Affairs.'

The future vice-chancellor of the Russian Empire, 'Peter the Great's Jew', knelt before Peter. The latter raised him to his feet. 'We are among friends here,' he said. 'Stand up. Learn two prayers, the *Paternoster* and the *Creed*, and come to see me here tomorrow. Our *pope* Ivan will baptize you. There is no church here, but that does not matter. You will be put in the tub where the soldiers wash.'

I know those prayers in Latin, Your Majesty: '*Pater Noster qui es in coelis, sanctificetur nomen tuum*'.

'You must say them in Russian,' said Peter. 'Until tomorrow then!'

Shafirov left, but not before he had been paid his five roubles.

The following day, Shafirov was plunged into a tub of holy water by the *pope* Ivan Voznesensky. Once baptized, he took the name of Pyotr (Peter). His godfather, the Czar, gave him three golden ducats and embraced him. 'Now,' he said, 'you are a Russian like us. Never forget it.'

Peter decided that his new recruit should be tricked out in a brand-new uniform. 'Aleksashka' Menshikov was present at the baptism. When Shafirov saw 'his thief', he spat in his direction and said to the Czar, 'Your Majesty will always have trouble with that one, "Once a thief, always a thief", says a Latin proverb'.

Shafirov and Menshikov remained enemies until their death. The memory of a few yards of stolen silk had the most serious repercussions on the affairs of state of the Russian Empire created by Peter the Great.

CHAPTER 22

THE AZOV EXPEDITION

Once she was rid of the 'Regent' Sophia, Nataliya governed with the help of the Naryshkin group. Peter's brother, Ivan the Simple, Grand Duke of Moscow, Czar of Kazan and Astrakhan, was left forgotten in his *pokoy* in the Kremlin to play with his puppets. His wife, Prascoviya Saltykov, presented him with three sons whose fathers, known to everybody, calmly walked about the Kremlin courtyards. Ivan V died in 1696 and was buried in the Archangel'sk Cathedral in the Kremlin.

As for Peter, he continued to concern himself exclusively with his *potechnyi* and he placed the task of government in the hands of the Naryshkins and his mother. It may be wondered why Peter let his mother take the reins of government. On this point Kurakin notes in his *Memoirs*: 'Czar Peter worshipped his mother. In her presence he was hardly recognizable, never drinking *vodka* or swearing. His mother married him to Eudoxia Lopukhin without his having seen his future wife in the *smotriny*, as befits a Russian Czar.'

Peter's marriage to Eudoxia Lopukhin (1689) took place with the greatest ostentation in the cathedral, but Peter came very late to the wedding: he had just spent the night with his mistress, Anna Mons, in the German Quarter.

Even after his marriage, Peter continued to live the life of a single man; for whole days, or even weeks, he was not seen at home. He lived and slept in friends' houses in the German Quarter. More and more he forsook the Russians for foreigners. He hated the old Russian traditions, manners, customs and churches. His marriage to Eudoxia Lopukhin, a girl of sixteen years of age belonging to a family of impoverished boyars, proved unhappy. If Peter did not sleep with Anna Mons or another of his mistresses, he spent the night in some brothel of the German Quarter, where he was known as 'Herr Peter'.

The young Czar was interested in navigation. He discovered the Dutchman, Timmermann, an ex-foreman of a naval shipyard, who taught him how sailing vessels were built, a subject for which Peter had a lifelong enthusiasm. Timmermann also

Paul I, 1754-1801, from a painting by Argounoff

[photo: Radio Times]

Nicholas I, 1796-1855, engraved by G. Cook

[photo: Radio Times]

x

Alexander III, 1845-94 [photo : Radio Times]

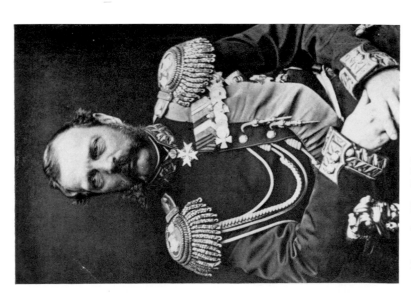

Alexander II, 1818-81 [photo : Radio Times]

taught Peter the arithmetic which Zotov had not succeeded in teaching him. Klyuchevsky has unearthed arithmetical exercises in Timmermann's hand in the young Czar's exercise-books. One example of this foreign 'master's' scholarship is: $4,325 \times 205 = 890,625$! There are other examples of equally surprising calculations!

One day, in a shed belonging to his uncle Nikita Ivanovich Romanov, Peter found a Dutch cutter which, as Timmermann explained, was designed to 'sail against the wind'. The Czar immediately decided to build a 'harbour' on the little River Yauza and another one on a 'pond' (called a lake for the occasion) at Pereyaslavl. He spent days in the Kremlin Naval Museum, created by constructors from abroad and particularly by Borel, whom Alexis had called in and who built the famous *Orel*. Peter had now only one idea: to provide Russia with a powerful fleet. The trade of ship-construction was, he said, the most noble of all occupations, more noble even than the Czar's.

Peter did not wish to become only the 'first Russian Admiral'; as 'sergeant of artillery' he was still busy with the two *poteshnyi* regiments, which he brought to the banks of the Moskva. It was near the village of Kozhukhov that what he termed the first 'large-scale manoeuvres and battles in the European fashion' took place.

The Scottish General Patrick Gordon was in charge of the manoeuvres and in this he was supported by Prince Romodanovsky and Prince Buturlin,[1] two relentless enemies, in charge of the regiments of Preobrazhensky and Semenovsky, which thoroughly hated each other. The manoeuvres were, in fact, a real battle which cost Peter dozens of lives and hundreds of wounded men. The 'manoeuvres in the European fashion' made a bad beginning.

After these 'exercises', the two commanders and General Gordon met together in the palace of the Ministry of War to discover 'the lesson to be inferred from these sham battles'. Buturlin and Romodanovsky came to blows at once and when Gordon attempted to intervene his face was reduced to a pulp. The young Czar quietened the members of his staff with his

[1] Prince Romodanovsky, whom Peter had appointed 'Generalissimo of all the *poteshnyi*' and 'King of Presburg', was also chief of the Czar's secret police, the '*prikaz* of Preobrazhensky'.
The Czar's second General, Buturlin, whom Peter appointed 'King of Poland' and 'Czar of Semenovskoye', was described by a contemporary as evil, hypocritical, who accepted bribes without scruple, whatever their source.

F

dubina, the stick which he habitually carried. 'Enough of this! We've had our fun at Kozhukov, now we'll go and play with the Tartars.'

The 'Battle of Kozhukhov' induced Peter to try his strength against the Turks who were in occupation of the mouth of the Don, thanks to their fortress at Azov. The war begun by Sophia against Turkey had resulted in neither armistice nor peace. Peter therefore attacked the fortress.

In the spring of 1695 an army of 30,000 men set out for Azov on Gordon's orders. The Czar took part in the expedition as a 'bombadier sergeant' of the Preobrazhensky regiment. The Russians were superior in number to the Turkish garrison. A powerful artillery and troops of engineers, with 'underground' experts, would, it was thought, bring about a speedy conclusion. But, after many assaults, all of them unsuccessful, the Russian army had lost nearly twenty thousand men; the Czar was obliged to raise the siege. A small detachment of Cossacks joined forces with Peter. Their Essaul, Stepan Aksakov, said, banteringly, 'We Cossacks took Azov with a small army. And what have you done with your thirty thousand men, your foreigners, your artillery and your engineers? What is the use of imitating foreigners? It is no use at all aping them.'

Peter could have had the Essaul arrested and executed but he knew very well that help from the Cossacks would perhaps be essential if Azov was to be taken. He grasped the Cossack officer and shook him so hard that he nearly strangled him. 'Don't you know,' he said, 'the Russian proverb, that "he who has begun a task shall finish it"? I shall finish what I have begun.'

Peter went back to Moscow with his army, leaving just a detachment of Cossacks at Azov. He stopped at Voronezh to establish the bases of the shipyards that were to produce the ships of his fleet of the Don and Sea of Azov. Thousands of Ukrainians were pressed into service in the naval shipyard of Voronezh.

Before his second journey to Azov, Peter called an important meeting of boyars and Moscow merchants in the Kremlin. The State needed a great deal of money to maintain its army, and it was therefore necessary to work out new measures of taxation.

'I would have you know,' said the Czar, 'that you are the owners of the serfs, the *kholopi,* and that every *kholope* who enlists in my army shall be granted his freedom by virtue of his enlistment. I must have soldiers and I will have them, even if I ruin all the boyars and merchants in the process.'

In his turn, Ivan Ivanovich Buturlin stood up and presented a pessimistic report on the state of finance, which received the applause of the boyars. Then Peter, drawing himself up to his full height, cried, 'You are not faithful subjects of mine. You are *derme*! I need 75,000 men. I shall have them, or your heads will fall into the pit of the Kremlin prison.' This precise, unequivocal language had its effect; the Czar was given his 75,000 and set out again. Some fifty galleys made their way down the Don. After a siege by sea and land, which lasted sixty days, Azov surrendered. But Peter had to call in the assistance of the Cossacks of the Don with their *Ataman* and their *chayka* (small rowing-boats). His fleet, under the command of 'Admiral' Lefort (the 'Swiss Admiral', who was born on the banks of the Leman and confessed that he had made but one trip in a boat in his whole life), was immobilized in the *Zatone*[1] of the Don. The Cossack chief Aksakov won the victory for Russia.

[1] The *Zatone*, at the mouth of the Don, were areas covered with shrubs and other vegetation which hindered the movement of the galleys.

CHAPTER 23

PETER GOES WEST

The Czar's return from the second Azov expedition was triumphal and was celebrated with a great feast in the Kremlin. In the cathedrals the *Te Deum* was sung. The people of Moscow, invited into the Red Square, were given kerchiefs on which were embroidered the words *Azov* and *Viktorya*.[1] The crowd, led on by a few *raskolniki* monks, took the word *Viktorya* to represent some pagan god whom the Czar was glorifying instead of rendering thanks to Jesus Christ. What most surprised the Muscovites was seeing Admiral Lefort and General Gordon make their entry riding in the imperial carriage while Czar Peter, in the garb of a sergeant of artillery, marched with the infantry. The angry people wondered whether the Czar was having a joke at their expense or whether this parade[2] was just another of the royal amusements from the Foreign Quarter of *Kukuy*. Tracts were scattered about the Red Square: Antichrist was soon to appear in the form of a bastard with a reddish growth on his right cheek and an enormous pubic freckle. The growth on Peter's right cheek was well known.

On his way to Holland, the Czar made a stop at the castle of Koppenbrügge, where he was welcomed by the Kurfürstin Sophie of Hanover and her daughter Sophie-Charlotta, Kurfürstin of Brandenburg, and her son the Crown Prince, heir to the throne of England. A crowd of pretty women of the German nobility soon surrounded the *enfant terrible* from the Kremlin. Peter was particularly keen to show his musical virtuosity and had a large drum brought, which he banged for hours. He confessed to the ladies that he scorned classical music and hunting, especially falconry, 'a stupid, traditional Russian sport'. His favourite occupations, he said, were travelling, building ships

---

[1] The word *Viktorya* has caused a good deal of misunderstanding in Russia. When Churchill visited Moscow during the Second World War and gave the V sign to the people, the Russians, who had no capital V in their alphabet just imagined that Churchill was promising them the second front, for which they were impatiently waiting.

[2] As a result of this parade in the Red Square the Muscovites named the Moscow prison *Lefortovo*.

and playing with fireworks. He showed his calloused palms to the ladies and said how proud he was at not having the hands of a 'degenerate aristocrat'. It is easy to imagine the sensation these words caused.

The music was followed by dancing. Peter found riotous amusement in lifting the ladies up at arms' length. He threw the Kurfürstin into the air and caught her. This colossus of a man did not know his own strength: a child of ten, the future King of England George-Ludwig, was presented to him, and Peter, deciding to kiss him, lifted the Crown Prince up by the ears!

At meals Peter refused to use his fork, and he had no use for a table-napkin. His conversation delighted the princesses, who found him very amusing, but 'not for long', for he was too uncouth for his company to be enjoyed every day. All these ladies saw in Peter a man who was intelligent, eccentric, a 'ladies' man' and rather crude. That day the Kurfürstin wrote in her diary: 'The Czar is a very good and also a very bad man. From the moral standpoint he is a perfect representative of his country.'

In 1697, Peter announced his intention of undertaking a long journey abroad in order to observe the 'way of life of others than the Russians' and to 'learn useful things'. The boyars' *Duma* was entrusted with the task of government while he was away. To the Preobrazhensky *prikaz*, whose head Romodanovsky remained, Peter allocated 'nine high judges' who were to deal with matters of importance. These nine were: the head of the *Razryadni prikaz*, Tikhon N. Streshnev; the head of the *Bolshoy Kazny prikaz*, P. I. Prozorovsky; the head of the *prikaz* of Kazan, B. A. Golitzin; the head of the *prikaz* of the *streltzi*, I. B. Troekurov; the boyars M. A. Cherkassy, *voevoda* Shein, Prince Dolgoruki, Prince Shcherbatov and the *dyak* of the *Duma*, N. Zotov.

The nine high judges were to assume executive and judicial powers while the Czar was absent. It was decided that they should hold session once a week, on Friday, in the *Preobrazhensky Prikaz*.

Impatient to leave Russia, Peter refused as far as he could to treat his going abroad as an official journey, because he knew quite well, he said, that official receptions could only waste time. All his life he hated formality and always felt that ceremonies were oppressive; he preferred to hide behind the pseudonym

'Pyotr Mikhaylov', 'a volunteer from the Czar's embassy', whose official chiefs were Franz Lefort, Artamon Golovin and the *dyak* Vornitzin. Peter's staff always included his interpreter, Pyotr Pavlovich Shafirov, his *aide-de-camp*, Alexander Danilovich Menshikov, a young negro Hannibal[1] and a dozen dwarfs for his entertainment.

He stopped for a few weeks at Königsberg where he met Frederick the Great, Elector of Brandenburg. The merchant's house where Peter took up quarters was so richly furnished that the Czar had to announce to Menshikov and his party that whoever touched the least object or stole anything would be hanged on the spot. Shafirov suggested that Menshikov's pockets be sewn up. Peter could not help admiring Prussian cleanliness and order. What amazed him most was the fact that doors stood open all day. In his Dutch-German dialect Peter was continually asking: 'Haven't you any thieves here? Aren't you afraid of robbery?' From the Prussian Colonel Steitner von Sternfeld Peter received instruction in artillery, firing of bombs and firearms in general. The Colonel awarded him a certificate, stating that his pupil was a 'competent master of artillery, with a sound knowledge of the art and ability to make use of it at will'. It was at Königsberg, too, that Peter had to intervene between Menshikov and Shafirov. Peter gave them a dressing down and shut them up in a keep for three days. When he came out, Shafirov claimed that Menshikov had been playing his old tricks and had stolen his watch.

Peter continued his journey into Holland, staying at Zaandam. There he worked as an ordinary employee in the naval shipyard of a private company. He rented a small room with the relatives of a Dutch carpenter who worked in Moscow. On Sundays, Peter visited the families of the Dutch technicians employed in Russia who had begged him to call upon the families they had left behind in Holland. Wearing the red jacket and white linen trousers of the Dutch workman, the Czar thought that by so doing he would avoid the curiosity of the crowds. He was quickly identified and followed about. On August 20, 1697, he stole out of Zaandam and reached Amsterdam, where he was admitted to the shipyards of the Dutch India Company on the recommendation of the burgomaster Wattsen. There he laboured day and night, surprising everybody by his enormous capacity for work and his mastery of the woodwork and ironwork in

[1] Ancestor of Pushkin.

boat-building. The Company laid a frigate on the stocks, and it was completed in eighteen weeks. A record!

He showed an interest in everything. The burgomaster had to go with him on his excursions and attended the lectures of the great doctor Ruish in his company. The Czar even watched surgical operations. On a visit to the anatomy room he noticed the body of a child. To the amazement of Dr Boergawe, the great scientist of the day, Peter stooped and kissed the corpse.

Visits to laboratories and operating-theatres excited him. He now wanted to be not merely a great boat-builder but a great surgeon dentist. He bought all the possible equipment for dental surgery and gave up all his other activities. He brought in his 250 Russian attendants and submitted them to oral inspection. If he detected a decayed tooth he pulled it out at once, despite the cries and protests of his 'patients'. He was endowed with great physical strength and in the early years of his dental practice he pulled out, not merely teeth, but pieces of gum as well.

All his life this passion for dentistry never left him. One of his *pokoy* contained several sacks full of extracted teeth! In the middle of a session of the council of ministers Peter would notice a face twisted with pain and exclaim, 'Oh, you son of a bitch, you have toothache and are hiding it from your Czar! Just wait a moment!' And, opening a drawer of his desk, Peter would take out a set of instruments with which he would draw a tooth from the howling wretch, who vainly protested that he had only a migraine. Towards the end of his life Peter's enthusiasm became even greater and he performed every possible kind of operation, including the amputation of limbs. Several boyars became victims of the royal surgeon.

Before he left Holland, Peter was invited to Utrecht by Stathouder William of Orange, who became William III of England. This meeting caused the Czar to decide upon a visit to England where the shipbuilding industry was even better organized than in Holland. He left at once for Deptford in order to improve his knowledge of the art of naval construction. The King offered him his best yacht and the Royal Society invited him to attend its meetings. At Richmond, he studied the making of shells and grenades. At Portsmouth he saw the British men-of-war and was amazed at the number and calibre of their guns, the weight of the shells, etc. Taking a notebook from his pocket, the Czar recorded all that he saw, and gave no heed to the polite observations of the English; had he not come to study?

In his honour the Admiralty arranged a naval battle off the Isle of Wight. Childishly happy, the Czar expressed a desire to load the guns on board the vessel where he was at the time. When the admiral in command of the fleet came and informed him that he could do as he wished, Peter threw his arms around him and kissed him so vigorously that he almost broke his ribs. The admiral had to take to his bed, and he never forgot the hug he had received from the Russian Bear. For his part, Peter never forgot the might of the British fleet.

The Czar or a member of his suite kept a careful time-table record in a diary. 'Visited the theatre and the *kostioles* (churches). Received visit from English bishops who bored us stiff for more than two hours. Invited the giant woman—four *archines* tall (7 feet 10½ inches); without stooping, the Czar passed beneath the outstretched arm of this giantess. Visited the Observatory. Went to the Tower of London, saw the Mint and the Prison. Saw the Houses of Parliament,' etc.

For two months Peter studied ship-design and mathematics. He also arranged for Captain John Perry, a canal engineer, to supervise the cutting of the Volga - Don canal. At the same time he succeeded in engaging the famous Dutch captain, Cornelius Kreis, as well as foreign commanders, boatswains, sailors, pilots, and artillery experts. By the Czar's orders they were quartered on Moscow nobles and merchants. Short of cash, Peter found an Englishman, Lord Peregrine, who came to his rescue by advancing £20,000 sterling for a tobacco monopoly throughout Muscovy. There was also a complicated question concerning a house rented by Peter and his suite. The English landlord presented a bill for a large amount because of considerable damage done to the house. The imperial purse generously supplied three times the sum requested.

Before he left England, Peter the Great received Bishop Burnet. The latter was aghast at his coarseness. After the visit, the Prelate declared, 'I am terrified by my talk with the Czar. He made me have doubts of divine Providence. I do not understand how Providence could have placed the destiny of such a great country in the hands of a man so devoid of moral sense. The incalculable power of the Czar is a defiance of divine Providence.' Bishop Burnet had forgotten Henry VIII.

CHAPTER 24

THE SLAUGHTER OF THE STRELTZI

At Vienna, Peter's journey was interrupted. There was bad news from Moscow: a revolt of the *streltzi* had just broken out (in the summer of 1698). The *streltzi* had simply announced that the Czar was dead and then requested that the Czarina Sophia should occupy the throne. (Sophia had remained in retirement in her convent.) Four regiments had risen in rebellion and were marching on Moscow.

The boyar *voevoda* Shein and General Gordon, with his seven regiments, encountered the *streltzi* on the Ryazan road and wiped them out. The 'high judges' hanged 150 of the rebels and beheaded fifty more. The questioning of the *streltzi* revealed complicity on the part of the Novodevichi convent where Sophia was living.

In Vienna, Peter received the high judges' report announcing the end of the revolt. Far from being calmed by this news, Peter became like a raging madman; the memory of those terrible days, from May 15-19, 1682, when his family was butchered by the *streltzi*, had never left him. The Czar gave orders to pack up and announced his desire to hold an enquiry in person. All the way back he spoke of nothing but the measures he would take against the rebels.

'Once for all,' he said, 'I will root up this accursed growth from the land of Russia. I'll teach them not to rise up against their Czar, even if it means killing several thousands of the rogues!'

Almost as soon as he arrived, Peter went to the offices of the secret police, in the *Preobrazhensky Prikaz*. There, the executioners were continuously occupied with torturing the accused men, breaking arms and legs. In his outbursts of rage, Peter had a good many heads cut off in his presence. The high judges stood by his side in terror, for the Czar accused them of 'magnanimity' and threatened them. 'What! You have only two hundred of the rabble to execute! You ought to lose your own heads! *Shapirka*,[1] make me out an invitation for the members

[1] The Czar's name for Shafirov.

of the diplomatic corps, so that they may witness the wholesale execution of the scoundrels.'

This wholesale execution began on October 10, 1698. Johann Georg Korb, the secretary to the Austrian Legation, has given a detailed description of this massacre:

'The Czar invited all the representatives of foreign princes and potentates to attend this exhibition of his merciless justice. In front of the barracks of the Preobrazhensky regiment stretches a piece of waste ground, surmounted by a hillock called *Kholmik*. It was there that the executions were carried out.

'The Yauza runs through the encampment of the Preobrazhensky regiment. On one bank of the river were waiting small carts filled with condemned men. No priest was allowed to be present, as the Czar considered the rebels were unworthy of such honour. Each of the prisoners carried two lighted candles. The procession and the executions began. The boyars and courtiers had to act in imitation of the Czar, who had seized an axe and was cutting off heads.

'Not far away was the howling crowd of wives and relatives of the condemned people, behind guards standing three deep. The victims' agonized cries mingled with those of the crowd.

'A hundred and thirty *streltzi* were taken out of General Shein's house; for them was reserved a death more terrible than decapitation, impalement and the wheel.

'At all the gates of Moscow had been set up, by the Czar's orders, double gallows, each intended that day for six rebels. Followed by the inseparable Menshikov, the Czar, wearing a green fur-lined coat, inspected the gibbets. Herded close together like cattle, the condemned came forward, their movement hampered by slabs of wood, and mounted the steps to the gallows. They crossed themselves three times, using two fingers, and covered their faces with their tunics, in accordance with custom. None of them waited for the officers to proceed with the details of their hanging; they put the rope round their own necks and threw themselves into space. Two hundred and thirty were hanged in this way.

'I noticed a strange scene which astonished me greatly; the Czar quickly climbed up on one of the scaffolds and spoke to a condemned man. The *streletz* listened to him and yelled out, "Get back, Antichrist!" He spoke a few words which I did not understand, crossed himself with two fingers, put his head into the noose and jumped. It was later explained to me that the Czar, recognizing a *streletz* who had distinguished himself at the capture of the Azov fortress, had decided to pardon him if he would agree always to cross himself with three fingers instead of with two as these traitors do. As for the words which the *streletz* used and which I did not understand, it seems that they had some reference to the Czar's mother.'

This testimony by Johann Georg Korb is one of the few authentic documents we have of those times. Alexis Tolstoy made use of Korb's account in his book *Peter I*, or, at any rate, in the first version of his novel. Stalin considered the soldier's contempt for his chief to be unthinkable and insisted *that the gallows scene should be cut out.*

Peter spared Sophia, but ordered that the leaders of the revolt should be hanged beneath her windows. To the chests of the corpses were pinned pamphlets and petitions to be addressed to Sophia 'after her coronation'.

Several Russian historians have attempted an explanation of the Czar's attitude in the matter of this execution. According to them, by forcing the boyars to take part in the killing of the *streltzi*, Peter thought he would bind them to him permanently and so prevent their return to the old Russian traditions. However that may be, one thing is certain: the mass execution of the *streltzi* was the first act in the stubborn struggle carried on by the Czar against Russian traditions in order to transform the Empire. A considerable number of *ukases* by Peter were necessary, among them the emancipation of women, the removal of the *Terems* and compulsory education for the sons of boyars and nobles. On the other hand, some of his edicts were strange: he ordered his subjects to shave off their beards at once and to wear Polish style of clothing. Those who objected were decreed enemies of the Czar and his régime. Whoever refused to be separated from his beard automatically became a 'traitor'. The law picked up the wearers of beards and broke down their obstinacy at police headquarters; after which, the recalcitrants' beards and hair were cut off, and sometimes their heads as well. The excessive length of men's and women's clothes was reduced. The Czar had, indeed, fixed the length of coats and dresses; in attending to this 'dress reform' he showed the zeal and earnestness always characteristic of him, whether it was a question of building ships, organizing an army or extracting decayed teeth.

Peter even fixed the number of buttons which a jacket might have; the police tore off any extra buttons. But the Russians were unwilling to wear the western-style clothes created by Peter on the lines of those he had seen when visiting Holland and England. A *ukase* forbade Russian tailors, *on pain of death*, to cut clothes in the Russian style.

The 'anti-beard' policy did a great deal of harm to Peter's reforms. The Russians became obstinate and were soon prepared 'to lose their heads rather than their beards'.

The police, already somewhat corrupt, reached a degree of venality hitherto never achieved: the beard-wearers paid the police, whose duty it was to cut off their beards, and so lost only a part of them; each encounter with the police cost them money —and a piece snipped from the beard. By the end of the day, 'a very ugly western goatee had replaced each handsome Russian beard'.[1]

Peter realized that he would never succeed in that way in 'disbearding' his subjects, and he decided to put a tax on beards. The beard thus became a constant source of revenue. A complicated set of regulations determined the 'amount of tax payable on a beard' in gold roubles:

For a noble, the equivalent of £100 (present day); first-grade trader, £250; second-grade trader, £150; free peasant, minor official or a man 'without definite occupation', £25; 'shopless tradesman', £50; watchman, £10; etc.

The peasant-serfs were permitted to wear a beard free of charge, provided they remained at home in the country. Otherwise, they had to pay one kopeck on entering a town and another on leaving.

In 1722, after defeating Sweden and reorganizing the Russian Empire, Peter shut himself up *for three weeks* so as to formulate a new law on the wearing of beards! According to this law, which prescribed in the minutest detail the 'permitted lengths' of beards for the different categories of wearers, only the peasant-serfs had permission to wear beards of unlimited length!

Through his 'agents' Peter learnt that many highly-placed dignitaries of the Russian Empire avoided losing their beards by bribing the police. He held a great feast in his palace at Preobrazhensky and sent invitations to the élite of his court. Going up to his senior boyar, *voevoda* Shein, the victor of Azov, and holding a huge pair of scissors, made for the occasion by the master

[1] According to Karamzin.

goldsmith of the German Quarter, Peter cut off his beard at a single stroke.

The dozens of dwarfs, who were just waiting for this to happen, drew their scissors and threw themselves upon the guests. The 'imps' made a hash of the beards of the most important personages in the Russian Empire. Peter looked on at the scene and howled with delight.

CHAPTER 25

THE SWEDISH WARS

The 'war against beards' was merely symbolical of Peter the Great's stubborn fight against Russian traditions. And who persisted in the old beliefs, unless it was the schismatics, the *raskolniki*? Who were the fiercest and most faithful defenders of the *raskolniki*, unless it was the *streltzi*? Why should the *raskolniki* rather lose their heads than their beards? 'Because,' said the *raskolniki popes*, our Lord Jesus Christ, His apostles and His saints, are represented in our ikons as wearing beards. If they wore beards, every true Orthodox Christian should do likewise.'

Peter got rid of his wife, Eudoxia Lopukhin. This marriage, which produced two sons (of whom only Alexis survived), did not suit him any longer. Eudoxia did everything in her power to please him, but without success. While he was on his travels, she wrote him many affectionate letters, which she signed 'Your Dushka' and in which she called him 'Lapushka'.[1] Her letters were not answered.

While he was in London, Peter wrote to the Czarina's confessor urging him to try to persuade her to take the veil. On his return, he did not visit her for three weeks, after which he had a talk with her in the house of the Postmaster, Vinnius. At the end of a quarter of an hour, as Eudoxia continued to show herself unwilling to take the veil, Peter, disregarding Vinnius's presence, had her driven off to a convent in Suzdal in a common sledge.

Menshikov and his friends knew very well why the Czar was so anxious to be rid of his wife. Peter, more than ever in love with Anna Mons, wished to marry her. He did not yet know— and was to remain in ignorance of the fact until 1701, three years later—that Anna Mons, the vintner's daughter, was the mistress of Keyserling, the Prussian Ambassador to Moscow.

According to the historian Waliczevsky, there was perhaps another reason which prompted Peter to obtain his freedom: Peter had a marked tendency to the crudest indulgence in dissolute living and his stay abroad had served to increase this

[1] Literally, 'little paw'.

tendency. His mother, Nataliya Naryshkin, had not been the best of examples to him. It is said that during one of his orgies Peter challenged the boyar, Tikhon Streshnev, who was known to have been 'intimate' with Czar Alexis's second wife: 'That man Ivan Mussin-Pushkin,' said Peter, pointing out a member of his suite, 'knows at any rate that he is the natural son of Czar Alexis, my presumed father. But what about me? Whose son am I? The Patriarch Nikon's? Or someone else's? Am I your son, Tikhon Nikitich? Speak! Come, speak out fearlessly. Speak, or I'll choke you!'

Peter seized him by the throat. Livid with fear and trembling in every limb, his eyes starting from his head, Streshnev gasped, 'Your Majesty—Sire—I implore you—let me go. I cannot answer my Czar as I should.'

'Why not? Come now!' said Peter.

'Sire,' was the reply, 'how can I express it? I was not the only one to visit Czarina Nataliya's bed.'

With nothing more to fear from the *streltzi*, Peter turned his thoughts to enlarging his Empire. His first concern was to open a 'window on the Baltic', which would provide Russia with enormous possibilities. Such access to the sea was vital.

It happened that a Livonian noble, Patkul, had just come secretly to Moscow with a proposal to Peter that he should conclude an alliance with the Livonian nobility, who were anxious to rid themselves of the Swedish yoke. Patkul was an educated and intelligent man; moreover, he was intimately acquainted with Shafirov and the boyar Sheremetev. In him Peter found the one who would provide the means for him to begin his thrust towards the Baltic Sea. Ingria,[1] Esthonia, Karelia and the Baltic coast would be annexed by Russia; Livonia would return to Poland.

In 1699, Peter concluded an alliance with Patkul. On January 12th of that year was signed the treaty of alliance between Russia, Denmark and Poland. But Shafirov, who drew up the diplomatic documents, although he was as yet no more than 'Postmaster-General', insisted that Peter should lose no time in signing a treaty of good neighbourliness with Turkey and so be free of any danger from the southern front. Shafirov sent to Constantinople a frigate with a powerful armament of English guns, so as to impress the Sultan. The frigate dropped

[1] A region of St. Petersburg.

anchor in the Bosphorus, beneath the very windows of the Sultan. On August 8, 1700, a Russo-Turkish *modus vivendi* was signed. Russia retained Azov. Peter was now in a position to open hostilities against his chief enemy, Sweden.

The anti-Swedish combination began disastrously. Charles XII, the 'soldier king', decimated the Danes and the Polish detachments from Livonia, and then turned upon the Russians, who had just taken the town of Narva. The Russian regiments encamped near Narva were commanded by the Duke of Croy and a few hundred foreign officers. On November 30th, Charles XII and his 8,000 troops forced the Russians back. Instead of counter-attacking, the Russian soldiers turned on their own officers and slaughtered them. The Duke of Croy and his staff took to flight and placed themselves under Charles's protection. Without loss of time, Charles attacked Augustus II of Poland, inflicted a heavy defeat upon him and drove him out of Livonia, so opening the way to the Polish throne for the 'Pretender', Stanislas Lesczinski, who had the backing, not only of Sweden, but of Versailles also.

One year later Peter the Great hit back by crushing the Swedes at Erestfer. In 1702, the Russian troops occupied Nöteborg and, in 1703, Marienburg and Nyenskans, so gaining a positive foothold on the Baltic.

The same year Peter appointed Shafirov as his 'private secretary' and made him responsible for establishing a few *ukases* to deal with home and foreign affairs and financial policy. Shafirov put into operation the plan proposed for dispensing with the 'boyars' *Duma*' and replacing it by the 'Private Chancellery'. It was Shafirov, too, who prepared the decree for the bureaucratization of the nobility. This decree was not confirmed until 1722, by the *ukase* of the 'Table of Ranks': every official holding the rank of active Counsellor of State became *ipso facto* a hereditary noble! Shafirov likewise devised the plan for a 'Governing Senate', the *ukases* of which would have legal force. Finally, it was he who formulated the exact details of the new Russian calendar. Being a prudent man, however, he took no part in ecclesiastical reforms, which were the personal concern of Peter the Great; the Russian Patriarchate was abolished and replaced (in 1722) by the Holy Synod, a council of metropolitans and archbishops conducted by an official appointed by the Czar.

At this time Peter the Great's activity became very strenuous.

After the Moscow fire of 1701, he built the Academy of Mathe-
matical Studies and Navigation. He forbade the construction of
wooden houses. Stone buildings were springing up everywhere.
No longer was one allowed to build how or where one liked;
buildings were to be 'in the western style'. A thorough clearing
away of the old streets resulted in the appearance of rectilinear
boulevards. A new arsenal was constructed in the Kremlin. The
first Russian newspaper made its appearance: the *Vedomosti*
('The News'), in January 1703. In the same year Peter laid the
foundations of the town of St Petersburg on the Neva.

But, abroad, war broke out again. In 1704, Peter captured the
town of Dorpat in Courland and then took Narva and the whole
of Esthonia from the Swedes. In 1706, Peter appointed Shafirov
head of the Ambassadors' *prikaz*, thereby keeping an old promise
made at Preobrazhenske.

In this year also the Volga region was in revolt, on the Don,
in the Ural district, the Ukraine and on the borders of the
Caspian Sea. Forty years after Stenka Razin, the Ataman Bulavin
rekindled the fires of rebellion. The Don Cossacks, joined by the
Old Believers and the 'defenders of the beard', declared a 'holy
war' against the 'Antichrist of the Kremlin'. Peter succeeded in
checking them, but a terrible famine devastated the land of
Russia and was followed by a serious economic crisis which was
to reach its peak in 1714.

During these difficult times, a fortunate event occurred:
Generalissimo Alexander Menshikov, who had drawn the claws
of the police agents at the Kukuy fair, achieved a brilliant
victory over the Swedes at the Battle of Kalish (1706). In a
striking manner Menshikov took full advantage of the struggle
in which Charles XII was engaged against Augustus II, King of
Poland, in the central European plain. By the treaty of Altran-
stadt, Peter's ally, Augustus II, had been obliged to abdicate in
favour of Stanislas Leszcynski and to give up Patkul to the King
of Sweden, who had him executed at Riga. Under daredevil
Menshikov's command the Russian armies probed deep into
Poland and Prussia. For the first time the chancelleries of the
west had to take into account a new European military power:
Russia.

It was the Swedish war that enabled Peter the Great to make
the acquaintance of the future Czarina Catherine I. Catherine
was a Livonian by birth, black haired, with arched eyebrows and
speaking a broken Russian. Her parents were Calvinistic Poles

whose exact name has never been discovered.[1] Before the Russo-Swedish war she was a farm hand. During the war she narrowly escaped the life of a military brothel by marrying the Swedish dragoon Johann Rabe, whom she accompanied as a sutler in his army service. She was delivered from the hands of her 'patron' by the Russians, who drove his regiment out of Livonia. Catherine took refuge in Marienburg, where she became a 'housekeeper' in the service of Pastor Glück. She soon became known in the neighbourhood as 'the most beautiful girl in Marienburg'. When the Russians took Marienburg, Catherine had just been captured by a detachment of Kalmuks. She became the mistress of Menshikov, who lived with her for some time until Peter the Great met her and took her away, giving his friend a handsome present in exchange.

In 1708, the Russian troops, ceaselessly struggling against the Swedes, were skirting the Minsk marshes in their withdrawal to Polesse so as to reach the Ukraine. The armies of Charles XII, after their victories in Poland where Stanislas had just replaced Augustus II, were approaching the Dnepr and threatening Smolensk and Moscow. Peter the Great's critical moment was soon to come. He withdrew to the Ukraine and waited for help from *hetman* Mazeppa and his Cossacks. He suddenly heard that, instead of marching on Moscow, Charles XII was making his way towards the Ukraine, to Chernigov and Poltava. At the same time a delegation led by two Cossack colonels, Kochubey and Iskra, apprised him of a secret alliance between *hetman* Mazeppa and Charles XII. Peter refused to place any trust in this information. He had the two colonels arrested and handed them over to Mazeppa. A Cossack tribunal sentenced them to death. The day after their execution Mazeppa withdrew his troops from the Ukrainian capital of Baturin and joined forces with Charles XII.

On June 27, 1709, near the fortress of Poltava, defended by the Russian garrison under their commandant Keller, Charles XII delivered the final assault. During the whole of the fighting Peter did not spare himself. He galloped over the battle-front, going to the most exposed points. His hat and saddle were riddled with bullets. The day ended with the utter defeat of the Swedes.

---

[1] Catherine was called Helen Catherine Skavroshchuk, but her brother was a Skavronsky and her uncle a Scavrech. Her family came to Livonia from Minsk in the Belorussian part of Poland, after adopting the Calvinist religion. Catherine was a Lutheran.

Charles XII and Mazeppa made their escape by way of the
Perevolochna road to seek asylum with the Sultan of Turkey in
Bender in Bessarabia.

Peter's delight know no bounds. He kissed everybody and
invited the Swedish generals to his tent, returning their swords
to them and calling them his 'masters and teachers'.[1]

Shafirov had not left Peter's side at Poltava for a minute, and
the day following the battle Peter made him vice-chancellor and
conferred on him the title of baron.[2] Catherine, summoned to
Poltava by Peter, stayed several months with the army and
arranged huge feasts for the officers and statesmen. Catherine
took great pleasure in Shafirov's company and spoke with him
in German or Polish. (She spoke Russian with a German accent,
which she never lost.) The new baron and vice-chancellor of
Russia became her firm friend, to the great displeasure of the
other dignitaries of the Empire. Peter, although very jealous by
nature, looked on them with a smile. 'Stupid things are being
said about Katka and Shapirka,' he remarked. 'Look at them!
Poor Shapirka has got only as far as the navel!'

The hatred between Menshikov and Shafirov persisted.
Shafirov did not scruple to repeat the story of the theft from his
Kukuy shop. Menshikov referred to him as a 'sheeny'. More
than once Catherine made an attempt at reconciliation between
her former lover Menshikov and Shafirov, but she never succeeded. Peter, who had become used to this hatred of many
years' standing, found their quarrels amusing. 'Listen, Shapirka,'
he would say, 'instead of wearing out your tongue on Aleksashka,[3] provoke him to a duel. I will act as your second. Will
you?' The invariable answer from Peter the Great's Jew was, 'I
don't fight with a thief'.

---

[1] The Swedish generals decided to remain in Russia and, after the Peace of
Nystad, agreed to become generals in the Russian army.

[2] The conferment of this title was made official in 1710.

[3] Menshikov.

CHAPTER 26

THE PEACE OF NYSTAD AND THE
EXECUTION OF
THE CZAREVICH ALEXIS

Turkey would not agree to the Czar's request to deliver Charles XII into his hands. The Swedish King had taken refuge at Bender, whence he continued with his diplomatic intrigues, while the Russian troops were thrusting deeper and deeper into Finland, Germany and Poland, where they reinstated on his throne Peter's puppet, Augustus II, and drove out Louis XIV's puppet, Stanislas.

Peter went on with his reforms. He often presided at the levees of the *ass ambleis*, at which the dignitaries of the Empire had, by his orders, to drain the 'Great Cup' or the 'Cup of the Two-headed Eagle'. The huge vessel was to be emptied at a single draught, and two guardsmen saw to it that there was no cheating. The Russian women admitted to these *assembleis* enjoyed increasing freedom and no longer tolerated their husbands' control.

The Kremlin, seat of power and intrigue, was doomed. The fortress of St Petersburg was built with all speed; Peter did not attempt to disguise his intention of making it his new capital. The workmen who took part in its construction on the marshes died in their thousands. The scourge and the rod took the place of the food stolen by the foremen. Often, Peter became a prey to despair and he one day confided to Shafirov, 'Explain to me why our Russians are such thieves'. 'I do not know, Sire,' was the reply. 'Ask Menshikov, who is more of a Russian than I am.' 'Oh, him!' said Peter. 'If all Russians were like him, there would not have been a stone of all my Empire left long ago.' 'Try to obtain a copy of his account with the Bank of England, Sire,' Shafirov said. 'There you will find a large part of the money voted for the construction of St Petersburg.'

Peter decided to create, alongside the political secret police, a new institution known as the *Fiskals*, a specially elected body of police accountants who recorded denunciations from whatever source and irrespective of their purpose. These *Fiskals*, under the

180

guidance of *Ober-Fiskal* Nesterov, had the right to conduct searches at any time or place, to inflict torture and throw the suspected persons into the Kremlin *yama*. Towards the end of Peter the Great's reign there were about 1,500 *Fiskals*. The *Fiskals'* ecclesiastical colleagues were known as 'inquisitors' and their chief as the 'grand inquisitor'.

Another institution, the *Pribilshchiki*, had as its objective the increasing of State revenue. Everything was taxed: births, marriages, deaths! More and more money was needed for the conduct of wars and the building of St Petersburg. The uninterrupted sequence of revolts was repressed with incredible harshness; the *raskolniki* distributed leaflets denouncing Peter's ancestry and referring to him as the 'false Czar' and the 'Latin and Lutheran Antichrist'. The first Russian secret printing-press was set up by a certain Talitsky, who printed pamphlets aimed at the Czar. He was arrested and the Senate sentenced him, together with his accomplices, to death by 'quartering after being smoked for three hours like a Baltic herring'. This cruel sentence aroused protests on all sides. Peter's son, Alexis, who had known Talitsky, shut himself up in the Kremlin cathedral for several hours, praying for the soul of the victim and severely condemning his father. This marked the beginning of the breach between father and son, an estrangement which ended a few years later with the tragic death of Alexis.

The war in the north went on, the Russian army capturing Riga, Viborg, Reval, Dvinsk and Pernau from the Swedes. Once the flanks of St Petersburg were secure and access to the Baltic was in his grasp, Peter had no further reason to prolong the war, but Charles XII, a refugee in Bender, refused, with the Sultan's support, to sign the peace.

The Russian ambassador to Constantinople, Andrei Tolstoy, succeeded in getting the draft treaty accepted but instead of ratifying it the Sultan charged the Russian ambassador with spying and imprisoned him in the dungeon of the Seven Towers. The Russo-Turkish war was resumed.

From the beginning of hostilities (1710) Shafirov displayed great acumen. He explained to the Czar that the only way to avoid war with the Ottoman Empire was to seek the intervention of Versailles, whose influence would weigh heavily with the Sultan and make Sweden give way. But Peter had confidence in the promises made by the Serbians Voych and Bogdan Popovich, the Bishop-Prince of Montenegro, Danilo, a few Greek priests and the Princes of Wallachia and Moldavia, who declared that when the Russo-Turkish war began the Christians in Turkey would rise in revolt. Relying upon this uprising Peter advanced towards Moldavia, taking Iasi by storm. But the *Hospodars* Princes took flight and the Christian inhabitants of Turkish soil, faced with massacre by the janizaries, entrenched themselves.

The Turkish army of 270,000 men with 244 cannon, under the command of the Grand Vizier, closed in upon Peter's 40,000 soldiers who were exhausted by weeks of forced marches across the burning steppe. Peter repeated all the mistakes made by Charles XII in his Ukrainian campaign and rejected the advice of his associates to make a prudent, temporary withdrawal. 'No,' said Peter, 'I am defending the whole of Christendom and I will not retreat one step.'

With their backs to the Prut, beset on all sides, threatened from every direction, their supplies cut off, harassed by the Turkish cavalry, the Russian soldiers waited for the end to come. Peter was in deepest despair. In his *Souvenirs*, Shafirov writes that he had to snatch the Czar's pistol from his hand; Peter did not want to be taken alive by the Turks. Historians have commented in different ways on his attempted suicide. One undeniable fact is that Peter fell seriously ill, stricken down by a sickness unknown in those days: nervous depression. Catherine, who had followed Peter as far as Iasi, was urgently summoned by Shafirov. In order to persuade the Grand Vizier to exercise patience, he sent him a large sum of money, with the promise of twice as much to follow when the armistice was signed. In due course Catherine arrived. Shafirov took her with him to the Turkish encampment, where they spent several days talking over the details of the peace treaty. Catherine and Shafirov occupied a double tent near that of the Grand Vizier, who often visited them by night to gossip and play chess with the vice-chancellor, Peter the Great's past-master at the game.

After several days' discussion, Shafirov signed the 'Treaty of Prut' on behalf of the Czar. He and Catherine returned to the Russian camp and the vice-chancellor submitted to the Czar the treaty he had concluded with the Grand Vizier. 'You are a wizard, Shapirka,' exclaimed Peter. 'How did you manage to get such a treaty from the Grand Vizier?' With a modest smile Shafirov took Catherine by the arm and said, 'It is not I, but she, who has saved Russia'.

Indeed, Catherine had given the Grand Vizier and the leader of the janizaries all her jewels—presents from the Czar—and a sum of 200,000 roubles in gold. It was a wonderful surprise for Peter who, on the eve of the armistice, was prepared *to give up all he had won from Turkey and Sweden*, except St Petersburg, and *for that he was ready even to sacrifice* to Sweden *the town of Pskov*, one of the oldest towns in Russia.

With Catherine's help Shafirov had succeeded in keeping *all that had been won in the northern war*. The Czar was compelled to relinquish only Azov and Taganrog and was to sign a peace with Charles XII, 'if it was possible to reach an agreement' (sic). This formula bears a strong resemblance to the preliminary talks which precede the summit meetings of the present day.

The Grand Vizier had asked, however, when signing the Peace of Prut (July 12, 1711), that Shafirov should be handed over to him as a hostage until all the clauses of the treaty had been fully implemented. The vice-chancellor's farewell scene was touching. Peter kissed Shafirov three times in the Russian manner. 'You have saved the fruits of my labour, Shapirka,' he said. 'You may remind me of the fact at any time. I am giving this ring to my wife, so that she may hand it to you on your return.' The Czar's very recent and very official wife, Catherine, wept as she embraced Shafirov.

Here, once again, history is wedded to romance. The historian Bantysh Kamensky supplies the following detail: 'Mischievous tongues claimed that Peter the Great's Jew had been permitted by Catherine to share her tent in the Turkish camp at the time of the Treaty of Prut discussion. After this adventure, Catherine, who was much taller than the vice-chancellor, always called him "My manikin".'

Shafirov therefore left for Turkey, where he stayed for three years, living a life of the most fantastic adventures, signing new agreements, meditating in various prisons, overthrowing the Viziers or buying them over. The Turks arrested the Grand Vizier and Kaya, the leader of the janizaries, as soon as they arrived in Constantinople and they were tried at once on the charge of having signed such a treaty and taken the vice-chancellor's money. They were impaled, and during the execution the molten gold from the roubles given by Shafirov was poured into their mouths. 'The Divan' wished to know the precise circumstances in which the money had passed to the Grand Vizier, but the vice-chancellor refused to speak and scorned their threats, pointing out his position as ambassador to the Czar, who 'alone could judge him'.

The Turks kept Shafirov in prison but, even from there, he continued to maintain contact with his foreign friends, Sutton, the English minister, Collier, the Dutch minister and others less known but equally influential. On August 5, 1712, Shafirov was allowed temporary freedom in order to sign a second peace treaty in the name of the Czar. On that occasion he succeeded in bribing the Grand Mufti, who declared that the annulment of the treaty of July 12, 1711, 'would be contrary to the teachings of the Prophet'. The historian Bantysh-Kamensky tells how the astute Shafirov managed to borrow money from the Greek usurers at rates of interest up to twenty-five per cent by offering them as security 'blank cheques bearing the Czar's signature', which he had taken care to bring with him. As a matter of fact, they were signed by Shafirov, but his master honoured them.

At last, in 1714, Shafirov was set free by the Turks and returned. Peter heaped favours upon him, despite the efforts of chancellor Golovkin and Menshikov, his eternal enemy, to discredit him. Catherine patronized him and invited him almost daily to come and play cards or tell her about the time he had spent in Turkey.

Three years had passed, and Russia was passing through a stage of grave economic crisis. In 1716, Shafirov, who had actually become the head of the new College of Foreign Affairs, which replaced the Ambassadors' *prikaz*, submitted a report to the Czar in which he recommended a closer bond with France. The task was to establish more friendly relations than those which obtained at the time and which had become bitter-sweet.

To coax the Versailles government, Peter decided to dispatch a professional diplomat, von Schleinitz, a German, but Abbé Dubois, the Regent's minister, told Mussin-Pushkin who had been sent by the Czar to prepare the way for his journey, 'We should prefer an ambassador from Russia to be a Russian. We have no confidence in von Schleinitz; all that we tell him is known in detail in Hanover, Vienna and Frankfurt.'

Prince Basil Dolgoruki was appointed to the position. Shafirov had devised a plan to bring about a closer association between Russia and France: to conclude a marriage between the Czar's second daughter Elizabeth and the young Louis XV. If the

Versailles government refused, one would consider the possibility of marrying her to the Duke of Chartres or the Duke of Bourbon. Shafirov had even foreseen that if the Duke of Bourbon married Elizabeth he would have a right to the Polish throne, and thus would be eliminated the question of Poland, a great source of disagreement between France and Russia.

The 'Old Pretender' to the throne of England, who had meddled in Franco-Russian relationships, suggested to the Czar through the medium of his representative Thomas Gordon that he should land in England in order to re-establish the Stuart succession. Once this Restoration was achieved, a Russian Grand Duchess could marry a new Francophile King of England and so create a dynastic union of England, France and Russia! There was certainly no lack of ideas.

In April 1717 the Czar and his ministers arrived in Paris. There, Peter gave free rein to his curiosity: he would go into shops or stop carriages and gossip with the coachmen or ply them with questions. Peter revisited museums and arsenals, waxwork shows, statue foundries and the Gobelin tapestry works. From the Invalides to the Observatoire, from Marly to Saint-Cyr, everywhere he asked questions and made notes. He reviewed the troops of the King's Household in the avenue of the Champs-Elysées, attended a meeting of the Académie des Sciences and a session of the Parlement. This was not the Peter who, in 1697, had shocked Bishop Burnet by his coarseness. Referring to Peter, Rambaud said, 'He is still the greatest of the foreign guests ever to visit Paris'.

During a big reception, the Czar took Louis XV in his arms, kissed him warmly in Russian style and whispered to the Regent. The same day the rumour spread among the courtiers that there was a mention of a marriage project between the Czar's second daughter Elizabeth and the King of France.

At the same reception in Versailles the Czar's minister had said to the Marshal of Tessé, 'Are you not alarmed at the tremendous power of the House of Austria? Put us in the place of Sweden and we shall provide all that you could have expected from her against Austria.'

The 'Russian marriage' was, moreover, intended to encourage a close connection between St Petersburg, the new capital of Russia, and Paris. But the marriage did not take place. Prussian diplomatic circles looked disapprovingly on this proposed Franco-Russian marriage and looked for other possibilities of a match for Elizabeth. In Paris also consideration was being given to a possible wife for Louis XV. Elizabeth of Russia was to remain single, but for her morganatic marriage with the precentor of the Imperial Chapel, Andrey Rozumovsky, who had been made a Count of the Holy German Empire.

Louis XV married the daughter of Stanislas Lesczynski, the dethroned King of Poland and unsuccessful candidate in the royal election of 1733, who received the Duchy of Lorraine as compensation. (On his death the Duchy was restored to the French crown.)

On August 4, 1717, M. de Châteauneuf for France, Baron von Knipper zu Knipphausen for Prussia and Golovkin, Shafirov and Kurakin for Russia, signed the following agreement in Amsterdam: 'The contracting parties undertake by their good offices to contribute to the maintenance of public calm as restored by the Treaties of Utrecht and Baden, this undertaking also to apply to those who intervene in the cause of peace in the north'.

The Czar and the King of Prussia agreed to the intervention of France between them and Sweden but, on the very evening following the signing of the document, during a private conversation with Kurakin Cardinal Dubois politely but firmly rejected the betrothal of Elizabeth of Russia to Louis XV. He put forward other candidates, such as the Duke of Chartres and the Duke of Bourbon. Peter the Great, taking offence at this, returned a categorical *nyet*.

In 1721, with the assistance of the French mediator Campredon, the war in the north which had lasted for twenty-one years came to an end. The Peace of Nystad (1721) was celebrated by Peter in the new Russian capital, St Petersburg, with a ten-day carnival.

Russia's situation was far from prosperous. War, rebellion, the building of St Petersburg and the Baltic ports had ruined the country and brought about the death of hundreds of thousands of Russians. Forced labour had added its quota of troubles. The rumours that Peter was the Antichrist, the son of Satan, the enemy of Holy Russia and the libertine who despised the Russians, had resulted in a wholesale migration of the Russian populace into the forest regions of the north; and the turncoats in their thousands were hiding in caves and grottoes. Russia resembled a 'huge madhouse set ablaze by ruffians'.[1] An officer

---

[1] The expression is that of a Prussian general in the service of Russia, von Bismarck.

of the Preobrazhensky regiment described the picture differently: 'A brothel on fire'; which cost him fifteen years' exile with hard labour.

The Czar's collaborators were always quarrelling. Menshikov, who had become 'His Most Serene Highness of Izhora', had stolen millions of roubles. Other 'servants' of the State also robbed, on a smaller scale of course, but it was enough to upset the budget.

Shafirov complained to Catherine of the 'unworthy servants of the Czar who undermined his work'. These 'unworthy servants' did not forget the vice-chancellor's complaint and spread malicious talk about him, accusing him of embezzlement and nepotism. It was stated that he was in collusion with the Vesselovsky brothers, ambassadors to Vienna and London, who refused to return to Russia. Shafirov felt constrained to box Golovkin's ears for calling him a 'sheeny', and right in the middle of the Senate Shafirov himself called Menshikov a 'thief' and Yaguzhinsky, the public attorney, a 'drunken sot'.

In 1723, in consequence of a denunciation made to the Ober-Fiskal, Shafirov was accused of being a Jewish necromancer and of practising the cabala. It was claimed that his son was circumcized. His daughters, Rebecca, Debora, Sulamit and Miriam, whose husbands' names were among the greatest in Russia, were blamed for never having agreed to change their Jewish first names for Russian names. His son, the young Baron Isaiah, had likewise refused to change his name.

1723 was the year of Menshikov's disgrace and Shafirov's death sentence. On February 15, a pathetic scene was enacted at the Kremlin: 'Bareheaded, the great Russian statesman, dressed in a simple garnet-red dressing-gown, was dragged to the scaffold. His head lay on the block and the executioner was about to raise the axe, when a messenger arrived from the Czar with a decree commuting his sentence to one of exile in Siberia for life.'

But Catherine had never forgotten the ring given to Shafirov, and there followed a further measure of clemency: the condemned man was permitted to withdraw to Novgorod. The banishment was of short duration. On the death of Peter, Catherine brought Shafirov back to the capital, restored his barony to him and, as a token of her friendship, placed in his hands the Czar's sword of solid gold, charging him to write the history of the reign of Peter the Great.

Shafirov died in 1737, after carrying out several delicate negotiations: he signed the peace of 1730 with Persia and took part
in the Congress of Nemirov; but he had lost his enthusiasm for
affairs of State. The man who had saved the Russian Empire in
1711 remained deeply affected by his sentence, brought about by
Menshikov. On his death-bed he was watched over by the young
Princes and Princesses Dolgoruki, Gagarin, Hovansky and Saltykov, and by his grandchildren.

The war in the North dragged on and discontent grew
throughout the land. A weak, but real, opposition began to take
shape around Peter's son Alexis. All that Peter loathed, everything against which he had always fought, the monks, the black
clergy, the *raskolniki*, the old beliefs, the Church, the *streltzi*,
all the old Russia seemed to want to support Alexis and to
cluster around him. That young man was tubercular, listless,
deeply religious, lacking in vigour and of low intelligence, and
had never forgiven his father for the way in which he had
behaved towards his mother Eudoxia or for his marriage to
Catherine.

After the victory of Poltava, Alexis had married Princess
Charlotte of Brunswick. He never loved this 'tall, thin, plain'
wife who had been inflicted on him by his father. He avoided
her or beat her, and was in love with Aphrosinya, his mistress, a
Finnish farm-girl, who was his constant companion. In October
1715, Charlotte died in giving birth to a son who was named
Peter. After his wife's funeral, Alexis received a long letter from
his father accusing him of subversive intrigues against him,
Czar Peter the Great. In alarm, Alexis followed the advice of his
friends, profiting from the fact that Peter was conducting the
German campaign, and fled to the court of the Emperor of
Austria in the company of Aphrosinya dressed as a boy. From
Vienna he continued to criticize his father's behaviour. In a
rage, Peter dispatched messengers all over Europe in an attempt
to find the fugitive Czarevich. Alexis escaped to San Elmo, near
Naples. Soon, running short of money, he went back to Vienna,
where Peter I's personal representative, Tolstoy, was waiting. He
was one of the Czar's most subtle sleuths and he inveigled
Alexis back to Russia, promising him a safe-conduct and a pardon. 'Go back, Alexey,' he said, 'you know quite well that your
father will find you, wherever you are, even if he has to dig you
out like an earthworm.' Alexis went back to Russia and was
taken under escort to the Kremlin, where Peter welcomed him

with these words: 'So the deserter from Naples is back? How shameful! What a disappointment for a father! My own son running to my enemies!' Alexis fell to his knees, beseeching his father to forgive him. The Czar was unmoved. One by one, he wrung from him the names of his supporters in Russia.

Tolstoy, Menshikov and senator Pushkin were appointed to head the Commission of Enquiry, which ordered the arrest of thousands of 'oppositionists'. There were delivered up to the executioner Kilkin, the leader of the network of 'Alexey's Supporters', Major Glebow, Eudoxia's lover, the Bishop of Kiev, Eudoxia's brothers and cousins, the entire Lopukhin clan and hundreds of boyars, including Prince Dolgoruki. The ex-Czarina Eudoxia was sent to solitary exile in a convent near Lake Ladoga. During the investigation of the 'Alexis affair' Menshikov had Aphrosinya arrested and thrown in the prison of the Peter and Paul fortress. There, on the wheel and under the lash, she put her signature to a statement in which she accused Alexis of being the head of a ring of conspirators acting against 'the life of the Czar' and the 'security of the State'. Menshikov got together a commission of 144, consisting of bishops, generals, senators and senior officials, to try Alexis. Peter presided over the court.

Alexis was found guilty of crimes against the safety of the State and sentenced to be flogged to death, the sentence to be carried out by Menshikov's executioners in the basements of the Schlüsselburg fortress on June 26, 1718.

Peter himself recorded the death, entering the time and place in the *Prison Journal*. The body of the Czarevich Alexis was thrown into the common grave of the Peter and Paul fortress.

CHAPTER 27

THE RISE OF ST PETERSBURG

When the Peace of Nystad was signed in 1721, Peter gave his whole attention to St Petersburg. Sumptuous premises, ministries and palaces sprang up everywhere. Kronslott (later known as Kronstadt), the fortress on the Island of Kotlin, was almost complete. Peter was becoming impatient. Undoubtedly, the little Palace of Peterhof, the work of Leblond, could already accommodate him and his family, but he wanted a 'Versailles'. The main official buildings were only just beginning to appear and many officials stayed in Moscow until 1740. St Petersburg did not become the true capital of Russia until that time, during the reign of Elizabeth.

The story of St Petersburg, with its palaces and its fortresses of Schlüsselberg and Peter and Paul, began with the death of Alexis. After his son's death, Peter made preparations for the accession of his other son, Peter, Catherine's child. One day, however, when the governesses were exercising the child Peter in the park of the Peterhof Palace, an unusually violent storm broke out so suddenly that they had no time to run into the palace with the Czarevich and took shelter in a small grotto, near the Monsters' waterfall, where they were struck by lightning.

Peter the Great was disconsolate at his son's death and spent whole days in lamentation by the empty little bed. Rumour laid the death at Peter's door and it was said that it was divine retribution for the murder of Alexis. Mad with rage, the Czar gave orders for the rumours to be cut short by cutting out the malicious tongues.

As for Paul, the other son of Peter and Catherine, he died mysteriously of an illness which struck him down in a few seconds and there was talk of poisoning. An enquiry conducted by the Preobrazhensky *prikaz* ended in the death of a few unfortunate people but found no explanation of the Czarevich's death.

Wishing to have heirs, Peter decided to conclude marriages for his daughters and nieces. His elder daughter, Anna Petrovna, married the Duke of Schleswig-Holstein in 1725, so establishing the Holstein-Gottorp-Romanov line. His nieces, Anna Ivanovna and Catherina Ivanovna,[1] married respectively the Duke of Kurland and the Duke of Mecklenburg. But Peter could not find a husband for his daughter Elizabeth, although he sent several portraits of her to all the courts of Europe. Versailles wanted no hand in a 'Russian marriage'. Madrid, Vienna and the German capitals held the same view. When at last one of the Imperial princes was found for the purpose, he died on his way to St Petersburg.

Peter became increasingly gloomy and taciturn; his associates were nothing but grasping individuals who tore to shreds his life's hard work. All of them were corrupt to the core.

Peter one day confided to his new *Ober-Kiskal* Malinin, 'It is essential to cut away the roots of the trouble, not the branches as you are doing. It is not enough to hang or behead the less important thieves; they must all be punished, whoever they may be, irrespective of their lineage. All of them!'[2]

Then to the attorney Yaguzhinsky he said, 'Prepare a new law. Anyone who robs the State and whose theft is estimated to be equal to or greater than the price of a rope shall be hanged with that rope.' Yaguzhinsky exclaimed, 'But, Sire, if this law is proclaimed, you run the risk of being left without any subjects at all.'[a]

On February 5, 1722, Peter personally drew up a decree relating to the succession to the throne. 'Every Czar will have personally to name his successor, choosing him as he thinks fitting.'

The Imperial dignitaries asked the Czar's personal secretary Makarov for elucidation: 'Suppose His Majesty wishes to pass on the throne to Vanka Kain?'[3] 'He will become the Czar of all the Russias,' was the imperturbable reply. 'Such is His Majesty's will.'

The year after the Peace of Nystad, 1722, Peter declared war on Persia on the pretext of avenging the Transcaucasian Armenians for the murderous attacks made upon them by the Persians. The Armenians had sent their Patriarch Nerses to ask the protection of the Czar. Nerses repeated the request made to Peter twenty-two years earlier by another Armenian, Israel

[1] The daughters of Peter's brother, Ivan.

[2] Klyuchevsky.

[3] A legendary character, the Moscow Cartouche.

Oryan; but on this occasion Peter decided to give protection to the Armenians and to send out from Astrakhan an expedition to move round the Caspian Sea and capture Baku.

Before he left, Peter confided a carefully sealed envelope to his secretary Makarov, with the words, 'If I do not return, you will give that to the Senate. Let it not be opened before my death, or you will pay with your head.'

The Russian expedition had hardly left Astrakhan, when Shah Tamasp's vassals revolted against him and dethroned him. In 1723 the Czar arrived at Derbent and received the fugitive Shah, who proposed an alliance against his vassals. The Czar agreed, and on September 3rd the Shah ceded to Russia the regions of Derbent and Baku and the provinces of Gilian, Mazanderan and Astrabad. In exchange, Peter restored the Shah to his throne, and Tamasp generously expressed his thanks to the Russian generals by presenting them with fabulously large sums of money.[1]

A few days after his return Peter fell a prey to violent feverish attacks, during which he smashed everything within reach. These fits of malaria (?) were accompanied by intestinal disorder. In the periods of freedom from pain Peter continued to show an interest in events in Central Asia and the Near and Middle East. He was several times heard to say that 'the war in the North had lasted too long and for that very reason had been a mistake'. In his view, Russia as a modern State should turn to the Near and Middle East and play the part of the 'leader of the modernized Asiatic powers'. Makarov related that the Czar had been impressed by the words of Abbé Dubois, the minister to the Regent Philip of Orleans: 'France must support the Sultan, since Turkey is the counterweight for the neutralization of Austria. If Russia were one day to replace Turkey on the chequer-board of Europe by applying military pressure to Austria and if Your Majesty's government guaranteed the integrity of Poland, then nothing would stand in the way of a Franco-Russian alliance. In these circumstances, Russia might go and seek compensation in Persia and India.'

[1] Part of this money was included in the *Register of the Persian Debt*, created in 1725 by order of Shah Tamasp.
   Among the successive custodians of the *Register* was Prince Dolgoruki. One of his descendants, 175 years later, handed over this *Register* to the banker Mitya Rubinstein (the father of Serge Rubinstein, assassinated in New York in 1955), who paid in the money and thereby established one of the greatest fortunes existing in the reign of Nicholas II.

Modern view from the river of the Kremlin at night   [photo: Charles Lewis]

XII

Early twentieth-century view from approximately the same point

[photo: Radio Times]

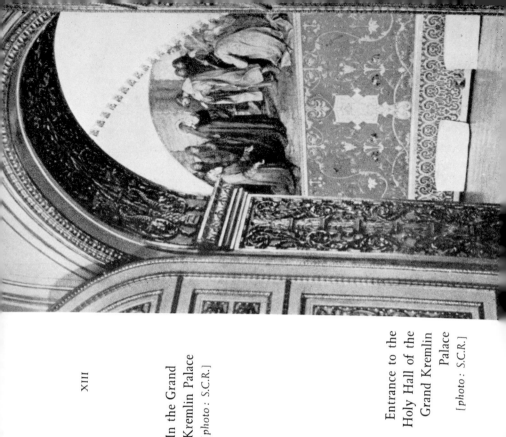

XIII

In the Grand
Kremlin Palace
[photo: S.C.R.]

Entrance to the
Holy Hall of the
Grand Kremlin
Palace
[photo: S.C.R.]

Peter, who was always complaining of the lack of funds for the industrialization of Russia, was very much drawn to India, which had the reputation of being enormously wealthy, and he conceived the notion of following in the footsteps of Alexander the Great, whose exploits he read over and over again. For this reason or another, England showed increasing hostility to Russia towards the end of Peter's reign. Dashkov, the Czar's ambassador to Constantinople, was therefore able to write, 'I have no worse enemy than my English colleague'.

It is important to remember the anti-Russian sentiments shown by England at this time if one wishes to penetrate the most exciting mystery of Russian history, a mystery which will be mentioned in a later chapter concerning the 'Affair of Peter the Great's Will and Testament'.

Peter's private life became stormier than ever when he heard of Catherine's relations with Anna Mons's brother, young Willi, whom the Czarina appointed court chamberlain. One night, after a stupendous drinking bout, in which his 'Synod of drunkards and gluttons'[1] took part, Peter returned home to see a shadowy form flit from Catherine's bedchamber and disappear rapidly into the park. He gave chase, but stumbled and sprained his ankle. The next day an enquiry established the fact that the figure was the chamberlain Mons. Mad with jealousy, he personally tortured the chamberlain. After the chamberlain's execution, Peter compelled Catherine to ride round the scaffold in a sleigh to look upon the bleeding remains of young Willi. Catherine, who had denied her guilt right to the end, maintained the most perfect calm because she knew very well that if she showed the slightest emotion Peter would strangle her at once. It is said that Peter, at a loss to find means of prolonging Catherine's mute suffering, placed her lover's head in a vase of alcohol and left it in his wife's bedchamber. The day following

---

[1] The Church wilfully obstructed the progress of Peter's reforms and he insisted on ridiculing it by creating a comical institution, the 'Synod of drunkards and gluttons', of which he took the modest title of 'Archimandrite'. He personally formulated its statutes: there were admitted to the bosom of the Synod only those who could drink a minimum of half a gallon of alcohol a day and eat 'three chickens and a quarter of a lamb or a whole ham and a quarter of a calf' per day. Some sessions ended with a sleigh-ride through Moscow, the sleighs being drawn by pigs and calves. After the death of the Patriarch Adrian, Peter decided to abolish the patriarchate and appointed a temporary 'Keeper of the Patriarchate'. The Metropolitan then begged Peter to stop his foolery with the 'Synod of drunkards and gluttons' and threatened him with resignation if he persisted in it.

G

Mons's execution, Peter confiscated Catherine's entire fortune, and had a close watch kept upon her.

The 'Mons affair' drove Peter out of his mind. All his life he had acted in servile imitation of the west but now he suddenly refused to believe in western technical superiority and became antagonistic to foreigners. His state of health grew worse and nervous depression began to take a tighter hold upon him. He saw before him nothing but blankness; he was 'acting alone in trying to draw Russia up to the *summit* and others were doing their best to pull her down'. In desperation he summoned Pososhkov, the self-trained peasant who had become a political economist, and asked his advice. Pososhkov said, 'Do as your father Czar Alexis did. Appeal to the nation, Pyotr Alexeyevich. Convene the *Sobor*. Let them make all the decisions and appoint your successor to the throne.' But Peter would hear no more. 'The *Sobor*!' he said. 'A gang of bearded ignoramuses! No, I will impose my successor and my will upon them!' 'Which successor?' asked Pososhkov. 'I will announce that at the proper time,' was the reply.

The reign was drawing to its close. The Czar's associates were beginning to realize it. Peter would walk about the streets of his new capital for hours at a time, alone and lost, gazing into vacancy, his face drawn and his hair standing up in the wind.

A few of his closest friends met at Menshikov's house and spoke with extreme frankness. His Most Serene Highness built up wonderful schemes: 'Catherine must succeed Peter. Then all I shall have to do is to obtain a divorce in order to marry her and become Czar of all the Russias.' Dreams in the wake of nightmares!

The Czar continued to wander about his capital, engrossed in his plans for the invasion and conquest of India. He stopped one day in front of the Admiralty, went into the admiral's office and said to him, 'I have decided to send a military and diplomatic mission to Madagascar.[1] That island will serve as a relay post on the way to India. Get me some frigates ready for the expedition.' A few frigates set sail but lost their rig on the high seas and had to return to St Petersburg. This setback deeply affected the Czar.

In the autumn of 1724, an abnormal rising of the level of the Neva threatened to flood Peter the Great's capital and a terrible storm broke over the city.

[1] *Histoire de la Russie* (Albert Mousset).

Peter walked by the Neva, watching the waves crash against the quay. He leapt into a fishing-boat and went as far as Kronstadt to observe the damage caused by the rising waters. On his way back he saw a boat capsize near 'Lakhta'. He hailed a launch and gave orders for the crew to be rescued. Suddenly he jumped into the launch, and for several hours he plunged into the icy water and brought the victims back on shore.[1]

Was he not aware that, at fifty-three years of age and sorely tried by illness as he was, such an experience might be fatal? Or had he chosen on this November day an occasion to pay for his errors and to obtain forgiveness for them? Did he imagine he could save his life's work by sacrificing himself in so heroic a manner? The fact remains that on returning to his palace he was gripped by a violent fever. His strength deserted him and he had to take to his bed. A few days later he made a last effort to dictate to his secretary a plan for a new expedition to the Arctic Ocean, to explore a different route by way of the Polar Circle which would lead to China and India. Peter wrote his last letter to Captain Behring inviting him to set sail in February in search of this route between Asia and America. The letter concluded with these words: 'Now that the Motherland is no longer in danger and is victorious on all fronts, the moment has come to consider new conquests, but this time in the realm of arts and sciences'.

This was his last message. In a few days he was once again in the grip of fever. With the coming of darkness there were heard the cries of a mortally stricken animal, and then a few throat-rattles. The name of Alyoshenka—the son who had been flogged to death in the Schlüsselburg fortress—was spoken several times in his delirium.

Peter motioned to Makarov to give him writing materials. Makarov put the paper down on the blanket and felt the Czar's burning hand. Propped up on one elbow Peter began to write: 'Give everything to ——'. He could not finish it. His head fell back on the pillow. He was dead.

It was five o'clock in the morning of January 28, 1725.

In the whole of this eventful reign the most surprising thing was the patience shown by the Russian people.

[1] According to an interpretation by Kurt Kersten: *Peter der Grosse*.

CHAPTER 28

CATHERINE I AND PETER II

Peter the Great had barely drawn his last breath, when the boyars congregated in the palace antechambers. They were of one mind in not wanting Catherine on the throne, which they were reserving for Alexis's son Peter, then ten years of age.

Menshikov, who had spent the night in the death-chamber and had fallen asleep in his armchair, was abruptly wakened by von Bassewitz, the Prince of Holstein-Gottorp's minister, who whispered to him, 'Wake up, Menshikov! There is not a minute to lose. If you do not act at once, we are due for the gallows and Catherine for the convent.' 'His Serene Highness the Prince of Izhora' awoke with a start and rubbed his eyes. What he saw was in no way reassuring. Surrounding the old marshal, Prince Repnin, the President of the Military Academy, were the Dolgorukis, the Saltykovs and the Golitzins. Outside, the people were calling for Peter, the son of Alexis, in application of the old Russian law of succession.

With no time to lose, Menshikov thrust his way through the crowd of boyars and dignitaries who were making very unpleasant observations on his presence. In the gallery he came upon his intimate friends, Count Apraxin and the crafty Ukrainian Metropolitan Feofan Prokopovich. 'Are you ready for action, Aleksasha?' asked Apraxin. 'Take Catherine and bring her on to the balcony. The Guard is ready.'

The arguing and bargaining of the 'great families' were interrupted by the roll of drums. The Guard, now assembled in the courtyard, yelled out, 'Give us our mother Catherine, the Czarina of all the Russias'. A thunder of *vivats* and cheers shook the palace: 'Long live Czarina Catherine I!' Menshikov, followed by von Bassewitz and Catherine, had just appeared on the balcony.

Prince Repnin, who had defeated the Swedes in Livonia, would have passed on to the balcony, but he was stopped by Buturlin, the commander of the Semenovsky regiment, who said, 'Where are you going, Prince? Do you not see the people cheering our Czarina?' Repnin answered, 'You mean Skavronskaya Skavrochuk, Buturlin?' Buturlin took the old marshal by the collar of his coat and shook him, saying in a hollow voice, 'Are you speaking of our beloved Empress, Repnin? Go back where you came from or I will smash your face in here and now.'[1] The yelling of the Guard smothered the drum-rolls: 'Long life to our Empress!'

Pastor Glück's serving-woman, the army sutler, Menshikov's mistress, Peter the Great's wife, with staring eyes and a barely perceptible smile on her lips, acknowledged the ovation with a movement of the head. Menshikov took the hand of the new Empress and led her to the great hall. There, before the dignitaries of the Empire, with a very low bow and in a firm voice which carried through the hall, Menshikov proclaimed, 'Mother of our native land, our Empress, I salute you in the name of our country'. Until the end of the century Peter the Great's Empire passed into the hands of Czarinas, who were chosen by the Guard.

Buturlin appeared in the presence of the dignitaries, wearing on his finger a gold ring set with diamonds, a present from the new Empress. He had come straight from Catherine's bedchamber. Catherine was happy to be rid of her terrible spouse and began her reign by drinking as much as the members of her late husband's famous Synod. Her court spent fabulous sums of money on vodka and champagne.

The Czarina instituted a Secret High Council, made up of Menshikov, Tolstoy, Ostermann, Apraxin, Golovkin and the young Duke of Schleswig-Holstein, which in fact ran the State. This 'Council' promulgated a few laws—such as the repeal of the State monopoly of oak coffins established by Peter the Great to punish the Old Believers who showed great enthusiasm for their oak coffins and had to pay 200 roubles for the privilege. The Academy of Sciences decided upon by Peter the Great was created. The lot of the *raskolniki* was made a little easier.

The Empress missed no opportunity to enjoy herself in her own way, arranging sumptuous banquets for the officers of the guard; the vodka flowed freely and, during these feasts, she would choose one or another of the officers of the guards regiments to spend the night with her.

Klyuchevsky relates that, during the morning of April 1, 1725, when the body of Peter the Great had been lying in the Peter and Paul Cathedral for hardly six weeks, the alarm-bell abruptly awakened the people of St Petersburg, who thought

[1] Klyuchevsky.

there was a fire or a Swedish invasion. Suddenly they saw Catherine leave the palace on the arm of a young captain of the guard, both of them drunk and laughing till the tears came. Catherine had played an April-fool trick on her people! The Russians of those times had no knowledge of 'April Fools' Day' and completely failed to appreciate their Czarina's joke.

Menshikov played a prominent part in the Secret Council but he had soon to give up the notion of becoming Catherine's husband and Czar of all the Russias. Catherine had reached the age when young men are preferable. With this woman who weighed nearly twenty stone indigestion was a chronic complaint. In 1727, she decided to undertake reducing treatment to lose the stoutness which prevented her dancing. Cardiac troubles ensued which gave Menshikov cause for anxiety. His Most Serene Highness decided that Catherine must not leave this world without making a will drawn up by him. But Catherine wished to proclaim her daughter Elizabeth Czarina. The nation acknowledged no other than the legitimate heir of Peter the Great, Pyotr Alexeyevich, Peter II.

It was at this moment that Vice-Chancellor Ostermann conceived the idea of harmonizing these two wishes: all that was needed was to bring about a marriage between the Czarevich Alexis and his own aunt, Elizabeth, the daughter of Peter the Great.

Ostermann, who was Peter's tutor, undertook to persuade the boy, who was entering his thirteenth year. Elizabeth was entering her seventeenth year and Ostermann had no difficulty in throwing her into her nephew's arms. Menshikov, in his displeasure, drove the wanton aunt from the Czarevich's quarters. The Prince of Izhora had his own plan, which was to marry the future Czar to his daughter. If he himself could not become Czar, he would become the Czar's father-in-law instead.

While Catherine, far from Moscow and the Kremlin, was gently subsiding in the arms of the young guards officers, there took place in the palace a great meeting, bringing together the members of the Secret High Council, the Senate, the Holy Synod, and the Officers of the Guard. This meeting chose Peter II as Catherine's successor. Menshikov came into Catherine's room and announced the news. 'I won't have it!' shouted Catherine. 'The throne shall go to Elizabeth. Peter will destroy the work of Petrus[1] so as to be avenged upon his father. You should under-

[1] Peter the Great was called Petrus by his intimates.

stand that better than anyone, Aleksasha.' 'Do not worry, Katya,' answered Menshikov. 'The boy is as tractable as his father. I will keep a hold on him and if necessary I will dispose of him as Petrus disposed of his son.'

Catherine looked contemptuously at Aleksasha. 'Do not compare yourself to him. Get out! You are nothing but dung. I am leaving the throne to Elizabeth.'

Menshikov paled, immediately left Catherine and went into secret conference with Ostermann and the Duke of Holstein-Gottorp's minister, von Bassewitz. Menshikov came out with a paper in his hand and went to fetch Elizabeth, whom he confined to her room after he had talked to her. Then he went back to Catherine. In the twilight of her bedroom she lay motionless. Shaken by the lively argument she had just had with Aleksasha, Catherine had taken a double dose of sedative and her heart had stopped beating while she was asleep. Menshikov gave a last glance at his former mistress, quietly closed the door behind him and went back to Elizabeth. 'Her Majesty,' he said, 'agrees to the text of the will which I have had drawn up. She asks you to sign it.' Elizabeth signed. She quite often did such things, for her mother had no head for documents.

The day after Catherine I died, May 7, 1727, the Czarina's 'will' was solemnly read:

1st successor: the Czarevich Peter.
2nd successor: Anna, Duchess of Holstein, daughter of Peter the Great.
3rd successor: the Czarevna Elizabeth.
4th successor: the Czarevna Nataliya, sister of Czarevich Peter.

After the coronation of Peter II, Menshikov took upon himself the title of Imperial Marshal and Generalissimo. The young Czar remained under the care of Ostermann, who prepared him for the idea of marrying Menshikov's daughter. Peter II, however, would hear no mention of any fiancée other than his aunt Elizabeth, who had also clung to her nephew. Peter was a fine example of the Russo-German type; the mingling of the Brunswick-Wolfenbüttel, Lopukhin and Naryshkin strains had produced a splendid result. Menshikov had to threaten Elizabeth with confinement in a convent to make her give up her nephew.

The young Czar soon began to feel his strength; the blood of Peter the Great flowed in his veins. He strenuously refused to follow his lessons with Ostermann, whom he called a 'scarecrow'. He also refused to sign the papers which Menshikov brought him. Peter II gathered around him young men of his own age; the young Prince Ivan Dolgoruki played the part of ataman. With his friends he meant to rule. Solemnly calling them together in one of the council-chambers, Peter II would apply to his 'Secret High Council', asking for opinions on one matter or another. Then he would note in his exercise-books the decisions taken and inform Menshikov and the real Secret High Council of them.

Menshikov realized the danger. He had the young Czar carried off to his own palace, where the first dignitary of the Empire and Generalissimo removed his Czar's breeches and administered the scourge, as he had already done in Peter the Great's reign when he beat the unfortunate Alexis, the father of Peter II.

A lackey witnessed this brutal scene, in which Menshikov, his face bloated and crimson with rage and drink, fixing on the child his deep-set eyes with swollen lids, roared at him, 'Learn, you brat, that I made your grandfather for what he was and destroyed your father for what he was not. In your family it was I who gave life and I who took it away when necessary.'

Menshikov did not stop there, with the allusion to the death of Alexis; while the valet was holding out a sponge and a bowl for Peter II to bathe his bleeding buttocks, Menshikov, who had had much to drink on that day, muttered something that so surprised the valet that he spoke of it for a long time afterwards and never forgot it. Menshikov claimed that all the accursed race of Naryshkins, Lopukhins and Skavronskys had shared his bed, without regard to their sex. This confession by Menshikov —always supposing that the valet who had been present the whole time did not lie—appears to confirm the view held by certain historians that Menshikov had sexual relations, not only with the dowager Czarina Nataliya, but with Peter I, whose homosexual instinct had been aroused by his 'Alexsasha'.[1] Poor Eudoxia's comforter and Catherine's lover, Menshikov appears to have been also Peter the Great's 'most intimate friend'.

After chastising the young Czar, Menshikov summoned the Metropolitan and ordered him to announce the engagement of the Czar and his sixteen-year-old daughter. But Peter II succeeded in making his escape, went back to Peterhof and called

[1] According to Alexis Tolstoy.

an urgent meeting of Prince Alexis Dolgoruki and a large number of high dignitaries of the Empire. Dolgoruki gave orders for
Menshikov to be arrested and brought to trial.

In September 1727 Menshikov, his titles forfeited and his
possessions and bank accounts taken from him, was banished to
the polar regions and sent to the little town of Berezov in the
extreme north-west of Siberia, where, in the company of his
daughter, Peter II's fiancée for a day, he died, abandoned by all,
after a period of the greatest distress when he was almost continually drunk.

But Prince Dolgoruki, who had become Peter II's confidential
adviser, tried soon after Menshikov's exile to repeat the stratagem which had failed the ex-generalissimo. Prince Dolgoruki
introduced his thirteen-year-old daughter Katya into the circle
of Peter's friends and gave sumptuous banquets in the young
people's honour. Following upon a banquet in which everyone
had imbibed an impressive amount of alcohol, Dolgoruki left
Katya alone with the Czar for a whole night. The next day,
Katya's brother, Ivan Dolgoruki, solemnly stated that honour
demanded that Peter should marry his sister, who had been com-
promised and disgraced for all time. This trick would have been
successful if, in the emergency, Ostermann, the avowed enemy
of the Dolgorukis, had not sent Elizabeth secretly to the palace.
The aunt found her young nephew to be in love with her but
undecided. She told him of her passion for him. It was but a step
from words to action; they had only to fall on the bed. Aunt and
nephew shut themselves up for several days in the 'Cupid and
Psyche' chamber of the Peterhof palace. Ostermann gave strict
orders that they were not to be disturbed.

Peter came out of the 'Cupid and Psyche' chamber to inform
Ostermann of his intention to marry his aunt Elizabeth in the
Kremlin. Moscow would once again become the capital of
Russia. St Petersburg would remain a commercial port. 'It is
time,' said Peter, 'to reconcile all the subjects of the Empire
which my grandfather gave us. Elizabeth and I will do that.'

The young Czar's decision was finally announced to the
people: 'Once again Moscow will be the capital of Russia and
the Kremlin the seat of the Empire created by Peter the Great.
The remains of Czarevich Alexis, furtively buried in the
Schlüsselburg fortress will be moved to the Kremlin and placed
in the Archangel'sk Cathedral together with those of Peter the
Great and Catherine I.'

An atmosphere of festivity pervaded the whole of Russia; the Muscovites spoke of a new era. The wearing of beards would be again permitted. Peter II evinced a firmness of character but was in no respect cruel, as his grandfather had been; German on his mother's side, he was a European, but he was also a Russian, respecting the traditions of old Russia, like his father whose attachment to those traditions cost him his life. The bells of Moscow found their voices again. The bearded *popes* told the peasants of the advent of the Saviour of Russia, 'Ivan Czarevich, sent by Jesus and the Holy Virgin' who had at last heard the nation's prayers. Ivan Czarevich! Is not that the oldest Russian legend, fed and preserved by the sufferings of a martyred people? The legend of a young and handsome Czar who, to save his people, went in quest of the 'Firebird' — Zhar-Ptitza — and brought it back to his country, which regained freedom and happiness.

Before leaving for Moscow, Peter spent a week with Elizabeth in the Peterhof Palace. On the day he left, everybody observed his radiant expression, in spite of the fatigue which nights and days of love had brought to his youthful face. During the journey he caught cold. When he arrived in Moscow with his suite of a hundred carriages, his body was afire with fever. The doctors diagnosed smallpox complicated by a malignant fever. In his delirium the Czar called, 'Lisa—Lisochka'.[1] The physicians took it in turns to stay at his bedside. All the time he called for his wife, his aunt, the daughter of his father's murderer. Masses were held in all the churches in Moscow and Russia; the people sang Mass and prayed, 'Long life to our Orthodox Christian Czar, Pyotr Alexeyevich!'

But fate refused Russia her Ivan-Czarevich. During the night of January 15, 1730, Peter II died of smallpox, in the Lefort Palace near Moscow. He was just fifteen.

[1] Diminutives of 'Elizabeth'.

CHAPTER 29

ANNA IVANOVNA

All the dignitaries of the Empire gathered in the Kremlin. The Secret High Council sat without intermission to find a successor to Peter II, whose death put an end to the male line of Peter the Great. There was certainly a will, which was discussed in the lobbies, but those in the know were well aware that it was a forgery.[1]

When Peter II died, the constitution of the Secret High Council was already very different from that of 1727, the year of Catherine I's death. The only representative of the new bureaucracy, created by Peter the Great, still to be found in the bosom of the Secret High Council was Chancellor Golovkin, supported by the two Princes Golitzin and the four Princes Dolgoruki. Vice-chancellor Ostermann still held a seat in the Council.

But the wind had changed; it was a wind of freedom which three years of the young Czar's rule had caused to blow fiercely upon the terrible *Preobrazhensky Prikaz*. The Russians had learnt to speak without fear.

The members of the Secret High Council decided, at a private meeting held in Prince Dolgoruki's palace, to take advantage of the situation and establish in Russia a monarchy on the lines of the western monarchies, with a council of the 'great families' to restrict the ever-dangerous autocracy of such an institution. But the Golitzin and Dolgoruki Princes, six in number, could not claim to represent all the Russian aristocratic families. There were at least twenty families with rights equal to those of the Dolgorukis and the Golitzins: such were the Tolstoys, the Apraxins, the Sheremetievs, the Buturlins, the Cherkasskys, the Trubetzkoys, the Saltykovs, the Odoevskys, the Baryatinskys, the Volkonskys and others.

At last, after interminable sessions in which there were

[1] It was Prince Alexis Dolgoruki who devised the 'will', and his son forged Peter II's signature. According to this 'will' the Czar passed on the throne of Russia to Katya Dolgoruki, his 'wife'. A *pope* named Tzibulsky testified to the authenticity of the marriage. When Dolgoruki showed the document to Golitzin, the latter advised him, 'Tear it up, Prince. It is a shameful thing for a Ryurikovich to become a forger.'

extremely lively exchanges, the Secret High Council agreed to propose as successor to Peter II the second daughter of Ivan IV (the feeble-minded), Anna, Duchess of Kurland and niece of Peter the Great.[1] Anna was considered to be a calm, thoughtful and thrifty woman; the *verkhovniki*[2] did not question her obedience to the régime, which was a sort of constitutional monarchy 'supported and restricted' by the 'great families'.

A messenger left the Kremlin for Mittau, the capital of Kurland, to convey to Anna the terms of her accession to the throne of Russia: she was to undertake to rule in accordance with the Secret High Council, never to make any decisions without the approval of the Council, to have all acts countersigned by the Council and not to bring into Russia her lover, a certain Buehren (Biron), a former groom at the court, an adventurer and embezzler from the prisons of Germany.

The *verkhovniki* were not ignorant of the fact that Anna was 'as poor as a church mouse'; Mittau, a sort of large village whose wooden houses were known for their 'Kurland bugs', did not provide Anna with enough money to permit her to dress in a manner befitting a duchess. The representative from the Kremlin promised that if she accepted the terms offered by the *verkhovniki* Anna would be given 8,000 roubles to prepare for her journey to Moscow. She requested 10,000 roubles, was given an assurance that the additional 2,000 roubles would be handed over on her arrival in Moscow and signed all that was asked of her.

The new Czarina, dressed in her new clothes, was in tears when she left Mittau; Biron and her pekinese were left in her 'Kurland slum'. Her lover, Biron, devoted most of his attention to the Duchess's dogs; she was particularly fond of the pekinese and never left them.

During the journey Anna learned that a part of the Russian nobility, hostile to the *verkhovniki*, were asking that she should not subscribe to the conditions which she had already accepted. Anna decided that she would first wait until the promised 2,000 roubles had been paid, before acting in one way or the other. Before she got to Moscow she stopped at the village of Vsekh-

---

[1] The Secret High Council had also put forward the candidature of Ivan's elder daughter, Catherine, wife of Charles Leopold the Duke of Mecklenburg-Schwerin. Golitzin rejected her candidature on the grounds that Ivan's daughter had an unbearable disposition and that her husband was mad.

[2] Members of the *Verkhovni Tayni Soviet* (Secret High Council).

svyatskoye. The Guard and a delegation of eminent persons came to greet her; the Senate Attorney, Yaguzhinsky, gave her the information she wanted concerning the state of mind of the capital.

The verkhovniki came to Vsekhsvyatskoye to conduct her to the Kremlin, but Anna refused to go until she had received the 2,000 roubles.

She was escorted to Moscow by the Guard. On the way, the officers told her, 'We Russians have long been accustomed to serve one monarch. Why should we be slaves to several tyrants like the verkhovniki?'[1]

Anna, who was as crafty as her mother, Prascovia Saltykov, was quick to understand the situation. When she arrived in the great hall of the Kremlin where she was to receive the verkhovniki, all the Muscovite nobility and the officers of the Guard, Anna Ivanovna took careful note of the comings and goings of the dignitaries, all the while fingering her talisman.[2]

In the evening, during a sumptuous banquet, Anna asked Golitzin for a 'small loan' of 5,000 roubles and he complied immediately. The feast was almost over, when the room was suddenly invaded by the officers of the Guard, one of whom knelt before Anna and cried, 'We desire an autocratic Czarina, we want no Secret High Council'.[3] Anna, whose reply had been prepared beforehand by Yaguzhinsky, the Senate Attorney, asked with the greatest candour imaginable,[4] 'What! Are you not conversant with the conditions imposed by the High Council? Have you not been consulted?' 'No, Your Majesty,' went on Major Skvortzov of the Semenovsky regiment. 'No. Those verkhovniki are traitors. If you so command, we will immediately place at your feet the miserable creatures' heads.' Anna turned to Prince Dolgoruki, who often presided over the debates of the verkhovniki, and said, 'You have been deceitful, then, Vassili Lukich!' Dolgoruki could not answer, for the officers of the Guard had already laid hands on him and were pushing him to the other end of the hall. To set the final touch to this comedy

---

[1] Klyuchevsky.

[2] According to the historian Waliszevsky, this talisman was one of Biron's fly-buttons. The Czarina was never without this talisman.

[3] Klyuchevsky.

[4] Anna was passionately fond of the theatre and the circus. Sometimes she even took male parts in the light-comedies performed in her 'palace' at Mittau. She had a distinct preference for the rôles of moneylenders and swindlers.

Anna picked up from the table the scroll containing the 'conditions' to which she had agreed in Mittau and, raising it up so that it could be clearly seen, she carefully tore it up—to the accompaniment of cheers from the Guard. In that way the constitutional monarchy was rejected, giving place once more to an autocratic régime.

Anna Ivanovna's reign began on February 25, 1730. The Czarina decided to thank the officers of the Guard who had raised her up from the position of an undistinguished Duchess of Kurland to that of Czarina of all the Russias. On April 4th Anna abstracted a large sum of money from the State Treasury and invited the officers, the Russian nobles and the diplomatic corps to a great banquet. At this feast the Czarina had at her side the groom Biron, whom she had brought from Mittau with her pack of pekinese and had installed in a small room adjoining her own quarters.

The festivities provided by Anna on this occasion were for a long time the talk of all Europe: hundreds of huge *ossetre* from the Caspian, *sterlets* and *belugas*, caviar, French and Italian wines, soup made from fish of the Volga, *selyanka*, countless hams from Siberia and the Ural regions, endless supplies of vodka and champagne, nothing was lacking. Everything contributed to the glorification of the new Czarina, 'skilled in thwarting the treacherous plots of a few great families animated by a desire to establish aristocratic oligarchy in Russia'. Anna displayed an extraordinary appetite, which drew certain comments that the Duchess of Kurland, accustomed to frugal fare in her capital of Mittau, was making up for lost time on good Russian food. The banquet was followed by a marvellous ball. The portly Anna opened the ball on the arm of Colonel Prassolov, so plainly showing the 'great families' of Russia that she would henceforth, in her rule, rely upon military strength. When the dancing was in full swing, women-servants from the Kremlin came and lined up before the Czarina, who called out, '*Nu, devki, poyte!*'

The girls sang; they sang without stopping, for hours, until they dropped, fainting, before the amused gaze of the Czarina.

Anna had no love for the Kremlin, every room and corridor of which reminded her of her unhappy childhood and her feeble-minded father, Ivan. She found pleasure only in Ismaylovskaya, a village near Moscow, where she had a small wooden Palace and her kennels, which took most of her time. She did not devote

herself to her subjects and affairs of State until she had attended
to her dogs and her lover. Biron went everywhere with her, to
the Kremlin, to St Petersburg or to Ismaylovskaya. It was he
who became the real ruler of Russia. He avoided appearing in
public and directed affairs from the wings. The Senate submitted
its authority to a sort of Czarina's 'Privy Council' or 'Council of
Ministers', the three members of which, Ostermann, Prince
Cherkassky and Golovkin, in fact constituted Biron's cabinet.
Klyuchevsky quotes from the files of this 'cabinet of ministers':
'Orders for hares from Tzna for the Czarina's kitchen. Payment
of bills for Anna's stockings and underclothing. Construction of
a urinal for the palace sentries. Investigation of the poisoning of
the Czarina's dog "Marko".'

In order to keep a watch upon her subjects, Anna instituted
the 'Secret Chancellery', which replaced the *Preobrazhensky
Prikaz* that had been dissolved by Peter II. This version of the
Oprichnina became a dreaded organization: a network of spies
covered the whole of Russia. The head of the secret Chancellery
received informers in person, admitting them by way of a secret
door in the Czarina's palace. It was clearly impossible to verify
the denunciations, which for the most part were 'inspired' or
'ordered' by the 'scoundrelly groom' Biron. One lost count of the
arrests and deportations, which decimated the 'great families'
and their most illustrious members. Torture-chambers were cun-
ningly equipped: certain instruments were imported from
Western Europe, in particular from the Iberian Peninsula. These
included the 'Spanish boots', the 'Nuremburg maiden' and the
'Pekin water-drops'. When all is said and done, these up-to-date
methods were only in the tradition established by Ivan the
Terrible and Peter the Great, and the secret Chancellery was but
a continuation of the *Oprichnina* and the *Fiskals*.

It was Biron who put into practice the principle of house
supervision and exile in Siberia. A special branch of the secret
Chancellery was concerned with the *ssylka*, but it was overwhelmed to such an extent by the number of cases, that it had
most of the time to give up its attempts to find out the names of
more than a quarter of those it deported; wholesale deportations
took place without reference to names. Here is a striking example
of the method employed: during a dinner given by a member
of the nobility, Krayevsky, someone unwisely referred to Biron
as a 'thief and son of a bitch'. This expression was reported by
one of the spies of the secret chancellery. Krayevsky was

arrested, together with his wife, his son and thirty other people identified by the agent as having been present at Krayevsky's dinner. They were all deported on the day they were arrested. The Chancellery files contain this laconic record: *Deportation of Ivan Krayevsky, his wife Avdotya, his son Stepan and 38 proche.* Thousands more were to follow.

During the whole of this period, called 'Bironovchina' by the people, there was seething discontent and rebellion was hatching. The Czarina knew all about this unrest and hoped to quell it with her police and the Guard. Peter the Great's Guard, composed entirely of Russians, did not seem safe to her. Far-sightedly she created a third regiment of the Guard, the Izmaylovsky, and placed in command of it a Baltic noble, von Loewenwolde, her chamberlain's brother. Anna controlled the composition of her regiment by obtaining recruits from the Ukraine, Esthonia and Kurland, and decided that the last vacancies should be filled by Russians. Anna had a weakness for Ukrainians, whom she considered to be less hostile to outsiders than the Russian. When, in 1733, members of the Holy Synod were to be appointed, she suggested that five Ukrainians, five Russians and one Belorussian should be taken.

Anna summoned the Metropolitan and informed him of her intention to alter the composition of the Holy Synod. The Metropolitan would have protested, but Anna cut him short. 'Never forget,' she said, 'that your Czarina is the head of the Orthodox Church. I have the right to determine the constitution of the Holy Synod and I mean to do so.'[1]

Biron became the object of a unanimous hatred which reached its climax about 1735. Several plots were exposed and even the army had its conspiracies. The Guard alone remained faithful to the Czarina and enabled her to govern with Biron and his two 'assistants', Count von Loewenwolde and the pekinese dog 'Eskimoss'.

The situation continued to deteriorate. So it was possible, according to Klyuchevsky, for the Polish diplomat Sapieha to tell the secretary of the French embassy, 'I believe that if this state of affairs continues the Russians will one day do with the Germans what they did with the Poles in the time of the spurious Dmitri: they will engage in a massacre'. 'Set your mind at rest,' replied the Frenchman, 'the Guard is on the Czarina's side and will put down all this disturbance.'

[1] According to Bantysh-Kamensky.

The Guard had much of the character of a constabulary; it took part in the collection of taxes, in the suppression of revolts, in the confiscation of the monastic lands and possessions, etc.

Klyuchevsky gives an admirable summing-up of Anna's reign: 'The reign of Anna Ivanovna is one of the darkest pages in our history, and the blackest spot on that dark page is the Czarina herself'.

Early widowhood had brought her to a completely amoral state; she was fond of intrigues, diplomatic and otherwise. The ignorant, ill-natured Duchess of Kurland, who, by the greatest fluke, became a Czarina, was a sadist.

Anna enjoyed listening for hours to her *karlitza* (midget) servant, a Kalmuk woman who told her weird stories of the old superstitions of the people of Astrakhan. This strange attachment which Anna felt towards her Kalmuk had a curious outcome, which became famous as *Her Majesty's Folly*. Anna decided to marry her Kalmuk to an old widower of the Russian aristocracy. She had an *ice house* built near the River Neva, a real ice palace. The Czarina herself took the newly-weds into this palace. Even members of the diplomatic corps were invited to this extraordinary performance, in which the *karlitza* was dressed as *Snegurotschka* and the bridegroom as *ded Moroz*.[1] Next day the couple were found dead in their Ice House. The Czarina gave orders for their bodies to be left there. This house, which was their tomb, melted in the spring and carried them away into the Neva.

Ostermann, who directed the foreign policy of this crazy reign, thought of himself as a 'diplomatic genius'. Like Anna, he had preposterous ideas. To please his Czarina he considered marrying the young Duchess Anne Leopoldovna of Mecklenburg, Anna's niece and heiress, to Prince William of England. The Earl of Newcastle, who did not for a moment consider the idea of this marriage at all seriously, let Ostermann's imagination have full rein and drew him into an anti-French coalition. France was then the enemy of Austria. Ostermann delightedly allowed himself to be led into this coalition. But the Earl of Newcastle's plans for the 'Great Nordic Coalition', to include Russia, England, Prussia, Denmark, Poland and the Netherlands, came to nothing, and Russia found herself alone with Austria in a war against France and Turkey. The Austrians asked for the military aid promised by Ostermann.

[1] The Snow Princess and Jack Frost.

Anna sent her friend Loewenwolde to Vienna in order to defer supplying this aid but the Austrians did not see it in that way, and they became insistent. In 1734, the Russian ambassador made a formal demand for Russian troops to be sent. Marshal Lacy, a Scot in the service of Russia, was given the order to set out. For the first time Muscovite troops were seen encamped alongside the Austrians near Heidelberg on the banks of the Rhine. The 'inspired diplomat', as Ostermann imagined himself, informed Cardinal Fleury, however, that Russia did not consider herself to be in a state of war with France.

At this time Russian troops entered Poland, dethroned Leszczynski in Danzig in 1734 and imposed on the Poles the Crown Prince of Saxony, who was crowned as Augustus III in Cracow. While giving assurances of his desire not to split up Poland, Ostermann ordered his ambassador in Warsaw to create a pro-Russian party and extract from the Diet a measure giving Kurland the right, as in the past, to proceed to the 'free election' of its Duke. This measure settled the fate of Kurland: the following year the Russian regiments, under orders from General von Bismarck,[1] entered Mittau. Biron was at once 'elected' reigning Duke and without losing time created Anna Ivanovna's second dog-kennel.

Ostermann, who was not a little proud of his 'success', prompted Anna to declare war on Turkey in 1735. He showed her the report from Vishnyakov, her ambassador in Constantinople: 'It will need but a battle, nay, the initial impact, for Turkey to be on the edge of the precipice. A few warships and the landing of 20,000 men will be enough to put the Sultan to flight and encourage revolt by Moldavia, Wallachia and Greece.'

The war began: unaided, one Turkish regiment overwhelmed the whole Persian army in alliance with Russia. Austria, which was to give support to Russia, did nothing, as usual, but stopped in Transylvania after occupying part of Bosnia, peopled with Serbians. The Russian commander-in-chief, who was to march on Azov, was prevented from doing so by Anna who, being frightened, decided to put an end with all possible speed to this war, so stupidly undertaken, and with this purpose in mind she convened the Congress of Nemirov, in which Russia, Austria and Turkey participated. This Congress quickly took on the semblance of a mad-house; the Austrians, Russia's allies, were 'astonished' at Russia's demands. Turkey, although at war with

[1] Ancestor of the 'Iron Chancellor'

Russia, supported her enemy when the Austrians put forward a claim to annex orthodox Wallachia.

The Spanish ambassador to Moscow, the Duke de Liria, wrote: 'The Congress now taking place in the Ukrainian town of Nemirov seems to have been arranged, not by Czarina Anna, but by her father, Ivan the Feeble-minded'.

The Congress produced no result, and the war went on. The Russian commander-in-chief, Field-Marshal Münnich, succeeded in occupying the whole of Crimea, including the Khan's capital Bakhchi-Saray, in beating the Turkish army at Stavuchany and making a triumphal entry into Iasi. He requested a 'personal contribution' of the prominent citizens, failing which he assured them that he would be unable to prevent his soldiers from setting fire to the town. Having transferred a very considerable sum of money to his 'personal account', Münnich called together the representatives of the leading Moldavian personalities. These representatives, who feared that they might be asked to make a further 'contribution', were relieved to hear the Russian Marshal speak of another matter. He asked them whether they preferred to be annexed by Russia or remain under Turkish domination. Happy that no further demands were to be made upon their purses, the Moldavian delegates acclaimed and proclaimed Anna as their 'Princess, deliverer of Moldavia'. Then they made off with all speed, declining the Marshal's invitation to dine. And while Münnich was sending a messenger to St Petersburg to announce to the Czarina her new title of Princess of Moldavia, Vienna was concluding a secret peace with Turkey to permit the Sultan to throw in all his forces against the Russians. Anna knew quite well that if this war, begun so victoriously, should end in disaster, the Russian nation would make her pay dearly for it. There was no madness in this madman's daughter! She asked France to mediate. De Villeneuve, the French ambassador to Constantinople, intervened with the declaration that he could secure peace only in the form of a cessation of hostilities. In vain did Ostermann offer him £15,000, the Order of St Andrew, a necklace and a ring set with large diamonds for his mistress; de Villeneuve held his ground and concluded the peace in the Versailles manner.[1]

As her only gain Russia obtained Azov, already twice conquered by the Cossacks and by Peter the Great, and lost by his successors. The fortified port of Taganrog had to be demolished.

[1] According to de Liria.

Russia could not fortify Azov or sail *merchant* ships in the Black Sea, the maritime trading being exclusively the right of the Turkish fleet. The districts around Azov were to be kept free of Russian occupation. After the Peace of Belgrade in 1739, all that Russia retained of her conquests was the steppes between the Dnepr and the lower Bug.

Versailles was therefore making Russia pay dearly for the presence of her troops on the Rhine and for the capture of Danzig. On account of her mediation France requested that the Marquis de la Chétardie, the *enfant terrible* of Versailles, should be accepted as French ambassador at St Petersburg. Versailles had realized that as long as the Ostermanns, the Birons and the Loewenwoldes remained in power, Russia would support the enemies of France.

In 1740 Anna fell seriously ill of an intestinal disorder. The Czarina, who wished to maintain her father's line of succession, summoned her niece Anna Leopoldovna and her husband Anton Ulrich, Prince of Brunswick-Lüneburg, and proclaimed their son, the three-months-old Ivan Antonovich, heir to the throne. She then appointed Biron as 'Regent until Ivan VI's majority'.

Biron confided to Anna, 'The Russians hate me and I am afraid'. 'Do not be afraid,' replied Anna. 'They are obedient. You have only to show them the *knout* occasionally and drink a glass of vodka with them.'

The Czarina died in September 1740. A posthumous *ukase* informed the nation of the name of the Regent. Münnich, displeased with the Peace of Belgrade, for which Ostermann was responsible, decided upon a *coup d'état*. He hated Biron, who had ordered the quartering of his friend, the minister Arthemy Volynsky, following an accusation of high treason. Münnich met the conspirators in the Military School, the School of Cadets, created by the Marshal. Major Semechnikov exclaimed, 'It is a shameful thing for us Russians to have a Biron for a Regent'. 'Yes, indeed,' added Captain Brovtzin. '*She* has made fools of us,' said a lieutenant of the Preobrazhensky regiment, 'but we can count ourselves fortunate. *She* could have entrusted the Regency to one of her quadrupeds instead of giving it to her favourite biped.'

Many Germans, including Colonel von Manstein-Levinsky,[1] were in the conspiracy.

Captain Brovtzin got together a large crowd of people on

[1] Ancestor of Marshal von Manstein-Levinsky of the Third Reich.

Vassilevsky Island and made a speech stigmatizing Biron's attitude. Cabinet minister Bestuzhev-Ryumin drew his sword and
made a vain attempt to arrest the Captain. Another of Biron's
ministers, Prince Cherkassy, came and arrested Pustoshkin,
Lieutenant-Colonel of the Guard and Münnich's delegate. But,
during the night of November 8, 1740, Münnich forestalled
Biron and a regiment of the Guard, by his orders, broke into the
new Regent's residence. The soldiers pulled the ex-groom from
his bed and scourged him in the presence of a crowd which
quickly collected to witness the whipping of the Regent of
Russia.

Biron was tried by the Supreme Court, sentenced to death,
pardoned and deported to Siberia. His vast fortune was confiscated.

On November 9, 1740, Anna Leopoldovna signed a manifesto
addressed to the Russian people, informing them of her appointment as Regent, which had been approved by the Holy Synod.
The Synod had, most certainly, merely accepted the *fait
accompli*.

Marshal Münnich, the German brought to Russia by Peter
the Great in 1721, was made Chancellor of the Empire. Münnich
was hostile towards Austria, at that time the enemy of France
and Prussia. The 'Most Christian Monarch's' ambassador, the
Marquis de la Chétardie, supported Münnich. On the other
hand, Anton Ulrich of Brunswick-Lüneburg, Anna Leopoldovna's husband, appointed Generalissimo of the Russian troops,
hated him. Under pressure from her husband, Anna dismissed
the anti-Austrian Münnich and replaced him by the agent of the
Viennese court, Ostermann. Thus, the Brunswick branch of the
Romanovs, represented on the throne by the Regent and her son
Ivan VI, carried on a pro-German policy.

Exasperated with the Germans, who continued to obstruct all
the roads to power, the ruling classes, as well as the common
people, turned their attention towards Elizabeth, Peter the
Great's daughter, the young Grand Duchess who had been
brought up in the French manner.

CHAPTER 30

THE ACCESSION OF ELIZABETH

The Marquis de la Chétardie, Cardinal Fleury's representative, was not inclined to wait with folded arms until Russian troops appeared once more on the Rhine. The French ambassador well understood that the Ostermann set, showing allegiance to Austria, would finally drag Russia into a war against France. The Marquis, an able and far-seeing diplomat, achieved his first diplomatic success—by removing Hungarian tokay from official Kremlin receptions. To do this he requested the Versailles court to send 50,000 bottles of champagne. Before long, champagne was prized as highly as vodka and took the place of tokay on the tables of the great Russian families. The enterprising Marquis next tackled the Romanov-Brunswick branch, which was following a violently anti-French and pro-Austrian policy.

The Russian economy was in a deplorable state. Taxes produced only a third of the revenue expected from them by the State. The Duke de Liria, one of the best observers of eighteenth-century Russia, wrote: 'Russia is coming to the end of her financial resources and is getting nowhere with her system of taxation. The despotic rule no longer recognizes the people's property rights and confiscates their profits on any pretext whatever.'

An excellent judge of the situation, the Marquis de la Chétardie, counting upon the venality of the Russian senior officials, asked Louis XV to make him a secret allocation of a very considerable fund amounting to some 5,000 roubles in pounds sterling and thalers, the favourite currencies of the St Petersburg dignitaries. The French Marquis had already chosen a successor to Ivan VI and his mother Anna Leopoldovna; this was Czarevna Elizabeth, second daughter of Peter the Great and Peter II's betrothed of a few months.

The Marquis carefully prepared the ground for action: he sent to St Petersburg an adventurer named Lestoc, who worked his spells upon the young Elizabeth. This Lestoc was a man of many gifts: he was a quack-doctor, surgeon, hypnotizer, mesmerist and spiritualist. This Huguenot from Havre succeeded

214

in winning Elizabeth's entire confidence. De la Chétardie also had Rambours, a French dancing master, sent to the Russian court, and he soon became a close friend of Peter the Great's daughter. There was also the *pope* Dubyansky, the Czarina's confessor, who was devoted to Elizabeth. The French ambassador himself took to Elizabeth, although she had 'the hips of a Polish cook' and 'did not care to wash very often'.[1] Elizabeth was passionately fond of everything French. The Marquis made the most of it and was assiduous in his loving attentions to her. She confided her troubles to him: how Anna Ivanovna would have put her into a convent if she did not agree to marry the Prince of Saxe-Coburg-Meiningen, alternative proposals which she avoided only by sharing Biron's bed. The Marquis listened patiently to all these confidences, and one evening he received a love-letter signed 'Lisochka'. Seeing this letter, Lestoc said to the Marquis, 'It is too late to draw back now. This night you must spend in the Grand Duchess's room!'[2]

The Marquis thus took an option on Elizabeth's accession to the Russian throne. At the same time, to Louis XV he was insistent that it was necessary to get Sweden and Turkey to attack Russia. A defeat of the Russian armies would facilitate the *coup d'état*. The Marquis was greatly helped in the further-ance of his plans by an unforeseen diplomatic incident. Zinkler, a Swedish diplomat, had been carried off to Poland by Russian officers who thought he was the bearer of secret papers relating to the Turco-Swedish alliance. As the Russian government denied Sweden any enlightenment of this incident, Sweden declared war on Russia on July 28, 1741.

A proclamation from the Swedish generalissimo to the 'brave Russian soldiers from Finland' stated that 'the Swedish army had crossed the frontier to avenge the wrongs done to their King by *German* ministers in control of Russia and to *liberate the Russian nation* from a cruel, intolerable yoke'. This proclama-tion had an unexpected outcome: part of the Russian pay corps from Viborg mutinied. Only General Keith's coolness and presence of mind enabled the revolt to be stamped out before it could spread.

The archives of the secret Chancellery gave a detailed descrip-tion of the state of mind of the Guard and the populace: 'The

---

[1] Waliszewski: *The Last of the Romanovs*, Paris, 1902.

[2] Since the time of Peter the Great, daughters of the Czars were known as 'Grand Duchesses', not 'Czarevinas'.

soldiers, who had sworn allegiance to Czar Ivan VI (aged eighteen months), argued the matter at some length. A corporal of the Guard cried, "Is it not a shameful thing that Elizabeth, the daughter of Peter the Great, is not allowed to ascend the throne?" All shared his indignation.'

In the offices of the Ladoga canal builders, where the manifesto appointing Ivan VI had just been posted, the clerks refused to take the oath, saying, 'To the devil with Ivan VI! We want Elisaveta Petrovna!'

Towards the end of November 1741, pamphlets compiled by the Marquis de la Chétardie and distributed by his agents appeared in St Petersburg. They accused Ostermann of being responsible for the Russo-Swedish war and of allowing himself to be bought over by Austria. The Guard began to show excitement. Prince Meshchersky advised Ostermann to expel the Marquis but the doyen of the diplomatic corps did not agree. 'To expel an ambassador,' he said, 'solid proof is necessary'. While Count Ostermann was seeking such essential evidence, Lestoc and the French Marquis's agents lost no time. They purchased the complicity of some dozens of the officers of the Guard, in particular Vorontsov, Shuvalov and Razumovsky, provoked the regiments to action and appeared before Elizabeth, asking her to head the Guard and proclaim herself Czarina of all the Russias. Elizabeth was hesitant, and Lestoc was obliged to carry her off to the barracks of the Preobrazhensky and Semenovsky regiments on the night of November 24, 1741. Elizabeth was there proclaimed Empress by the officers, whom the Marquis de la Chétardie had previously plied with large quantities of champagne. Elizabeth undertook to pardon all those who had been sentenced to death and in the middle of the night made her way to the palace of the Regent and her son.

Elizabeth burst suddenly into Anna Leopoldovna's bedroom. 'Get up, little sister!' she said. The Regent was not alone; her friend, Yulia Mengden, was her bedfellow. Roused to indignation by this discovery, Elizabeth slapped the Regent's 'mistress' in the face, went into the room occupied by the little eighteen-months-old Czar and kissed him. She then dispatched the Guard to arrest Duke Anton of Brunswick-Lüneburg, the Generalissimo of the Russian armies. The Duke had not slept at the palace since his wife's association with Yulia Mengden but occupied a camp-bed at the Ministry of War. It was there that his arrest took place.

The night of November 24th was filled with cheering. Elizabeth, accompanied by officers of the Guard, Vorontsov, Shuvalov, Razumovsky and her 'surgeon' Lestoc, rode through the capital in her carriage, to the acclamations of the crowd.

The next day, that of Elizabeth's accession, there was very nearly a *pogrom* of the Germans in the town. The crowd, inflamed by the pamphlets, invaded the homes of the senior German officials and dragged them into the street to lynch them. Elizabeth had to intervene in person. 'My father,' she said, 'invited the Germans here in the service of Russia. Many have served us loyally. I will give them protection.'

Ostermann, Loewenwolde and Münnich, as well as Golovkin and von Bismarck, were arrested the day after the *coup d'état*. Yielding to Lestoc's entreaties, Elizabeth, five days later, published a manifesto denouncing Ostermann's crimes. She accused him of having, among other things, had a hand in the affair of Catherine I's will. A court of justice, made up of two generals and three prominent personages, sentenced Ostermann to be quartered, but Elizabeth, faithful to her vow never to inflict the death penalty, pardoned him. Ostermann was sent to Berezov in Siberia, to the same town where Aleksasha Menshikov had died. Münnich and Golovkin were pardoned just as they were mounting the scaffold, and they also were sent to Siberia.

The Holy Synod, which bowed so obsequiously before Ostermann when he was the all-powerful Chancellor to Anna Ivanovna and Anna Leopoldovna, ordered Masses to be said in celebration of the 'departure to Siberia of that servant of Satan, Andryushka Ostermann'.

INTERLUDE IN
ST PETERSBURG

1741-1918

Elizabeth was to reign for twenty years. The first thing she did was to be crowned in the Uspenie Cathedral in the Kremlin, and the second was to desert the old capital for St Petersburg. Since 1712 Moscow had become the second capital, and this permitted the 'shaven' and the 'bearded' to live in reconciliation several hundred miles apart. St Petersburg, thirty-eight years after its founding by Peter the Great, presented no very delightful aspect in the early days of the reign. Let the facts be judged from the account given by Algerotti, a diplomat of that time: 'On entering St Petersburg, you find that the town is less beautiful than you thought when you viewed it from a distance. St Petersburg is situated on the banks of a great river and is made up of several islands. The site which it occupies is a spongy marsh and is surrounded by a vast, sinister forest. The materials which have gone into its construction are of no great value and the design of the houses is that neither of an Inigo Jones nor of a Palladio. The mixed architectural styles combine French, Italian and Dutch elements. The last-named usually predominate and it is not surprising; it was not without effect that Peter the Great's studies took him first to Holland. It was at Saardam that this new Promethus found the flame with which he inspired his nation. It was in memory of the days spent in Holland that he planted along the streets those long rows of trees which are to be seen everywhere in St Petersburg and dug the canals which certainly have not the same usefulness as those in Amsterdam!

The great imperial figures of Russia must surely have come and settled here with reluctance, for Moscow and the Kremlin will, for the Russians, always remain the real hub of the country. Only the premature death of Peter II prevented a permanent return to Moscow. The people think that Moscow will not become the capital of Russia until a 'real national government' concerns itself with its interests.

218

To return to St Petersburg, it is very obvious that the palaces of the Russian imperial grandees, situated on the banks of the Neva, were built as a result of obedience and fear rather than as a matter of choice. The walls are already full of cracks, and one wonders why they have not fallen down. Concerning this, a Russian diplomat recently remarked to me that everywhere else ruins were produced naturally but here in St Petersburg they were built!

Despite the diplomat Algerotti's tart observations, St Petersburg soon became the fabulous 'Palmyra of the North' admiringly spoken of in all the courts of Europe. Under Elizabeth were founded the Academy of Fine Arts (1757) and the first Russian theatre (1756), and the building of the Academy of Sciences was completed. Wonderful palaces sprang up along the Neva and, by 1750, St Petersburg already had nearly a hundred thousand inhabitants. The French language and literature made a deep penetration into the upper layers of St Petersburg society. Many foreign scholars arrived in the new capital on the Neva to attend the lectures given by one of the most eminent physicians of the eighteenth century, M. V. Lomonossov.[1] Besides the architects Shevakinsky and Korobov, who built wonderful palaces such as the Sheremetiev Palace, the Italian Rastrelli constructed the Winter Palace, the Smolny Monastery, the Stroganov Palace, the Vorontz Palace and many other architectural masterpieces.

In the building of her sumptuous Winter Palace, Elizabeth asked that the cost should not be considered. Quite clearly, no expense was spared. But the Kremlin was, until March 1918, to be very much what Versailles became on the evening of October 6, 1789—a soulless monument, a historical monument and an imperial tomb, the Czars' Saint-Denis.

With the death of Elizabeth on December 25, 1761, and the weakling Peter III's accession to the throne which Catherine the Great was soon to occupy, the French Revolution was near at hand. The world was in commotion. Through the interplay of coalitions, imperial wars were often to mingle Russian history with that of France, and even, if the Kremlin remained deserted, the course of history beyond the Niemen must be briefly indicated without pleasant indulgence in anecdote. The Kremlin was to be visited, and prayers said in its cathedrals, but to the nostalgic Russians, who had so often cursed it, it became the symbol of what had been, more lamented every day as it receded

[1] Encyclopedist, scholar, physician-chemist (1711-65).

into the past. The long interlude of 177 years—nearly two centuries—was none the less fascinating to all the historians in the
world. Spiders wove their webs on the gilded ceilings of the
abandoned Kremlin, and just as untiringly wove them about
people on the move. Let us take a bird's-eye view of Russian
history during this interlude.

'This time,' says M. Alfred Fichelle,[1] 'with Elizabeth's
accession, a real Russian was to rule over Russia.' Brought up in
the German manner, the Czarina had also come under French
influences, even in the privacy of her bedchamber, and this
influence coloured her vocabulary in her rôle of lover. She continued the work begun by her father. She did a great deal for the
nobility and nothing for the serfs. She was liberal with her
affections—but she never permitted affairs of State to become
mixed up with her passionate love-affairs. On the whole, her
reign was a happy one, and Russia is indebted to her for having
named as her successor the sickly Peter, her sister Anna
Petrovna's son, whom she married in 1745 to Sophia of Anhalt-
Zerbst. Sophia became a convert to the Orthodox Church and
took the name of Catherine. Peter III reigned for six months,
from December 1761 until his abdication on June 28, 1762. In
that brief space of time he had tried, as they say, to 'reverse
steam'; he had shown himself to be anti-Russian, anti-Orthodox
and so far anti-clerical as to fill his coffers with Church money.
It was beyond all reason. The helpless Senate, then in abeyance,
rose against him with the backing of the Russian Church,
naturally, and the support of the Guard, which was loyal to
Catherine. Before the end of 1762, the bells of St Peter and Paul
tolled the knell above his coffin. The official record states that he
had succumbed to an attack of colic combined with a cerebral
hemorrhage. It was rather overdone. With less consideration,
gossip had it that his loving wife Catherine had simply had him
murdered. St Petersburg knew all about the methods practised
in the Kremlin for centuries.

Too many eighteenth-century French writers, from Diderot
to d'Alembert, have praised Catherine's enlightened and rather
generous hospitality for it to be necessary to stress it here. To the
French encyclopedists, who were sometimes short-sighted and
whose motives were not always disinterested, Catherine was the
symbol of intelligent royalty in comparison with some of the

[1] *Histoire Universelle*, III, Encyclopédie de la Pléiade.

unfortunate decisions taken by Versailles. At the bottom of their hearts the Russians did not think so highly of her.

Catherine's reign was long, lasting until 1796 — after the French Revolution. She was in a position to judge how far the 'enlightened' ideas dear to her French friends could lead. Her dream of turning her Empire into a powerful State was almost realized. Sympathetic towards the nobility and harsh in her attitude to the common people, in July 1774 she had to put down a large-scale revolt led by the Cossack Pugachev, who posed as Peter III. She did it mercilessly, and horrible were the convoys on the road to Siberia. Having placed her friend Stanislas Ponyatowski, who was perhaps her lover also, on the throne of Poland, she was attacked by the Turks in 1768. The struggle was fierce and was marked by appreciable success: she gained an opening to the Black Sea, Azov became definitely Russian in 1783. The Russo-Turkish war was resumed in 1787. The Peace of Iasi (1791) merely confirmed the facts established in 1783. The Poles having, in her opinion, shown too much enthusiasm for the French Revolution, even to the point of adopting the Constitution in 1791, Catherine with the help of Prussia cut off a good slice of Poland. It must be admitted that she could die happy and proud of the results obtained, when death came suddenly upon her on November 5, 1796, while she was sitting on her chamber-pot. The greatest Russian poet, Pushkin, has summed up Catherine's reign as follows:

> Endeavouring to make herself attractive to Zubov
> The old woman lived a gay life, not to say a wanton one.
> She drafted the 'Instruction' and also burnt fleets.
> She came to her end on a chamber-pot.
> Since then darkness has covered the face of Russia.
> Russia, Oh! Russia, unhappy land!
> When Catherine squatted
> Your glory departed.

For saying much less than this in his *Journey from St Petersburg to Moscow*, Radishchev had taken the road to Siberia—on the enlightened orders of the Czarina.

Paul I's reign was wild and brief. From the ringing of the Kremlin bells on the occasion of his anointing, until 1801, five years later, St Petersburg experienced storms almost as violent as those which the Kremlin had known under Ivan the Terrible.

It is probably true that just before she died Catherine had advised Alexander quite simply to get rid of his father, Paul, the heir to the throne, and that as a dutiful son he had told him everything. It is understood that Paul had a pack of Great Danes sleeping at the foot of his bed and that he slept with loaded pistols under his pillow. The memory of Peter III's 'colic' haunted him. On the throne, his morbid condition made him odious. Ruinously obliging to his few favourites, harsh towards the soldiers he intended to lead as Frederick the Great had done, unreliable, showing little concern for the army corps sent to meet Bonaparte, the irresistible conqueror in Italy, he succeeded in making everyone hate him; and on the night of March 11, 1801, a conspiracy of officers under the leadership of Bennigsen put an end to this crazy reign by assassination. At the time of the Czar's murder, Count Pahlen, the ringleader of the plot, went into Alexander's room. The latter, who was aware of the events that had taken place that tragic night, was in full uniform and weeping in the arms of his wife Elizabeth. Pahlen shook him and said, 'Enough of this acting the child. Come, it is time to rule.'[1] Alexander did not have to be told twice.

With the dawn that followed this murder, in which Alexander was involved, by a coincidence which the chancelleries did not find very strange, an English squadron was entering the Sound. There is not always an iron curtain in the way of liberal ideas, and those of the French Revolution, although in the garb of the First Consul ('Déjà Napoléon perçait sous Bonaparte'[2]) were winging their way from steeple to steeple across an astonished Europe to the gilded domes of the Kremlin.

In September and October, 1801, on the occasion of the coronation, there was a semblance of activity in the Kremlin. Alexander and his wife Elizabeth were staying in the rooms that had been occupied by Nataliya Naryshkin, Peter the Great's mother.

Alexander was twenty-four. There was dancing in the old *terems*, there was much drinking, there was flirting in the secluded gardens adjoining the cathedrals. The Czar lost no time in seducing young Mme Kussox, *née* Helen Tukhashevsky (a name which will be heard again later), and he also made the acquaintance of Maria Antonovna Naryshkin, who was for a

[1] Constantin de Grunwald: *L'Assassinat de Paul Ier* Hachette.

[2] 'Already the Emperor Napoleon was showing through the Bonaparte": Victor Hugo.

long time to be his official mistress. She was distantly related to Marie Walevska. Alexander then returned with his court to St Petersburg to deal with more serious matters. Educated to the ideas of the century, as they say, Alexander had liberal sentiments, but not excessively. He dreamed of an English-style constitution with which he would have liked to incorporate a few ideas from France without, however, ceasing to be an autocrat. That was an objective difficult of realization and in trying to achieve it he was aided by three of his counsellors, Stroganov, Czartorysky and Novosiltsev. He quickly accorded his ministers a greater degree of liberty, left the rein slack on the Senate—but not for long—and, while still imposing a considerable number of restrictions upon them, he authorized landlords to free their serfs. Hardly fifty thousand of those serfs were able to obtain their liberty. At that time Alexander had a counsellor, a *pope's* son, Speransky, who might have done great things. He was the author of a liberal constitution, an Imperial Council consisting of eminent people and local representation (the Three Orders). Alexander kept merely the Council, and that he convened on one occasion only, in January 1810.

He who was to become 'his dear brother Napoleon' was stirring up Europe. The English squadron's entry into the Sound was followed by talks, the result of which was that in 1805 Alexander found himself again by the side of England, Austria, Naples and Sweden, and saw the sun set over Austerlitz on December 2, 1805. In the political arena Alexander's Russia was *a sombra*.

With the help of Prussia he decided to have his turn in 1806. Great Frederick was dead, and Prussia was beaten in turn at Jena and Auerstedt. Napoleon's armies were at the Russian frontier. Despite the communiqués which appeared in the Paris *Moniteur*, the Battle of Eylau (February 1807) was, in fact, indecisive, although Napoleon probably won it on points; but at Friedland, on June 14, 1807, he was victorious. Alexander took fright and, to the surprise of his advisers, his former allies and the whole of Europe, he reversed his alliances.

It was not now a question of meagre Polish fare; Alexander and Napoleon felt their appetite was keen enough for them to tear hungrily at Europe and the East. Running in advance of their armies, their dreams reached out as far as India. More than once, on St Helena, Napoleon's thoughts turned back to his great dream. Did he believe in it? No doubt he did, for there

was a time when Alexander, led on by the Mediterranean story-
teller, also believed it—on the Tilsit raft—but not for long. It
became a pretty picture in retrospect. Between Tilsit and Erfurt
(September-October 1808) what was left to the Summer Palace
and Saint-Cloud of those imposing schemes for the capture of
Constantinople (the great Russian dream) and the conquest of
India (the great Napoleonic dream after the Egyptian expedition) (?). Not very much. England remained under arms and on
the watch. After his temporary defeat the Czar was raising his
head again. Spain was the imperial Achilles heel, and Talleyrand
was afraid. When the Prince of Benevento was afraid, he resorted
to treachery; and he was often afraid. From the time of Erfurt
onwards, there was on the banks of the Neva less dreaming
about Constantinople, and India lay dormant in the portfolios of
the imperial army's geographical service. Once again Alexander
was playing the turncoat towards Maria Naryshkin, the beautiful Pole. And yet, notwithstanding the official records, Napoleon
and the Czar were related 'on the wrong side of the blanket'.
The 'right side' had availed so little throughout the centuries,
although on the famous raft Napoleon had asked his 'great
friend' for the hand of his sister, the Grand Duchess Catherine,
in marriage. Alexander, who was slightly deaf, pretended not
to hear, and Napoleon did not repeat his offer. Moreover,
Josephine still reigned in Paris. But that did not present a major
obstacle.

'I predict war against any power that refuses the Emperor's
proposal of marriage,' Cambarcérès confided to Talleyrand.
'Insolence will be paid for!' said Napoleon at a later date to
Caulaincourt, his ambassador to St Petersburg. In 1810 he
declared, 'This Austrian marriage has definitely put me on bad
terms with Alexander. He has not forgiven me for not marrying
his sister!' It is difficult indeed to write history in the presence
of eye-witnesses.

St Petersburg did not look favourably upon these interviews;
the old, deep-rooted politics condemned them. It was not even a
question of resuscitating Poland in order to satisfy the 'ogre's'
appetite; and everybody knows that, in the arms of Marie
Walevska, he had promised that. Furthermore, there had been
Marie-Louise, but for him the map of Europe was unchanged.
Alexander was watching. Napoleon was making his preparations. Napoleon just needed time to have the King of Rome
privately baptized, before the Grande Armée was on the march,

with eyes looking steadfastly towards the east. War broke out
on June 23, 1812.

At first, everything happened as if there were no Russian
army. The Niemen was crossed and the march went on until,
without a shot being fired, Vilno was taken, on June 26. But
already the Grand Armée was finding the provisioning arrangements inadequate and the staff was showing signs of anxiety.
Would there be a lack of bread? Alexander was not ready. He
was thinking of peace and he sent Balashov as emissary to the
Emperor's headquarters in Vilno with the message, 'Let the
imperial troops withdraw to the other side of the Niemen and
there will be serious talk of peace'. That would have meant loss
of face for Napoleon. He could not make up his mind to it, yet
declared that he was 'keeping his ears open to any suggestions of
peace'. With clumsy irony he asked Balashov, 'To get to Moscow,
what is the best road to take?' 'There are several,' was the
answer. 'Charles XII went by way of Poltava.' (That led to
disaster, as one knows.)[1]

Barclay de Tolly retreated at Drissa and Bagration gave way
before Davout at Mokhilev. There was no decisive battle, but a
continuous harassing and fleeing phantoms. Already, by the end
of July, the Grand Armée, exhausted by its fruitless advance,
was showing signs of weakness. There were hardly any dead, but
stragglers in plenty.

Before Smolensk on August 16th Napoleon thought he had
his chance; the fighting was fierce, but the Russians set fire to
the town and withdrew. The road to Moscow was a long one!
For the time being, that to St Petersburg was even longer. But
for Napoleon, Moscow was a symbol, 'the moral and religious
centre, the witness to history'.

Bagration criticized Barclay's perpetual retreats. 'Barclay,' he
told Alexander, 'is leading our guests straight to Moscow.'
Alexander recalled Marshal Kutuzov, the 'old fox from the
North', whose only failing in the eyes of some people was that
he was over-fond of the champagne bottle. It was he who, on
September 6th and 7th, at the approaches to the old capital,
engaged in that murderous battle called Moskova by the French
and Borodino by the Russians. The Moskva, in fact, was not concerned in it, for the engagement took place on the banks of the
Kolocha, one of its tributaries. But the name is of no importance.
Napoleon was a sick man and relaxed his vigilance. The battle

[1] Emile Tersen: *Napoléon*, Club Français du Livre, 1959.

H

was a series of terrible head-on clashes between army corps. The cost to the French was 50,000 casualties, including fifty generals; to the Russians, 58,000 men. The Imperial Guard was held in reserve and Kutuzov made an orderly retreat. The road to the Kremlin was open. But at what a price! At the head of his horsemen Murat entered Moscow on September 14th. The Kremlin was again to live through brief times of tragedy.

In *War and Peace*, Tolstoy describes the entry into Moscow. Napoleon, sitting in a chair in the Salute Hills, was waiting for the boyars to bring him the keys of the capital, as had been done in other towns which he had captured. But the boyars did not come. Moscow was deserted. The 10,000 inhabitants who remained raided the brandy stores. A French officer wrote to his wife, 'This damned town of Moscow with its Kremlin! You go looking for boyars and you find nothing but drunkards, Russian and French!'

Napoleon spent the night of his arrival in Moscow in the vicinity of the Drogomilovsky Gate and the next day he set up his headquarters in the Kremlin. When he reached the famous citadel, he exclaimed, 'At last I am in Moscow, at last in the Kremlin!' It was a brief moment of satisfaction, the only one that destiny vouchsafed to him during the Russian campaign. That night a sinister red glow lit up the sky. The whole town, or almost all of it, was burning; the flames sprang up in fifty different places at once. From the suburb of Pokrovka to Arbat, alone the main roads, Tverskaya, Nikitskaya and Povarskaya, it was one line of fire.

Who was responsible for this conflagration? French historians have accused Rostopshin, the governor-general of Moscow; the Russian staff laid the blame on the Marquis de Chambray, acting on Napoleon's orders. Tolstoy claimed that the fire was caused by thousands of marauding soldiers, who, in order to light their way into the houses which they were looting, had taken improvised torches with them. Russian testimony refers to the agents left by Rostopshin to set fire to the town.[1] There also exists indirect evidence from the British General Wilson, who was his country's representative with the Russian command and who witnessed the burning of the Rostopshin Palace at Voronovo near Moscow, an act which was the work of Rostopshin's own hand.

For a long time Napoleon watched the fire through the win-

[1] Serge Glinka and Dmitri Buturlin.

dows of the palace in the Kremlin and then exclaimed, 'What a terrible sight! What an extraordinary revolution! What men they are! They are Scythians!'

The fire soon reached the Kremlin. In the courtyard of the palace occupied by Napoleon the French grenadiers shot the Russian police agents whom they suspected of being responsible for the burning. Flames were springing up all around. It was too late to leave for the Petrovsky Palace in the suburbs. Accompanied by his marshals, Napoleon ran down the great staircase and dashed through the smoke in an attempt to reach the Spassky Gate. But there, also, flames were rising on all sides. They had to make use of the underground passage of the Kremlin, that one which the boyars had used in 1682 to escape the wrath of the *streltzi*. That night the Emperor slept in Petrovskoye Castle. On September 18th there was heavy rain in Moscow and the fire was put out. The following day the Emperor returned to the Kremlin and sent for the Russian State archives dealing with the Pugachev revolt. Closeted with Lesseps, the French consul in Moscow, and with Caulaincourt, Napoleon put the question to them, 'Suppose Pugachev's exploit was repeated? What if the peasants were incited to rebellion and the Cossacks massed against the Czar?' Lesseps replied, 'For that we should need a false Dmitri, and we haven't one'.

The Emperor summoned to the Kremlin Mme Aubert-Chalmais, a Frenchwoman who had lived long in Moscow. She dissuaded him from 'playing the Pugachev card'.

About October 15th Napoleon called his marshals together in the Kremlin and formed a Grand Council of War. He proposed to burn what was left of Moscow, to blow up the Kremlin and march on St Petersburg, where MacDonald would join forces with the Grand Armée.[1] But he gave up the idea in the face of opposition from his marshals. Later, when in exile on St Helena, he wrote, 'It was the same distance from Moscow to St Petersburg as from Smolensk to Moscow. I thought it better to go and spend the winter in Smolensk and leave the attack on St Petersburg until the spring.'

The autumn of the year 1812 was exceptionally mild, a rare occurrence in those parts. The golden leaves from the trees in the Kremlin lay thick in the alley-ways, and Napoleon was strolling in front of St Basil's Cathedral, which he called 'the mosque'. He turned to Caulaincourt and said, 'Autumn in

[1] Jean Jacoby; *Napoléon en Russie*.

Moscow is as mild as in Paris. In this season the Kremlin is just like Fontainbleau.' With the ghost of a smile he added, 'So this is a sample of that terrible Russian winter with which M. de Caulaincourt frightens children!' And he went on in his high-pitched voice, 'Travellers from afar can lie with impunity'.

Marshal Berthier came to see the Emperor and urged that they should leave Moscow before the rainy season set in. It was high time to withdraw to winter quarters; and, besides, strong concentrations of Cossacks had been observed near Kaluga and Tarutino. The Emperor's face clouded and he flung out at Berthier, 'So you want to go to Grosbois to see the Visconti?' (She was Berthier's mistress.)

On the night of October 17th Kutuzov's troops attacked, overthrew Murat, deflected him to his left and cut off his retreat. It was only with difficulty that Murat regained the initiative and restored the situation.

As soon as Murat's report of this battle was received, Napoleon gave orders to leave Moscow for Kaluga, but Kutuzov engaged him at Malo-Yaroslavetz and threw him back on the Smolensk road.

The retreat of the Grand Armée was beginning. Snow was now falling and, squelching in the mud and cut off from their supply bases, harassed day and night by Kutuzov, Bagration's cavalry and the Cossacks of Davidov and Platov, Napoleon's soldiers fled. Napoleon's forces, which numbered more than half a million men to begin with, were reduced to no more than 60,000 when they crossed the Beresina; only 30,000 reached France. The victorious Kutuzov besought Alexander to halt at the Niemen, for the 'final crushing of Napoleon would, in the long run, only help England and Russia's enemies'. The Czar replied, 'He and I cannot both be masters'. There was already the threat to co-existence.

Pillaged, blackened, lifeless, the Kremlin was silent once more.

Alexander believed in Providence; he was the man destined 'to war against the Antichrist'. 'The Moscow fire,' he said, 'lit up my soul and filled my heart with an ardent faith such as I had never known before. I do not heed the advice of Kutuzov and the others, who are weary of war and are in a hurry to build up the ruins and sow the scorched earth.' In 1814, flattered by some and laughed at by others, he entered Paris and proclaimed the Holy Alliance, which was to unite sovereigns and peoples!

A pleasant dream which, like all dreams, was quickly dispelled by the wind of reality and conflicting interests. By 1816 Russia was alone again, in the grip of a monarch who was as autocratic as his predecessors and whose declared liberalism was merely produce for export. He pretended not to know that around him, roused no doubt by their contact with Europe, officers were thinking of liberty. One could see little sign of liberty in Russia when he died at Taganrog in the Crimea on December 1, 1825. His dreaded adversary had gone to his grave four years earlier.

Here and there secret societies became active: The True Sons of the Motherland, The Welfare Union, The Northern Society, The Southern Society, all of whose aims had two points in common: a constitutional government and an end to serfdom. The Union for the Common Good went so far as to approve the French Republic.

It was this uneasy Russia that, on Alexander's death, Nicholas offered to his brother Constantine, who was then in Warsaw, happy in his morganatic marriage. After some delay, Constantine declined the throne. Without waiting for his reply, the Societies went into action. Once more the throne was shaken by a *coup d'état*, but Nicholas was alert, and the famous plot of December 14, 1825, ended in bloodshed in St Petersburg and even further away in Russia, where a regiment had rebelled. As a lesson to others, five men were hanged and more than 150 of the conspirators were sent on the customary road to Siberia.

Nicholas I had every intention of ruling, and he did so for thirty years, with varying success and ever-increasing power. It was in his reign that, with respect to Pushkin and the *Huntsman's Notebook* by Turgenev, certain pages were suppressed. Since then a considerable number of writings have been obliterated.

The track of the first railway was laid on the steppes. In 1834, Nicholas matched the Paris - Saint-Germain line with his Petersburg - Tsarskoye Selo railway. Seventeen years later Moscow, the second capital, was connected by rail with St Petersburg. Progress—material progress—crossed the Niemen. With some diffidence, and under-staffed, a few factories appeared here and there and industry began to expand.

But the question of bond-service was ever present. The nobility banked on both autocracy and orthodoxy, the systems which for centuries had proved profitable. Abroad, ideas were developing. Herzen and Bakunin were spreading their doctrines. One day in 1847, Dostoyevsky was arrested with the members of the

'Brotherhood of St Cyril and St Methodius' and, wrongly considered as one of the 'socialists' of this group, was sentenced to death. He managed to escape the gallows but sampled four years of Siberia, to which he testified in his harrowing book, *Recollections of the House of the Dead.*

Nicholas tried to keep faith with the ghost of the Holy Alliance but in France the nephew had replaced the uncle and one day the Turks became the allies of the French and the English. Nicholas died on March 2, 1855, not knowing what would be the outcome of the war in the Crimea.

It was his son, Alexander II, who had to clear the account. The door to the straits remained closed. When, in 1855, at the age of thirty-seven, the new Czar ascended the throne, he inherited a war and a domestic situation which was hourly growing more dangerous. At all costs the problem of bond-service had to be solved and the liberally minded Sovereign devoted himself doggedly to the task. In his Slavonic studies, Alfred Fichelle gives the following statistics: 'At the time of the new Czar's accession (1855), the Russian serfs numbered some twenty million peasants in the service of the Crown. Four million seven hundred thousand were working on endowed estates and in the mines and factories, twenty-one million *belonged* to the wealthy landlords and one million five hundred thousand were in domestic service. Chief among Alexander II's concerns was the abolition of serfdom. (In 1858 and 1859 the police of the Third Buro had to record 176 cases of peasant revolt.)'

Even if the nobles and the landlords were in agreement with the Sovereign in principle, they showed marked differences in the application of the principle. In the eyes of the nobles, the land was theirs almost by divine right, and the great landlords were not far from sharing this view. The division of the estates appeared to be an insurmountable problem: the peasantry claimed the right to the property. The question was much debated but no agreement was reached, and in the meantime there was growing discontent throughout the length and breadth of Russia. It was not until March 1861[1] that the question was settled by decree—and so unsatisfactorily that almost everybody was displeased with the result. But by that decree the peasant gained the right to his personal freedom and the possibility of ownership of his house and land. There came into being the institution of the *Obshchina*, or rural property, which

[1] Two days after the assassination of Alexander II.

from afar foreshadowed collective ownership. It may be said, without fear of contradiction, that it was equally unwelcome to both sides. In buying back their land the erstwhile serfs found that they were more heavily taxed than before. A certain communal autonomy was instituted, the magistrature was re-cast in a more liberal mould, and education and the army experienced statutory changes. This liberalism had only one outcome: the strengthening of hidden opposition which had been increasing since the middle of the century. There were more than one indication that this opposition would break out at some distant date. However it may be, Alexander II figured as a reformer, although it was most certainly too late. Throughout the vast, crumbling Empire revolutionary ideas were spreading by way of the works of exiled intellectuals. In the heart of Russia secret societies were rapidly increasing in number and, unfortunately for the Russian monarchy, which had wakened too late to universal realities, the last two Czars, Alexander III and Nicholas II, were frightened creatures who clung to the past. The revolution, as yet, was marking time, but in the way that athletes do, to flex their muscles before the race.

Little can be said of Alexander III's reign, 1861-1894, except that it was one of almost continuous movement in a backward direction, and, whether he was wrongly inspired or badly advised, he tried by wayward action to consolidate his authority and endeavoured to achieve isolation behind his frontiers, hostile to everything which was not Russian — to the East as to the West.

Right at the beginning of his reign, Nicholas II, who had become initiated in government affairs during his father's illness, declared his determination to defend the principles of autocracy energetically. Through his mother, Princess Dagmar of Denmark, he inherited the 'rotten' blood of Hamlet, Prince of Jutland. In obedience to the vagaries of an erratic will, the last Czar of all the Russias, by virtue of his character, recalled the shade of the Shakespearian hero.

Fate willed that by marrying Alix, Princess of Hesse-Darmstadt, Nicholas II should combine the heavily charged heredity of the Romanovs and the House of Denmark with the no less heavily charged inheritance from the House of Hesse. Alix had in her blood the baleful haemophilia of Hesse. It was therefore probable that the future Czarevich would inherit this unfortunate predisposition. But was Alix not the favourite granddaughter of Queen Victoria, who had brought her up in Osborne House in the Isle of Wight?

The premonitory signs of the future tragedy of Ekaterinburg appeared in the life of Nicholas II the day he married Alexandra Feodorovna, ex-Princess Alix.

His reign began in sinister circumstances. On May 14, 1896, in the Kremlin, the imperial crown was placed on his head. The occasion was marked by a great feast given by the Emperor to his people in the huge field of Khodynka near Moscow. Some 300,000 people were to take advantage of the free entertainment and presents offered by the Czar. The peasants from the vicinity of Moscow mingled with the people of the ancient capital in the field of Khodynka. When the distribution of the presents began, a terrible jostling movement transformed the crowd into a stampeding herd. There was fighting for the presents, and there were not enough of them. The police were powerless to control the rush of humans crashing into one another with incredible violence. The staging collapsed, trapping and killing 7,500 people. Everybody expected the coronation festivities to be interrupted by a period of mourning, but the Czarina was intent on ignoring the occurrence. She decided to hold a ball in the great hall of the Kremlin on the day following the Khodynka catastrophe. Another magnificent ball was given on the day of the mass burial of the victims. Wishing to prevent the funeral procession from passing through the town of Moscow, the authorities issued orders for common graves to be dug on the very spot where the public festivities had been held in the field of Khodynka. On that spot were buried the bodies of the unfortunate people who had come to seek a royal gift. More than half of them were put into the graves without identification, so great was the haste to turn the page of that unhappy chapter.

The day following this burial an anonymous letter was discovered in the Czarina's boudoir. The contents of the letter were divulged by Zinayda Tzankova, lady-in-waiting to the Czarina, in her Memoirs: 'Nicholas and Alexandra Romanov had no wish to interrupt the coronation festivities in spite of the Khodynka catastrophe. They were not one whit concerned for thousands of their subjects who had met a tragic death. The day is not far distant when the people of Russia will show equal lack of concern for Nicholas and Alexandra Romanov. Their bodies will be lost from sight in a pit, as were those in Khodynka.'[1]

[1] William de Queux: The Tragic Czarina.

Next day, in the corridors of the Kremlin between the Czar's chambers and those of his wife, a second letter was found. It contained a prediction made by a Siberian prophetess from Irkutsk: 'The Romanov dynasty will become extinct thanks to a German wife who will pass on a terrible disease to the Czarevich.' In spite of all its investigations the Okhrana never succeeded in discovering the writers of the letters. Extremely depressed, the royal couple returned to St Petersburg.

After the coronation, revolutionary activities became more formidable than ever. The militant union for the liberation of the working class, the creators of which were Lenin and Martov, was established in St Petersburg in 1895. In Munich in 1900 there appeared the first issue of the Iskra ('The Spark'), which was to cause the explosion. Soon the Iskra emigrated to London. Already there were heated discussions, and those who kindled the revolution had split into two camps, the Bolsheviks and Mensheviks. Until October 1917, during the Ten Days which shook the World,[1] nobody could say which would prevail.

The Empire, unsuccessful in its European objectives under Nicholas I and Alexander III, was no more fortunate in its designs on the East under Nicholas II. It should be remembered that in 1904 and 1905, in the Russo-Japanese War, Port Arthur was captured and the whole of the Russian fleet of thirty-eight ships, under the command of the hapless and incompetent Admiral Rozhdestvensky, was utterly defeated in a few hours by Admiral Togo at the crushing Battle of Tsushima. That was on May 14 (27), 1905.[2] Peter the Great's dream was fading away. No longer could Russia claim to protect her sea-routes, or even to defend herself at sea against any third-rate power.

Between the surrender of Port Arthur and the Tsushima disaster, a revolution, quickly and fiercely repressed, had flared up in St Petersburg, an outbreak of which the capture of Port Arthur was but the cause and distant signal. A strike was called, involving 200,000 of the capital's workers, more or less centred around a pope, Gapon, whose dealings with the police have since been verified. There was also the event known as 'Bloody Sunday' which took place on January 9 (22), 1905, in front of the Winter Palace, where Gapon had organized a procession

[1] Title of John Reed's book.
[2] Here and in later pages the first date given is that of the old Russian calendar, which was thirteen days behind that of the present day.

with the object of handing to the Czar a list of respectful demands. Nicholas was not present. The Guard became alarmed and opened fire. Barricades were set up in all parts of the panic-stricken capital. There were further strikes. The aspect of Russian society was changing abruptly. At the news of Tsushima, the crew of the old battleship *Potemkin*, at anchor off Odessa, turned her guns on the town. Then, to avoid reprisals, they gave themselves up to the Rumanian authorities. The Czar called upon the services of a skeleton *Duma*, which would be elected by property qualification and could hardly be said to represent the country. At Portsmouth he treated for peace with the victorious Japanese—but tempers were running high; to borrow a metaphor used in different circumstances, the dying Russian monarchy 'was spluttering'.

On October 17 (30), 1905, a manifesto was published, which gained much approval. It was concerned with close collaboration between the government and the people and with universal suffrage. It was quickly realized that the author or inspirer of the manifesto was none other than Witte, the Czar's chief minister. Those holding liberal views applauded it. 'Nevertheless, it appeared that they were clearly outdone by the councils or *Soviets* of the workers' representatives. That was the first occasion on which the name 'Soviet' was employed; it was to come into spontaneous use again in 1917.'[1] By a *ukase* of December 11, 1905, universal suffrage was firmly instituted, but the Czar reserved to himself so many powers, by comparison with those enjoyed by the *Duma*—a body existing merely to record His Majesty's wishes—that this caricature of a parliament was from its first session doomed to failure, and it gave up the ghost on July 8, 1906.

It is not only in recent times that faked elections have been known; the second *Duma* of 1907 was so elected. It sat for barely three months and had to give way on a question of parliamentary immunity. Meanwhile, the peasants were given the option of not joining in with the *Obshschina*—communal ownership—and had the right to own the land which they cultivated. But the workers, who received instructions from abroad, were secretly active. Since the first two had done so little, it is surprising that there were preparations for electing a third *Duma*, unless it was that in spite of its strength popular pressure was ineffectual. This third *Duma* had a comfortable royalist majority

[1] *Le Monde Slave*, Encyclopédie de la Pléiade, p. 874.

and, no doubt for that reason, those who were known as the Oktyabrists were able to gain a hearing, but they were no longer thought to be dangerous. The Poles and Finns were granted small freedom rights. The only clearly revolutionary event that took place in those days occurred at Kiev in 1911: it was the assassination of the prime minister Stolypin, who was no doubt considered by right-wing extremists to be too tolerant of the demands made by the peasantry. The *ukases* and the half-hearted representations of the *Dumas* were unavailing; the revolution was afoot and, in the words of Poincaré (August 1, 1914), 'the diplomatic horizon clouded over'. The red flag was thrusting its way into the steppes. Instructions were arriving from Geneva and London, where Lenin was watching the course of events. The story of the war is well known—even its false rumours, such as 'The Cossacks are three days' march from Berlin!' Strikes, incompletely settled, were causing disturbances in St Petersburg. As in France, Russia experienced a very short burst of national unity. But the defeat at Tannenberg on August 30, 1914, followed by the retreat in Mazovia, broke down the first impulsive rush of an army that was large on paper but in reality badly appointed, lacking supplies and railway transport.

Turkey's entry into the war, on the side of the central powers, increased the difficulties of a hard-pressed general staff, and while Nicholas was at the front the Czarina, in control of home affairs, was under the influence of Rasputin, a dubious character and drunken miracle-monger, who undertook the impossible task of curing the Czarevich. Rasputin was all-powerful. In view of the bad news from the theatre of war, the libidinous monk—his autopsy revealed what may be termed his 'power'—suggested that he should go and pronounce a blessing on the armies. The Grand Duke Nicholas Nicolayevich cabled a message to him: '*If you come to G.H.Q., I will have you hanged like a dog*'.

Suspicion was aroused, by way of Stockholm, that Rasputin was a German agent and he was further accused of causing the death of Lord Kitchener, who had left for Kronstadt at the head of a British mission and had never arrived. On May 24, 1916, the cruiser *Hampshire*, with Kitchener on board, was sunk off the north of Scotland by a German submarine. Kitchener's death was the straw that broke the camel's back; the Intelligence Service and the British Ambassador decided to put an end to the matter. Informed of their intention, the French Ambassador, Maurice Paléologue, tried to dissuade them. Indeed, there was no assurance that once Rasputin was gone the Czarina would not find some other charlatan, perhaps one more dangerous.

On the night of December 16th, four conspirators met in Prince Yussupov's palace. They were: Felix Yussupov, the monarchist representative of the *Duma*, Purishkevich, Doctor Stanislas Lazovert and Captain Sukhotin. Prince Yussupov was the chief conspirator.

Prince Yussupov, who was married to the daughter of a Grand Duke, was descended from Kutuzov on his grandmother's side and from the Hohenzollerns on his grandfather's. Young, lively and intelligent, he was popular in all quarters of the capital. He was known for his great wealth and his thoroughly eastern lavishness.

The British Ambassador had vaguely mentioned to Paléologue his plan to make Yussupov a *constitutional* Czar, a 'Russian Louise-Philippe'. Sir George Buchanan thought that the wonderful fact of being Rasputin's assassin would be sufficient for the Russian Constituent Assembly to make Prince Felix a constitutional, non-autocratic Czar of all Russia.

At dawn on December 17 (31), 1916, after a tragic scene in the best style of a Dostoyevsky or of Gogol's *Diary of a Madman*, the body of the murdered Grisha Rasputin was thrown into the Neva.

Events showed Maurice Paléologue to have been right. The Czarina held on to her 'spirits'. She secured the services of a medium, Protopopov, the Minister of the Interior. This Protopopov communed with 'the spirit of Rasputin', whose decisions he passed on to the Czarina, and she in turn informed the Czar. The imperial rule was moving towards its disastrous end.

In addressing the *Duma* with reference to President of the Council Sturmer and Minister of the Interior Protopopov, Milyukov used words that provide a good illustration of those times: 'A government,' he said, "as deplorable and rascally as the present one Russia has never had. Its Ministers are imbeciles; except the President, who is a traitor.'[1]

Milyukov was not very wide of the mark in what he said. Protopopov, the Minister of the Interior, stated to anyone who would listen to him that he felt strong enough to defend the czarist régime and the Orthodox Church 'against unpleasant eventuality'.

It is true that in the slums, where wretched conditions had

[1] V. Marcu: *Lenin*, Payot.

prevailed for centuries, there was as yet no thought of insurrection. The power of the Czar was too great. The more distressing daily life became because of it, the more it was hated and the more inaccessible its walls became in the eyes of the masses. Unlike the Grand Dukes, the bankers, the manufacturers and the senior officials, the man in the street could not peep through the keyholes of the private rooms of absolutism. The prelude to the 1917 revolution, the greatest that history has ever had to record, was not played in the dark recesses of conspiracy, nor yet in the slums of the Vyborgskaya Storona, the working-class district of St Petersburg, but in the palaces and the most magnificent houses in the capital. On the very morning of the great day there was vague talk of a palace revolution. Even in Kerensky's socialist circles all were agreed that a popular uprising was *impossible* at the moment.

On February 23 (March 7), 1917, St Petersburg awoke to a temperature of seventy-seven degrees (Fahrenheit) below freezing-point. Twelve hundred locomotives became immovable blocks of ice; 57,000 railway trucks, with food supplies for the capital, were immobilized. The bakeries were empty. Panic ran through the working-class suburbs. Hungry people came out on strike. Men and women poured into the streets, the men calm, the women weeping and cursing.

Suddenly, all these Russians remembered their distress, the sacrifices they had made, the husbands, sons and brothers, who had fallen in that horrible carnage which was Russia's first world war. And suddenly they stopped believing in their saints, their heroes, their little father Czar Nicholas and the St George medals issued to those who had come back maimed from the front. One after another the factories became idle; men and women made their way to the town centre. The bakeries and shops were plundered.

The anger of the people, and their hatred of the régime, were mounting hourly. The Bolshevik Secret Committee called upon the populace to act.

On the morning of February 24th almost all the factories in the suburbs had stopped work. The bridges leading to the centre of the town were held by troops from a garrison of 100,000 men, but men who were very unsure of themselves. The Cossacks hurriedly brought by Protopopov from the front were even less confident. On February 26th a miracle took place: the Cossack regiments, reputed to be the mainstay of the existing order, fired on the police and not on the crowd. By the end of February all authority had vanished.

Three centuries of Romanov domination were swept away in three days. In the path of the wind of revolt the walls of autocracy crumpled like a house of cards. All day long crowds of hollow-cheeked people passed beneath the windows of the bourgeois residences. The men wore workmen's caps and army greatcoats. They carried banners with blood-red letters, 'Bread, Peace, Liberty'. On the night of February 26th Rodzyanko dissolved the old *Duma*. The following night, the soldiers who had joined in the demonstrations occupied the Taurid Palace. A provisional government assumed power. It was the end of the Romanovs.

So it was that a riot that took place in front of the empty bakeries of the capital swept away the Romanov Empire with bewildering rapidity. It was the final incident in a historical trail blazed by the insurrections of the Razins, the Bolotnikovs, the Pugachevs and the Bulavins, by the revolts of the peasant serfs and the Decembrists and the revolution of 1905.

The fall of the Romanovs brought with it a temporary lawlessness. On March 2 (15), 1917, a provisional government was created, including Prince Lvov. The czarist police, hated by the populace, were replaced by a militia, the inadequate strength of which could not guarantee the most elementary safety measures in town or country. The Czar's governors gave place to 'provisional government commissars' unprovided with any real power. A *Soviet* of manual workers, peasants, soldiers, black-coated employees and Cossacks was in control of the government and deprived it of all freedom of action. The Russian people, reliving the 'period of disturbances' which followed the disappearance of the Ryurikovichi dynasty, were preparing for a long spell of civil war.

The slogan given by the Soviet to the February Revolution was 'Bread, Peace, Liberty'. These words were posted up everywhere, even on the Kremlin walls, alongside the ikon of the Iberian Virgin, the most sacred relic in Russia.

The provisional government was unable, in the middle of a world war, to provide bread and peace. As for liberty, the Russian people had seized it and made full use of it for nine months. There was a succession of meetings of all kinds and strikes were called. In the South of Russia, near the sea of Azov, a former peasant-teacher, Nestor Makhno, instituted the 'Free Commune' of the Gulyay-Pole and proclaimed the 'revolutionary principles' of Bakunin: 'Acknowledging no activity but destruction, we declare that the forms which such activity shall take may be extremely varied—from a bullet in the base of the skull to a running noose. The Revolution sanctifies everything, without distinction.'

An uprising began in the peasant body, which demanded the dividing up of the estates, the centuries-old dream of the Russian peasantry. Soldiers at the front deserted and went back to their country districts to take part in this division of the lands. The provisional government had the insane idea of starting a new offensive against Germany with the aid of a half-decimated army. This offensive failed disastrously and Prince Lvov gave up the presidency, which passed to the barrister Kerensky on July 8 (21), 1917.

Kerensky invoked full powers to re-establish the death penalty for treason and desertion to the enemy, to disarm the civil population and prohibit demonstrations. An extremely popular speaker, this 'tenor of the revolution' conceived the notion of forming a few battalions of women 'shock troops', under the command of Madam Bochkareva. These troops proved to be the only military force on which he could depend. After proclaiming the 'Government of National and Revolutionary Welfare' and then resigning with his ministers, Kerensky formed a 'coalition' government on July 25 (August 7), 1917.

In order to consolidate national unity, Kerensky, a moderate socialist, decided to convene the 'State Conference' (Gosudarstvennoye Soveshchane) in Moscow.

The old capital of Russia and the Kremlin were thus again becoming the centre of political life. Some moderates would have definitely established it as the capital, but their idea did not find support from Kerensky and his friends. Moscow had the reputation of being a 'reactionary' capital. It was in Moscow, indeed, that in August 1917, after the 'State Conference', General Kornilov's famous plot was hatched, the prelude to the Bolshevik revolution of October 1917. A number of political adventurers acting under the direction of the self-styled Zavoyko, that puppet of the armament manufacturer Putilov, had succeeded in persuading General Kornilov to overthrow the Kerensky government by a military *putsch*. On August 25 (September 7), Kornilov ordered his troops to march on Petrograd. Kerensky

refused to resign and called upon the Left to 'defend the Revolution'. The Soviet mobilized the Petrograd workers and the
Kronstadt seamen, most of whom were anarchist, and the *putsch*
was broken. The parties of the left, in particular the Bolsheviks,
decided to make the most of the situation and throw over
Kerensky in his turn. He no longer had any support in the
country, whether from the right or the left. Trotsky, the president of the Petrograd Soviet, and Lenin, the head of the Bolshevik Party, who had both been living secretly in Finland since
the abortive revolt of July 1917, formed a revolutionary military
committee, the *Revkom*, which directed the insurrection of
October 25 (November 7), 1917. Kerensky, who had only the
women's battalion of Bochkareva and the corps of cadets to
defend him, managed to make his escape disguised as a woman.
On the eve of the Bolshevik *coup d'état*, Lenin arrived in Petrograd, wearing a red wig lent to him by Stalin, and still wearing
it[1] he presided over the Politburo of the Bolshevik Party which
was to form the first Soviet government. Two people's commissars, representing the left-wing revolutionary socialist party,
were included in it.

So began the Soviet period in Petrograd, a period which saw
the disruption of the Empire. The borderland provinces broke
away from the mother country and created new states. The
Ukraine proclaimed its independence, thanks to the support
given by German bayonets. Caucasia separated from Russia. The
peoples of the Ural and Caspian regions followed suit. Russian
Central Asia was subjected to attack from Moslem guerillas
(*basmachis*), Turcomans and Kazakhs. The Cossacks revolted
under the leadership of Kaledin, Denikin, Alexeyev, Krasnov
and Kolchak. After crushing the detachments of Red guards, the
Germany of Wilhelm II imposed upon Soviet Russia, in March
1918, the harsh Treaty of Brest-Litovsk, which was to give legal
sanction to the disruption of Russia.

It was at this time, March 1918, that Lenin decided to transfer
the capital to Moscow. After two centuries the Kremlin again
became the seat of Russian government. Internationalist though
he was, Lenin was one hundred per cent Russian and was aware
that the unification of Russian territories could be achieved only
through Moscow and the Kremlin. It was from there that Ivan
Kalita, the 'Unifier of Russian lands', had operated.

---

[1] This comic episode is reported by Trotsky.

PART II

FROM THE REVOLUTION
TO THE
PRESENT DAY

CHAPTER 1

STALIN ENTERS THE KREMLIN

For seven of the 'ten days which shook the world', the struggle for power was at its bloodiest in Moscow and the Kremlin, the very heart of Holy Russia. During that time a cold snow-laden wind blew through the deserted streets of Moscow, carrying with it the proclamations of the Provisional Government, speeches by Lenin, theatre bills and proclamations of the workers' and peasants' councils. At the street corners stood groups of men, leather-clad sentries, soldiers with slung rifles and lorries packed with sailors and infantrymen laden with cartridge-pouches. The shop windows were boarded up. On October 28th began the battle of the streets. To direct the insurrectionist movement the Bolshevik Party had appointed a committee of five, who received from the Smolni in Petrograd the order to go into action. Some orders bore the signatures of V. I. Lenin and L. Trotsky. The Muscovite Soviets of workers and soldiers had created a military Revolutionary Committee, as had been done in Petrograd and most other towns. They had at their disposal about 10,000 trustworthy men, Moscow factory workers, as well as the majority of the soldiers of the garrison, in particular the 193rd reserve regiment and the 56th, 57th, 196th and 250th infantry regiments. The forces which had remained loyal to the Provisional Government were grouped around the municipal Duma, forming a Committee of Public Safety. Both the opposing parties had thousands of agitators and vied with each other for the support of the Moscow regiments. At daybreak on October 28th officers and cadets of the military colleges took the offensive. Their units forced the entrances to the Kremlin and shot the soldiers of the 56th regiment who were in occupation. The Revolutionary Committee replied with a general strike of all the factories. Barricades were set up in Moscow. On that day was born the 'revolutionary romanticism' of that period, the period which was to be the prelude to the civil war that devastated Russia for four years and was so admirably described by Alexis Tolstoy in his *Road of Torment*. Having taken the Kremlin by surprise, the Whites held the centre of Moscow for a week, while the Red guards were in control of the suburbs. After seven days of desperate fighting between the workers and the demobilized soldiers on the one side and the cadets, officers and students faithful to the Constituent Assembly on the other, the suburbs devoted to the Moscow proletariat decided the issue. Red reinforcements arrived daily from Kolomna, Serpukhov, Ivanovo-Vosnessensk and Vladimir. On November 1st the Red artillery went into action. The next day the Whites evacuated the streets called Nikolska, Ilinska and Varvarka, leading to the Kremlin, and their officers abandoned their headquarters at the Continental Hotel. The fighting went on beneath the embattled walls of the Kremlin. The pupils of the 5th School of Cadets were the last defenders of the Provisional Government. On the evening of November 2nd[1] the Red guards under the command of M. V. Frunze pierced the main defences of the Kremlin. At nine o'clock the military Revolutionary Committee of Moscow cabled to the Smolni in Petrograd: 'The Red guards are victorious, the Junkers and White guards are giving up their arms and the Committee of Public Safety is dissolved. The bourgeois forces are completely beaten and surrender unconditionally.' To the Smolni in Petrograd V. I. Lenin triumphantly announced the fall of the bastion of Russian bourgeoisie. Moscow and its Kremlin were in the hands of the Red guards.

The taking of the Kremlin confirmed Lenin's undisputed authority. The same day the Council of Commissars published a declaration of the rights of Russian peoples, proclaiming the equality and sovereignty of all these peoples and giving them the right to self-determination. All privileges of ancestry and religion were abolished, together with nobiliary titles. There was now no other title than 'Citizen of the Russian Republic'. The Soviet régime was beginning to take root throughout the whole extent of Russia and the transference of the Government and Bolshevist Central Committee to Moscow was awaited.

The year 1918 was a decisive one in the formation of the young State. Felix Dzerzhinsky's Cheka played an important part in it.

Plot followed plot; the monarchists and the moderate Revolutionary-Socialists (the Kerensky supporters) organized daily attacks on the Soviet leaders. The left-wing Revolutionary-Socialists, two of whose leaders had a part in the government

[1] November 15th of the new calendar.

and lived in the Kremlin with Lenin and Trotsky, decided to do away with Lenin, who had signed the Peace of Brest-Litovsk. Indeed, these left-wing socialists asked for the repeal of the treaty and a proclamation of revolutionary war against the Kaiser.

Towards the end of June 1918 an infernal machine was discovered in an underground room of the Kremlin. The Cheka made an inquiry and learnt that Cherepanov, an anarchist connected with the left-wing Revolutionary-Socialists, was printing pamphlets announcing 'the destruction of the Kremlin and the reign of Bolshevik oppression'. Then the Cheka discovered and wrecked an attempt to poison the Kremlin water. Every day pamphlets were found stuck to the walls.

Dzerzhinsky wanted to arrest all members of Cherepanov's organization, but Lenin opposed the suggestion; Cherepanov's father was a friend of Lenin's brother and had been hanged in 1887. Young Cherepanov had inherited from his father the principles of 'revolutionary populism', contrary to the Marxism of Plekhanov, Lenin's teacher. It should not be forgotten that Alexander Ulyanov was also an ardent 'revolutionary populist' and that, if Alexander III had pardoned him, the Russian revolution of 1917 would probably have taken place as a struggle between the Ulyanov brothers.

On the night of July 4, 1918, the Central Committee of the left-wing Revolutionary Socialists, *sitting in the Kremlin*, decided to direct an insurrection against Lenin and the Bolsheviks. The sailor Popov, in charge of the Cheka troops,[1] was appointed to lead the uprising.

Alexandrovich, a prominent Revolutionary-Socialist and vice-president of the Cheka, was detailed for liaison duties between the garrison troops, who were 'in sympathy with' the left-wing Revolutionary-Socialists, and the Kremlin garrison.

The insurrection was planned as follows: (1) Assassination of Count Mirbach, the Kaiser's ambassador to Moscow. (2) Storming of the Kremlin and arrest of the *sovnarkom*. (3) Convening of an extraordinary congress of the Soviets to repeal the Treaty of Brest-Litovsk and declare war on Germany. (4) Election of a new Soviet government by the left-wing socialists and the Bolsheviks hostile to the Treaty of Brest-Litovsk (the Bukharin-Uyatakov group).

---

[1] Popov was the left-wing Revolutionary-Socialists' representative, with Alexandrovich, in the Cheka. He held important positions there by agreement with the Bolsheviks.

Only one detail in all this programme was successful—the first, viz. the assassination of Count Mirbach. On July 6th a left-wing Revolutionary-Socialist, Blumkin,[1] provided with forged papers (procured by Alexandrovich) from the Cheka, appeared at the German Embassy with his accomplice Andreyev and asked to speak to Mirbach about one of his relatives, a German officer who was a prisoner of war in Siberia. Blumkin entered the Embassy and threw two bombs which wiped out Mirbach and wounded several German diplomats. The German Embassy telephoned to the Kremlin an urgent request for a protective force. Popov and Alexandrovich launched the revolt.

At dawn on July 7th the rebels occupied Trekhsvyatitelsky Street in Moscow and began the bombardment of the Kremlin. Popov, at the head of a small party of sailors, occupied the Cheka and arrested Dzerzhinsky. Alexandrovich, made chief of the Cheka by the rebels, had Dzerzhinsky brought to his office to protect him from the anarchists' vengeance. Pamphlets flooded the streets; appeals were made throughout the capital, urging the people to revolutionary war against Germany.

The rest of that day, July 7th, was spent in negotiations. The Kremlin garrison, consisting of Letts, refused to surrender, and Popov decided to blow up the *sovnarkom* palace where Lenin was housed. Strong intervention by Alexandrovich, who considered that after such an action no Bolshevik would take part in denouncing the Treaty of Brest-Litovsk, alone saved Lenin and the *sovnarkom*.

While the rebels were wasting time in argument, Trotsky brought up loyal troops with all speed. At 2 p.m. on July 8th the rebels surrendered. At four o'clock a communiqué from the *sovnarkom* announcing the end of the revolt was posted on the walls of the Kremlin.

About 600 people were arrested and taken to the Kremlin to appear before the Cheka. Twenty-three erstwhile revolutionaries were sentenced to death and executed as 'White guards'. Alexandrovich, also sentenced to death, was visited in his cell by his friend Dzerzhinsky, who handed him a revolver to save him the shame of execution by the firing-squad. Alexandrovich refused to take his own life and was shot with his comrades in the prison-yard of Lefortovo, where only the 'privileged' were executed; the others awaited death in the cellars of Lyubyanka Square.

---

[1] Pardoned in 1919, Blumkin entered the Communist Party and became an important official of the Cheka. He was shot as a 'Trotskyist' in 1929.

The mistake which the left-wing Revolutionary-Socialists made was in wanting to continue the war at a time when five and a half million Russians were dead or wounded, when agriculture was in a state of complete neglect, when the intellectual élite were divided and the State ruined. This mistake, this madness, was paid for by certain of the better revolutionary elements with their lives.

The summer of 1918 was terrible; civil war was raging, there were revolts, insurrections, riots and, in addition, famine and typhus, which broke out in June and lasted almost to May 1921. A veritable plague of lice descended upon Russia. On the Troytsky Gate of Moscow appeared a huge notice: 'Comrades! Either socialism must conquer the louse or the louse will conquer socialism! Everyone must play his part in fighting lice!—LENIN.'

To destroy the lice gigantic fires were lit near the Kremlin walls. Heaps of dirty linen, articles of clothing and household cloths were flung on the fires. The people's commissars carried the war against lice into the remotest regions of Russia. A policlinic was set up to fight the vermin. Until Stalin's death the Kremlin policlinic remained one of its most mysterious places.

On August 31, 1918, the following communiqué appeared in the Moscow newspapers:

The Kremlin,
30 August, 1918, 10 p.m.
Attempt on the life of the President of the Council of people's commissars, comrade Lenin.

Attention, everybody!

A few hours ago a criminal assault was made upon comrade Lenin. There must be orderly calm! Everybody must keep his head! Let us take a grip of ourselves! Let us close our ranks!

Yacob M. Sverdlov.
(President of the Central Executive Committee.)

That night, Doktor Riessler, Count Mirbach's successor at the German Embassy, telegraphed to his government that Lenin's days were numbered; he had been shot three times full in the chest. The shots had been fired by a poorly-dressed woman, Fanny Kaplan, a member of the Revolutionary-Socialist party who had been exiled to Siberia in the time of Nicholas II.

On the same day, August 30, 1918, a young student, Leonid Kannegiesser, wishing to avenge the death of a friend who had been executed by the Cheka, shot and killed Trotsky's friend Uritsky, head of the Petrograd Cheka.

A terrible wave of 'Red counter-terror' spread over Russia. Zinoviev, the President of the Regional Soviet of Petrograd, ordered the shooting of a thousand people who had been arrested as hostages. In Moscow, the Dzerzhinsky Cheka shot more than two thousand people. Fanny Kaplan's attack on Lenin caused a chain reaction with more than twenty victims!

Fanny Kaplan narrowly escaped the firing-squad immediately after the attack, but Lenin ordered her to be confined to a small room in the Palace of Facets.[1] After the shooting, Lenin was moved to the Kremlin at the same time as the Cheka's 'black-maria' was taking Fanny Kaplan there.

When he arrived at the Kremlin, Lenin, supported by his companions, went slowly up the staircase to the third storey, where he had been living since he left the ground floor of the Kazakov Palace in July 1918. He was laid on his bed; beads of sweat stood out on his forehead; his torn shirt revealed two gaping wounds near his shoulder. Livid with pain, he groaned, 'My heart . . . it is painful . . . very bad . . . my heart! . . . Has my heart been damaged?'

An injection of morphine settled him. One hour later, Sverdlov sent a telegram to Trotsky, 'Volga front. Return at once. Ilyich wounded. Possibly dangerously. August 31, 1918. Sverdlov.'

Trotsky returned with all haste to Moscow, where already the first shots of the Cheka's execution-squads could be heard as they dispatched the 'bourgeois hostages'. Lenin held out his hand to him and said simply, 'You must be protected better than I was. If we both went, do you consider that Sverdlov and Bukharin would be effective replacements?'

Trotsky recorded in his book *My Life*: 'I left as soon as I had Sverdlov's telegram. In Party quarters in Moscow spirits were low and depressed, but unshaken. Sverdlov showed this firmness more than anybody. The doctors declared Lenin to be out of danger and soon to be convalescent. To the Party I expressed my hope of rapid successes in the East and, without further delay, I went back to Svyazhsk. Kazan was retaken on September 10th and two days later the Fifth army captured Simbirsk. It was not unexpected; Tukhachevsky, in command of the army,

---

[1] On October 3, 1918, when Lenin himself had just decided to spare Fanny Kaplan, Sverdlov ordered her to be shot.

had promised me at the end of August that he would take Simbirsk by September 12th at the latest. I received his telegram: 'Order carried out — Simbirsk taken'. Lenin, who was much better, sent a telegram of hearty congratulations to Tukhachevsky on the capture of his native town of Simbirsk (Ulyanovsk).'

Without Lenin's being aware of it, a short-length film was made, entitled Lenin walking in the Kremlin. The press published hundreds of articles on Lenin's attempted murder and the injuries he had sustained. According to Vishnyak, when Lenin had read them all he said was, 'I find these articles distasteful. They are all about me. I consider this un-Marxist way of giving prominence to a personality extremely harmful. It is a bad thing, entirely unacceptable and pointless. All those pictures too! And that silly film! How can one avoid all this publicity? What is the reason for it all?'

Lenin had asked to see Fanny Kaplan and speak with her. The conversation, which took place in Lenin's own quarters with three guards in the next room, made a marked impression on him. He sent for Sverdlov and told him, 'I am asking for this woman's life to be spared'. A stormy argument followed and lasted several days. Sverdlov and Trotsky considered that he showed a lack of 'revolutionary logic'. Thousands of people had been executed, following upon Fanny Kaplan's attack. How could one spare the person responsible? But Lenin could not be persuaded and, in spite and in defiance of him, it was necessary to carry through the unanimous decision of the Politburo. It was one of the few battles that Lenin lost to his associates.

On September 17, 1918, Lenin presided over the session of the Sovnarkom with his arm in a sling.

The civil war went on and the famine was acute. The state of the Policlinic was precarious for lack of supplies. Malkov, the commandant of the Kremlin, and Bulanov, the Cheka representative, were given the responsibility of ensuring food and medical supplies. The Policlinic grew rapidly in importance. Sverdlov and the Health Commissar, Semashko, saw to its proper organization. Famous doctors were appointed 'personal medical advisers' to the Soviet leaders. Such were Pletniev, Kazakov and Fominsky. The ever-mistrustful Sverdlov assigned to these duties his confidential assistant Genrikh Grigorievich Yagoda, a native of Nizhni-Novgorod: he was a chemist. At the same time the chemist Yagoda became the 'representative to the Kremlin Policlinic'. Thanks to Sverdlov his promotion was extremely rapid. This obscure chemist and toxicologist, who had destroyed a number of Nizhni-Novgorod's cats and dogs in his experiments, was to become the chief of the Soviet secret police during the Stalin period. He 'initiated' the series of 'Moscow lawsuits', which included that of Kamenev and Zinoviev in August-September 1936.

In his book *My Life*, Trotsky relates that Stalin met Yagoda in the rooms of his 'intimate friend' Vorontzov, the deputy-commandant of the Kremlin. It was thanks to Stalin that this Vorontzov, a sailor who, although a young man, had a considerable criminal record, became the assistant to Malkov, the Kremlin commandant. Peter the Great's methods were still applied.

Sverdlov's sudden death aroused no suspicion in Lenin, for everyone in the Kremlin knew that Sverdlov was a consumptive. His premature death could not but benefit Yagoda—and Stalin, who had been his enemy since their quarrel over an actress. While Sverdlov lived, Yagoda could never have been appointed to the Cheka. Yagoda had one day asked Sverdlov to grant him the post of supply chief to the Board of Health and Sverdlov had coldly replied, 'There is a Russian proverb which says that you don't let a pike loose in the fish-pond'.

When Sverdlov was dead, Yagoda was appointed to the Cheka, in charge of the 'Secret Operations Department' and in control of the information channels which provided the Cheka with details of counter-revolutionary activities. This department commanded secret financial resources and had a large supply of jewels and furs[1] with which to reward its women informers, who were often aristocrats, actresses, singers or prostitutes.

Trotsky records that at Sverdlov's funeral Lenin delivered a speech devoted to the memory of the first Soviet president, a warm-hearted speech in which, 'without actually mentioning Stalin, he referred to suspected intrigues against Sverdlov and recognized that certain people had been unfair to this fearless and blameless revolutionary'.

To quote Trotsky further, 'Kamenev told me, with his usual cynical geniality, that in 1923 Stalin had suggested to him and

---

[1] In his lifetime Sverdlov would never have entrusted the store of jewels and furs to Yagoda or have permitted Stalin's appointment as secretary-general of the Party in 1921, at the time of the Tenth pan-Russian Communist Party Conference.

to Zinoviev that they should get rid of me by "Florentine methods". And then I thought of the others, especially of Sverdlov, a doomed consumptive, whose speedy death suited Stalin particularly well.'

After Sverdlov's death, the People's Commissar for Nationalities, Stalin, found his progress increasing with bewildering rapidity. Thanks to Vorontzov's influence, he was allocated a small two-roomed apartment in the Kremlin, rather far from Lenin's quarters and those of Trotsky and other Soviet dignitaries. There he received his emissaries, intermediaries and agents. Yagoda was a frequent visitor. He brought flowers for Nadezhda, Stalin's wife, and medicines for his father-in-law, he attended the 'civil marriage' and waited for his reward, which he eventually received in 1920. Stalin was often visited by a Georgian named Ordzhonikidze. Yagoda tried in vain to win this man's liking but the Georgian detected something strange in the chemist and in his eager, candid way said as much to Stalin, who answered, 'Sergo, you are not a good Leninist. An eminent Bolshevik once said that no garbage should be overlooked in a great household.'

In 1919-20, with civil war raging and the White Army at Tula, from which position it threatened Moscow, Stalin had not changed his attitude towards Trotsky. He already saw in him, however, his most dangerous rival. A brilliant speaker, a first-rate journalist, an untiring organizer of the new army and a gifted theorist, Trotsky was recognized by all as second to Lenin in Soviet Russia. At that time Stalin could work for only third place and had to be careful not to offend Trotsky. That is why, while continuing to receive Zinoviev, Kamenev, Voroshilov, Ordzhonikidze and Yagoda in his small apartment in the Kremlin. Stalin made several attempts to put himself on closer terms with Trotsky. The incompatibility of these two pretenders to the inheritance was, however, too great for them to be able to agree.

In Trotsky's words: 'Stalin tried several times in those days to get closer to me. Of course, he did so in his uncultured, obsequious way, as if each time he felt his inferiority. One day, when I was passing through the Kremlin corridor near Kollontay's rooms, the door of which was ajar, I saw Kollontay at the telephone and heard a few words of what she was saying. Suddenly, Stalin appeared at the end of the corridor; his eyes were glinting with the crafty expression of those who listen at doors.

He came towards me, took me by the shoulder in a friendly manner and held out his hand to me, saying, "It's Dybenko now, you know. It's he she is speaking to. She has asked him to come from Petrograd as soon as possible. He's not unwelcome in that quarter, with his height of nearly six feet six." In distaste, I shook off his grasp and, without having taken his hand, I answered, "It is their own business. Let us not indulge in scandal, like a couple of caretakers." Stalin turned pale with anger.' He never forgot Trotsky's contemptuous behaviour on that occasion and never forgave him for it.

CHAPTER 2

THE DEATH OF LENIN

The tenth Russian Communist Party Congress in March 1921 accepted the new economic policy (NEP) put forward by Lenin. Confronted by resistance on the part of the peasantry, he had decided to call a halt to militant communism: the requisitioning of corn was replaced by a 'corn tax', the *prodnalog*. In a speech of far-reaching importance Lenin announced the reconstitution of the monetary system, based on the gold standard as in capitalist countries: 'When socialism prevails,' he said, 'mankind will recall the part played by gold in the capitalist systems. We shall raise a wonderful memorial to gold: a huge public urinal in gold will take the place of the golden calf of the pagans.' Lenin then recalled the total victory of the communists in the civil war. The last White regiments had been liquidated, and likewise the anarchist insurrection of the Kronstadt sailors, by Tukhachevsky's troops.

That was, if not the last of Lenin's speeches, the most significant of his final days. His health began to fail. He had increasingly to delegate his duties to the new secretary-general of the Party, elected at the tenth Congress after nomination by Zinoviev: Joseph Vissarionovich Stalin, otherwise known as Sosso Bezovich Dzhugashvili.

From now on, Lenin spent most of his time on an estate called 'Gorki', some twenty miles from Moscow, in an unfrequented spot, on a hill surrounded by fields and woods, an ideal setting for his enforced leisure. It was a two-storey house, with white pillars which stood out against the green of the park. At the end of this park was a pond, to which Lenin was in the habit of going, wearing a Russian shirt and with a bath-towel over his shoulder. He would bathe, go rowing, pick flowers or gather mushrooms. Since the attempt on his life by Fanny Kaplan, he was closely guarded; occasionally, as a diversion, he would hide amongst the bushes or get lost in the forest. The panic-stricken guards would find him half an hour later with some children who were fishing in a stream in the vicinity of 'Gorki'.

Towards the end of 1921, Lenin complained of giddiness,

253

strain and sleeplessness. His headaches became more frequent. One day he had a fit of dizziness which made him reel and he was obliged to hold on to a piece of furniture for support. The doctors made every effort to calm him, telling him that it was merely a question of fatigue. Dejectedly he replied: 'No. I feel it is the first stroke of the gong.' A few days later Lenin said to his associates, 'Mark my words, I shall end up as a paralytic.'

In the spring of 1922 the doctors prescribed complete rest for V. I. Lenin. He went back to 'Gorki'. It was there that he had his first seizure. He lost the power of speech and movement of the right arm and leg. The paralysis became progressive. He could neither speak nor walk. He was aware of all that went on around him but could not refer to it.

Trotsky states in My Life: 'Those who had long been preparing to oppose me—and Stalin was the chief of them—played for time. Lenin's illness was such that it could result in a tragic crisis at any moment. That was the time of the forming of the troyka, consisting of Stalin, Zinoviev and Kamenev, which was was intended by Stalin to act in opposition to me in his struggle for personal power. But a miracle happened: Lenin recovered!'

Mark Vishnyak records: 'His wife Krupskaya had a difficult task to perform: to restore in part her husband's intellectual faculties. She taught him to write with his left hand and to spell. Like a child Lenin obeyed her, practising his reading and writing and doing his exercises with care.'

By July 1922, as a result of a great and unparalleled effort of will, Lenin was able to write and walk, and even to discuss politics. By October of that year he returned to the Kremlin and resumed his work in the Politburo and the Sovnarkom. He made a public appearance at a congress of the Comintern, when he delivered his last speech, his 'swan-song'.

In the middle of this speech his voice suddenly became faint and could hardly be heard; he forced himself to say what he had to say; he was bathed in sweat. Clara Zetkin ran to him and kissed his hands. Lenin took her hand and placed it to his lips.

The signs of paralysis returned; his right arm and leg were useless. Bedridden, he stayed in the Kremlin, keeping in touch with the political situation. He suggested to Trotsky that the latter should become the first deputy president of the Council, so that in the event of his death authority would automatically fall to Trotsky. He dictated his 'last will and testament'. Lenin's estimate of the six most prominent figures in the Party was as follows: Bukharin was an 'academic' and a 'non-marxist'. Pyatakov was an able but too bureaucratic administrator. Kamenev and Zinoviev 'had been reluctant to give unreserved support to the Soviet revolution in November 1917'. Trotsky was clever, and a good administrator, but his failing was over-confidence in himself. As for Stalin, he was disloyal to the comrades, misused his power to achieve personal ends and was so crude that he had no place in the communist body. He must be relieved of his post as secretary-general. Zinoviev and Kamenev must not be reproached for their wavering in November 1917, nor should Trotsky be taken to task for his 'earlier un-Bolshevik attitude'.

Stalin reduced this list to one name—his own. He had the first four shot and contrived Trotsky's murder in Mexico City!

It is noteworthy that towards the end of his life Lenin had a sharp exchange of words with Stalin concerning Krupskaya, who openly supported Trotsky. Stalin was abusive to Krupskaya on the telephone and angrily requested her not to meddle in the affairs of the Politburo.

Lenin had his second seizure in March 1923. His right side was completely paralyzed. He found it difficult and painful to take food; the nerve centres of his throat and palate were more seriously affected than on the first occasion.

According to Mark Vishnyak, Lenin left the Kremlin about the middle of May, 'this time never to return'. But the Soviet historian A. Loginov records that Lenin did go back on October 19 and 20, 1923. What was the reason for this unexpected appearance? Why this superhuman effort which brought on such cruel suffering?

At that time the Soviet government was anticipating the savage outburst of the German revolution. Trotsky was asking that 'any risk should be taken to help German comrades'. Ambassador Victor Kopp faced Count Zamoyski, the Polish minister, with these alternatives: either that Poland would act as a bridge between Soviet Russia and Red Germany or else that she would incur the risk of being wiped off the map of Europe by those two countries.

That is the explanation of Lenin's return to the Kremlin. The Bolshevik leader had always declared that the advent of Soviet Germany would sound the knell of world capitalism, and he wanted at all costs to be present at the meeting of the Politburo when the fate of the German revolution was decided.

Some influential Russian communists had already been sent in secret to Germany: Radek, Pyatakov, Unschlicht, Sokolnikov, Alexandrov, Gruzenberg, Eiche, Kviring, Skripnik and others.

Lenin was in a very low state. He had to be taken back to 'Gorki'. He was even incapable of uttering a single syllable of the word 'revolution'. Patiently Krupskaya kept repeating: 'R - e - re -v- rev- o- revo - l - revol - revolu - revolu - ti - revoluti - on- revolution.' Lenin made desperate efforts but only a few sounds came from his throat: 'G . g . ggg . . . ue . . . gguevo'.[1] His head would fall back on the pillows, great tears would glisten in his eyes and spill down his cheeks. He was in a terrible state. He shouted, moaned and howled. Story has it that the dogs of the village nearby answered his inhuman cries. The peasants of the neighbourhood would cross themselves and wipe the tears from their eyes. The 'Gorki' estate, beneath a mantle of snow, echoed during those long winter nights with the heartrending screams of the tortured Lenin.

At about that time Trotsky suddenly fell mysteriously ill. Doctors could not effect a cure; they diagnosed, by turns, intestinal influenza, typhoid fever and infective gastritis. Becoming increasingly weak, Trotsky was compelled to take to his bed and give up all work. Prostrated by sickness, Trotsky sought rest at Sukhumi on the Black Sea. It was at that very time that Lenin felt better and summoned Stalin to him. Stalin went to see him, returned to the Kremlin and announced to the *troyka* that the 'Old Man' could not withstand his terrible suffering any longer and that he urgently requested the Polit-buro to 'put him out of his misery'.

At seven o'clock in the evening of the 21st of January, Lenin passed out of this life.

In *My Life* Trotsky writes:

' "The Old Man is in terrible pain," Stalin said. "We might cut short his suffering." I was watching Stalin and closely examining his face for some expression of pity for a comrade in pain and misfortune; I saw nothing there but a sly, fleeting smile. "The Old Man is in pain," Stalin said again. "He is asking the Politburo to put him out of his misery." Zinoviev and Kamenev looked at each other. Zinoviev had spent all his politi-cal life with Lenin; he had grown up with him and worked under his orders. But Zinoviev and Kamenev had nothing to say.

[1] Like a real Russian aristocrat Lenin spoke with an impediment: he had difficulty in pronouncing the letter 'R', which he replaced by 'G'.

Interior of the Cathedral of the Assumption

[*photo : Charles Lewis*]

Interior of the Uspensky Cathedral` [*photo : Charles Lewis*]

The Golden Room of the Garret Palace
[photo: Educational and TV Films]

Lenin's study in the Kremlin, as he last used it [photo: S.C.R.]

'Then I stood up and asserted that we were bound to take care of Lenin until the end, that it was our duty to the Party. In the end Zinoviev and Kamenev backed up my opinion.

'Stalin was silent. Then, with an enigmatic smile he said once more, "The Old Man is in pain and is begging for his release".

'It was long after that dramatic session of the Politburo that Zinoviev and Kamenev joined with me. At the time, I mentioned Lenin's request for the poison-cup, but they refused to make any comment; it was as though they were still bound by some conspiracy to Stalin.'

I

CHAPTER 3

STALIN'S TROYKA

With Lenin's death broke out the fierce struggle between Trotsky and the *troyka*, Stalin-Zinoviev-Kamenev. Centred in the Kremlin, this struggle was not one whit less intense than those between the Princes of Moscow and the Princes of Ryazan, Tver and Novgorod-Seversky. In the heart of the triumvirate Stalin was content, for the time being, to play an unobtrusive part. He took care not to appear too often at the front of the political stage. He was no orator or pleader of causes, and rarely spoke in the meetings. His guttural Gori accent, offensive to the Russian ear, the slow delivery of his didactic speeches, the paucity of his imagination and his pompous manner, recalling that of the old-fashioned seminarists, did not endear him to his audience. Instead of making speeches, therefore, Stalin preferred to employ his time in attempting to obtain a hold upon the Party 'machinery'. At all strategical points he placed local secretaries, in whom he had complete confidence, and he made all ready against the day when the *troyka* should break up.

He succeeded in his designs nearly everywhere, but not at Leningrad. There, Grigory Zinoviev, a prudent and experienced president of the 'Commune', sent back to Moscow all the *apparatchiki*[1] he received from Stalin. Zinoviev, whose real name was Radomysselsky, was one of Lenin's favourite disciples and thought he would one day succeed him. He was president of the Comintern and already saw himself as 'leader of the world revolution'. In Leningrad he was preparing for his 'world communist administration'. A long-winded speaker—he was known as *vodoley* (the water-pourer)—high-falutin and arrogant, he regarded Stalin as a negligible quantity and allowed him complete freedom of action in the bosom of the Central Committee of the Communist Party. Zinoviev failed to recognize a truth which was obvious to any observer of Russian politics, viz. that he who has control of the Central Committee of the Communist Party of the USSR has control of the whole country. The fact that the October revolution broke out in Leningrad led him to

[1] Party officials.

258

believe that the master of Leningrad (Zinoviev himself) was the master of the USSR.

Kamenev, who was 'head of the communist organization of Moscow', was an intelligent man, a brilliant journalist and an outstanding orator. But he had no political ambition. He was a handsome man; his strong, typically Russian face, his fair hair and beard, gave him the look of a genuine Muscovite 'lord'. Yet Kamenev, properly named Rosenfeld, was Russian only on his mother's side. His father, Boris Rosenfeld, was a medical expert in Tiflis. It was there that Kamenev joined forces with Stalin, who was then a seminarist. Kamenev was converted and married his first wife, a Greek Orthodox Russian, but he continued to eat Jewish Passover bread. By marrying Olga, Trotsky's sister, Kamenev quickly became his brother-in-law's political enemy and rival. Olga urged her husband to achieve a popularity equal to Trotsky's. Kamenev was a gentle person who was very reluctant to admit the excesses of the revolution, the massacres and the blood spilt by Trotsky.

The relationship between Kamenev and Trotsky became increasingly strained; the quarrel took a serious turn after the execution of Captain Shchassny (promoted rear-admiral by the Kerensky government), who commanded the fleet at Kronstadt. In accordance with the Treaty of Brest-Litovsk, Soviet Russia was to hand over the Baltic fleet to Germany. Shchassny, keen socialist and patriot that he was, refused to surrender the fleet and scuttled his ships. Although the sailors were communists and anarchists, they supported Shchassny, who became the hero of Kronstadt. But Trotsky, as head of the armed forces, committed Shchassny to court-martial and appeared in person at the trial so as to prefer the charge and obtain a conviction. 'When high-ranking officers,' he cried, 'decide to make a reputation for themselves in time of revolution by acts of insubordination to the Revolutionary Government, they must put up with the consequences of such conduct.'

Since the President of the War Revolutionary Council—Trotsky's title at the time—demanded the death penalty, the court could hardly do otherwise than give such a verdict unanimously. Shchassny made an appeal for mercy to the Executive Central Committee but, on Trotsky's order, the sentence was declared 'irrevocable'; Shchassny faced the firing-squad in the yard of the barracks where the court-martial was held.

The unjust decision of the court was met with an outburst of disapproval. In full session of the Politburo[1] Kamenev accused Trotsky of being jealous of Shchassny's popularity with the fleet of Kronstadt, his feudal possession in 1917. After this incident relations between the two brothers-in-law became worse, and they avoided meeting each other.

This quarrel was followed and aggravated by another. A young Englishwoman, Claire Sheridan, had come to Moscow with her brother, an officer in the Royal Navy. A self-styled journalist, painter and sculptress, she claimed to be a distant relative of Winston Churchill and a descendant of Richard Sheridan, one of the leading Whigs, the great orator, dramatist and composer, who had defended the principles of the French Revolution against Pitt in the House of Commons. Claire Sheridan soon became the 'darling' of the Kremlin. She was welcomed by the Soviet dignitaries, whom she immortalized by making busts of them. Felix Dzerzhinsky himself became one of her most ardent admirers. As for Kamenev, he was so taken with her that he invited her to live at the Kremlin; Miss Sheridan was accorded the suite occupied by ex-Czarina Maria Feodorovna in the new palace. Kamenev's admiration grew and he invited her to the Livadya Palace in the Crimea, customarily reserved for members of the Politburo on holiday. He spent all his days in the company of the beautiful English girl. He even wrote verses to her—on English bank-notes, to show his contempt (as Lenin had done) for these notes, which at the time carried a hundred per cent guarantee.

The idyll was abruptly shattered by Trotsky: the *Osobyi Otdel*, the military Cheka, with Unschlicht at its head, accused Claire Sheridan's brother of being a member of the Intelligence Service and of having come to the USSR as a spy. While Kamenev was admiring the bust of himself and that of Dzerzhinsky,[2] the Grand Inquisitor of the Russian revolution, and was congratulating Claire Sheridan on her artistic achievements, her brother was expelled from the USSR. Trotsky requested 'an end to the scandal' and the expulsion of the English girl who yet had made busts of him and other members of the Central Committee. The matter went to the Politburo. Stalin, who could ill conceal his satisfaction, refused to order the expulsion demanded by Trotsky, but administered a 'friendly'

[1] The following entry is found in the court archives: 'Performed a heroic action by succeeding in depriving the enemy of the Kronstadt fleet.'

[2] This bust is at present in the Revolution Museum in Moscow.

reprimand to Kamenev for his 'bourgeois flirtation'. Kamenev returned with Claire Sheridan to the Kremlin. She remained there a little longer to finish the busts of her friends, the Hindu Nath Roy and his wife, who attended the meetings of the Comintern and who also lived in the Kremlin.

Nath Roy was a tall, slim man, with a very dark skin and curly hair. He and his wife, who was statuesque from every point of view and who wore extremely revealing light clothing, became the intellectual hub of Kremlin society. Wives of people's commissars, actresses and ladies of the new Soviet aristocracy surrounded them. Trotsky often appeared in this circle; it was said that he was very much attracted by Roy's wife. And then the 'Kro'[1] Department of the GPU, supported by the 'Ino'[2] Department, submitted to the presidency of the Council some information from a Mexican source: Roy was a member of the Intelligence Service. Kamenev had taken his revenge.

These intrigues, antagonisms and tussles provided the material from which Stalin, patient and unwearying, wove the web of his future domination. He called upon the services of a Czech engineer named Karlik for the installation of the first automatic telephone line in the Kremlin, the *vertushka*. Karlik had installed 300 dial instruments, when Stalin suddenly ordered him to stop the work. At the same time he gave instructions for Karlik to be expelled. The Czech left Moscow, took a train at Ryazan station and disappeared without leaving the slightest trace. All measures by the Czech authorities and Karlik's family proved fruitless. Not until 1929, after the flight of Bazhanov, Stalin's private secretary, was the mystery made clear. Stalin had had the new automatic telephone exchange installed *in his private study*. A special installation made it possible for him to listen to every conversation by the first 300 subscribers living in the Kremlin, the highest Soviet officials. The officials often spoke frankly on the telephone, and Stalin spent hour after hour at his listening-post in his study, gleaning first-hand reliable information about the state of mind of his friends and enemies.

To return to Karlik, he was quite simply 'liquidated' by Yagoda's personal agent, Kryuchkov,[3] who accompanied the Czech to the frontier.

[1] 'Kro' was concerned with counter-espionage and counter-revolutionary activities.

[2] 'Ino' was concerned with the Cheka, and propaganda abroad.

[3] Kryuchkov was shot with Yagoda in 1938.

It took Trotsky a long time to realize that his principal enemy was neither Zinoviev nor Kamenev, but Stalin. He showed himself to be but a poor strategist in his struggle within the Party. After his banishment, when he was asked what his cardinal error had been, Trotsky tried to find a 'Marxist' explanation for his defeat. Why did he need to disturb the ashes of Karl Marx? The simplest explanation points the purely strategical fault that, instead of concentrating his early attacks on Stalin, he had chosen the wrong target and had aimed at Zinoviev and Kamenev. By so doing he had helped Stalin to change the *troyka* into a personal dictatorship. After that, Stalin had only Trotsky to fight and Trotsky could do no more than join with Zinoviev and Kamenev, the very men whom he had politically annihilated by his criticisms and tirades.

It was during the year 1924 that Trotsky and his supporters conducted an extremely violent campaign against Zinoviev, then president of the Comintern, and Kamenev, president of the Moscow Soviet. The starting-point of this campaign was the 'defeat of the German revolution' in 1923. In his usual controversial way Trotsky, in his book *The Lessons of the October Revolution*,[1] returns to the charge against Zinoviev and Kamenev and accuses them of having had the 'wind up' (*sdrefili*) in October 1917, when Lenin decided to use force to overthrow Kerensky instead of waiting for the convening of the Constituent Assembly, in which the Bolsheviks and their left-wing allies might hope to obtain a parliamentary majority. Trotsky publishes his 'factual' reproof in order to emphasize that Zinoviev had been unwilling to help the German Revolution of 1923 by all the means available to the Soviet government, which included military assistance, and had shown this unwillingness despite the fact that he had the support of Kamenev who had the following of most of the Politburo.

Fiery as usual, Trotsky at that time accused Zinoviev and Kamenev of 'defeatism', almost 'treachery', in respect of the revolution. A series of meetings took place in Moscow. The communists in the capital, particularly the young people, demanded that the Party Congress should be convened, that the Central Committee and the Politburo should be re-elected and that 'traitors' should be removed. In his turn, Zinoviev

---

[1] The revolution of November 7, 1917, took place on October 25, according to the old Russian calendar, but with the westernization of the calendar the Bolshevik revolution continued to be known as the 'October Revolution'.

organized meetings in Leningrad at which Trotsky was referred to as a 'Menshevik traitor who had come among the Bolsheviks to disrupt Lenin's party'.

With the beginning of the discussions there were some rather serious incidents. Brawls took place in the Baumann district of Moscow. The huge 'Elektrozavod' factory hooted its director's speech. This director was a Zinoviev supporter, Nicholas Bulganin. Molotov was booed at the meeting of the Faculty of the School of Advanced Technology. The secretary of that body, Georgyi Malenkov, was set upon by Trotskyist students. The 'democratic' opposition and that of the Trotskyists combined under the leadership of Sapronov, Shlyapnik and Drobnis. The Party, together with Stalin, came in for criticism. The immediate re-election of the district committees of Moscow was demanded. The Politburo began to have misgivings. The head of the Cheka, Dzerzhinsky himself, was hooted on the occasion of the meeting of the directorate of the 'Hammer and Sickle Factory'.

Stalin occasionally appeared with the executive of the Party Central Committee, where he thought he was safe from all intrigue. Even there, the office staff, the caretakers, the typists and the 'fundamental communists' belonged to the democratic opposition. The secretary-general was also booed by his subordinates.

Suddenly a strange epidemic burst out in Moscow. The Party members fell ill in hundreds after eating in communal restaurants. They were suffering from a gastric infection which confined them to their beds for several weeks. The doctors were ordered to grant sick-leave more liberally than usual. The capital became empty of fighting personalities. Then suddenly, Trotsky, who had hardly recovered from his gastric illness, fell ill again, and this time seriously. Having been moved to the Kremlin Policlinic, he very nearly died. He refused to be attended by doctors on the staff. His friend, Dr Feodor Alexandrovich Getier, had him sent to a rest-house in the Crimea and saved his life.

In the autumn of 1924, Stalin ordered a severe purge of the various centres in the capital. A Party Control Commission, led by Shkiryatov and Soltz excluded over 50,000 communists from the Party on the grounds that they were 'careerists'. All students had to show that they did not enter the colleges merely as an 'easy means to a career'.

Towards the end of autumn, the source of opposition in

Moscow was liquidated and the *troyka* enabled to continue its reign in peace.

Joseph Stalin's power was now growing daily. Since his name will appear on nearly every page in the rest of this book, a clearer and more objective picture of this 'uncultured' politician, who sent hundreds of former Bolsheviks to the cellars of the GPU and persecuted the best of the Party, may be attempted. It should never be forgotten that, of all the stories that were current about Stalin, most of them came from the pen of the exiled Trotsky, who never forgave him for ruining his political career. Because of his skill as a pamphleteer and journalist, Trotsky managed to create a picture of Stalin which, though undoubtedly interesting, was incomplete and biased.

What were the characteristics of the man Stalin? No political leader attracted so much world interest as this son of a Gori cobbler. In ten years he silently established himself in the Kremlin and seized in his muscular grasp the fate of a nation of 165 million souls. In a quarter of a century he raised the USSR to the position of second world power; millions of men saw in him the long-awaited Messiah, the Prophet of the Golden Age. He was not liked, and even his closest associates feared him.

Dzhugashvili Stalin: a man of average height, solidly built, with a body that had withstood all trials and every privation, a yellowish unhealthy face, furrowed by wrinkles that both revealed and disguised a deep and intensive experience of life, a low forehead hidden by a thick head of hair, extremely keen and searching deep-set eyes, a mouth hidden by a heavy black moustache which also partly covered a cruel chin. He dressed modestly, even poorly: a pair of cavalry boots, a khaki shirt, no decorations, an old military cape over his shoulders and on his dark head a shabby cap. His way of life was that of an ascetic. As far as possible he stayed out of the limelight, effacing himself behind those who showed themselves and who held the front of the stage. In all his movements could be detected a great desire to look like Lenin; his postures were all copied from those of the leader of the Russian revolution. He worked relentlessly, inside the Kremlin, that ancient seat of Czars, haunted by the spirits of the past. Every stone there served as a reminder of the shadows of Ivan IV, Boris Godunov, the *streltzi*, the *kramola*, Nikon, the *raskolniki*, Peter the Great.

For eighteen hours a day he worked in the tiny office of his modest quarters or in his *sovnarkom* office.

Taciturn and resolute, with strong nerves inherited from his mountain people, he listened and noted, letting each man say what he had to say. Only when he had heard the last speaker would he get up and, in a low, strong, confident voice, give his orders and dictate a decision which would affect millions of human beings. He might smile, as an Aztec mask might smile.

After conferences and meetings he returned to his modest three-roomed flat, two rooms of which had at one time housed servants. The furnishings were plain: an old armchair by the window, coarse linen curtains; on an unpolished wooden table the eternal samovar, a glass of tea, a tobacco-pouch and two or three pipes packed by his wife Nadya, the mother of his two children. His meals were less than frugal—a piece of herring and a few potatoes; his only luxury was a glass of Caucasian wine. While he was at work, he drank countless glasses of tea.

Before the door of his flat a sentry was on guard day and night. The only people allowed in were those supplied with a special pass countersigned by the commandant of the Kremlin. Visitors were very few. Work absorbed his whole attention. He spoke little, even to his wife and children. In his suburban *dacha* he worked almost as hard as he did in the Kremlin. For relaxation he played the pianola. A few photographs of himself with Lenin and Voroshilov decorated the walls. After the war he added to them a photograph of his son Basil in uniform and one of his favourite actor, Nikolas Chekassov, in the rôle of Ivan the Terrible.

Although he did not like leaving his desk, he sometimes made a sudden appearance at the Party Secretariat. The panic-stricken staff awaited his orders or his criticisms. He would stop and stare for a few seconds at a secretary and say, 'Listen you! You are just like a he-goat my mother had in her village. But the goat did not wear pince-nez.' The staff laughed respectfully. Stalin would light his pipe and, with his slow, deliberate tread, leave the room.

His ascetic way of life developed a certain shyness in him, especially in regard to women. An incident of the Yalta Conference may be recalled: Stalin, in his brand-new suit which fitted him too tightly, was not at ease with the ladies who accompanied Roosevelt and Churchill. He took their hands in a rather comical way, as if he did not know what to do with them. Suddenly, he jerked forward in the 'German' style and kissed their hands very elegantly in the manner of the old royal courts. He then blushed like a schoolboy and his hands shook.

All his life Stalin thought himself persecuted and shunned company. To what extent did he make himself the mouthpiece of Ivan the Terrible who was personified by his favourite actor Cherkassov? Nobody can say, but it is known that he himself revised the scenario of the film.

CHAPTER 4

INTRIGUES WITHIN THE KREMLIN

Towards the end of 1924, it was rumoured in the Kremlin that the *troyka* envisaged a great purge of the Party; the figure suggested amounted to thousands of people. Panic began to spread through the USSR. Simultaneously, the *troyka* decided to create a diversion: the Control Commission staged proceedings for 'individual purge'. Marshal Simeon Budenny had to answer to the Control Commission for his 'unfortunate action' in having killed his wife. The Pillared Hall of the House of Workers' Syndicates[1] was filled to overflowing[2] during the three days of the hearing of this strange action. Budenny, under interrogation from Soltz, an Israelite from Vilno, beat his breast and promised 'never again to commit an act of which the Party might not approve'. Budenny admitted that on the day of his crime he had 'had just a very little more to drink than usual'.

No doubt, the case was not of interest in itself: a badly made soup, a marshal who had drunk a little too much, an uneducated old Cossack woman and the habit, established by civil war, of settling arguments with the help of a Mauser 7·65. This entire action was preceded by skilful propaganda which held the attention of the Muscovites and made them forget the gastric epidemic. It is obvious that in this action Stalin had purposely appointed Soltz in order to amuse the Muscovites; after three days of talk and laughter, judgement was pronounced: 'a severe reprimand and a warning of expulsion from the Party if the offence was repeated'.

Standing perfectly to attention Budenny heard the finding of the court and promised 'never to do it again'. It should be noted that the judgement of the Central Control Commission was only a Party judgement. But according to the traditions of the Russian Communist Party, which were derived from those of the imperial nobility, the members of the Party who were not debarred from

---

[1] It was in this hall that the 'Moscow lawsuits' were conducted. The 'Beria case' was heard there, in the absence of the accused, and a series of other important cases.

[2] Reported in the *Souvenirs* of Dumbadze, a defaulting Chekist.

the Party by the Control Commission could not be tried by a State tribunal for the same offence.

After the Budenny proceedings another action was staged by Stalin (for the amusement of the Muscovites): that of Krassnoshchekov, the president of the Commercial and Industrial Bank. Krassnoshchekov was accused of 'moral degeneracy' and 'abuse of power for sexual ends', unworthy of a communist, as well as 'misplaced intimacy with representatives of the capitalist world' and 'excessive appropriation of the special fund for expenses'. Krassnoshchekov was expelled in advance from the Party by the Control Commission. Soltz again presided at the trial.

The Krassnoshchekov case was attended by an extraordinarily large number of the public. The witness for the prosecution, a domestic servant employed at the Bank, related in detail how the accused made love to her, how he used to come to the Bank 'wearing a capitalist-style hat' (it was a bowler hat) and how she had been dismissed because the 'foreign capitalists were displeased with her behaviour as an honest Russian proletarian'.

The accused replied that he had never tried to 'flirt with the old hag' and that he had discharged her because, when bringing tea into a reception of foreign bankers, she 'dipped her fingers into the glasses as a sign of her contempt for the capitalists she was to serve'.

Those present were convulsed with laughter, but Soltz howled, 'Be quiet, you fools! You are insulting a proletarian and a comrade!' Turning to Krassnoshchekov he said, 'You should be ashamed at having fallen so low as to dismiss a comrade merely because she dipped her fingers into capitalists' glasses!' The sentence was six years' hard labour 'on account of comrade Dasha's fingers'.

After providing such relaxations, Stalin decided to strike a decisive blow at Trotsky: the Politburo had to debate the question of the appointment of a new president of the Revvoyensoviet to replace Trotsky. The motion was put by the second secretary of the Central Committee, Vyacheslav Molotov. It was first debated in the *Orgburo*[1] for more than a week in an attempt to find a new candidate to head the War Ministry. Stalin wanted the post to go to his personal friend Klim Voroshilov, his Tsaritzin comrade during the civil war and his companion-in-

[1] The *Orgburo*, the supplementary committee to the *Politburo*, was presided over by Molotov, whereas Stalin was president of the Politburo.

arms in Poland at the time of the unsuccessful offensive against Warsaw.

Voroshilov at that time commanded the military region of Northern Caucasia and was based at Rostov on the Don. But most of the military saw in Voroshilov 'Stalin's man', and Lashevich was put up as a candidate. He was an old Bolshevik who had been political commissar in the Ural district at the time of the civil war. Lashevich obstinately refused to undertake a task which he thought himself incapable of fulfilling. He there-fore proposed Mikhayl Frunze, in command of the military region of the Ukraine and the Crimea and victor of Wrangel. A man who had so distinguished himself could not fail to be wel-come to the Trotskyist military men. Frunze was known to be loyal to Trotsky and would not attempt to conspire with Stalin and the troyka against the president of the Revvoyensoviet. For these reasons the Politburo accepted Frunze's candidature.

The troyka knew quite well that the recall of Trotsky could provoke resistance within the army or, indeed, result in attempts at a coup d'état. Trotsky, who was a sick man and absent from Moscow, showed not the slightest inclination to resist, but there was the fear of possible military uprisings that would take place without consulting Trotsky. The troyka particularly feared the head of the Political Directorate of the Red Army (the PUR), Vladimir Antonov-Ovseyenko, the old Bolshevist who had led the attack on the Winter Palace during the insurrection of November 1917 and who told Molotov at a meeting of the Orgburo, 'If you lay a finger on Trotsky, you will start a blaze!'[1]

Stalin therefore decided to act with the greatest discretion, despite the advice of Zinoviev who wished to be rid of Trotsky as soon as possible. The president of the Comintern came to Moscow from Leningrad three times a week and held endless secret conferences. Kamenev was sometimes present at these meetings, but most of the time he was closeted with Stalin, expounding methods of putting an end to Trotsky without incurring the risk of a military pronunciamento.

Stalin made up his mind to work in stages: first, Trotsky had ardent supporters at the Commissariat for War, and it was there-fore advisable to replace them by supporters of the troyka; secondly, once the ground had been prepared, a decisive blow could be struck by dismissing Trotsky.

[1] The head of the 'PUR' was, ex officio, a member of the Orgburo of the Central Committee.

The Politburo, or the *troyka* (since it had a majority in the secret Directorate of the USSR) decided to send a delegation to Trotsky in Caucasia in order to put to him a plan for the modification of the Commissariat for War.

Concerning this delegation Trotsky comments in *My Life*:

'A delegation from the Central Committee came to Sukhumi to discuss with me certain proposed modifications in the directive personnel of the War Ministry. *Basically, it was a pure farce.* The changes in the personnel had been made long before, *with all speed*, behind my back. All Stalin, Zinoviev and Kamenev were doing was to give the matter some semblance of legality.'

Having prepared his ground at the Commissariat for War in this way, Stalin dismissed Trotsky. A secret circular letter was sent to all local secretaries of the Party stating, among other things, that:

'Comrade Trotsky's illness puts the Central Committee in the painful position of having to consider his replacement for the Presidency of the Revvoyensoviet of the Republic. Comrade Trotsky has deserved well of the Republic. Public opinion must be prepared and the members of the Party in your region made ready to accept this important change in the direction of the Revvoyensoviet, to which the Central Committee has decided to appoint in place of comrade Trotsky comrade Frunze, an old Bolshevik and wartime captain of long service who has the affection of the Party and the country.'

The extent of Stalin's prudence can be seen. The full meeting of the communist Central Committee in the Kremlin, where the decision to make the change was taken, proved a stormy occasion. Some members abstained and requested that a medical certificate should be produced concerning the state of Trotsky's health. But the danger did not lie in that quarter; the real trouble was Karl Radek, Trotsky's most enthusiastic supporter in 1924-5, who had just decided to join with Antonov-Ovseyenko and wanted to appeal directly to the senior officers of the Red Army.

About the end of December 1924 a secret meeting took place in the Kremlin, in Radek's quarters. There were present Radek, Antonov-Ovseyenko, Tukhachevsky, Putna, Yakir, Primakov, Fabricius and Feodorov.[1] Yakir was Frunze's assistant in the

_____
[1] All who were present at this meeting were executed in 1937 and 1938.

command of the 'Ukrim' region. Primatov was in command of the Red Cossacks of the Ukraine. Fabricius held the command in Transcaucasia. Tukhachevsky, formerly in charge of the Volga and Ural districts and the victor of the Kronstadt and Tambov rebels, was a national hero in the USSR. By bringing together these generals and the head of the 'PUR' (the army representative of the Central Committee of the Communist Party), Radek considered he was establishing a 'military centre' of sufficient authority in the army, an authority which was unquestioned and which could not be suspected of being anti-communist.

After a lengthy discussion it was decided to send a delegation to Sukhumi to ask Trotsky's consent to a plan evolved by Radek. This plan proposed (1) the military occupation of the Kremlin and arrest of the *troyka*, (2) an extraordinary meeting of the Party Congress to re-elect the Central Committee of the Party and the Politburo, (3) the temporary appointment of Trotsky as Secretary-General of the Communist Party until the election of a new Central Committee of the Party.

The delegation arrived in Sukhumi but Trotsky refused categorically to become the Secretary-General of the Party, that is, the dictator of the country. 'I refuse,' he said, 'to be the grave-digger of the revolution. By carrying through this plan we shall merely open the door to the third anti-Soviet force which will bury us all beneath the debris of the counter-revolution.'[1]

Stalin must have got wind of the 'Radek plan' and the *pronunciamento*. Sending a telegram to Rostov-on-Don, he brought to Moscow some elements of Budenny's First 'Army of Horsemen' with its Don Cossacks. With Budenny came Voroshilov, the commander of the military region of Northern Caucasia. Stalin surrounded himself with his faithful supporters.

Like the Czars before him, Stalin called upon the Cossacks for support. Once again the 'constant Cossack' was to intervene in Russian history. A Cossack squadron occupied quarters in the Kremlin, and the *troyka* could henceforth sleep peacefully.

The *troyka* took the necessary steps to add to its power. The first concerned Lenin's mummification. The building of a mausoleum was decreed; there, the embalmed body was to lie for all time. This new relic, a new 'St Vladimir', was intended to restore confidence to the Russian muzhik and satisfy his need

[1] Victor Serge.

for medieval and Byzantine types of worship. To be sure, such relics did not come within the scope of Marxism or dialectic materialism. By creating them, Stalin and his friends were pandering to demagogy and popular taste. By government decree Professor Vorobiev and the biochemist Zbarsky, who embalmed Lenin, were decorated for their work.

The embalming produced a profound disgust in opposition quarters. A Trotskyist pamphlet was distributed in Moscow declaring that 'the voice of Lenin severely condemns those who seek to retain power by recourse to medieval means in having him embalmed and placed in the mausoleum'.

The Soviet historian Loginov notes in his book *Our Kremlin* that, after Lenin's death, an opposition group proposed that a memorial to Lenin should be raised on the Kremlin hill. 'The monument,' it was stated, 'will have to be erected, not in some place in the Kremlin, but *in place of the Kremlin*. The Kremlin must be destroyed!' 'For how long,' asked a Russian revolutionary and ardent populist,[1] 'are we to preserve the bones of Ivan the Terrible? Are we going to preserve for ever this monument of the sufferings of the people and the blood spilt by the Czars? Must we for ever keep this horror museum that testifies to slavery and shame and is fit only for the refuse-bin of history?'

Stalin believed, on the contrary, that there was every indication for making such an 'ideological concession' in order to link up the broad masses of the population with the new power. Although he had probably not read Gustave le Bon, Stalin was guided by that brilliant sociologist's great maxim, 'Revolutions merely change the surface of a country; underneath it remains the same.'

In his revolutionary faith Lenin had thought he could transform a feudal Russia into a socialist Russia by installing 'electric light in every *izba*'. When he died, history played a trick on him by making his own corpse a relic.

After Trotsky's elimination from the Commissariat for War, the *troyka* considered that its power was firmly established, but the new president of the Revvoyensoviet, Frunze, was soon seen to be an independent person capable of unexpected initiative. He soon got into touch with the generals appointed by Trotsky and became their best friend and protector. Wishing to restore the full prestige of Red Army officers, Frunze set up a committee for the purpose of re-establishing the officers' 'code of honour'

[1] This was the anarchist Adashev, one of the Red Army's aviation organizers.

in the old army style. At the same time he brought before the Politburo the question of a *habeas corpus* for officers: an arrest could not be made without the previous consent of the commanding officer of the military region.

To assert his authority, Frunze ordered a meeting of the commanders of the military regions, and at the meeting the president of the Revvoyensoviet read the agenda, by which he made changes in the command without first having obtained the consent of the Politburo.

This came near to defiance, and Zinoviev and Kamenev requested Frunze's dismissal. Stalin was opposed to such action. Frunze, who had just been appointed in Trotsky's place, could not be ousted without incurring the risk of serious trouble in the army. An impulsive man, Frunze was more dangerous than Trotsky. In his past there had been a few incidents that marked him as something of a 'terrorist'. In 1905 he had killed a police superintendent at Ivanovo-Voznessensk. When in the central prison of Irkutsk, he had been the leader of a riot in which forty-five people had met their death. In private conversations with his friends Frunze said that he would not let himself do as the 'intellectual' Trotsky had done and that he would 'have his enemies' blood before they had his'. The president of the Revvoyensoviet came to the meetings armed with a Mauser, although custom required that weapons should be left in the cloakroom. One day, when Zinoviev referred to this, Frunze answered, 'A soldier should not go unarmed, and I am a soldier of the revolution'.

Stalin and his henchmen were faced with a new problem: Trotsky had shown weakness in the struggle within the Party; he had not dared to make a *coup d'état*. But if Frunze, urged on by the Trotskyist generals of the Red Army, revolted against the Politburo with Trotsky at his side, what would happen? Nothing any good for the *troyka* could come of it. It was necessary to act before Frunze became more firmly established in the War Ministry and took complete control of the country's military machinery. First of all, therefore, the commanders of the military regions had to be replaced by supporters of Stalin and Zinoviev.

Stalin's personal telephone number (122) and his office number (034) were permanently engaged. The *vertushka exchange was transferred to Stalin's private quarters.* The Secretary-General of the Russian Communist Party was preparing to eliminate Mikhayl Vassilievich Frunze.

CHAPTER 5

THE DEFEAT OF TROTSKY

Before Frunze's elimination, Stalin was to suffer a humiliating experience: at the time of the pan-Russian Party Congress, Lenin's widow, Krupskaya, who hated Stalin and supported Trotsky, requested the reading of her late husband's will, in which Lenin emphasized the necessity for removing Stalin from the position of Secretary-General and for replacing him by 'another comrade who would be more loyal and who would not abuse his power to settle personal accounts'.

The will was read in secret session of the Congress. It was one of the great events in the history of the Soviet State. In his book, *With Stalin at the Kremlin*, Bazhanov, Stalin's former secretary, comments as follows:

"It was distressing to see Stalin. Sitting on one of the tribune benches, with his head bowed and his eyes half closed, he did not move. Only the slightly heightened colour in his face told of the tension within him. Immediately after the will was read, Zinoviev asked to speak on behalf of the Leningrad representation. He proposed that the debate should not be opened. So Stalin was saved.'

It is recorded that at the Party Congress the St Andrew Hall of the Kremlin was plunged into darkness because of an electrical breakdown. Candles were lit and by their light Stalin, pale and tight-lipped, silently heard the reading of the will. At the end, Stalin rose to his feet and said, 'I wish to be the first to request the execution of Ilyich's will. I offer my resignation.' Zinoviev leaped up, exclaiming, 'The matter has been decided by Congress'. 'In that case,' was the solemn reply, 'I submit to the will of the Party.'

Then the electricity came on again and the Kremlin hall lit up. Congress had confirmed Stalin's position. Nobody, not even Trotsky, made a move to ask for his dismissal. Making the request for Lenin's will to be executed was on that occasion enough to win the case for Stalin. Such is the way of history.

274

A few days after this never-to-be-forgotten session, Zinoviev presented his 'account' to Stalin: he asked him to transfer a dozen local secretaries who had recently been promoted by the Secretariat, all of them Stalin men. The Politburo, on which the Secretary-General had a majority, refused to agree to Zinoviev's request. The latter had left for a holiday at Kislovodsk with several other members of the Politburo whom he was determined to convince of the justice of his request. Zinoviev sent a telegram to Stalin, asking him to come to Kislovodsk for a 'private meeting'. The meeting took place in a cave and was for that reason humorously styled 'the meeting of the troglodytes'. Stalin, Zinoviev, Kamenev, Lashevich, Rudzutak, Kalinin, Bukharin and Tomsky took part. Molotov and Dzerzhinsky telegraphed their support of the 'Stalin group'. Zinoviev, Kamenev and Frunze were the only supporters of the 'Zinoviev motion'. The 'Stalin motion' was therefore adopted.

Quite rightly, Zinoviev saw in this a direct warning, and he hurriedly left Kislovodsk for Leningrad to prepare for battle against Stalin at the Fourteenth pan-Russian Congress of the Communist Party which was called for December 1925.

For the Secretary-General it was not Zinoviev, but Frunze, who was the danger now. In October 1925, by a decision of the Secretariat of the Central Committee, all people's commissars were invited to undergo medical examination at the Kremlin Policlinic. It was found that Frunze had a gastric ulcer, and the President of the Revvoyensoviet had to undergo an operation. He decided to postpone the event, for he had a weak heart, but the Policlinic advisers insisted. Frunze died on the operating-table on October 31, 1925.

The report of the autopsy was published by the Commissar for Health, Semashko, who had opposed the operation. It contained these words: 'The presence of a gastric ulcer is noted, an ulcer *completely cicatrized*'!

There were all kinds of rumours. Pamphlets appeared, accusing Stalin of having recourse to the surgeon's knife in order to be rid of Frunze.

The day after Frunze's death, Klimenty Efremovich Voroshilov was appointed President of the Revvoyensoviet. This time Stalin had control of the army. Voroshilov, his constant comrade in arms, was also 'co-opted' to the Politburo as a temporary member. Voroshilov's first proposal was to change the name of Tzaritzin to Stalingrad. Stalin returned the compliment by renaming Lugansk, Voroshilov's native town, Voroshilovgrad. Zinoviev then asked that the town of his birth, Elizabethgrad, should be known as Zinovievsk.[1] Wishing to appear impartial, Stalin also suggested changing the name of the little town of Pulkovo,[2] near Leningrad, to Trotsk.

The split in the *troyka* came about in December 1925, in the course of the Fourteenth pan-Russian Party Congress. Zinoviev spoke after the Secretary-General; with the backing of forty-five of the Leningrad representation, Zinoviev severely criticized Stalin, his politics and his administration. Zinoviev spoke of the 'stalinization' of the Party and requested its 'destalinization'.[3]

The 'right-wingers' of the Politburo, Bukharin, Rykov and Tomsky, who despised Zinoviev and Kamenev because of their complete lack of political principles (and because of the cynicism with which they changed their attitude with regard to Stalin and Trotsky), thought that Trotsky would refuse to support the 'Leningrad opposition' with his authority. But, for once, Trotsky showed a complete lack of political principle; although his struggle against the *troyka*—which had as its starting-point his book *The October Lessons*—had been constantly directed against Zinoviev and Kamenev, Trotsky decided to win over the 'Leningrad opposition' against Stalin. The struggle took a personal turn.

Trotsky's wife, Nataliya Ivanova Sedov, supplies the following testimony: 'Endless meetings were held at the Kremlin, either in our rooms or in those of Kamenev, Zinoviev or Karl Radek. The sincerity shown by Zinoviev and Kamenev was as obvious as their delight in at last being able to speak freely and discuss every problem without reserve. Collaboration with Stalin, who, because of his intellectual make-up and his lack of general culture, had little understanding of the language of ideas, was indeed a heavy task. Kamenev got his own back in little ways by telling stories and mimicking Stalin's awkwardness, his Georgian accent and his elementary education.

But these 'games' by Kamenev, Zinoviev and their new ally Trotsky merely stirred up hatred: Kamenev's 'Caucasian anecdotes' were matched by 'Jewish anecdotes' from Stalin's friends. The new triumvirate of the opposition—Trotsky,

---

[1] Now called Kirovsk.

[2] Pulkovo is well known for its Observatory on the Russian meridian.

[3] Nikita Khrushchev's 'destalinization' is therefore no new idea, but in 1925 the word 'destalinization' meant only the dismissal of local secretaries who were loyal to Stalin.

Zinoviev and Kamenev — consisted entirely of Jews. A strong current of anti-Semitism was apparent and pervaded the whole of the Stalin epoch.

In this struggle within the Kremlin, thorough use was made of an extremely powerful weapon, viz. calumny. The opposition accused Stalin of preparing his own 'Thermidor' and betraying the revolution. The Stalin group denounced the oppositionists for having made preparations for a *coup d'état*, for seizing power through insurrection, and a military *pronunciamento*.

It has been seen how obstinately Trotsky refused to listen to the advice of military men like Radek, Drobnis and Antonov-Ovseyenko. In spite of that, the group consisting of Sapronov, Drobnis, Smirnov and Perepechko spoke openly of an 'insurrection of the Commune', of a 'conspiracy of equals',[1] of the need for Russian 'Babeufism' in response to the machinations of the 'Stalinist Thermidorians'.

The 'young communists', the *komsomols*, took an active part in the struggle. The leaders of this organization called in the local secretaries to 'reason' with them. Stalin frequently stayed up until dawn with their representatives in his rooms. The Secretary-General was, indeed, bent on dispelling the rumours that he was a 'Thermidorian' and wanted to bury the revolution. His most important ally at the time, Bukharin, gave the following watchword to the peasants: 'Increase your wealth so that you may be able to provision the Soviet State and supply it with raw materials'. The opposition, which employed any means to discredit Stalin, quoted only the first three words, 'Increase your wealth' and accused Stalin and Bukharin of preparing, not only for 'Thermidor', but also for 'the Directory'.

In 1926, the opposition turned to direct action with the masses. A campaign of 'private meetings' of Party members was decided upon. Zinoviev, Kamenev, Trotsky, Smilga, Preobrazhensky, Radek, Ivan Smirnov and others formed small 'conspiratorial groups' as in the days of the Czars. The problems of the 'permanent revolution' were debated at these meetings, while the students watched at the doors for fear of a visit from the GPU. Some of these meetings took place even in the Kremlin. The situation became extremely thorny for Stalin. The anti-government movement was penetrating the sacred precincts.

[1] The writer Ylya Ehrenburg, who lived in Paris at this time, wrote *The Conspiracy of Equals*. In this book he describes in 'very Muscovite' language the struggle between these two groups at the Kremlin.

While the communist workers were going to Trotsky, Zinoviev, Kamenev and Radek in the Kremlin to hear anti-Stalin and anti-government speeches, long lines of peasants and provincials were filing past Lenin's mausoleum. But, one day at the Nikolsky Gate, 'oppositionist' students distributed leaflets containing words spoken by Stalin to Zinoviev before the latter went over to the opposition: 'To consolidate our régime we need a relic. We need a Red mummy at the Kremlin. Then the people will forget the saints of the Orthodox Church and will come to worship the remains of the Red St Vladimir, Ilyich.'

A detachment of the Cheka immediately surrounded the Red Square and arrested a dozen students who were handing out leaflets. They were sent to Siberia. Two of them who were found to be carrying arms were shot. The first blood had been shed.

But the Cheka-GPU did not merely concern itself with hunting down opposition students. Powerful enemies of the young Soviet State were awaiting a favourable moment to counter-attack and they were encouraged by the arguments of Clemenceau, Millerand, Churchill, Hoover and Baron Tanaka.

White Russian emigration to foreign countries had from the start created a large number of terrorist organizations to fight the Soviet power. The first of these organizations was the famous 'Azbuka' of the two monarchist leaders, Purishkevich and Schulgin. This organization was based in Yugoslavia, with another 'parallel' centre in Paris and its 'Working Committee' on Rumanian soil, first at Kyshinev and later at Bucharest. 'Azbuka' carried out a few acts of sabotage in the port of Odessa. (It made an underground tunnel in order to blow up the Cheka building there. The explosion was only partly successful.) A second terrorist organization, an extremely dynamic one, was formed in Paris by General Kutepov. A remarkably attractive women, Zacharenko-Schultz, was put in charge of it. Three secret expeditions to Russia were organized to blow up the Cheka building, the Central Committee of the Communist Party and the Kremlin buildings which included the presidency of the Council, the Sovnarkom.

The terrorists were to some extent successful. The bomb placed in the Cheka building in Lyubyanka Square destroyed the left wing of the building and killed seventy-five people. Another bomb in the premises of the Committee of the Communist Party exploded, killing thirty-five Party members and wounding some dozens of them, including Bukharin himself. A third explosion succeeded in Leningrad. Almost all the terrorists were captured by the Cheka, except Rodyonov and Bessonov, who escaped abroad.

The anti-communist Ukrainians also organized terrorist detachments in Poland with *hetman* Tutunik at their head. They managed to blow up a few railway junctions and assassinate a few dozen communists at Kiev, Zhitomir, Ekaterinoslav and Odessa. Tutunik was eventually caught on Soviet soil and shot at Kiev. With the exception of the Ukrainians, the White terrorist activities were for the most part subsidized by financial groups in Paris, London and Tokyo.

Apart from the monarchist organizations there also existed the active groups of anarchists of 'Batko' Makhno. Makhno himself had sought refuge in Paris but 1,500 of his former army comrades lived in Rumanian Bukovina, where they were working as woodcutters. Every year, a small band of forty or fifty 'woodcutters', armed to the teeth and well appointed, crossed the frontier into the USSR, where they blew up trains and bridges, assassinated the communist leaders, etc. In 1930, the Swedish financier Ivar Kreuger concluded an agreement with Makhno through one of his directors, Vladimir Bogovut, a friend of the turncoat Soviet diplomat G. Bessedovsky. Kreuger, displeased because the Soviet government had cancelled his permit to exploit the aspen forests, decided to lend his support to an armed peasant revolt in the Ukraine. Arms and munitions were bought from England to equip a veritable small army of 3,000 Makhnovians, who were to break out in the Ukraine in the summer of 1931 by the help of collective action and peasant uprisings. The GPU got wind of all these preparations from one of its agents, Sterligov, living in Bulgaria. The Soviet government requested Rumania to disarm the Makhnovians immediately and backed up the request with the threat that the Red cavalry would move into Bessarabia and Bukovina. The suicide of the match king, Kreuger, in March 1931, deprived Makhno of his main support.

Besides these important organizations there existed a few dozen local organizations: in Czechoslovakia, that of Serge Masslov, head of the Russian Peasant Party; in Yugoslavia, that of Ksyunin and Gutchkov, former Minister of War in the Provisional Government; in Germany, those of Shabelsky, Gumansky, Dzhaparidze; Petluras (Ukrainian) and Dashnak

(Armenian); in Esthonia, the remains of Youdenich's army headed by Ivanov; in Latvia, the peasant organization under the leadership of Sokolov-Krechit; in Turkey, that of the Crimean Tartars under Ibrahim Mustafovich Ibrahimov; in Bulgaria, that of the Russian Revolutionary Socialists with Lebedev and Pronin. Obviously, the Cheka-GPU of the Kremlin had to maintain an implacable struggle against all these terrorist organizations, most of which were kept going by foreign capital. It should not be overlooked, moreover, that the White terrorist organizations in Manchuria, Mongolia and Japan were as numerous as those mentioned above.

Millions of money were swallowed up by these terrorist activities. For instance, Ivar Kreuger spent more than a million dollars and Sir Henry Deterding about five million. As for the Japanese, the Mitsui Trust had a special credit of fifty million yen for organizing subversive anti-Bolshevik activities.

One very striking episode in the Cheka's struggle against the terrorist counter-revolutionaries was the 'Lockhart Plot', important enough at the time to receive mention.

The summer of 1918 was one of the most difficult times for the Soviet power in the Kremlin. Famine was raging in Russia, for the Ukraine was occupied by the Germans, Caucasia was cut off, Siberia and the Volga region were held by the Constituent armies and insurgent Czechs.

It was then that a plot developed in the Kremlin itself, the plot of the Kremlin Latvian Guard. This force was composed of the Latvian battalions under the command of Colonel Berzin. The Cheka heard that several Latvian officers had been approached by the secret agents of Bruce Lockhart, the British Chargé d'Affaires and principal member of the Intelligence Service in Russia, to encourage them to mutiny against the Soviets, assassinate Lenin and Trotsky and set up a new power in Moscow, a moderate Russian government.

A serious danger threatened the Kremlin, for, although the Latvian battalions had a high percentage of Bolsheviks in their ranks, a strong non-Bolshevik majority, particularly among the officers bought by foreign gold, could direct the conspiracy and repeat the affair of Paul I's assassination by agents of the Intelligence Service in March 1801 by murdering Lenin and Trotsky in their Kremlin quarters.

Dzerzhinsky, the head of the Cheka, decided to act. He called in Colonel Berzin and Captain Peterson, two Latvian officers who were a hundred per cent Bolshevik, and suggested that they should get in touch with Lockhart's agents, offering to dispose of Lenin and Trotsky for the sum of $1 million.

Lockhart swallowed the bait. He saw the Latvians in a private flat where one of his most important Russian agents lived, paid them $200,000 'on account' and formulated the plan for the Kremlin coup d'état. By this plan, a squad of the Guards, led by Berzin, was to enter Lenin's and Trotsky's rooms after nightfall and assassinate the two Bolshevik leaders. Simultaneously, anti-Soviet forces in the Upper Volga region[1] (Yaroslavl-Rybinsk) were to rise up against the Soviet authority and establish an anti-Bolshevik government. The new dictator was to be Sakinkov, the former leader of the Socialist-Revolutionary terrorists who had fought the Czar and, by his popularity and energy, the most eminent character among the anti-Bolsheviks.

Lockhart was photographed when meeting the two Latvians, his conversations were overheard and written into the official record by Cheka agents in an adjoining room. The trap set for His Majesty's diplomat was crude, but Lockhart fell into it. On the day of the proposed coup d'état, a revolt did indeed break out in the Upper Volga. Savinkov, persuaded that the Kremlin would be 'cleared' of Lenin and Trotsky by Latvian Guards, gave orders to march on Moscow. Meanwhile, in the Kremlin, the Cheka carried out the arrest of Lockhart's liaison agents and the British Chargé d'Affaires and his staff were bundled out of Russia.

Savinkov took refuge abroad, where he continued to fight the communists until 1924.

Savinkov's organization was centred at Prague, where Masaryk was aiding the anti-Bolshevik Russians. To entice Savinkov into Russia, the Cheka formed an organization of double agents, the 'Trest', which convinced him of the presence of 'insurrectionist centres' in Russia. Persuaded that it was necessary for him to go there to inspect these non-existent centres in person, Savinkov secretly crossed the Russo-Polish border and was arrested at Minsk by the Belorussian Cheka agent, the German Baron von Pillau.[2]

Tried by the Supreme Court of the USSR, Savinkov made a full confession and was sentenced to death, but was reprieved by

[1] Berzin claimed to have a whole network of agents at his disposal in this region.
[2] Shot by order of Yezhov in 1938.

the Executive Central Committee, and the sentence was commuted to ten years' solitary confinement with hard labour. Instead of being held in a prison, Savinkov was confined to a small flat in the Cheka building in Lyubyanka Square. Dzerzhinsky occasionally took Savinkov out in his limousine and showed him Soviet Moscow and the Red Kremlin. During one of these drives Savinkov obtained a promise from the head of the Cheka that he would be liberated and sent abroad to fight the enemies of the Soviet rule. Savinkov declared that he realized how meaningless were the counter-revolutionary activities; he saw the necessity for all Russian patriots to support the new Kremlin Government. True to his promise, Dzerzhinsky made a request for Savinkov to be released, but the Politburo refused. At the Kremlin there was no confidence in the former terrorist leader who, once he was out of the country, might renew the fight.

When he learned the news in his flat at the Cheka, Savinkov opened the window and jumped from the fifth floor to the stones of the inner courtyard. He left a letter for Dzerzhinsky, which the latter published in *Pravda*: 'I am sorry,' wrote Savinkov, 'that you appreciated neither the sincerity of my repentance nor my eagerness to blot out my crimes against the Nation by a complete reconciliation with the power established in the Kremlin by the Nation. I cannot go on with this life in my gilded cage at the Cheka. The past weighs too heavily upon me. Being unable to pay for my crimes, I can only atone for them. That is why I have decided to take my life. I am grateful to you, Felix Edmundovich, for the candid talks between two revolutionaries whom fate has placed on opposite sides of the fence. As I am about to die, it is to you that I turn to ask for my last greeting to be conveyed to the people, in whose name I am sure history will accord us absolution for all the blood we have shed in the fight for the well-being of Russia! Farewell, Felix Edmundovich!'

By Dzerzhinsky's order a plaque was put up in the inner courtyard of the Cheka with the inscription, 'Here died B. Savinkov, a lapsed revolutionary'. The plaque was removed by Dzerzhinsky's successor.

By the end of 1926 the battle within the Kremlin became still more intense. But already Zinoviev and Kamenev were showing signs of fatigue; they might be expected at any time to agree to a compromise. Trotsky, the mainspring of the new opposition, the 'Bloc'[1]—which replaced the *troyka*—showed firmness. But suddenly he fell ill again, of the same mysterious malady as in 1924. Dr Krause, who had come specially to Moscow from Berlin, stated that Trotsky should go immediately into his Berlin clinic for observation. Trotsky's relapse occurred very opportunely for Stalin.

When Trotsky came back from Berlin in 1927, the efforts of the opposition had assumed an almost insurrectionist character. The Kremlin gates were guarded by double detachments of the GPU and the special Guard of the Politburo under the command of the head of Stalin's Secretariat. The rooms where the full Central Committee of the Party met were kept closed, except on session days. The keys were held by Stalin or the head of his Secretariat, Tovtukha, soon to be replaced by Leon Mikhaylovich Mekhlis.

Nobody could now visit Trotsky in his Kremlin flat without first having obtained a special pass signed by the commandant of the Kremlin. Officials of the Council Presidency and the Executive Central Committee were searched, and also their offices. The opposition was becoming increasingly mad.

It was then that Yagoda instituted his first 'plot'. After Dzerzhinsky's sudden death on July 20, 1926, his place was taken by Menzhinsky. But the real head of the Cheka-GPU was Menzhinsky's chief assistant, Yagoda.

This 'plot' was a complete fabrication: a former Czarist officer was supposed to have procured arms for the oppositionists who thus could have taken the Kremlin by storm and massacred the Politburo. This officer 'confessed' and faced the firing-squad, while the members of the opposition were arrested. One of the latter was the secretary of the 'Union of Co-operative Supply Stores', a protégé of Stalin's wife, Nadezhda Alliluyeva. The result of the 'plot': seven men shot.

Kamenev, Zinoviev and Trotsky were asked for explanations before the Central Committee in plenary session. Zinoviev and Kamenev denied that they had had any hand in the 'plot', but Trotsky could not contain his anger; from the top of the rostrum in the St Andrew Hall of the Kremlin he pointed to Stalin and cried, 'There's the real conspirator against the Communist Party! It is you, Dzhugashvili, who are the unspeakable grave-digger of the Revolution!'

[1] The 'Opposition Bloc' was the name given to the Trotsky-Zinoviev-Kamenev alliance.

After this incident, Nataliya Ivanovna Sedov noted in her *Diary*:

'Pyatakov was the first to come back to our flat after the meeting. Very pale and downcast, he poured himself a glass of water, drank it eagerly and said, "It was worse than anything. And why did Leon Davidovich[1] say that? Stalin will not forgive even his great-grandchildren for it!" Pyatakov was too upset to explain clearly to me what had happened. I learned later that Stalin had made a threatening gesture to Leon Davidovich, had stood up and, controlling himself with difficulty, had slammed out of the hall. I realized that the break was irreparable.'

At the end of October 1927, Trotsky and Zinoviev spoke for the last time before the Central Committee, and were then immediately debarred from further participation.

On November 7, 1927, Trotsky, Zinoviev and their friends left the Kremlin, never to return. It was the tenth anniversary of the Revolution. Ten years had been long enough to eliminate the man who was Lenin's first-lieutenant and the organizer of the Red Army.

On December 2, 1927, the Fifteenth pan-Russian Communist Party Congress opened at the Kremlin. Stalin spoke for seven hours forty minutes. Then Molotov gave a full report on agriculture. Congress adopted the first Five-Year Plan and the Rural Collectivization Project. At this Congress, Zinoviev and Kamenev renounced Trotsky.

On January 16, 1928, Trotsky was exiled to Alma-Ata in Kazakhstan. In January 1929 he was banished from the USSR. At the same time a special commission 'purged' all the suspect 'tenants' of the Kremlin.

[1] Trotsky.

CHAPTER 6

ALLILUYEVA'S SUICIDE

Trotsky's banishment merely aggravated the struggle within the exile's influence was still very great. His popularity, especially with the army, was much greater than that of Voroshilov, who placidly carried out Stalin's orders. Soviet youth, turbulent and enthusiastic like youth the world over, continued to offer resistance to Stalin. Trotsky did his utmost to increase this resistance. His son, Leon Sedov, became the central figure in a secret organization controlled from abroad. Several collaborators from the GPU, close friends of Trotsky, formed in the very heart of Kremlin in spite of the dismissal of Zinoviev and Kamenev. The the police force a Trotskyist secret society which built up an intense anti-Stalin activity. The Kremlin walls were occasionally covered with posters that referred to Stalin in more than ungracious terms.

It was in Stalin's native Georgia that there was open Trotskyist opposition. Mdivani, Kavtaradze and Okudzhava made speeches against Stalin, which resulted in their arrest. In his villa on the Isle of Prinkipo, where he lived for several years, Trotsky established his international headquarters and received there members of the Comintern to prepare them for action against the 'grave-digger of the international communist movement'. Yagoda sent his secret agent, the Latvian Franck. But Yagoda himself was not entirely free from danger. The former chemist was as proud as he was clever; he wished at any price to take part in the activities of the literary and artistic circles of Moscow and he was easily able to do so because of his brother-in-law, Leopold Averbach, a brilliant literary critic.[1] Yagoda took over a flat in the Kremlin in order to receive literary personalities and actors of stage and screen. So it was that in the first 'State Circus' the song-writer Sokolsky could he heard singing couplets dedicated to Yagoda. The nominal head of the secret police, Menzhinsky, took almost no further part in GPU affairs. A talented pianist, he gave up his flat in the Kremlin to go and

[1] He was shot as a result of the Great Purge of 1938.

285

live in the GPU building in Lyubyanka Square, where he spent his time playing the piano.

Stalin was quick to realize the danger which might face him from men like Yagoda in revolutionary times. In a conversation with his friend Gogohya, a Georgian relative by marriage of Nadezhda Alliluyeva, Stalin declared that 'Yagoda would one day end up in his own GPU cellar'. But at that time Stalin still had need of Yagoda, and Yagoda knew it. In a hurry to replace Menzhinsky, who was taking so long to die, the ex-chemist inaugurated the 'system of concentration-camps as a source of cheap labour'. The liquidation of the NEP made it possible for him to organize the first of these camps in the former monastery of Solovki Island in the White Sea. Yagoda made use of his 'concentration-camp resources' to construct a canal between the White Sea and the Baltic. A very capable organizer, he improved the system of 'labour groups' and the 'Communes for corrective labour'.

This side of the police chief's activities could not be displeasing to Stalin, who had no personal liking for the aesthetic intellectual Menzhinsky. While Menzhinsky was still living, Yagoda was already the undisputed master at Lyubyanka Square. After the death of the former People's Commissar for Finance, Stalin had Yagoda accepted by the Politburo as chief of police. Stalin had decided upon this appointment with some apprehension; he was beginning to experience symptoms of that same illness which had so opportunely put Trotsky out of action at critical moments in the fight against the opposition. A heart attack— the first of a series which resulted in his death in 1953—seized the Secretary-General during his indisposition.[1] Stalin refrained from ordering an enquiry, which would have been troublesome at that time, contenting himself with spending all his time in his small flat in the Kremlin, while looking for a country house for himself in the neighbourhood of Moscow.

In that way Stalin thought he could remove himself to a distance from the GPU and its chief. His bodyguard ensured his personal safety. He found a refuge some twenty-eight miles from the capital. It was a former *dacha*, set in a splendid park, with a pond, lawns and gardens. Nadezhda Alliluyeva named this

[1] The one-time Soviet diplomat Raskolnikov was the first to unveil the complex and sinister relationship between Stalin and Yagoda. He did so even before the lawsuit of March 1938 which resulted in Yagoda's execution. Raskolnikov's revelations corroborate some of those made by Nikita Khrushchev in his secret report.

dacha 'Gorinka' (not to be confused with the Gorki property where Lenin died) and became attached to her new home. She was not, however, to enjoy it for long. Twenty years younger than her husband, she was an unsophisticated woman who would never give up her modest employment at the Co-operative Supply Stores. But she was on excellent terms with the 'Communist Youth'. At that time, Soviet sexual morality was very broad. To be sure, the 'phalansterian free love' of Kollontay was no longer practised, but the morals of the young people who met at Alliluyeva's house were very different from those of Stalin, who had the outlook of his Caucasian mountain-folk and the narrow views of a provincial bourgeois.

Alliluyeva and Stalin differed also in their political ideas. Alliluyeva would have liked to see a deep democratization of the Party and adhered to the conceptions of the Sapronov, Smirnov, Drobnis, Boguslavsky group, which fell in with the Soviet youth of the times.

The quarrels between husband and wife sometimes took so violent a turn that Stalin had to send their children, Svetlana and Basil, to stay with Alliluyeva's parents, so that they should not see their father and mother quarrelling. Yagoda, who wished to 'please' Stalin, had a close watch set upon the *Komsomols* who visited Alliluyeva and was quick to discover among them a few 'terrorists in disguise'. Thirty-seven 'terrorist' *komsomols* who were connected, or supposedly connected, with Leon Sedov and his terrorist centre were arrested. The Latvian Franck, who had spent five months with Trotsky at Prinkipo and was Sedov's liaison agent, 'confessed' to having re-entered the USSR with the express purpose of preparing the way for Stalin's assassination. Franck furnished proofs of his stay at Prinkipo: photographs of Trotsky and his son, letters from Sedov and instructions written in chemical ink. This double agent, suddenly repentant, gave the names of a dozen *Komsomols* as accomplices. Most of the young people were friends of Alliluyeva. The enquiry was conducted by Yagoda in person and the record given to Stalin.

Was Stalin convinced of the truth of the accusations brought against the young communists in Alliluyeva's circle or did he allow Yagoda to take action in order to appease his hatred of his wife's young friends? Did he suspect his wife of infidelity or was he bent on political revenge? Was he, in 1932, already a prey to the persecution mania referred to by Nikita Krushchev in his report? It is difficult to say. All that is known is that on

October 5, 1932, Alliluyeva went to Stalin's rooms in the Kremlin and telephoned to her husband at the Party Central Committee. At the conclusion of a fairly long conversation, Alliluyeva
shot herself through the heart.

Her suicide was passed off by the Moscow press as 'sudden
death'. After lying in state in the Hall of Pillars, her body was
buried in the cemetery of the Novodevichi alongside the grave
of Yoffe, a Bolshevik who had also committed suicide as a protest
against her husband's politics. At Stalin's order, a magnificent
sculptured stele was erected over his second wife's[1] grave.

[1] Stalin's first wife was Catherine Svanidze, who died in 1909. They had a
son, Yasha, who was shot by the Germans in a camp of Russian prisoners of
war. Yasha had been brought up in Tiflis by his grandmother Catherine
(Keke) Dzhugashvili.

CHAPTER 7

THE ROAD TO DICTATORSHIP

Nadezhda Alliluyeva's death affected Stalin deeply. His young wife was devoted to him and he was very much attached to her. This was the second time that death had struck at his private life. His first wife, Catherine Svanidze, whom he had loved very much, had died of galloping consumption. At her funeral, Stalin had opened his heart to his friend Iremashvili. The latter reported in his *Memoirs* (published in Berlin in 1924): 'He looked dejected and greeted me as a friend, as he used to do. His drawn face mirrored the suffering caused to this hard, relentless man by the death of his partner. The shock must have moved him very deeply, for it was impossible for him to hide his emotion.

'When the modest procession reached the cemetery gates, Stalin grasped my hand strongly, pointed to the coffin and said, 'That woman softened my heart. She is dead, and with her go *my last feelings for humanity.*' Putting his right hand to his breast, Koba[1] sighed, "Here is *emptiness, unspeakable emptiness*".'

This episode, which took place in 1910, long before the Revolution, throws light on Stalin's state of mind in November 1932, when his second wife died. The Kremlin was full of rumours that he wished to become the dictator of Soviet Russia. Ryutin, the local secretary of the Party in Moscow, and his friends said so openly. Ryutin did not scruple to call Stalin *the future Lord Protector of Russia.* There was rigorous collectivism throughout the countryside and it resulted in the victimization of countless peasants, who were imprisoned, deported or herded like cattle in trucks of unknown destination. It is known that, in Trotsky's words, Ryutin secretly printed a brochure in which he referred to Stalin as an *agent provocateur* whose aim was to 'bury the revolution'.

After he had lost his wife, Stalin became the target for frenzied attacks by his enemies. Leon Mekhlis, the new head of his personal secretariat, an eminent historian and journalist,

[1] Stalin's youthful nickname.

appears to have reminded Stalin of the occasion of the death of Anastasya Romanov, the wife of Ivan the Terrible. The boyars who contributed to the Czarina's death exploited the situation in order to make veiled attacks upon the Czar. The historical parallel was disturbing to Stalin. Soon after Alliluyeva's death he had a rather serious heart attack. When he had recovered, he decided to conduct a stubborn fight against all his enemies, in which respect he was again acting as Ivan the Terrible had done. From that time onwards, Stalin imitated the Czar, not only in his policy, but also in his private life. The first symptoms of persecution mania appeared in Stalin as they had appeared in Ivan the Terrible, after the death of his wife. But another woman entered the life of the Secretary-General. She was Rosa Kaganovich.

Thanks to her, the 'Gorinka' *dacha* was completely modernized. Stalin had several buildings constructed near this villa to house the fifty members of his bodyguard. Machine-guns were placed in the turrets. A signal system was installed along the road from the *dacha* to the Kremlin. This system followed the Arbat through Moscow and was used to inform the police of the movements of Stalin's car and his guards.

Stalin married Rosa Kaganovich, entrusting to her care the upbringing of his children. Twice a week his third wife held receptions at 'Gorinka', while, at the Kremlin, Stalin was working out with Yagoda plans for the complete annihilation of the Soviet *Kramola*.

Yagoda's secret files contained proofs of the fierce and persistent hatred in which he was held. The 'right-wingers' Rykov and Bukharin were in negotiation with the Trotskyists and Zinovievists for the overthrow of Stalin. Bukharin said to anyone who cared to listen, 'What can you do when faced by an adversary of this sort? This worthless product of the Party is a Gengis Khan.'

In his dejection, Stalin confided in Bukharin (knowing full well that he would repeat his remarks to his enemies and the waverers in the Politburo: Molotov, Kalinin and Voroshilov), 'If they want a fight to extinction, they shall have it. Why are you against me, Kolya?[1] Why will you not take your seat by me and direct the Party and the country? You and I, I and you, will govern Soviet Russia. I am alone now, terribly alone, surrounded by a lot of "fools". What is Molotov but an official?

[1] Bukharin.

Nothing more. And Kalinin? A crafty but unimportant village mayor who would like to end his days drinking tea with four lumps of sugar instead of two. And Voroshilov? A *feldwebel* like his father before him, neither more nor less. Join with me and help me to set up the young communists, and let all that gang go to the devil. Why do you hate me, Kolya? After all, we are as Himalayan peaks in the Politburo.'

Voroshilov was told of this conversation by Bukharin himself, and asked Stalin for an explanation. Stalin denied everything, declaring that these slanders were 'a despicable invention of an enemy of the Party'.

Meanwhile, in the 'Gorinka' *dacha*, Rosa Kaganovich was performing the duties of a very gracious hostess, receiving her friends from Nizhni-Novgorod, first and foremost of whom was Nadezhda Bulganin, a doctor like herself. As the historian Nikolaevsky says, 'Gorinka' was becoming a real 'Nizhni-Novgorod Society'. It was within this society created by Rosa Kaganovich that Stalin found his surest and most devoted collaborators.

Molotov began his career at Nizhni-Novgorod (now Gorki) in 1918, as Party Secretary and President of the Regional Soviet. Kaganovich also began there, in 1918-1919, as President of the Workers' Syndicates and Party Secretary, and Nicholas Bulganin as Deputy Leader of the Osobyi Otdel. Mikoyan went there from Baku at the end of 1919 to accept appointment as Party Secretary and stayed until 1922.

Nicholayevsky, who wrote a study of the Volga in the Russian revolution, gives much space to 'the Nizhni-Novgorod Association', which 'conquered the Kremlin thanks to Nadezhda Bulganin, schoolfellow and university friend of Rosa Kaganovich'. It was because of this 'Association' that Malyshev (the 'Kremlin's strange invalid' and head of the rocket industry) achieved a brilliant career, as did also Saburov (president of the Plan after Voznesensky), Pervukhin (ambassador to Berlin), Baybakov, Ponomarenko, Ignatev, Pospelov, Shepilov, Mikhayl Suslov (at present 'No. 3 at the Kremlin') and many others.

Stalin was also looking for a way to attract the young people in order to create a 'faithful relief force'. Zhdanov, Andreyev, Malenkov, Yezhov, Shcherbakov and Kossygin were brought in by Mekhlis, the head of his private secretariat. Kaganovich and Bulganin brought with them the young Ukrainian, Nikita Khrushchev, the secretary of an administrative district of Moscow and political commissar for the construction of the capital's underground railway. From Leningrad occasionally came Seryozha Kirov, the secretary of the Party Committee in Leningrad, and from Tiflis the Georgian Lavrenti Beria, head of the Caucasian GPU and Party Secretary in Tiflis. Of all these, the closest friend of Stalin was probably Kirov. He was a Siberian by birth and a gifted student of the Tomsk Institute of Technology, whose real name was Kostrikov. He took part in the civil war of 1918 on the banks of the Volga, where he made Stalin's acquaintance and quickly became his confidential friend. Few of Stalin's circle can boast of having been so heaped with honours as Kirov.

When Stalin offered Kirov a copy of his *Questions of Leninism* he inscribed it 'To my friend and dear brother Seryozha Kirov'.

The year 1933 was spent in the application of compulsory collectivism and the deportation of peasants, on pretext of pursuing the fight against the *Kulaks*.[1] Preparations were also made for the Seventeenth Pan-Russian Party Congress to be held early in the following year.

When the Congress met in January 1934, Kirov proposed that it should be named *The Victors' Congress*; the St Andrew's Hall was filled with wild applause. Stalin remained motionless. Did he suspect some trick? The Congress ended with the election of a new Central Committee[2] and a new secretariat. By secret decision, never published, Congress abolished the title of 'Secretary-General' so as to 'return to the Lenin tradition'. Nikolayevsky points out that, from the time of the Seventeenth Congress, Stalin signed no more decrees as 'Secretary-General', but merely as 'Secretary of the Central Committee of the Russian Communist Party'. That is proof that the title was abolished by the 'Victors' Congress'; it was to pay dearly for its boldness.

1934 passed much more calmly than the previous year. It was rumoured that Stalin had had a second heart attack in March and that he was about to give up his duties as Party leader and retire to the Black Sea coast.

During the evening of December 1, 1934, the capital of the USSR heard that Serge Kirov had just been murdered in Leningrad by a GPU official, Nikolayev. Stalin, Voroshilov, Molotov, Kalinin, Mikoyan, Kaganovich, Zhdanov and Andreyev left at

[1] The wealthy peasants.

[2] In his 'secret report' Khrushchev stated that, between 1936 and 1940, Stalin had about seventy per cent of the delegates of the Victors' Congress executed.

once by special train for Leningrad, after promulgating the harsh law of December 1st directed against the opposition as responsible for Kirov's assassination. Yagoda, the head of the GPU, requisitioned a railway engine from Moscow station and left for Leningrad two hours after the Politburo.

A telegram sent by Yagoda to the GPU provincial heads ordered the immediate liquidation of about a thousand people who had been arrested for 'counter-revolutionary intrigues'.

Once again the spectre of terror appeared in the Kremlin as it did in August 1918, after Fanny Kaplan's assault upon Lenin. This time the reckoning was to prove more bloody than that of the days before the September equinox of 1918.

The 'Law of December 1, 1934' has often been compared to Couton's law of the 22nd Prairial, Year II, which hastened the downfall of Robespierre. It is difficult to make a reliable estimate of the number of victims of the law of the 22nd Prairial. As for that of December 1934, there were probably some thousands of victims who met their fate between 1934 and 1940, including about 300 members of the old Bolshevik Party Guard, the 'Companions of Lenin' who directed the October uprising against Kerensky, as well as hundreds of long-service communist fighters. This law also enabled Stalin's successors to liquidate Beria and almost the entire 'upper crust' of the MVD between 1953 and 1956.

By a grim irony of history, the law of December 1, 1934, which was the Russian equivalent of the 9th Thermidor of the French Revolution, was not rescinded until 1957, by Nikita Khrushchev, after his victory over the members of the 'anti-Party': Molotov, Malenkov, Kaganovich and others.

CHAPTER 8

THE LIQUIDATION OF THE OPPOSITION

The Kirov affair will always be one of those mysterious stories of the Kremlin for which an explanation cannot be found. In his Report to the 22nd Party Congress Khrushchev declared that the Kirov affair 'still remained obscure' but that he had ordered a thorough inquiry into it. Khrushchev concludes: 'It is quite possible that the whole of the dismal affair may have taken place without Stalin's knowledge'.

But Stalin was too astute a politician not to take advantage of the assassination in order to liquidate many of his enemies. In Leningrad a new GPU leader was appointed. He was a certain Zakovsky, whom Stalin received in person at the Kremlin so as to make his intentions known to him. This reception took place in his private rooms. Yagoda *was not invited*; he who for some time had borne the title of Commissar General for State Security (and worn a uniform as ornate as a marshal's), realized that his position was very unsafe. From the summer of 1935, he took to drinking, no doubt to dispel the notion that his disgrace was imminent. He could not but end his days in the GPU cellar, near the boyar Kuchka's *yama*.

It was certainly because he wished to save his neck that Yagoda devised his 'Kremlin plot' in the summer of 1935. The Kremlin commandant, the Latvian Peterson, and the woman doctor Rosenfeld of the Kremlin Policlinic (who had attended Allilluyeva) were accused of planning a *coup d'état* and of intending to poison Stalin and his secretarial staff. All those who were in any way connected with this story were shot. They included the doctor's husband, a talented painter. Kamenev was taken from the Verkhneuralsk prison and brought to Moscow, where he was tried, found guilty and sentenced to a further ten years' imprisonment in addition to the five-year sentence already imposed. A series of lawsuits ensued. The judges mercilessly applied the Law of December 1, 1934, and sentenced large numbers of people *in their absence, on records supplied by the police.*

While the terror was on the increase, Stalin often sought the seclusion of his 'Gorinka' *dacha* to rest and share the company of the 'Nizhni-Novgorod Association' and his assistants, Malenkov, Zhdanov, Yezhov, Mekhlis, Andreyev and Beria. Stalin was most often seen with Yezhov, who had been appointed fifth secretary of the Communist Party Central Committee and who, among his other duties, was Director of Literature. Molotov did not hide the fact that he considered this to be a strange choice; Yezhov, an uneducated dwarf, a former Rostov factory worker, suspected before the revolution of being an informer of the Czar's police, was the man who was to restore literature to a position in keeping with 'the general line' and bring writers to heel.

At that time Boris Pilnyak was working at his new novel *Island Woods*. When it was finished, the novel was sent to Yezhov, who found in it 'counter-revolutionary' tendencies. He gave Pilnyak *a list of fifty passages to be amended*. After a stormy argument with Yezhov, Pilnyak said to a friend, 'This sinister dwarf will have me thrown into prison in the end. With people like that, there is not a single adult in the land who does not risk being shot one day !'

Pilnyak's prophecy came true. The author of *The Bare Year*, *Ivan da Maria* and *The Machines and the Wolves* was shot by Yezhov in 1938. For his part, Stalin undertook the disciplining of the two most famous contemporary Russian writers, Gorki and Alexis Tolstoy. Maxim Gorki was to write a novel on the subject of Ivan the Terrible and Tolstoy was engaged in writing his novel about Peter the Great. But Gorki avoided appearing at the 'Gorinka' *dacha*; this 'second Kremlin' was repugnant to him. Alexis Tolstoy went there on several occasions but said one day that it was impossible to write there under pressure from people like Yezhov and malicious press critics. Stalin gave him reassurances, took him home in his car and was lavish in his protestations of friendship. Next day, *Pravda* ceased its attacks on Alexis Tolstoy.

But, in the very heart of the GPU there was a strong, secret current of opposition. Pamphlets found their way even into the corridors used by the secret police. Some collaborators of the GPU were accused of distributing them and disappeared into the Lyubyanka cellar. In order to gain the necessary time to obtain the prisoners' confessions, Stalin sent to the GPU his regrettably famous circular, to which Khrushchev refers in his Report: the police employed methods of torture. And that, in spite of the Soviet law formally forbidding it!

Hundreds of accused people confessed to everything that was required of them so as to shorten their time in prison and die as soon as possible. The suicides of members of the Central Committee such as Skrypnik, heads of local committees, writers, ordinary workers and low-ranking enthusiasts assumed the proportions of an epidemic. The old Lenin Guard began to disappear like the Moscow snow in the April sunshine.

It was in this atmosphere that Stalin decided to strike his great blow: during the night of August 14, 1936, the Moscow radio announced that in five days' time the legal proceedings against the 'Trotskyist-Zinovievist Centre' would begin.

The 'Case against the Thirteen' opened in Moscow on August 19, 1936. In the dock were Zinoviev, Kamenev, Evdokimov, Bakayev, Smirnov, Ter-Vaganyan, Holtzmann, Rheingold, Dreitser, Lurie, David, Bermann-Yurin and Olderg. 'This is the third time,' said Kamenev calmly, 'that I have been tried by the Soviet court.' It was only the second time for Zinoviev. Andrey Vyshinsky, the former Menshevik, was prosecuting.

To the amazement of the whole world, the accused men confessed to having organized Kirov's murder at a time when Ivan Smirnov had been nearly two years in a prison cell, when Zinoviev was in exile in Kurultay, a small town in Kazakhstan, and Kamenev in Minusinsk, both of them under strict surveillance. They also confessed to having premeditated and prepared other attacks *on all members of the Politburo except Molotov*. No material evidence was forthcoming.

One of the accused, Holtzmann, confessed that he had met Trotsky's son Sedov at the Hôtel Bristol in Copenhagen, and had received 'instructions for Stalin's assassination'. Now, in 1936, Copenhagen was one of the few capitals without a 'Hôtel Bristol'. Was the attorney of the USSR and future Foreign Minister, Andrey Vyshinsky, careless in his preparation of false testimony?

On August 25, 1936, one hour after the verdict was pronounced, the prisoners were executed in the cellar of the NKVD. Zinoviev, a dying heart-case, was taken there on a stretcher.

At the beginning of September came the announcement of Yagoda's dismissal and the appointment of Nicholas Ivanovich Yezhov as head of the NKVD. Yagoda was appointed 'Postal Commissar'.

Now began the era of *Yezhovchina,* which recalled that of the *Bironovchina* in the time of the Czarina Anna Ivanovna. Yezhov arranged for Zakovsky to be appointed as his deputy. This Zakovsky, a coarse, brutal and sadistic individual, was all-powerful in the prisons and torture chambers. His favourite expression was, 'If even Karl Marx fell into my hands he would confess to being an agent of Bismarck!'

At the beginning of the winter of 1936-7, some hundreds of officials of the NKVD were liquidated as 'traitors and Fascist spies'.

In January 1937, a second legal action, the 'Case against the Seventeen', was opened in Moscow. The second tumbrel sent by Yezhov to the executioner contained Yuri Pyatakov (Vice-Commissar for Heavy Industry), Karl Radek (Rector of the Chinese University of Sun Yat-Sen and close friend of Stalin), Sokolnikov (economist, diplomat and financier), Serebryakov (ex-secretary of the Central Committee), Muralov (formerly in command of the military region of Moscow) and others. The 'spontaneous confessions' recorded by Vyshinsky were even more improbable than those of the 'Case against the Thirteen'.

In this action, Radek suddenly 'confessed' to having been approached by Marshal Tukhachevsky to work up a *pronunciamento* at the Kremlin. At that moment, Vyshinsky interrupted Radek and forbade him to speak of Tukhachevsky. Radek was silent, but everybody realized that Stalin was already preparing an action against Tukhachevsky, the first Vice-Commissar for Defence and the Red Army's Chief of Staff.

During the night of February 1, 1937, all the accused, except Radek and Sokolnikov, were shot. Three years later, Radek was strangled in his prison cell at Irkutsk.

But already the rumour was circulating in the Kremlin that preparations for an action against Marshal Tukhachevsky were under way. In Paris a White-Russian, General Skoblin, a double agent of the NKVD and the Gestapo, was entrusted with the task of establishing proof of Tukhachevsky's connivance with the staff of the Wehrmacht; double agents of the NKVD were sent to Berlin with this objective.[1]

In the Spring of 1937 the marshal was transferred to the military region of the Volga, then arrested and brought back to Moscow. Tried with his friends, he was condemned to death and shot in the Lefortovo prison yard with seven Soviet generals. The

[1] *L'Affaire Toukhatchevsky,* Laffont, Paris, 1962.

execution of Tukhachevsky and the seven generals was soon followed by that of some hundreds of officers of all grades in the Red Army. War was not far off.

It is known today that the SD chief, Heydrich, the future hangman of Czechoslovakia, was congratulated by Hitler for the part he had played in the Tukhachevsky affair. General Skoblin was likewise generously rewarded by the Gestapo and the NKVD for his services in the same affair, before being implicated in the kidnapping of General Miller.

Yezhov made daily reports to Stalin. He added to the 'proofs' of plots and conspiracies hatched against him and also showed him his 'plan of action' for the NKVD with the names of the condemned men already written in. On every possible occasion the Soviet press mentioned the name of Nicholas Yezhov, 'the glorious head of our counter-espionage service'. Pictures of Yezhov appeared alongside those of Stalin. It was whispered that Yezhov was to take Molotov's place as President of the Council.

During the summer of 1937, from the distant Maritime Province, came news of Russian victories over the Japanese in Mongolia. These were followed by other equally brilliant successes. In the military firmament a new star was rising: General Zhukov. Mekhlis, appointed to Gamarnik's position as head of the Political Directorate of the Red Army, left the Kremlin for a prolonged tour of inspection in the Far East and in order to boost the morale of a group of officers who had been unsettled by the Moscow lawsuits. (Garmarnik, for his part, had taken his own life, *as a wise move*!)

Between March 2 and March 13, 1938, the third legal action of the Kremlin was heard. If possible, it was even more shocking than the others. Twenty-one people were brought to trial. They included: Nicholas Bukharin, the most distinguished of the communist theorists; Rykov, Lenin's successor as President of the Council; Yagoda, the former NKVD chief; Rakovsky and Krestinsky, one-time ambassadors; Rosenholtz, the ex-Commissar for Foreign Trade; Chernov and Grinko, the former Commissars for Agriculture and Finance; several famous physicians and surgeons. All 'confessed' to being spies of Hitler or the Mikado and, with the exception of Rakovsky, all faced the firing-squad twenty-four hours after the verdict.

After ridding himself of the oldest Russian communists of the former Lenin Guard, Yezhov began to exterminate the foreign communists who were living in Russia. The Poles were the first to be dealt with, as 'Pilsudski agents'. Among the victims, all of whom had re-established their good name in Poland, were, in particular, the senior Party officials Maria Koszutska (known as Wera Kostszewa), Julian Lenski, Edward Proshniak and Jerzy Ring, as well as the writers Bruno Jasienski, Wandurski, Adolf Warski, Henryk Walecki, Henrykowski and Sofia Unszlicht.

After the Poles, the German 'comrades' were 'liquidated', as 'Hitler agents'. Among them were: Kupferstein, leader of the 'Red Front', who had killed two Nazi officers during a street battle; Kupferstein's wife; Heinz Neumann, Heckert and Remmele, members of the German Communist Party Central Committee; Schubert, a member of the Reichstag; Werner Hirsch, Thaelmann's secretary, who had escaped the concentration camp and fled to Russia; the journalists Züsskind (*Rote Fahne*), Kurt Sauerland (*Aufbau*), Herber (*Die Internationale*), Borozz (International Correspondence); Rudolf Hauss, the military writer; Felix Halle, a jurist and President of the 'Friends of the USSR'.

The turn of the Bulgarian, Yugoslav, Hungarian and Chinese communists came next. They were cooped up in the secret prisons of Yaroslavl (which had once housed the Csar's hard labour prisoners), Uman and Irkutsk. Bela Kuhn was calmly strangled at Uman by the sadistic Kratov, chief warden of the prison. Liu-Shao-Chi, now the President of the Chinese Republic, was arrested as a *'friend of the traitor Radek'* and sent to Butyrki prison. He owes his freedom to Voroshilov, who knew him personally. Marshal Tito, who was then living in Moscow, owes his life to 'extremely cautious behaviour' (confirmed in one of his recent speeches) and an outward impression of 'complete submission'. Tito left to join the International Brigades against Franco in Spain and after the defeat he avoided returning to Russia and went to Yugoslavia to continue his underground activities.

The official President of the Comintern, Dmitrov, a brave and loyal man, was merely a figurehead. Stalin gave Yezhov, in addition to the duties as head of the NKVD, the task of *directing the Comintern*. Thus an ignorant, sadistic hangman was given control of the international communist movement. The shadow of Ivan the Terrible hung once again over the Kremlin.

The old citadel resembled a mad-house: the chief of the secret police in the land of socialism did nothing but exterminate communists. No Thermidor could have wiped out the old Lenin

Guard with the ferocity of Yezhov and his successor Beria. In his report to the 20th and 22nd Party Congress Nikita Khrushchev revealed the workings of the extermination procedure: the NKVD arrested Party local secretaries and Soviet presidents in the provinces, accusing them of running secret terrorist organizations for the purposes of sabotage, spying, creating diversions, etc. Confessions were extorted by the use of the cruellest and most subtle tortures. After that, the NKVD arrested the minor officials on the charge of supporting their 'criminal superiors'.

It is difficult to say how this bloodthirsty tragedy would have ended, the tragedy of a land over which hovered the shadow of a sadistic dwarf, if the latter had not become involved in trouble with his chief assistant, Lavrenti Beria, who had been moved from Tiflis to Moscow. Yezhov, who suspected Beria of wanting to supplant him, unearthed a secret file concerning the Beria of 1914-18, when the Georgian Menshevik collaborated with the Moslem Party (mussavatist) of Baku, in league with the British occupation. Beria defended himself by unearthing a secret file concerning the Yezhov of Rostov, Yezhov the informer in the pay of the Czar's police.

The Beria-Yezhov contest ended with the defeat and disappearance of the dwarf, after a commission of the Politburo headed by Mikoyan (ex-secretary of the Party at Rostov-on-Don) had brought from Rostov evidence of Yezhov's earlier activities. In order to avoid the scandal of an official trial of the 'glorious head' of the NKVD—especially as his predecessor, Yagoda, had only just been executed—Stalin ordered Yezhov to be confined in a lunatic asylum. There, one day, the dwarf was found, like Judas Iscariot, hanging from an aspen, with a placard tied round his neck. On it was written, 'I am just filthy carrion'; but the writing was not his.

CHAPTER 9

THE SHADOW OF WAR

Alarmed by the breakdown of the Red Army command, which followed the shooting of officers of all grades, Stalin gave orders for the setting-up of a rehabilitation commission under the leadership of Molotov. The commission re-established about 1,500 officers who had been held in concentration camps. The present Marshal Rokossovsky was released from a camp in the Ural district where he had been confined after several interrogations by the NKVD, during which he was beaten black and blue and had his teeth knocked out. A few other marshals and generals, including Rodimtsev and Rybalka (tanks), Zhigarev (aviation), Nedelin (artillery), Sokolovsky, Grechko, Zakharov, and admirals Kuznetsov and Tributz, as well as a host of colonels, majors, captains, lieutenants[1] and others, were also liberated, restored to their positions and rewarded with special leave and gratuities. And that, after hearing Beria's personal account of 'Yezhov's crimes'.

While re-establishing the army men, Stalin ordered the arraignment of all the senior party officials, the 'conspirators', before the High Court Military Collegium. The president of this court, the Latvian Ulrikh, and the attorney Andrey Vyshinsky, received their instructions from Stalin himself or from his new secretariat chief, General Alexander Poskrebyshev, the most contemptible of all the secretaries in his employ. The military court sat *in camera*, according to the Law of December 1, 1934, and sent some thousands of senior officials either to the cellar in Lyubyanka Square or to Lefortovo Prison. These persecutions went on until September 1940. Beria, the head of the NKVD, was directly answerable to Stalin for this 'continuous purge' which lasted for two years.

It was during the 1938-40 period that Stalin's life underwent a change. Quarrels between the dictator and his third wife became increasingly frequent. But Stalin was not now the

---

[1] Among the young officers to become known at a later date may be mentioned the future General Berzarin, Berlin Commandant in 1945, Colonel Tulpanov, Colonel Grebennikov, Colonel Mikhaylov and Major Maslennikov.

recluse of preceding years; he was coming out of his shell. He was often to be seen at the Bolshoy, at receptions and festivals. He was often accompanied by Alexandrov, a young professor of philosophy, who became his favourite and who was entrusted with the task of working out details of the Marxist-Stalinist ideological questions. Alexandrov read through the texts of the pamphlets and brochures which appeared with Stalin's signature. His duties made him the ideological adviser on the theatre, the cinema, the fine arts, the ballet and literature. Alexandrov held receptions on behalf of the Central Committee Union and made the most of the occasions to introduce Stalin into artistic society and the intellectual élite of Moscow. Rosa Kaganovich was seldom invited. She took her revenge by setting against Alexandrov her 'salon friends', Zhdanov, Bulganin, Andreyev and others, except Lazare Kaganovich, who refused any part in his sister's schemes.

A violent 'philosophical quarrel' broke out in the Kremlin as in the days of Nikita Pustovyat's *raskolniki*. Professor Alexandrov attacked Zhdanov's work on western philosophy, accusing him of not having understood Marx. Instead of trying to justify himself on the subject, Zhdanov produced a letter from Stalin who had read the manuscript of his work and fully approved it. But Alexandrov was convinced of the 'philosophical heresy' and his study on western philosophy (written to counter Zhdanov's work) was put on the 'index'. The professor's fall from grace was expected, but Stalin, while approving of the 'philosopher' Zhdanov, meant to retain Alexandrov as head of the Propaganda Department[1] of the Central Committee. A small room in the Kremlin, near the Palace of Facets, was set aside for Alexandrov's 'receptions' and only the 'chosen ones' were admitted. It was soon learnt that Georgi Malenkov of the Central Committee was a frequent visitor. It was there that he met his second wife, Helen Khrushchev (not related to Nikita).

Now that he was Alexandrov's friend, Malenkov took up the cudgels against Zhdanov and continued the battle until the latter's death, on August 31, 1948.

Meanwhile, the Kremlin learned that the dictator had made up his mind to break with his third wife. A divorce was obtained. Rosa disappeared from the Kremlin and the *dacha*. She left for the Ural district, where she married a doctor of the Sverdlovsk Policlinic. Stalin was left alone with his daughter.

[1] Agitprop.

Svetlana was the image of her mother. Beautiful, intelligent and gentle natured, she took charge of his flat in the Kremlin and also of his other villas and *dachas*. Stalin dearly loved his daughter. She reminded him of Nadezhda Alliluyeva, about whom he felt a deep sense of guilt, and for that reason he often visited the cemetery of the Novodevichi Convent with Svetlana. There, they spent hours in silence, on a small seat in front of the monument above the grave. The cemetery was empty. NKVD agents stood on guard at the entrances and exits and closed the approach road.

The keepers, until the dictator should leave, waited in a small building of the convent where Sophia, Peter the Great's sister, once lived in retirement. Then Stalin, his eyes moist with tears, stroked his daughter's head; and they both went back to the 'Gorinka' *dacha* or the Kremlin.

Sometimes Stalin was visited by a brilliant singer, the 'Moscow Carmen', a Tartar woman from Astrakhan and the widow of a Soviet diplomat. Or else it was another woman who called upon him, a renowned parachutist. Who was to be the fourth Mrs Stalin?

One of the most frequent of Stalin's visitors in the Kremlin was a young Soviet diplomat, George Astakhov,[1] a specialist on Far Eastern and Middle Eastern affairs. Astakhov was soon to leave on an extremely secret mission to Berlin, with the object of contacting the government of the Reich and concluding an economic and political agreement between the USSR and Germany. Stalin gave him a last word of advice and did likewise for another visitor: the Secretary-General of the Ukrainian Communist Party and former secretary of the Moscow Committee, the dynamic, intelligent Nikita Khrushchev.

The Kremlin had indeed been aware for some time that the Third Reich wished to separate the Ukraine from the USSR. The Ukrainians supporting Colonel Konovalets, whose organization was the 'UWO',[2] prepared for an uprising to take place when Germany attacked Russia. Stalin therefore sent Khrushchev to Kiev to sound the Ukrainians and secure the neutrality of the

[1] It was Astakhov who left Tokyo for Shanghai in 1927 to take part in the organization of the Fourth Chinese People's Army under the command of Chou-Teh, together with the Political Commissar Liu-Shao-Chi, today the President of the Chinese Republic.

[2] Ukrainian War Organization. Colonel Konovalets was assassinated in Rotterdam, where his organization was centred, on the eve of the Second World War.

Ukrainian nationalist elements, former members of the 'borobist'[1] Party.

Stalin rarely went to 'Gorinka', and more than ever he spent his days and nights at the Kremlin. He was often closeted with Beria in the small office overlooking the Borovitsky Gate. The new head of the Foreign Section of the NKVD, Semirensky,[2] frequently came to see him in this completely isolated office, where even high officials of the NKVD were not allowed without a special pass. Maxim Litvinov, head of the Russian Commissariat for Foreign Affairs, was no longer a guest at the Kremlin. Beria's replacement, Dekanozov, became the real Foreign Minister of the USSR[3] and was assisted in his task by Potemkin and Palgunov,[4] Mikhaylov and Kuznetzov.[5]

President of the Council Molotov became responsible for supervision of the Commissariat for Foreign Affairs, before assuming the leadership of it in May 1939. During one of its conferences in the Kremlin, concerning a possible *rapprochement* with the Third Reich, Stalin decided to put to Hitler, through Astakhov as intermediary, a 'preliminary condition', viz. that the Third Reich should give up its 'Ukrainian project' and its 'plan for an expedition against the Soviet Ukraine'. This plan was the last word in Colonel Beck's stupid and criminal policy, through which he hoped to save a desperate Poland by collaboration with the aggressor against Czechoslovakia and the Ukraine.

The end of February 1939 saw the convening of an important meeting in the Kremlin. About twenty-five people took part, including Litvinov, for whom it was his 'swan-song'. Litvinov[6]

[1] The 'National Ukrainian Communist Party', which was amalgamated with the Russian Communist Party in 1919 at the Congress of Kiev and gave rise to the 'Ukrainian Communist Party', the K.P.U.

[2] Suspected of being responsible for the murders of Reiss, near Lausanne in 1937, and Trotsky, in August 1940.

[3] Dekanozov, the last Russian ambassador to Germany before June 22, 1941, later appointed Vice-Commissar for Foreign Affairs. Back with the M.V.D., he became Vice-Minister for State Security. He was executed in December 1953, during the Beria trial.

[4] Director of the Press Bureau to the Commissariat for Foreign Affairs during the war, Palgunov, with Lozovsky, was in control of the censorship of the foreign Press in Moscow.

[5] The present Assistant-Minister for Foreign Affairs.

[6] In February 1939, Litvinov was still a member of the Communist Party Central Committee. He lost his place on this committee as a result of his attitude during the meeting of February 1939.

protested vigorously against the new turn in Soviet foreign policy. He warned Stalin that Hitler could never go back on the essential undertaking stated in *Mein Kampf*: the liquidation of Bolshevism. But Stalin was of the opinion that it would not be difficult to deceive Hitler, to lull him into a state of confidence and so deflect from the USSR the immediate threat of Nazi aggression. Stalin considered that a policy of economic co-operation with the Third Reich, implying deliveries of petroleum and raw materials, was the best of guarantees for warding off a conflict between Germany and Russia. All were in favour of this idea, except Litvinov, who was courageous enough to vote against the Secretary-General, which cost him his seat on the Central Committee. On a proposal by Malenkov, Litvinov was excluded.

In March 1939 the Eighteenth Congress was held in the Kremlin. Stalin hurled vehement accusations against the Western powers and declared that the USSR would not pull other people's chestnuts out of the fire for them. Nikita Khrushchev followed Stalin and spoke of the Ukrainian problems. Then the new Central Committee was elected. Litvinov was no longer a member of it.

In May of that year, Molotov became Commissar for Foreign Affairs in addition to being President of the Council.

A new conference was held in the Kremlin in June 1939, with the full Central Committee and several people's commissars. At this conference the Secretary General of the Ukrainian Communist Party, Nikita Khrushchev, submitted his report of the Ukrainian situation. Khrushchev asked that the Soviet Government should adopt certain principles held by the Ukrainian irredentist movement of the *Soborna Ukraina*[1] to remove from the 'UWO' Ukrainians the power to develop an anti-communist insurrectionist movement. As the new leader of the 'UWO', Melnik, who succeeded Konovalets (assassinated at Rotterdam), had shown himself to be as dangerous as his predecessor, Stalin strongly supported Khrushchev. The unification of Ukrainian territories, with Kiev, the capital, as the centre, was to become one of the main objectives of Russian foreign policy after the Kremlin conference of June 1939. It is an ironic twist of history that this same Kremlin which, in June 1709, after the victory of Poltava, witnessed the disappearance of *hetman* Mazeppa's

[1] 'The Greater Ukraine', which was then split up among Russia, Hungary, Poland and Rumania.

Ukrainian Cossack State, should, in June 1939, be instrumental in realizing the greatest dream of the Ukrainian people.

The 'Greater Ukraine', with its forty million inhabitants, became a living reality.

The name of Nikita Khrushchev will henceforth always be associated with the historic act of the creation of a 'Greater Soviet Ukraine'.

CHAPTER 10

THE RIBBENTROP AGREEMENT

Historians have perhaps not yet fully appreciated the decision of the Moscow Conference to take advantage of the international situation as it was in May and June 1939 to drag from the Third Reich the concessions concerning the re-unification of the Ukraine. In Burmistenko's *Memoirs* are very interesting passages relative to these decisions: 'I went to Moscow with Khrushchev. An important conference was to decide the question of our closer relationship with the Third Reich.[1] On the journey Khrushchev had a long talk with me. He said that an agreement with Hitler's Germany was not impossible. He added that he had made a report to the Politburo that use should be made of such an agreement in order to create the Soviet Soborna Ukraina and so remove once for all the question of Ukrainian irredentism, that stubborn enemy of the USSR. "Germany must allow us," said Khrushchev, "to combine with Soviet Ukraine *Kressy*,[2] Polish Eastern Galicia, Carpathian Ukraine, Bessarabia and Bukovina. Berlin would certainly be prepared to pay a high price for an agreement with us, and we must make the most of it. It is a historic occasion which may never come again." During our stay, Khrushchev took part in an important meeting at the Kremlin which was to approve the signing of an agreement with Germany. Our ambassador in Berlin had informed us that von Ribbentrop was prepared to come to Russia to sign such an agreement. Molotov considered that they should not precipitate matters, but first negotiate with the British and French "to push up the price". But Stalin wanted to hurry. He was afraid that *at the last moment Chamberlain might manage to force Hitler to action against the* USSR. In the end, Khrushchev supported

[1] In his 'secret report', Khrushchev accused Stalin of having signed the agreement with Ribbentrop, without consulting the Politburo. In his *Memoirs*, Burmistenko claims that the criticism is not justified. The Molotov-Ribbentrop agreement appears to have been signed with the consent of the members of the 'Kremlin Conference'.

[2] The name *Kressy* is given to that part of Volynia and Podolia occupied by the Poles in 1918 and 1919 and conceded to Poland by the Treaty of Riga (1921) between the U.S.S.R. and Poland.

Molotov. When our visit was nearly over, Khrushchev told me that Stalin and Molotov (who had just been made Foreign Minister) were fully in accord with his views. He was rubbing his hands together in his delight, saying that he would bring to his country what no other statesman had ever been able to bring. "I shall be the Ukrainian Cavour!" he told me, after the Conference.'

There followed three further meetings. One of them, under the chairmanship of Voroshilov, fixed the details of the programme of talks with General Ironside, who had come to Moscow to conclude with Stalin an Anglo-Franco-Soviet pact. The second meeting, presided over by Mikoyan, worked out the list of products and raw materials available in the event of a financial and trade agreement with Germany. Molotov conducted the third of these meetings, which brought together the experts of the Commissariat for Foreign Affairs to discuss negotiations with Sir William Strang, permanent secretary at the Foreign Office, who was in Moscow on a special mission. As is well known, all these meetings resulted in the Molotov-Ribbentrop agreement of the end of August 1939.

In Burmistenko's Memoirs, again, there is a description of this period: 'In August 1939, I made another journey to Moscow with Khrushchev. The Ribbentrop agreement had just been signed. Stalin called a full meeting of the Communist Party Central Committee to ratify it. There was much excited talk in the Kremlin. Many communists did not see the need for the agreement with Hitler. All believed that he would betray us at the first opportunity and would make an attempt to combine with Great Britain to attack us. I called on a friend of mine, a Ukrainian called Grechko, the foreman of works at the Kremlin and a cousin of the officer in charge of the military region of Kiev. Grechko told me in confidence that a special circular had been issued giving instructions for the historical monuments of the Kremlin and objects of value in the museums to be protected. Boards and sandbags were also being got ready for the protection of the walls and towers. I told Grechko that I did not believe there would be war between Germany and Russia, but he replied that his cousin, General Grechko (now Marshal Grechko), did not share this view and that almost all of the Soviet army men believed that war between the USSR and Germany was inevitable. Grechko told me that his cousin had attended an important military conference and that Voroshilov was very much concerned about the situation because he had no faith in Hitler's sincerity. He also told me that Stalin was influenced by his new personal adviser, Vyshinsky, when it came to questions of foreign policy, and that Vyshinsky[1] had convinced him that the British and the French would not risk a war with Germany after our agreement with Ribbentrop. At a private meeting of a dozen trustworthy people in Stalin's rooms, Vyshinsky explained his view: the Ribbentrop agreement made it possible to localize the war between Poland and Germany, which was sure to break out any day.'

There has been much discussion of the motives which persuaded Stalin to conclude this pact with Hitler. Many historians hold the view that Stalin wished to provoke a general conflict in Europe, in which the USSR should remain neutral 'and pull the chestnuts out of the fire for herself'. It has been said that it was a capital error on the part of Stalin, who did not realize that once war had begun between Poland and Germany a world war would be the inevitable result and Russia would be involved. In attempting to probe the 'secrets of the Kremlin' one may consider the most reasonable explanation to be that Stalin and Vyshinsky firmly believed that the agreement with Ribbentrop would tend to localize the war between Germany and Poland and so avoid the outbreak of a world war and a Germano-Soviet conflict.

This view held by Stalin and Vyshinsky was not a Marxist one but it was genuine. Through the breaking up of Poland, the USSR meant to achieve the unification of Ukrainian territories and re-establish footholds in the Baltic regions of Latvia, Lithuania and Esthonia.

Burmistenko states that 'after the signing of the Ribbentrop agreement, Stalin gave a small banquet in the Kremlin for a few members of the Central Committee. Khrushchev was there too. At this banquet Stalin proposed a toast to the Greater Ukraine and said that in future all Ukrainians would march in line with the USSR. After the banquet Stalin invited the thirteen members of the Politburo[2] to an at-home in his dacha. There was much talk of the success of Soviet foreign policy in consequence of the pact with Ribbentrop.

[1] In 1939, Vyshinsky was not yet deputy Foreign Minister of the U.S.S.R., a position to which he was appointed in 1940.

[2] There were fourteen members of the Politburo at this time: Stalin, Molotov, Mikoyan, Kalinin, Zhdanov, Malenkov, Andreyev, Voroshilov, Shcherbakov, Beria, Voznesensky, Shvernik, Ponomarenko and Khrushchev.

'Khrushchev told me how pleased Stalin was at the Ribbentrop agreement. He said that the Germans had proved more generous than he expected and that a secret clause in the agreement was a source of great satisfaction to the USSR.'

It is interesting to compare Burmistenko's recollections with certain passages to be found in the *Secret Archives of the Third Reich*, published in the United States: 'During our interview at the Kremlin,' notes von Ribbentrop, 'every time we came to speak of the Ukrainian lands that were to join up with the USSR, according to our agreement, Molotov adopted a most rigidly uncompromising attitude. I do not think it was a personal attitude, for Stalin was just as uncompromising as Molotov on questions of Ukrainian territories. I was curious to learn more details about this attitude. Now, our agents were unable to tell me anything definite on this score although, I understand, they had a *very well placed informer* at the Kremlin, in the offices of the Foreign Ministry. They knew that there was a Ukrainian among the top Soviet officials and that it was *his* influence which was responsible for the uncompromising attitude shown by Molotov and Stalin.' The 'mysterious Ukrainian' was none other than Nikita Sergeyevich Khrushchev.

War between Poland and Germany broke out on September 1, 1939. On September 3rd, Great Britain and France declared war on the Third Reich. By the end of the month there was no Poland left. By a second Molotov-Ribbentrop agreement the land was shared by the USSR and Germany; the Poles paid the price for Colonel Beck's blindness.

The beginning of the war showed no justification, therefore, of the theory held by Stalin and Vyshinsky that France and Great Britain would not take part. But, although not justified by events, Stalin's theory was well founded, since the declaration of war on Germany was *artificial*. Gamelin engaged in no military operation for the relief of Poland. It was the 'phoney war', which, according to the Trotsky formula at Brest-Litovsk in 1918, was 'neither war nor peace'.

A feeling of triumph pervaded Moscow. The measures taken to protect the Kremlin were rescinded. Soviet newspapers praised 'brilliant comrade Stalin', who had succeeded in 'thwarting the intrigues of the British imperialists and maintaining peace for the citizens of the USSR in the face of an imperialist war'.

At the end of October 1939, Stalin was again the victim of a slight heart attack. He was nearly sixty. His doctors were very anxious but neither the public nor the foreign diplomats had a hint of the warning to Stalin. On the contrary, preparations were going forward for celebrating his birthday in December 1939.

In all Soviet newspapers there were enthusiastic articles glorifying his genius and thanking him for the 'happiness and well-being' brought to the people of the USSR, peasants, and workers of all kinds. Lydia Timashuk,[1] a medical student, suggested that there should be instituted at the Kremlin a 'medical competition for the maximum prolongation of the life of comrade Stalin, so precious to the USSR and all progressive humanity'.

The 'precious life' was giving cause for anxiety. The doctors prescribed three months' complete rest and a long stay by the Black Sea. A spot was chosen between Sochi and the watering-place Gagry. A competition was organized, inviting plans for a luxurious villa to be built on the Black Sea shore and to be called 'Nadezhda' in memory of Stalin's second wife. The prizewinner was the architect Ophan and the Commissariat for Building allocated considerable funds for speedy construction of the new villa.

On the eve of Stalin's sixtieth birthday, there was a family trouble in the dictator's rooms at the Kremlin. His fondness for his daughter, Svetlana, has already been noted. Svetlana was being courted by one of her fellow students of the Faculty of Arts in Moscow University, Mark Friedmann, and a romantic attachment between the two young people was beginning to take shape. Both were members of the 'Communist Youth'. Svetlana decided to speak to her father of her intention to get married. Stalin took the suggestion very badly. As a result, instead of going to the Zag's[2] to attend to the marriage formalities, the unfortunate student was summoned by Beria, who outlined for him the prospect of a few years spent in the province of Magadan on the north Pacific coast of Russia. But the gentle Svetlana threatened that she, too, would go to Eastern Siberia if anything happened to her fiancé.

One day, Svetlana disappeared from the Kremlin. Stalin gave

---

[1] She gained world-wide notice in December 1952 because of her denunciation of the 'white-coated murderers', which brought about the arrest of twenty-three doctors of the Kremlin Policlinic.

[2] The civil registry-office for marriages.

way to the deepest despair and ordered Beria to find his daughter for him within twenty-four hours and to report progress hourly to him. Svetlana was discovered in the house of one of her friends, who lived in the outskirts of Moscow, and was restored to her father. The tussle between father and daughter resulted in a compromise. Svetlana was to give up the idea of marrying Mark Friedmann, and, instead of going to Magadan, he was to take up an insignificant appointment at Sverdlovsk in the Ural district.

After celebrating his sixtieth birthday, Stalin decided to leave for Sochi, where he was to stay until March 1940. In the west, the 'phoney war' dragged on. Stalin thought that his absence from Moscow for the winter of 1939-40 would be in no way prejudicial to the conduct of affairs of state. A very special telephone line was installed between the Kremlin and his villa. While staying on the verandah which encircled his house, Stalin could listen to arguments by members of the Politburo when it was in session. The direct line enabled him to take part in the discussion. His views were broadcast from a loudspeaker installed in the conference hall.

The Kremlin did not recover its liveliness until the spring of 1940, when France was invaded by the Wehrmacht. Paul Reynaud, who had become President of the Council in place of Daladier, had been urging Stalin to sign a 'pact of friendship', to supplement the Boncour-Litvinov agreement. Ivanov, the Secretary to the Soviet Embassy in Paris, appears to have met a representative of Paul Reynaud's cabinet and begun preliminary talks with him on the subject of a friendship pact. Reynaud's objective was to alarm Hitler by threatening possible intervention on the part of the USSR during the Battle of France and by so doing to tie down a certain number of German divisions in the East. Reynaud stated that he was prepared to send Alexis Léger as ambassador to Moscow as an indication of the great importance he attached to this post. But, for answer, Stalin, it appears, requested the appointment of Pierre Cot. A special meeting of the Politburo was held in the Kremlin to decide upon the most suitable measures to take for the relief of France without, however, giving Hitler sufficient excuse for breaking the Molotov-Ribbentrop pact.

Two days after this meeting, the German *Panzers* were rushing towards Laon, Douai and Dunkirk. The speed of the German tanks made the 'Soviet safety-valve' unnecessary. However, the

USSR had already undertaken a reshuffle of divisions on the Eastern border of the Reich. This re-grouping did not save France, but it made such an impression on Hitler that he did not dare to attempt the invasion of England in the summer of 1940, for fear of being attacked in the rear by the Soviet army.

The rapid and dramatic breakdown of France made Stalin aware that the danger of conflict between the USSR and Germany was more real than he had thought. A few meetings of the Higher War Committee, presided over by Voroshilov, were devoted to the consideration of a programme of 'preventive measures'. In November 1940, Molotov left for Berlin to obtain from Hitler a whole series of elucidations and concessions. The only effect of all this was to accelerate the German attack.

On June 22, 1941, the Wehrmacht crossed the Soviet border. The Germano-Russian war began with a terrible kick from the Nazi boot at the ants' nest of a Soviet army still disorganized in its higher ranks by the purges carried out by Yezhov.

CHAPTER 11

CHURCHILL IN THE KREMLIN

The day the Nazis entered the USSR, Stalin, who had been President of the Council since May, was in his villa at Sochi. It took him twelve days to get back to Moscow; during that time, Molotov took charge of the Government and the Central Committee in his place. Once back in Moscow, Stalin settled in a small *dacha* in the village of Tarassovka, twenty miles northeast of Moscow, on the banks of the Klyazma.

On July 3rd, Stalin went to the Kremlin and made a broadcast speech. In this historic speech he appealed to the country to make a supreme sacrifice in resistance to the aggressor. Then he went back to Tarassovka, where he remained closeted with his personal adviser Marshal Boris Shaposhnikov, a former colonel of the Imperial Staff. Three days later he returned to his rooms in the Kremlin and resumed control of the country.

On July 12, 1941, Molotov and Sir Stafford Cripps, the British Ambassador, signed the Russo-British alliance in the presence of Stalin and Shaposhnikov. After shaking hands with the diplomats present, Stalin and Molotov went to St George's Hall for an extraordinary meeting to consider the steps taken for the country's defence. It was at this meeting that Beria reported the formation of the *Smersh* section for dealing with spies, saboteurs and deserters. Shcherbakov, the secretary of the Party Committee in Moscow, submitted his report on the passive and anti-aircraft defence of the Kremlin and the capital. He proposed that the Kremlin walls should be repainted to make them look like a row of houses. Lenin's mausoleum of red and black marble, in the middle of the Red Square, was to be covered with sandbags and *disguised as a chalet*. The Mokhovaya highway leading to the Kremlin was painted a zigzag pattern to look like *roofs* from the air. Drapings were hung on the Bolshoy Theatre, with *dummy entrances* underneath. The front of the Grand Palace of the Kremlin disappeared beneath a network of green branches. The five red stars shining on the top towers were concealed with grey fabric. The gilt domes of the churches were enclosed with dark scaffolding and the pale-green roofs of many important buildings were repainted *blue and brown*. The camouflaging of the Kremlin and the capital was a masterpiece.

Three lines of anti-aircraft defences were established in the forests around Moscow. Beneath the shade of fir trees and birches were grouped in concentric circles vast numbers of searchlights. Deep pits were dug in the fields and clearings covered over with leaves and branches for the installation of anti-aircraft batteries. Balloons with their cables linked together formed an almost impenetrable screen. The underground railway stations were fitted with steel doors and special air filters.

These preparations—and many others—saved the Kremlin from destruction, although, at the most critical moment of the Battle of Moscow, the front was only about ten miles distant from the capital.

The first great bombardment of Moscow and the Kremlin took place on July 21, 1941, one month after the outbreak of hostilities. Stalin and the members of the Russian Defence Council[1] went down to the Kremlin shelter, which had been constructed 115 feet below ground at the exact spot where the Kremlin subterranean tunnel turns towards the Moskva. From that shelter the Defence instructions were issued.

The defence of Moscow was so well organized that, even in November 1941, in the middle of the Battle of Moscow, a twelve-minute military parade was held by Stalin in the Red Square. He took the salute standing on Lenin's mausoleum. On the evening of November 7th, Stalin made a great speech in the Mayakovsky underground station.

The Germans did their utmost to destroy the town and the Kremlin. On the bodies of German airmen of the 'Condor Legion' (famous for its operations in Spain), which came to Russia with the 53rd air squadron (based on Minsk) and the 55th and 26th squadrons (based on Borissov and Bobruysk), were found formal instructions to destroy 'the monument of Russian barbarism, the Kremlin'.

General Gromadin, head of the Moscow anti-aircraft defences, and Basil Pronin, president of the Moscow Soviet, published the following report on the bombardments suffered by Moscow and the Kremlin for ten months: dead, 1,088; incendiary bombs, 35,000 - 40,000; explosive bombs, 200 - 300; German aircraft destroyed, 1,100.

[1] At the beginning of the war, the Russian Defence Council consisted of Stalin, Molotov, Malenkov, Voroshilov, Voznesensky and Beria.

The last Nazi air raid on Moscow took place on April 5, 1942.

The years 1941, 1942 and 1943 were dramatic: the war was fought on Russian soil. The battles of Moscow, Uman, Kiev and Kharkov, the titanic struggle for Stalingrad and the tragic siege of Leningrad (which claimed a million civilian victims who died of cold, hunger and disease in Peter the Great's capital) could not break down the resistance of the Russian nation. Stalin, in his shelter, attended to the conduct of the war. He soon dismissed Marshals Voroshilov and Budenny, who could not adapt themselves to modern warfare, and replaced them by Zhukov and Timoshenko in charge of the two fronts, north and south, in November 1941 at the critical point of the war. By taking these steps and appointing as his personal adviser Marshal Shaposhnikov (who had come out top of the Imperial Staff Academy promotion list in 1909) Stalin restored the situation in the Russian Staff which had been seriously disorganized by his Great Purges of 1937-9. He found a whole cluster of new stars among the younger colonels and generals: Solovsky, Vassilevsky, Rokossovsky, Antonov, Konev, Malinovsky, Chernyakovsky, Tolbukin, Govorov and Vatutin, to mention only some of them.

Ivan Kalita's old Kremlin became the symbol of the struggle for the safeguard of the national heritage of eternal Russia. The towers of the Kremlin, over which hung the hammer and sickle, watched over the victory, as they had done in 1812 at the time of the Napoleonic invasion.

When Stalin gave the word of command for the 'patriotic war', he did not mention the proletariat, internationalism or the brotherhood of the workers. His message, dated 'The Kremlin, July 10, 1941', was as follows: 'Russian soldier, it is your duty not to die without first having killed *at least one of the enemy!* If you are wounded, pretend to be dead, wait for the Germans to come, choose one and kill him! Kill him with your rifle, your bayonet, your knife, kill him with your teeth! But do not die without leaving behind you a dead German. That is an order from your mother country in peril of death.' At the same time, by Stalin's order, all school books had to contain these patriotic lines:

> Who would dare to take from us the Great Bell?
> Who would dare to move the Czar-Cannon?
> Who so insolent to refuse to bow
> Before the sacred gates of the Kremlin?

Thus, in the face of mortal danger from the enemy at the very gates, Stalin entrenched himself behind the legendary sanctity of the old fortress of Ivan Kalita, the Unifier of Russian Lands. The victory of the 'patriotic war' of 1941-5 was, first and foremost, a victory for the Kremlin.

Within these precincts ,which were reasserting their symbolical significance, Stalin and his Politburo received visitors from abroad during the war. Of all these receptions, the most dramatic was perhaps that of Churchill, Russia's inveterate enemy.

Churchill went to Moscow to discuss with Stalin all important aspects of the war. He arrived on August 12, 1942, in the company of Harry Hopkins, President Roosevelt's representative, and left on August 15th.

Stalin suspected that the British were unwilling to open the second front in Europe so as to prolong the blood-letting and bring about the extermination of both Russians and Germans in this Russo-German war which was the only fierce conflict at the time. The operations in North Africa, by their scope and the forces employed, were no more than unimportant skirmishes by comparison with the gigantic battles being fought in the great plain of Eastern Europe.

The moment he arrived, Churchill was responsible for a misunderstanding. As he left the aircraft, the Prime Minister made his famous 'V' sign and got into his car. The Russians thought that this two-finger sign was a reference to the second front. The news flashed through Moscow that Churchill had come to announce the opening of the second front. To dispel the rumour and prevent disappointment, the *Crocodile* published the following story: 'A foreign diplomat was asked how the second front could be created. He replied that there were two ways in which it could be done, the natural and the supernatural. The natural way would be for the Archangel Gabriel and his heavenly hosts to put in an appearance; the supernatural would be for the British to arrive.'

The story was immediately taken up by a Moscow theatre. It made Harry Hopkins roar with laughter but it did not suit Churchill, who complained to Molotov when he first visited the Kremlin. Laughingly, Molotov told Churchill that fortunately the Russians had regained their sense of humour since the beginning of hostilities. Molotov told Churchill an anecdote which was going round and in which Churchill, Hitler and Stalin were supposed to figure: 'In Heaven, God was disturbed by the noise of battles and sent St Peter down to find the man responsible for the trouble. Stalin was the first to be brought up, because (added Molotov) God does not like atheists. "Is it my fault?" said Stalin. "Can I help it if I am attacked? It is that scoundrel Hitler who is to blame." St Peter then brought Hitler, who said, "Why am I here? Great Britain declared war on me. It is Churchill who is to blame. It was he who influenced Chamberlain." It was at that very moment that you, Mr Churchill, arrived in Heaven (said Molotov). It was a solemn occasion, for you were threatened with the Last Judgement. It was no doubt to avert this danger that you are supposed to have said, "What is there against me? Look! Can you see any place where there is an Englishman really at war?' Churchill did not move an eyelid, but quickly changed the subject.

The evening of August 12, 1942, was taken up by a discussion which lasted three hours ten minutes. Stalin meant to speak exclusively about the second front and was very insistent. He went so far as to point out that, for lack of a second front and with the threat of a German invasion of Caucasia, Russia might have to reconsider all her obligations to the Allies. To this reference to a possible compromise in the East, Churchill replied that the only place where Great Britain could open a second front at once was the Mediterranean, which would give access to the Balkans. This remark startled Stalin, who stated that the USSR would consider the opening of a second front in the Balkans to be an unfriendly act. Hopkins calmed Stalin with the assurance that Roosevelt was convinced of the uselessness of a front in the Balkans.

On August 14, 1942, at nine o'clock in the evening, in the Catherine Hall of the Kremlin Grand Palace, Stalin held a reception for Churchill and Hopkins. Churchill's entrance created a sensation: he was wearing a blue zip-up jacket with an open-neck shirt *and no tie*, whereas the Russians were all in formal dress. Seeing Churchill so strangely garbed for an official reception, Stalin pulled a face, which put Churchill in a beastly mood. The dinner began on a sub-acid note.

The menu was in no way inferior to those of the banquets given the Czars in the Catherine Hall. It included: hors-d'œuvre, caviar, white balyk, smoked fish from the lower Don, cold ham, bear ham, 'foie gras', cold game with mayonnaise, cold duckling, Siberian grouse, sturgeon jelly, fish pies, patties, various salads, cheeses, butter, toast, mushrooms with cream, hashed game with herring and potatoes, 'meunière' mince, cream soup, consommé, beetroot consommé (*borshck*), sterlets in champagne, turkey, chicken, wood-grouse, roast lamb with apples, cucumber salad, cauliflower, asparagus, ices, sherbet, coffee, 'petits fours', roasted almonds, Caucasian fruits, champagne from the Crimea, French champagne 'Veuve Cliquot', *rosé*, Caucasian red wines, red Bordeaux and Burgundy, Crimean white wines, 'Chäteauneuf du Pape' special 1911 and 'Château Yquem' 1919 for the dessert.

Churchill, who came from an England that was rationed to the limit and where even Buckingham Palace had dried eggs, had a few things to say about it.

At the meal a great many toasts were drunk. Stalin became more cheerful as the atmosphere warmed up, whereas Churchill became increasingly gloomy. There was suddenly a very awkward moment, when the British Ambassador, Sir Archibald Clark Kerr, proposed a toast to Stalin. Everybody stood up, with the exception of Churchill. Leaning back in his chair and pulling his shirt collar open still wider, the Prime Minister, addressing His Britannic Majesty's Ambassador in his deep voice, said, 'Haven't you been long enough in the diplomatic service to know the rules of etiquette? An ambassador must always address the Foreign Minister of the country to which he is accredited and not the President of the Council.'

Stalin was overjoyed at being present at this quarrel between Churchill and his ambassador. He stood up with a smile and said, 'I should like to propose a toast to which there can be no response. I drink to the health of the officers of the Intelligence Service who are doing such important work. I know that nobody could reply, because the officers of the Intelligence Service are not in the habit of making themselves known.' An unforeseen incident then occurred. Whereas the British guests remained quite unruffled, the United States naval attaché, Captain Jack Duncan, who had already sampled all the wines, the vodka and the champagne, stood up and said, 'I can reply to the toast by the President of the Council on behalf of the Intelligence Service, because I belong to it'. Stalin burst out laughing, left his seat, went and had a drink with Duncan and spent the remainder of the evening with him. They left the Catherine Hall, arm-in-arm, about one o'clock in the morning.

During the evening of August 15, 1942, Churchill returned alone to the Kremlin, without Hopkins, to have a final discussion with Stalin. The interview took place in Stalin's private flat on the second floor, in a small drawing-room which had once been Nadezhda Alliluyeva's bedroom. Churchill intended to try to efface the impression caused by his dress and his behaviour; his ambassador had told him that the Russians had been very much annoyed by what they considered to be a 'lack of respect shown at a formal reception held by Stalin at the Kremlin'. The interview was a long one. Taking advantage of Stalin's good mood, Churchill decided to broach certain questions so far unresolved. Then Stalin answered, 'Do you not think, Mr Churchill, that we should have something to eat? I am hungry, and when I am hungry I am a bad negotiator; I don't give way. At home in Georgia they say that a hungry man is a disagreeable man.'

Stalin rang the bell and Svetlana answered it. Stalin kissed her on the forehead and said to Churchill, referring to something which his guest had written about the nasty characters in the Kremlin, 'Does it surprise you that I should kiss my daughter? I am reputed to be a monster. And you certainly believe that all communist leaders are "nasty characters", do you not?' Pavlov, the interpreter, states that Churchill made no reply to this. Svetlana went out and brought some food. She acted as hostess for her father and Churchill, who continued their talk until four o'clock in the morning. It was the longest conversation ever to take place between a Russian head of State and a foreign head of State, the longest witnessed by the walls of the Kremlin.

In his *Memoirs*, Churchill avoids giving a complete and precise account of his nocturnal conversation in Stalin's rooms at the Kremlin. He does not mention, either, the unfortunate incident occasioned by his dress at the formal reception held by Stalin. Stalin said later on, 'I should like to see Churchill's face if I dared to attend a reception at Buckingham Palace wearing no tie or dressed as a North American Indian'.

At a banquet given by Stalin to his marshals and generals in celebration of the Red Army's twenty-seventh anniversary, he was able to inform them that in 156 weeks of fighting the Russians had accounted for 7,000,000 of the enemy, destroyed 90,000 guns, 70,000 tanks, 60,000 aircraft and had recaptured nearly 400,000 square miles of territory. The Russian losses amounted to 5,000,000 men, 48,000 guns of all sizes, 49,000 tanks and 30,000 aircraft. The Anglo-American lend-lease was in the nature of nine thousand million dollars. Stalin omitted to give the number of Russian civilians who had met their death in three years of the most terrible bloodshed the world has known since the invasion by Baty's hordes in the thirteenth century.

The year 1945 ! The war was over. Stalin offered an imposing banquet to his entourage. It was one of the greatest receptions held by the master of the Kremlin.

CHAPTER 12

DEATH OF A DICTATOR

The enormous effort put into the war by Stalin, in guiding the course of his country and directing military operations, took toll of his already failing health. He had already suffered two heart attacks, one of them very serious, in 1944, when it was thought that he would die, and the other in the summer of 1945. The doctors earnestly advised him not to spend more than three or four months of the year in Moscow, and those in spring and summer. In line with this heart weakness went an increasing persecution mania. Several times a year he changed the leaders of his personal guard and began to suspect the closest of his associates. In his 'secret report', Khrushchev tells how Stalin spoke to him one day: 'You seem strange today, comrade Khrushchev. Why don't you look me straight in the eye? Why do you try to avoid my glance?'

All the people who came to his office were searched, without exception. Vyacheslav Molotov, arriving in Moscow from London, where he had been attending the meeting at Lancaster House, forgot that his revolver was still in the pocket of the overcoat he was wearing. One of Stalin's guards noticed the bulge in the coat pocket and literally leaped at Molotov and snatched off his raglan. Molotov complained, but Stalin sided with the MVD sergeant.

Although Beria was moved to a new post in 1946, to superintend matters concerning atomic energy, the Ministry of the Interior (MVD) and the Ministry of State Security (MGB) continued to function under his guidance. As chief of police he was replaced by Victor Semenovich Abbakumov, an Armenian from Armavir. Two former chiefs of Stalin's personal guard, Merkulov and Kruglov, were appointed as his assistants. The whole of the Kremlin secret police were henceforth under the supervision of the head of Stalin's Secretariat, General Alexander Poskrebyshev. But even he, when visiting Stalin, had to leave his revolver with the leader of the guard who, in turn, was under surveillance from two other men, the Political Commissar of the guard and the Commandant of the Kremlin.

After Svetlana's marriage in 1945, Stalin felt lonely and lived with his son Basil, who had been made colonel in 1945, major-general in 1948 and lieutenant-general (aviation) in 1952. But Basil preferred the company of his service friends to that of his father.

Stalin's other son, Yasha, had been shot by the Germans. Stalin offered a large reward to anybody who could show him Yasha's grave, for he wished to have him buried at Tiflis near his mother and his first wife.

Every time Stalin came to stay at the Kremlin, he would go to the cemetery where Nadezhda Alliluyeva was buried and spend hours sitting there.

Of all the members of the Politburo, only Voznesensky, the lively young president of the Gossplan, continued to visit this lonely man, who often consulted him on economic questions. But, one day, the visits came to an end. Voznesensky, a member of the Politburo, had been thrown into prison. His colleagues saw in this a direct threat and decided to show their reaction. Molotov, Bulganin and Mikoyan continually pressed for an explanation. Boria made a similar request on behalf of the Politburo, but Stalin drily replied, 'That is my business'. A few days later he told Molotov, 'You wanted to know where Voznesensky is. Well, he was shot yesterday.'

In his Report, Khrushchev stated that the reasons for Voznesensky's execution were obscure. The turncoat Rastvorov declared that Voznesensky's book *The War Economy of the United States* provided the reason. Stalin considered this book to 'imply deviation from established principles', but the author would not admit the 'deviation' and was arrested. The MGB included him among the Party members implicated in the 'Leningrad plot'.

The 'plot' attributed to Popov, the secretary of the Leningrad Party Committee, and to about a hundred communists of that area, was 'discovered' by Merkulov and Abbakumov. It aimed at the assassination of Stalin during a meeting of the Central Committee. When the 'Leningrad affair' was investigated, a statement was recorded from a certain Maskalov, a well-known Leningrad communist and a friend of Voznesensky. He stated that during a friendly conversation with him Voznesensky had 'confessed' that he had become a member of the American secret service during the war, while he was in the United States, where he had gone in 1942.

Israel's first ambassador to Russia was Mrs Golda Meierson-Meier. When she arrived in Moscow, the very warm welcome she was given by others of her race provoked a new fit of anger in Stalin. He was always telling his associates that the Jews in Russia had not been able to adapt themselves or become acclimatized like other minorities and constituted an ever-present danger. Every Muscovite Jew had foreign connections and the 'USSR was threatened by the danger of Zionism'. Stalin was also very displeased by the agreements concluded between Israel and Western Germany with support from Washington.

Stalin had brought to light the old colonization project of the Jews of Birobidzhan, a region near the border of China and Siberia. At the Kremlin there was talk of rules of behaviour and restrictions to be introduced in respect of the Jewish minority. These restrictions went almost as far as the laws which applied to this minority under the Czars. It was one of the reasons why some members of the government opposed Stalin, which caused him to break into fits of rage. These members were: Nikita Khrushchev, whose son-in-law was of Jewish origin; Voroshilov, who had married a woman of Jewish extraction; Molotov, whose wife was a Jewess; Kaganovich, who was himself a Jew; even Beria, whose mother was half Jewish.

In 1952, when he had deported several dozen Jewish intellectuals, writers, actors and others, had banned the Jewish press and had closed the Jewish theatres in Soviet Russia, Stalin decided to act. The Egyptian *coup d'état* had put Nasser's revolutionary junta in power and accelerated a *rapprochement* between the USSR and the Egyptian government. Vyshinsky, *one of those who had worked hardest in the establishment of Stalin's anti-Semitic policy,* was entrusted to undertake secret negotiations with Cairo for the purpose of concluding an 'anti-Zionist pact'. The Nineteenth pan-Russian Congress of the Communist Party was to give effect to Stalin's plan for the liquidation of the Politburo and its replacement by an anonymous Praesidium entirely without influence.

In October 1952, in the great hall of the Kremlin, Malenkov made the opening speech of the Congress. One month later, on the denunciation made by Dr Lydia Timashuk, house physician to the Kremlin Policlinic, the MVD arrested the Jewish doctors of the Policlinic on the charge that they had promoted a scheme for assassinating Stalin and some generals and marshals of the Soviet army by 'medical means'.

The Dictator wished to secure the benevolent neutrality of the army so as to settle accounts with those whom, in his mentally sick condition, he considered to be his future murderers.

Sinister rumours passed through the Kremlin. There was talk of the imminent arrest of Molotov, Beria, Mikoyan, Voroshilov and Kaganovich. It was said that Leo Mekhlis, the very man who had built up the legend of the 'brilliant leader', had fallen mysteriously ill at Saratov and had been brought to Moscow for treatment in the MVD infirmary—in Lefortovo prison.

Khrushchev's 'secret report' reveals how Stalin determined to arrest several members of the Politburo, including Molotov and Voroshilov, how he called the latter an agent of the Intelligence Service, how he made up his mind to deport Israelites *en masse* from the USSR, how he ordered Ignatov to obtain 'by any means, torture included', confessions from the Jewish doctors, and threatened him by saying, 'If you do not obtain confessions from those doctors, you will have your own head pulled off'. In this affair of the 'white-coated murderers', Ignatov had blindly to follow out the instructions given to him by Poshrebyshev.

The months of January and February 1953 were a veritable nightmare. Mekhlis passed quietly away in the MVD infirmary. Several secretaries of the members of the new Central Committee Praesidium (including Khrushchev's secretary, Ivan Klyachko, a Ukrainian from Kiev) were arrested. On February 10th, the news of Mekhli's death was received. It was rumoured that his last visitor had been General Poskrebyshev, who had got the dying man to sign a document. What document could this be?

In this terrible state of affairs it was reported on March 1, 1953, that Stalin had died suddenly during the night. All day long there was neither denial nor confirmation of this report, but in the evening a communiqué signed by the Central Committee of the Russian Communist Party informed the country and the world: 'A great misfortune has fallen upon our people and upon the Communist Party. Comrade Stalin has had a cerebral haemorrhage.'

At the beginning of March, the too zealous Poskrebyshev was arrested by Beria and he has not been seen since then. On March 5th, despite 'the greatest efforts to save his life', Stalin finally 'died a natural death'.

Here, now, is the final mystery of the Kremlin, the mystery surrounding the circumstances of Stalin's death.

The world press, in 1957, published the sensational statements of the Russian ambassador, Ponomarenko, relating to Stalin's last moments. In broad outline, this is what he said: 'In February 1953, Stalin called together the twenty-five members of the Praesidium—at that time, an exceptional procedure. The "white-coat plot" had just been exposed. The most eminent Soviet doctors, most of them Jewish, had been arrested for attempted medical assassination of the military and civilian leaders. *Pravda* made a great to-do about the Zionist plot against the USSR. Stalin therefore submitted to the Praesidium a decree providing for the deportation of large numbers of the Jewish population to Central Asia. This measure was, in fact, in process of being carried out. When Kaganovich and Molotov mentioned that such a deportation would make a disastrous impression abroad, Stalin flew into a rage. Then Kaganovich threw his Party-membership card down on the table and said that Stalin was disgracing the country. Confusion ran riot through the Assembly. Suddenly the dictator, who was suffering from a weak heart, collapsed. Immediately, Beria cried, 'We are free at last! The tyrant is dead!' But, alas, Stalin opened his eyes. Then Beria, on his knees and wringing his hands, begged forgiveness of the master he had betrayed. Stalin died without regaining consciousness. Had Stalin been allowed to die, or had there been, as widespread rumour had it, joint action against him by his successors, those of greatest consequence in the régime today?

Here is a version attributed to Ehrenburg: 'Soon after the Nineteenth Russian Communist Party Congress, in October 1952, it was obvious that Stalin was suffering from persecution mania in an acute form. In his conversations he asserted that his oldest colleagues, like Molotov, Mikoyan, Voroshilov and Kaganovich, were conspiring to murder him. When, in December 1952, the 'doctor scandal' broke out, we realized that Stalin's state of mind constituted a grave threat to the country. His persecution mania apart, Stalin was perfectly lucid, and, driven on by his disorder, he was making preparations for a veritable massacre, the almost total extermination of the Central Committee elected by the Nineteenth Party Congress.' To judge from this account, his death came none too soon.

After playing the part of a Danton, a Marat, a Robespierre, of a Barras and even of a victorious Bonaparte, Generalissimo Stalin seemed to want to prepare for his last combat in the Babeuf fashion, as a 'leader of equals', against those who, by his own actions, enjoyed privileged positions in the régime.

Fate had placed Stalin in a period of history when the advent of a 'unifier of lands'—a new Ivan IV and a new Peter the Great—was vitally necessary to Russia.

Just so long as he had conformed to the 'prescribed plan of history', he had been 'great' and 'brilliant', despite his cruelty, his terrifying amorality and his blind dogmatism. But as soon as he felt compelled to change that plan, he was doomed to vanish like the victims of his purges, for whom the interest of the Russian nation was waning in the face of some subtle ideology culled from nineteenth-century Marxism. The idea has been well expressed by Leo Tolstoy: 'Men who are called "great" are so only in so far as they are content to guide the course of history in which fate has set them. As soon as they rebel and show resistance to historical necessity, there is only one outcome for them, just as "it is but a step from the sublime to the ridiculous", and they must disappear from the international scene.'

Why did Stalin set himself against the fate which would have made him the architect of a new Russian State? Why had he to go back to the period from which the revolution had forged so far ahead? Nikita Khrushchev supplied the answer when he was staying in Belgrade: 'It was a case of reversion to the influences of one's youth, as often happens to men in the twilight of their lives, when pure reason begins to cloud over with shadows from the past.'

Koba-Stalin began his career as an equalitarian revolutionary. He said as much to Emil Ludwig. 'I became a revolutionary in my youth,' he said, 'for I wanted to establish freedom and social equality in place of oppression.'

His disappearance from the scene created a vacancy to be filled by another, and it was Nikita Sergeyevich Khrushchev who was destined to occupy his chair in the Praesidium of the Central Committee.

And now the story of the Kremlin has caught up with us and appears less of a mystery. We know how Beria, all-powerful for a moment with the death of Stalin, was later shot, and his place taken by Malenkov, who soon faded out before the Bulganin-Khrushchev combination. We know of the text of the famous Secret Report read by Nikita Khrushchev on February 25, 1956, to the Twentieth Party Congress, at which he denounced Stalin's mistakes and attacked the 'cult of personality'. Since then we have witnessed the eclipse of Marshal Bulganin, who was allowed to claim his right to retirement. We have seen Khrushchev greeted in many lands — in India, Burma, Pekin, Belgrade and Berlin. At President Eisenhower's invitation he arrived in the United States, at Andrews Air Force Base, Md, USA, on September 15, 1959. It was a type of reception that was to continue generally throughout the most photographed and televised visit ever made by a foreign dignitary to this country. And on April 2, 1960, he woke in the morning at Rambouillet, in Francis I's tower, before catching his plane to return to the Kremlin.

In Soviet Russia a new era has begun: the Khrushchev era. The appalling example of the Stalin period, the seamy side of which was disclosed by Nikita Khrushchev himself at the Twenty-Second Party Congress in October 1960, will help to provide the Russian people with fresh food for thought. The younger Russian generation is beginning to understand what things were really like in their country during the past thirty years, and after having repudiated Stalinism they are ready to identify the name of Nikita Khrushchev with a new era in the history of Russia. From this new era they expect greater happiness, better living standards, more freedom, wider achievements in the fields of science, education and technology, and above all, peace in their time. What place will the Kremlin, with its thousand-year-old history, play in the future? Only Nikita Sergeyevich Khrushchev, a clever, versatile, seasoned statesman and patriot, can answer this. But if this book contributes towards an understanding of the age-old sufferings of the Russian people, misguided and ruled by tyrants of one kind or another, it will have more than fulfilled its purpose.

INDEX

VERMONT   COLLEGE
    MONTPELIER, VT.

        Date Due